MICHAEL JACKSON'S
MALT WHISKY
COMPANION

Michael Jackson's

Malt Whisky
Companion

LONDON • NEW YORK • MUNICH
MELBOURNE • DELHI

Design Nick Harris, Rebecca Painter, and Edward Kinsey
Editorial Carla Masson and Elizabeth Stubbs
Research Owen D. L. Barstow and Cathy Turner
Photography Steve Gorton and Ian O'Leary

Additional material
Dave Broom, Jürgen Deibel, and Martine Nouet

FOR DORLING KINDERSLEY
Senior Editor Simon Tuite
Senior Art Editors Joanne Doran and Sue Metcalfe-Megginson
DTP Designer Louise Waller
Production Controllers Sarah Sherlock and Heather Hughes
Managing Editor Deirdre Headon
Art Director Peter Luff

Fifth Edition published 2004 by Dorling Kindersley Limited
80 Strand, London, WC2R ORL

PENGUIN GROUP

2 4 6 8 10 9 7 5 3 1

A CIP catalogue of this book is available from the British Library

ISBN 1 4053 0234 8

MD159
Colour reproduced by Colourscan, Singapore
Printed and bound in Italy by Graphicom

Discover more at
www.dk.com

CONTENTS

*Before dinner or after?
With coffee, chocolate, or a
cigar? These are just some
of the moments for malt.
There are suggestions with
every entry ...*

INTRODUCTION
A SECRET NO LONGER

IN MY LATE TEENS, I was introduced to malt whisky by a fellow journalist in Edinburgh. I was young to have discovered spirits, especially one thought to be for adults only. My first malt was Glen Grant 12-year-old, flowery and seductively sweet. An older colleague warned that the kiss of spirits led to moral decline, but it was too late. I had lost my virginity to a single malt.

The sensuous pleasures are still being delivered with every dram, but a good four decades later, I have spent more time in the ascendant: clambering up the granite slopes of the Grampians in search of water sources; high in the Spey Valley, bracing myself as Macallan tries to sow barley against a headwind; feeling the salt stinging my face as high seas break against the rocky shores of Islay. Even the southerly climes of Spain and Missouri offered snowy hillsides when I went prospecting for the resiny European oak and the sweeter American variety, which are required to make casks for Macallan and Glenmorangie respectively. There was a welcome warmth in the flames, smoke, and steam as the coopers of Andalusia and Kentucky wrestled 100-year-old oaks into roundness. A cooperage can be Dante-esque, but that is as close as I have been to the *Inferno*. The disposition of gods and angels are important too, as I have been reminded on the sites of abbeys in Scotland and temples in Japan. All of these influences make themselves felt in its aromas and flavours; the spirit of earth, wind, and fire reaches the glass. But where to raise the glass? A soft morning in Cork or Antrim is one pleasure, a foggy evening in Nova Scotia or Northern California quite another; the rituals of Kyoto's old town something else.

It is the experience offered by the whisky itself that has always been my greatest interest. In trying better to understand this, I began 30 years ago by reading authors such as Barnard, Bruce Lockhart, Daiches, Gunn, and McDowell. They told me about the process of whisky making, its lore, history, and geography, but little about aroma or taste.

At that time, malt whisky was very much a local drink in the Highlands. Even in Edinburgh many pubs were innocent of malts. Those that did stock this most rooted of Scottish drinks rarely had more than one example. Glens Fiddich, Farclas, and Morangie were to be seen here and there, but not much else. Scotland's great national drink was almost a secret.

I had written the odd short piece on the subject in the 1970s, but started more serious research in the 1980s. In those earliest days, my questions about single malts were not welcomed by some of the more conservative souls in the industry. Malt whisky, in their view, belonged only in blends. Their myopia was perhaps forgivable: blended Scotch whisky was the world's most popular drink, and its sales were built on brand loyalty. Attempts to describe aromas and flavours and explore connoisseurship might unsettle such loyalties. This was whisky, not wine or food.

Writing on whisky was a lonely business, but I was given great encouragement by Wallace Milroy and Derek Cooper. My first book on the subject was *The World Guide to Whisky*, published in 1987, and this was quickly followed by malt whisky book in 1989.

No other writer had attempted so thoroughly to describe the taste of individual whiskies, discussed so many, or taken the controversial step of scoring them. In that first edition, there were fewer than 250 tasting notes. By the fourth edition, the tally had gone past 750. In this new, fifth edition, I have exceeded 1000. Keeping up is ever more difficult, not only because of the numbers, but also due to the many bottlings that bear a vintage date or celebrate a special occasion. They flirt for a moment, and then are gone. While I am forever keen to include new bottlings, I hesitate to exclude old ones. This is not just to boost the numbers. It is also to recognize that, while the distillery, merchant, importer, or distributor may long have sold out, the consumer might still find the bottling in one of America's huge drinks supermarkets or in a stylish malts bar in Tokyo or Sapporo. Where a bottling is now hard to find, I have indicated that.

The diversity of malts has greatly increased consumers' interest in whiskies of all types. Their questions are being answered by a growing number of writers. In the United States, the magazine *Malt Advocate* was established in 1987 to cover both beer and whisky, but has increasingly concentrated on the latter. *Whisky Magazine*, founded in 1998 in Britain, has an international audience. Malt whisky can no longer be regarded as a minor interest reserved for Caledonophiles.

WHAT'S NEW?
TRENDS IN MALTS

M ALT WHISKY IS BLOSSOMING AS NEVER BEFORE: new distilleries, new styles, new stars. New products line the shelves in airport shops and specialist wine merchants. How can whisky be simultaneously deeply rooted and dynamic? There are trends and fashions, but they arise from passion and individuality.

MICRODISTILLERIES

The term "micro" is more commonly applied to the very small breweries that have blossomed in the United States, especially during the 1980s and 1990s. In San Francisco, the Anchor Steam Beer brewery, a survivor from the California Gold Rush, has been an inspiration for the micro movement. Steam Beer has a fermentation system traditional to the West Coast, and in the 1990s, the company launched a traditional interpretation of rye whiskey. The rye is malted, and no other grain is used. Distillation takes place in a pot still. The brewery and distillery are in the same premises, on Potrero Hill, a rehabbed neighbourhood of design studios and art galleries. Several versions of a single malt rye have been produced and marketed. Old Potrero was first reviewed in the fourth edition of this book. At that time, several other small enterprises, some of them based in beer breweries, others originally established to make grape brandies or fruit *eaux-de-vie*, were beginning to produce malt whiskies. Like the first microbreweries, the new small distilleries began in the wine regions of the west, but have now spread further afield (*see pp. 434–38*).

Rye revivalist
A single malt rye is just one revival from Fritz Maytag, of Anchor Brewing. In addition, he also makes gin, wine, and cheese.

On Cape Breton Island, in the province of Nova Scotia (meaning "New Scotland"), Canada, the Glenora distillery seems finally to be on a firm footing, after 10 years of intermittent production and sporadic bottlings. It is a handsome distillery, with a restaurant and

Born-again Bladnoch
Small is beautiful in this typical distillery hamlet. Instead of a church tower, a pagoda. Buddhists in Bladnoch? No, it is the vent on the retired maltings.

hotel, in a dramatically beautiful location in an area noted for its festivals of Scottish music.

In a wintry location across the Atlantic, the world's northernmost whisky distillery ran its first spirit at the end of 1999, at Gavle, on the Baltic coast of Sweden. The Mackmyra distillery has been established on a site that made vodka in the 1800s.

In a region known for the cultivation of malting barley, the town of Lahti, Finland, has for eight years enjoyed beer brewed at the Teerenpeli bar ("the flirt"). Publican Anssi Pyysing and wife Marianne began to buy malt whisky from Scotland and finish it in sherry, brandy, and rum casks. In 2002, they installed a small still and began to produce single malt.

In Ireland, plans have been announced to open a new distillery in Kilbeggan, County Westmeath. This venture is not connected with the former Locke's distillery, which matures whisky from Cooley.

The Gwalia Distillery, near Aberdare, in Wales, released its first whisky on 1 March 2004, St David's Day. The nation's patron saint surely enjoyed the meaty, spicy, minty, Penderyn Single Malt. The whisky bears the name of the village where it is distilled, in the Brecon Beacons National Park.

In the Scottish county of Fife, work is proceeding on a distillery to be called Ladybank. The plan is to use barley from identified local farms. Meanwhile, a nearby farm, called Daft Mill (sic), has obtained planning permission for a distillery. At the opposite end of Scotland, plans were also announced for the Shetland Isles' first legal distillery, Blackwood. They aim to start distilling late in 2004.

While the term "microdistillery" is not widely used in Scotland, it could be applied to these projects, and perhaps to several others. The common feature is that these are not owned by national or international groups, and are not in the business of building "brands".

The use of barley contracted from local farms to produce identified bottlings has also been a feature at the old-established Springbank distillery of Campbeltown. In 2001, its owners began work on the refitting of the Glengyle distillery, which had been silent for 75 years.

In the Lowlands, the Bladnoch distillery, which had been closed for 10 years, reopened as a "micro". The aim is to operate part-time, producing whisky primarily for bottling as a single malt, with an emphasis on local sales.

The notion of "down-sizing" an existent distillery to make it viable has also been pursued by the renowned merchant Gordon & MacPhail, which bought the silent Benromach distillery on Speyside. This has been completely re-equipped for smaller-scale production.

Pending the opening of the various planned distilleries, Scotland's smallest distillery was Edradour. This was returned to private ownership in 2002, when it was acquired by Andrew Symington of the independent bottlers Signatory. Thus was endorsed the notion that small is beautiful.

RECOGNIZING JAPANESE MALTS

It was not quite as dramatic as the 1976 "Judgment of Paris", in which some of the great French châteaux were outscored by Californian vineyards, but *Whisky Magazine's* 2001 "Best of the Best" judging had a similar significance for Japanese malt whisky.

Each edition of the magazine carries a blindfold judging of new releases, usually a dozen or 20. There is also always a tasting of a similar proportion based on a region, country, or style. After the first two or three years of the magazine, all the whisky regions, countries, and styles had been sampled, so it was decided to compare the highest scorers from those tastings with the "winners" from each flight of new releases. Prior to the inception of this new "contest", a total of around 300 whiskies had been reviewed by the magazine's two regular critics, who had awarded metaphorical "medals" to about 50 of the best of them.

These "best" whiskies were now judged blindfold in Edinburgh, Kentucky, and Tokyo, by panels whose membership read like a *Who's Who?* of the whisky world. The samples were kept within categories, albeit broader, so that the whiskies were judged more or less like with like. A Lowland Scotch did not find itself being compared with a bourbon, nor a Canadian with a Japanese. Nonetheless, there was still a highest scorer in the entire tasting. It was a 10-year-old, single cask malt whisky from the Nikka Distillery of Yoichi in Hokkaido, Japan.

Soon afterwards, a 1986 vintage of this malt was made available to members of the Scotch Malt Whisky Society as a monthly selection. That such a body

Winning whisky
The most Scottish-looking distillery in Japan makes the most Scottish-tasting whisky. This distillery was built in the 1930s in the fishing village of Yoichi, north of Sapporo, Hokkaido.

should select a Japanese whisky was deemed worthy of a celebratory dinner at the society's headquarters, which are in an historic wine cellar in Leith. The guest of honour was Takeshi Taketsuru, son of Masakata Taketsuru, who founded Nikka and was the original consultant on whisky to Suntory. At the dinner, the digestif was the Nikka 1986. It is a complex, wintry whisky: smoky, peaty, leafy, and resiny, with a suggestion of garden mint.

It was decided to hold the "Best of the Best" every alternate year. In 2002, another single cask ten-year-old from Nikka was among the high scorers, but it was beaten by Suntory's Hibiki 21-year-old, a minty, spicy, creamy whisky, described by one Scottish whisky maker as being "unspeakably good".

THE FASHIONABILITY OF ISLAY

The openings and reopenings that excited malt lovers at the end of the 1990s and beginning of the 2000s have a westerly bias. The most exciting reopenings have been on the western whisky island of Islay, which is renowned for the intensity of its malts.

The Ardbeg distillery reopened under new ownership just before the last edition of this book was published in 2000, and has released about 20 bottlings since (*see pp. 97–101*). Then when, in 2001, Bruichladdich reopened, also under new ownership, there was a sense of confirmation: Islay really was experiencing a revival. Bruichladdich has since released a dozen bottlings (*see pp. 149–57*).

Soon afterwards, Bunnahabhain, which had been experiencing a lengthy silent season, also went back into production. This meant that all the workable distilleries on the island were in operation. At the time, Port Ellen, which closed in 1983, still had its full complement of

Bruichladdich's back
Opening day, and Jim McEwan, one of the principals, introduces past managers of the distillery.

distillery buildings, but no equipment. Plans to retain the 19th-century former kilns but demolish a pagoda and the still-house building were disclosed in 2002. An "official" bottling of Port Ellen had been released earlier, with a recommended price of £110/$170. It was believed that two or three further bottlings might be released, the last by the middle of the current decade. Port Ellen has become something of a cult whisky. It is by no means the only malt from a dismantled distillery, nor is its product the rarest, but the combination of location and quality seals its status (*see* "Regional Variations", *pp. 54–63*).

MULTIPLE MALTS

A single malt, by definition, emanates from just one distillery, but the converse does not apply. A single distillery can make more than one malt: either by using a different configuration of stills or different levels of peating. Only a handful of distilleries have done this in the past (*see, for example, Glenburgie and its Lomond stills, p. 246*). The most interesting example is the Springbank distillery, which combines both approaches. The original Springbank whisky is distilled in an odd configuration, described as two-and-a-half times, from medium-peated malt. A second whisky, Longrow, is double distilled, from heavily peated malt. A third, Hazelburn, is triple distilled, from unpeated malt. The first Hazelburn is expected to be bottled in 2006. The use of different peating levels was one of the first innovations from the new owners at Bruichladdich. The original Bruichladdich is lightly peated, but two more assertive spirits are now distilled, under the names Port Charlotte and Octomore. When Shetland's proposed Blackwood distillery was announced, the principals indicated that both unpeated and heavily peated whiskies would be produced.

Singles shop

It looks like an ordinary corner shop, but Eaglesome's in Campbeltown is a shrine to malt whisky. It was bought by the owners of the Springbank distillery and the bottlers Cadenhead. Together, they line its shelves with rare whiskies.

IDENTIFYING THE CASK

By definition, a bottle of single malt contains whisky from just one distillery, but it is usually a marriage (or "vatting") of several production runs, drawn from a variety of casks. The most traditional types of cask are hogsheads, butts, or puncheons that formerly contained sherry. These may be made from either European (usually Spanish) or American oak. The type of sherry might be anything from from the delicate fino to the rich Pedro Ximénez. Sherry casks are expensive, and Scottish distillers today more commonly use barrels that formerly contained Kentucky bourbon or Tennessee whisky. These casks are made from American oak.

Some Scottish distillers have begun to itemize (on labels, boxes, or accompanying booklets) the type of casks used in the maturation of a particular whisky. The information supplied might include the type of sherry formerly contained in the casks, and the number of times they have been filled with whisky. Some connoisseurs like to have this information for its own sake, but it also helps the potential buyer to understand what to expect from the whisky. For example, "first-fill" casks impart much more aroma and flavour than "refill" casks.

WOOD FINISHES

This trend, reviewed in the fourth edition of this book, has proven to be more than a fad. The Glenmorangie distillery, which pioneered the technique in the mid-1990s, has stepped up the frequency and diversity of its wood finishes, which now number about 20. Some prized examples have included Côte de Nuits (launched in 2000), Côte de Beaune (2001), and Sauternes (2002). Perhaps feeling it had been on too rich a diet, Glenmorangie put down its wine glass for a moment at the end of 2002. But although the year was finished, the last whisky wasn't. Missouri Oak Reserve was matured throughout in new American barrels.

Some of the most innovative essays have emerged from William Grant & Sons. First came a version of the honey-tasting Balvenie finished in casks that had previously matured an Islay malt (believed to be Laphroaig). This was followed by Glenfiddich Caoran, its Gaelic name referring to the embers of a peat fire. Caoran achieves its peaty character by spending time in Islay casks. A further version is Glenfiddich Havana Reserve, which is finished in rum casks.

While the industry still sometimes perceives malt whiskies as being rarefied, the counter argument is that their individuality and colour attract attention to whisky as a whole. Techniques from the world of malts, such as wood finishes, are also beginning to influence blends.

The finishing touch

Glemorangie was a pioneer of distillery bottlings at cask strength and of wood finishes. Dr Bill Lumsden, one of the new generation of whisky makers, has a special interest in wood. While a wide variety of cooperage from the wine industry is used in "finishing", the principal maturation of Glenmorangie is usually in American white oak from the Ozark mountains.

The first two examples were The Famous Grouse Islay Wood Finish and Port Wood Finish. William Grant's own blend, bearing the company's name, is even more innovative, with a version finished in casks that previously contained a strong, typically malty Scottish ale, from the Caledonian Brewery of Edinburgh. This is labelled William Grant's Ale Cask Reserve.

The term "wood finish" implies that the whisky first had its normal maturation, usually in either bourbon or sherry wood, and has then been reracked into a wine barrique, port pipe, madeira drum, or whatever, for the finishing touch. This often only lasts for six months, but may occasionally last for a year or two.

The technique is controversial on several counts. The finishing of Speyside whiskies in Islay woods raised a difficult question: if there is any residual Islay whisky in the "empty" cask when it is filled, isn't the result a vatted malt rather than a single? It would follow that, if there were any residual port, sherry, or madeira, the end result would not be a pure whisky of any kind.

Some traditionalists object in principle, on the grounds that "finishing" is a marketing device, and not traditional. While such vigilance has protected the integrity of Scotch whisky, it assumes that nothing has ever changed. The likelihood is that the first Scottish distillers had used herbs in their whisky, and that they did not mature it. Were they "traditional"?

Today, the contribution of wood to aroma and flavour is increasingly appreciated, not only in respect of finishes. An interesting regime reviewed in the fourth edition of this book was that applied to the 16-year-old version of Bushmills Malt: equal proportions of whiskey (the Irish spelling) are matured in sherry butts and first-fill bourbon barrels, then married in port pipes. Bushmills has produced a number of wood finishes but, like several other distilleries, has also released malt whiskies matured throughout in woods other than the traditional sherry or bourbon. Bushmills' owners, Irish Distillers Limited, have records showing that their predecessor company was buying marsala, malaga, and madeira casks in the late 1800s and continued to do so until the eve of the First World War.

CASK STRENGTH

Cask strength whiskies were a novelty a decade ago. The extent to which this has now changed is illustrated by the number of recent bottlings in this style from United Distillers (now Diageo). The company's rare malts, for example, were an early recognition of connoisseur interest in whisky at "full" strength. Diageo later added a selection of limited bottlings under the rubric "cask strength". In the 2000s, the company introduced versions of more than 30 malts sub-titled "natural cask strength".

As the term "cask strength" implies, the spirit enjoys a variety of potencies on its way to the bottle. It is usually collected from the still at an average strength between the mid- or lower 70s and upper 60s. It is sometimes reduced with water to the mid-60s before being filled into casks. The water is felt to "open up" the spirit and help it to mature.

During ageing, a substantial volume of spirit is lost through evaporation. The size of this "angels' share" varies considerably, and is influenced by many factors. Among them are the height at which the casks are stacked, the style of construction of the warehouse, the ambient temperature, the age and size of the cask, the weather during its years of maturation, and the duration of the storage. Customs and excise allows the angels to take a maximum of 2.5 per cent of the volume per year.

Depending on these factors, a sample drawn from the cask could still be in the 60s, or may have dropped into the 50s or lower. So the term "cask strength" does suggest something more potent than usual.

The appeal to the consumer might diminish if evaporation had taken the alcohol below the levels at which malts are conventionally sold: 42 per cent (for "De Luxe" or "Export" bottlings) or 40 per cent. The industry has taken action to make the latter an international minimum.

Unless a whisky is very old indeed, it is unlikely to have reached either of these levels by evaporation. In conventional bottlings, the strength is normally reduced by dilution with water.

The only distilleries with bottling lines are Springbank (which also produces Longrow and Hazelburn); Bruichladdich (whose new owners installed the equipment); and Glenfiddich (with sisters Balvenie and Kininvie). These are therefore the only distilleries that can reduce their whiskies with the same water as they use in distillation. They therefore regard their whiskies as being "château-bottled". All the others use central bottling plants and reduce with de-natured water.

Similar standard or minimum strengths are applied to spirits in many countries, and are widely enshrined in laws, duties, and taxes. Many of these measures have their origins in legislation passed at around the time of the First World War. Concern about levels of drinking during this period gave rise to Britain's laws on pub hours, and Prohibition in the US and several other countries. During this period, whisky was sold at 37.2 per cent in Britain.

Whisky has always in a small way been available at cask strength, in that it was once supplied in the wood to country houses, farms, shops, and even bars. The very independent family distillers of Glenfarclas notably carried on the cask strength ideal in some of its bottlings. They were one of the inspirations behind the founding in 1983 of the Scotch Malt Whisky Society, which grew from a group of friends who formed a syndicate to buy at cask strength.

The independent bottler Cadenhead and some of its competitors have since become protagonists of cask strength. In 1990, Glenmorangie commercially pioneered the rediscovery of this notion with its "Native Ross-shire" bottlings. Explaining the appeal of such

It's a steal

When Glenmorangie first bottled its whisky at cask strength in 1990, it sported a mock-rustic label design. Had the consumer stolen the whisky?

editions, a marketing man at Glenmorangie said: "This is as near as you can get to sneaking up to the distillery in the middle of the night and tapping a cask. It is whisky as at source."

The term "cask strength" indicates that the whisky has not been reduced, but it could be a vatting of several production runs, from several casks. The person in charge of the vatting will choose his casks to achieve a desired character in the end result. He may also aim for what is considered to be a desirable alcohol content. Consumers may still wish to add water but, in the case of a cask strength whisky, they (rather than the bottler) choose how great the dilution.

Despite the potential of the alcohol to anaesthetize the palate, some whisky drinkers do like to drink their malt at cask strength. Some whiskies matured in sherry casks can "fall apart" if substantial amounts of water are added; and it might be argued more generally that a whisky which is rich, malty, and creamy in style should, indeed, be allowed to show its texture without being watered.

VINTAGE EDITIONS

The grape may be far more temperamental than the grain, but barley has its moments. Weather over the growing season may produce a richer or more delicious barley in a particular year. The quality of the distiller's water may vary according to the weight of rainfall and the depth and speed of mountain streams. A cold winter may make for a more effective condensation of vapours, and therefore a cleaner, creamier spirit. Despite all of this, it has been argued that the spirit differs more from one batch to the next than it does between years. Whatever the quality of the spirit, the weather during maturation is almost certainly more important, simply because its influence is exerted over a number of years.

Changes in production methods over the years are also an influence. In general, most malt is today less heavily peated than it was, stills are run faster, and cuts of spirit are wider. Occasionally, some quirk of the moment, or even a particular distillery manager, reverses such "progress" for a year or two.

A vintage edition contains whisky from just one identified year. Some malts, such as Knockando, quote on their labels the dates of distillation and bottling, rather than simply the age. Others, such as Glenfiddich and Balvenie, have in recent years made it an annual ritual to delve into their stocks and select one or more casks of very old whisky to bottle as a vintage edition. The Glenlivet Vintage, a selection from the 1960s and 1970s, was the first such official bottling from a distillery company. It was reviewed in the fourth edition of this book. In 2002, Macallan made vintages from 1926 to 1972 available, and published *The Definitive Guide to Buying Vintage Macallan*. Since 1996, the distillery has also made vattings that attempt to match the character of rare bottlings from 1841, 1861, 1874, and 1876, with more to come. This unusual venture is known as "The Replica Range".

SINGLE CASK

Many "vintage" bottlings are from a single cask, hence the term "single cask", as are many "cask strength" bottlings. Each of the three terms makes a slightly different promise, but they can overlap or coincide. Their growing popularity reflects the desire of discerning consumers to be better informed about the products they buy, to be able to exercise choice, and sometimes to prefer individuality to consistency.

UNCHILLFILTERED

Conventional malts are usually chilled before being despatched. The drop in temperature causes them to become cloudy. The haze comprises protein and other elements, which have dropped out of suspension. These are then removed by filtration. This pre-empts a protein haze forming if the purchaser of the whisky keeps it in the fridge, or adds ice to his drink.

As true whisky lovers do neither, they do not require such mollycoddling. In removing the haze, chill filtration also strips out some flavour elements, notably including fatty acids. "Unchillfiltered" is a clumsy term to find on a label, but it should be welcomed nonetheless. It indicates a whisky for people who like their meat on the bone or their bread crusty.

High society
The tasting panel at the Scotch Malt Whisky Society chooses treats for its members. The avoidance of chill filtration was part of the society's raison d'être.

WHY MALTS?

AN INSTANT GUIDE TO THE PLEASURES OF THE PURSUIT

AT ITS SIMPLEST, MALT WHISKY HAS A STARTLING PURITY. The snow melts on the mountains, filters through rock for decades, perhaps even centuries, bubbles out of a spring, then tumbles down a hillside, until it finds land flat enough and warm enough to grow barley. The water irrigates the barley in the field; persuades it to germinate in the maltings; infuses its natural sugars in the mash tun; becomes beer when the yeast is added; vaporizes in the still; becomes liquid once more in the condenser; enters the cask as spirit, and leaves it as whisky.

THE FLAVOUR of malted barley is always present to a degree, clean, sweet, and restorative, but there are many other elements. The rock from which the water rises will influence the character of the whisky. The vegetation over which it flows can also be an influence. In the process of malting, the partially germinated grain is dried, sometimes over a peat fire, and this will impart smokiness. The yeasts used in fermentation can create fruity, spicy flavours. Similar characteristics can be influenced by the size and shape of the stills, which also affect the richness and weight of the spirit. Further aromas and flavours are assumed during maturation in the cask, from the wood used, its previous contents, and the atmosphere it breathes (*see pp. 72–3*).

For people who enjoy a spirit with flavour, malt whisky at its most robust is a world champion. The flavours in a blended Scotch are usually more restrained, as they might be in a cognac. Those who suffer from fear of flavour might feel safer with white rums or vodkas.

THE INDIVIDUALITY of malts is what makes each so different. Naturally enough, they appeal to people who are individualists. A smoky, earthy, seaweedy, medicinal malt from the coasts or islands of Scotland is a spirit of unrivalled power on the palate. A Speysider may be sherryish, honeyed, flowery, and often very complex. Lowlanders are few, but they can be appetizingly grassy and herbal.

Glass of 2004?
Tasting glasses after a master class at Bruichladdich. Malt lovers like to learn – classes, tastings, and whisky festivals are popular. Finding flavours and aromas is a sensuous activity.

THE MOMENT for a malt may simply be the occasion for a sociable drink, but some pleasures are more particular: the restorative after a walk in the country or a game of golf; the aperitif; even, occasionally, the malt with a meal; the digestif; the malt with a cigar, or with a book at bedtime.

Martine's cuisine
In Paris, writer Martine Nouet conducts classes in cooking with whisky. She drinks whisky with her meals.

THE MEAL Although malt whiskies are more commonly served before or after a meal, they very happily accompany some dishes, most obviously sushi. Some malt-loving chefs also like to use their favourite spirit as an ingredient (*see p. 441*).

THE EXPLORATION Malt drinkers rarely stick to one distillery. They enjoy comparing malts from different regions, and familiarizing themselves with the aromas and flavours of each. To do this is to explore Scotland by nosing-glass. This armchair exploration often leads on to the real thing.

THE DISTILLERIES are often in beautiful locations. Some have their own distinctive architecture. Most are quite small, and it is not unknown for visiting malt lovers to strike up long-term friendships with distillery managers or workers.

THE VISIT Malt lovers often become passionate about Scotland itself. Whisky tourism extends beyond visits to distilleries. The principal whisky regions (the Highlands, especially Speyside; and the Islands, especially Islay) are set in countryside offering outstanding opportunities for walking, climbing, bird-watching, and fishing. Islay has a festival of whisky and folk music in late May; Speyside has festivals in spring and autumn; and the distilling town of Pitlochry has a summer theatre festival.

THE CONNOISSEUR Just as wine enthusiasts progress from comparing vineyards or châteaux to assessing vintages, so malt lovers develop their own connoisseurship. A single distillery may offer malts of different ages, vintage-dated malts, a variety of strengths, and a diversity of wood finishes. As new bottlings are constantly being released, there is no end to this pleasure.

THE COLLECTOR Every lover of malt whiskies sooner or later becomes to some extent a collector. It may not be a conscious decision. It can just happen. A few casual purchases, the odd gift. For the collector's friends, birthdays and Christmas are suddenly easy. Some collectors have backgrounds in the trade. Some buy two of every bottle: one to drink, the other to keep. Such collectors pour scorn on those who do not drink any of their whisky. The most serious collections are often found in countries with a nostalgia for the Britain of gentlemen's clubs, leather-upholstered Bentleys, and rugby union. There are famous collectors in Brazil, Italy, and Japan.

Sukinder's stash
In London, Sukhinder Singh started with miniatures. Now he has 2,500 bottles in his private collection, and is a whisky merchant.

THE INVESTOR 1 — AUCTIONS Even if it was not bought for that purpose, a collection soon begins to represent a valuable asset. Collections that began after the Second World War started to come up for sale in the 1980s. In 1986, the Scottish branch of the famous auction house Christie's began to include whiskies once a year in its sales of fine wines. Within two or three years, whisky had been separated from wine. Christie's Scotland then closed, and its whisky expert, Martin Green, moved to Scottish auctioneers McTear's.

Some single malts have appreciated fivefold or even tenfold (although some bottles have proven to be fakes, so care should be exercised). In 2002, a well-authenticated single bottle of 62-year-old Dalmore fetched £25,000 (about $38,000). In the 1990s, importer and distributor Norman Shelley bought 76 bottles of Macallan, ranging from current 30-year-olds to 1856 bottlings, for an undisclosed price. Within two or three years, his collection was valued at £231,500 (about $360,000).

THE INVESTOR 2 — EN PRIMEUR Some distillers have at times sold newly filled casks "en primeur", but this has not been a great success. The cost of storage during maturation, and the payment of duties and taxes, complicates the calculations. No one can be certain how well the cask will age, nor how saleable a single cask of whisky will be when it is mature. While the distillers involved have been perfectly respectable, some investment companies have behaved less scrupulously. Care is advised.

THE ORIGINS OF
MALT WHISKY

WHILE GRAPE VINES HAVE their roots in prehistory, barley staked out the beginning of civilization. As hunter-gatherers, human beings picked wild fruits such as grapes, but this source of refreshment and nutrition had a short season and a propensity to rot (or spontaneously ferment) into wines. Fruits take up rainfall from the soil and turn it into highly fermentable, sugary juice. Wild yeasts trigger fermentation, and this process creates alcohol. Perhaps the hunter-gatherers enjoyed the effect, but wine did not provide them with any much needed protein.

When human beings ceased to be nomadic and settled in organized societies they did so in order to cultivate crops. The earliest evidence of this, between 13,000 and 8000 years ago, occurs at several sites in the fertile crescent of the Middle East. The first crop was a prototype barley, and the first explanation of its use is a depiction in Sumerian clay tablets of beer making. This is sometimes described as the world's first recipe of any kind.

HALF-WAY TO WHISKY

To grow barley, transform it into malt and then into beer, is half-way towards the making of whisky. While it is easy to obtain the sugars from fruit – peel me a grape, take a bite from an apple – grain is less yielding. The first step toward the unlocking of the sugars in barley and several other grains is the process of malting. This means that the grain is steeped in water, partially germinated, and then dried. The Sumerian civilization was on land that is today Iraq. It may be that malting occurred naturally while the barley was still in the field, as the water rose and fell in the flood plains of this land. This is described poetically on clay tablets in "A Hymn to Ninkasi" *(see p. 26)*.

It seems likely that at this stage the Sumerians had no more precise aim than to make grain edible. They did so in the form of beer, though pictograms and relics suggest a grainy, porridgey beverage consumed through straws. This depiction bears a startling resemblance to the "traditional" beer still brewed in villages in some parts of Africa.

Road to the Isles
A few miles from the Bushmills distillery in Ireland, this remarkable rock formation heads for Fingal's Cave, Staffa, and Mull. The first whisky road ... or the first whisky legend?

WHEN YOU POUR OUT THE FILTERED BEER OF THE COLLECTOR VAT, IT IS [LIKE] THE ONRUSH OF TIGRIS AND EUPHRATES. NINKASI, YOU ARE THE ONE WHO POURS OUT THE FILTERED BEER OF THE COLLECTOR VAT, IT IS [LIKE] THE ONRUSH OF TIGRIS AND EUPHRATES.

Grain and water meet ...

... in the "Hymn to Ninkasi" (c. 1800BC), found on tablets at several sites in Iraq. Translated in 1964, by Miguel Civil, of the Oriental Institute of the University of Chicago. The first evidence of malting?

If the cultivation of grain originally radiated from the first civilization of the Ancient World, the crop itself varied from place to place. To the east, the Chinese and Japanese grow rice, which is fermented to produce saké. To the north, the Russians use rye to make kvass. To the west, barley is brewed. The words "brewed" and "bread" have the same etymology, and, in Germany, beer is sometimes known as "liquid bread".

The soft, sensuous, delicate, capricious grape and the tall, spiky, resilient grain compete to make the world's greatest drinks: fermented and distilled. The weather divides temperate Europe into wine and beer belts. Wine is made in the grape-growing south: Greece, Italy, France, Iberia. Beer belongs to the grainy north: the Czech Republic, Germany, Belgium, and the British Isles. All of these countries also produce distilled counterparts, but the real emphasis on spirits is in the colder countries. The spirits belt links Russia, Poland, the Baltic and Nordic states, and Scotland.

Modern-day Iraq is due south of Armenia, and the Greek historian Herodotus tells us that the Armenians made "barley water". So perhaps the brewing of barley malt spread by way of Armenia, Georgia, and the Ukraine. The Greeks also called all "strangers" Celts. The Romans called them Gallic people, and a part of Turkey is known as Galatia. The term "Galatian" was also used by the Roman author Columella to describe the two-row "race" of barley, preferred today by many brewers.

Sites that were Celtic settlements are even today known for the brewing of beer, notably sites in Bohemia, Bavaria, and Belgium. Many of these sites later gave rise to abbeys, with breweries. Most of the early brewing sites in England, Scotland, and Ireland are on the locations of former abbeys. So are the distilling towns of Cork and Midleton in Ireland. The northeast of Ireland and the western isles of Scotland have associations with St Columba, who urged his community of Iona to grow barley. In 1494, Friar Cor, of Lindores Abbey in Fife, placed on record in the rolls of the Scottish Exchequer the purchase of malt "to make *aqua vitae*". He probably wasn't the first malt distiller, but he left us the first evidence.

THE ART OF DISTILLATION

It is easy to see how spontaneous fermentation provides a natural model for the first brewers. Evaporation and condensation occur in nature, too, but it is not clear when, or where, distillation was first practised. To distil is to boil the water, wine, or beer, collect the steam, and condense it back into liquid. This drives off certain substances (for example, the salt in water) and concentrates others (such as the alcohol in wine or beer). The process was used by Phoenician sailors to render sea water drinkable, by alchemists, by makers of perfumes and, eventually, in the production of medicines and alcoholic drinks.

One theory has the Phoenicians bringing distillation to Western Europe, via the Mediterranean and Spain, whence it crossed the sea again to Ireland. Another theory has the art spreading by way of Russia and the Nordic countries to Scotland.

The fermented raw material – wine or beer – is boiled to make steam, which, being wraith-like, may have given rise to the English word "spirit" or to the German "*Geist*" (ghost), especially since condensation brings it back to life in a restored (and restorative) form. The "water of life" they call it: vodka, a diminutive form, in Slavic countries; aquavit, in various spellings, in Nordic lands; *eau-de-vie* in French; and *usquebaugh*, in various spellings, in Gaelic. This last became *usky*, then whisky, in English. All of these terms at first simply indicated a distillate, made from whatever was local.

All spirit drinks were originally made in a batch process in a vessel that superficially resembles a kettle or cooking pot, and malt whisky is still made in this way today. But this "pot still" was an inefficient purification vessel, and, in the early days, if the spirit emerged with flavours that were considered disagreeable, they were masked with spices, berries, and fruits.

"PLAIN MALT"

In the mid-1700s, a distinction was made in Scotland between flavoured spirits and "plain malt". As the first industrial nation, Britain shaped its beer and whisky with the early technologies of the Industrial Revolution: England's "bright beer" was a copper-coloured pale ale, rather than the more "evolved" golden lager of Continental Europe, which was made using more advanced techniques. Scotland's whisky remained a pot-still product, with its own inherent flavours, turned to an attractive complexity.

Most of the northern European countries use a generic term such as "schnapps" for a spirit, and offer both plain and flavoured examples. More specific flavourings include caraway and dill, traditional in the aquavit of Scandinavia; and juniper, together with botanical flavourings such as iris root and citrus peel, in the gins of northern Germany, the Low Countries, northern France, and England. Flavoured or not, many grain-based spirits outside Britain employ a column still, and most are not aged.

The elements that go to make up a Scottish malt whisky are the local water; a grist comprising malted barley only; traditionally, a degree of peat; pot stills, usually designed and built in Scotland; and ageing in oak casks. The last of these elements gradually became more significant from the late 1700s onwards.

BLENDED SCOTCH

Like most drinks production, the distilling of malt whisky in Scotland was originally a sideline for farmers. In the coastal coves and Highland glens, illicit distillation was rife. Legislation in 1824 to regulate this activity began the shaping of today's industry. That process was largely finished by the legislation of 1909–15, which initially arose from a trading standards case in the London borough of Islington.

For the farmer-distiller, a few casks of malt whisky might be a hedge against a rainy day. A farm distillery would not have a bottling line. The casks could be sold directly to wealthy householders, to hotels or pubs, or to a licensed grocer, a Scottish institution similar to an

Blending the bottles
The "medicine bottles" on Richard Patterson's workbench contain the latest samples taken from casks of malt whiskies normally included in Whyte and Mackay's blended Scotch. Every cask is slightly different. Patterson checks colour, nose, palate – and adjusts accordingly.

American country store. (The outstanding example of such a shop, and still active, is Gordon & MacPhail of Elgin.) One or two renowned distillers might sell their whisky to a wine merchant, sometimes as far away as Edinburgh or London.

Each farmer's whisky would vary from one year to the next, and supply would be irregular. So rather than run out of farmer McSporran's fine dram, the licensed grocers would vat the malts and sell the result under their own label. Some became famous: names such as Chivas Brothers, Johnnie Walker, and George Ballantine. Among the wine merchants known for their bottlings, two in London are still active: Justerini & Brooks and Berry Brothers & Rudd.

Vatting turned to blending when, in the mid-1800s, the column-shaped continuous still was patented. This type of still, operated on an industrial scale, can produce whisky that is lighter in flavour and body. It can also produce whisky more quickly, at a lower cost, and in larger quantities than a pot still. Column-still whisky provides the bulk of a blend, while a combination of pot-still malt whiskies add character and individuality. The volume afforded by blended Scotches, and their less challenging style, helped them become the world's most popular spirits at a time when much of the globe was embraced by the British Empire.

Mountainous Scotland, with its long coastline, had provided mariners, explorers, engineers, teachers, soldiers, and administrators for the empire. Each turned out also to be a propagandist for the virtues of his country's greatest product.

BORN-AGAIN MALTS

More than 90 per cent of malt whisky still goes into blends. Scotland has about 100 malt distilleries, of which about two thirds are working at any one time. All but a handful are owned by international drinks companies whose products include blended Scotches. A blend can contain anything from six or seven malts to 30 or 40. The drinks companies like to own the distilleries whose malt whiskies are vital to their blends. They also exchange malts with one another.

The big drinks companies have been growing through mergers since the 1920s. A round of mergers after the Second World War left the handful of remaining independent distillers feeling vulnerable. William Grant & Sons, producers of Glenfiddich and Balvenie, decided they no longer wished to rely on supplying blenders, but to actively market their whisky as a single malt. The industry view was that single malts belonged to the past, and that the dominant position of the blends could not be challenged. Happily, Grant's were not dissuaded.

ABERLOUR

ESTD 1879

WAREHOUSE № 1
SINGLE CASK SELECTION

SPEYSIDE MALT SCOTCH WHISKY
AGED 11 YEARS

BOURBON CASK MATURED

FILL DETAILS

☑ 1ST   ☑ 2ND   ☐ REFILL

CASK NUMBER... 10122 ....

FILLED INTO CASK ... 6/1/1998 ...

BOTTLE NUMBER... PRESELECTION ...

70cl

HAND FILLED AT ABERLOUR DISTILLERY
THE ABERLOUR GLENLIVET DISTILLERY CO. LTD.
ABERLOUR ~ SPEYSIDE ~ SCOTLAND

57.2 vol

THE WORDS USED ON
THE LABEL

CONTROVERSY was aroused in 2003 when Cardhu single malt was relaunched as a pure malt. What is the difference, and why did it matter? This book is primarily concerned with malt whisky, but also looks briefly at grain whisky. The main body of the book, the A–Z section, is devoted only to single malt Scotches, but a section at the back deals with products from other countries – these are malt whiskies, but not Scotches. All of these overlapping terms are employed in labelling. What do they say about the liquid in the bottle?

MALT Cereal grain that has been partially sprouted – in preparation for the release of its fermentable sugars – then dried in a kiln. The grains look drier and slightly darker after being malted for distillation. The grain is always barley if the end result is to be malt whisky in the Scottish or Irish style. Other grains can be malted and used in other whiskies, as in the case of Old Potrero rye.

For the beer brewer or whisky distiller, the process of malting in part parallels the crush in wine making or brandy distilling. The premises in which it takes place is called a maltings. The grains are first steeped in water, to encourage their sprouting (or partial germination). Traditionally, the sprouting continues with the grains spread on a stone floor. They are constantly raked, or turned with a shovel, to keep them aerated. Floor malting requires a lot of space and is labour-intensive, but is felt by many to produce the most delicious result. There are several other methods, including ventilated boxes and rotating drums.

Just as grapes are also eaten or used to provide juice, so malted barley is used, either as whole grains or milled, in breads, cakes, and milk shakes. A syrupy, water-based extract of malt sugars is sold as a tonic. An ever-evolving series of barley varieties is used for malting. These are required to produce plump kernels and clean, sweet malt sugars. The farmer distinguishes between malting barley and feed barley for cattle.

Almost all types of whisky employ a proportion of malt. Those that employ no other grain are known as malt whisky. Single malt whiskies are often referred to simply as "malts".

Detailed dram
Malt lovers like to know what they are drinking, and Aberlour provides every last detail when you make your own vatting and bottling at the distillery's visitor centre.

Mountain men?

These pot-bellied creatures are the whisky stills at Ben Nevis. The pot-still shape is more evident when the whole vessel is visible.

WHISK(E)Y A spirit drink originating from Scotland and Ireland – but produced in a variety of styles in other countries – distilled from malted barley and other grains, and matured in oak. Its complex aromas and flavours originate from the raw materials, manufacturing process, and maturation. These distinguish whiskies from the more neutral grain spirits in the schnapps and vodka families.

There is a misunderstanding that there are British and American spellings of this term. However, it is not the nationality of the writer, or the country of publication, that should determine the spelling. It is the type of whisk(e)y: thus Scottish and Canadian "whisky", but Irish "whiskey". American styles, such as Kentucky Bourbon and Tennessee whiskey, generally favour the "e", but some labels dissent.

MALT WHISKY Whisky made only from malted barley. Typically distilled in a batch process, in a copper vessel resembling a kettle or cooking pot.

SINGLE MALT WHISKY Malt whisky produced in a single distillery, not vatted or blended with whisky made in any other distillery. Scotland has by far the most malt distilleries: just under a hundred, of which between 80 and 90 per cent are operating at any one time. Ireland has one distillery that can produce only malt whiskey, namely Bushmills. Malt whiskies are also distilled on a more limited scale at Cooley and Midleton in Ireland, though both of these also produce a range of other styles. Some very serious malt whiskies are made in Japan, and a scattering elsewhere in the world.

SCOTCH WHISKY This term can be applied only to a whisky made in Scotland, and matured for at least three years. No other nation can call a product "Scotch", although any nation can call a product whisky. Scotland's status is not widely understood beyond its borders. It is not a region but a nation, and has been for almost 1000 years. For the past 300 years, it has been part of a union, and this was not altered by the recent restoration of the Scottish Parliament. Scotland, England, and Wales share an island called Great Britain. These three nations and Northern Ireland (a six-county province) form the United Kingdom.

SINGLE MALT SCOTCH WHISKY Single malt whisky made in Scotland.

SINGLE CASK A bottling made from just one cask.

VATTED MALT If malt whiskies from different distilleries are combined, the result will be called a vatted malt. This might be done to create a desired character, perhaps the flavour of a region. This term assumes that all the whiskies in the vatting are malts.

PURE MALT A term that is likely to fall out of use because its meaning is insufficiently clear. It has been employed in some cases to indicate a single malt and in others to signify a vatted malt. When Cardhu switched from the former category to the latter, the term "pure malt" was used. Other distillers protested, arguing that the consumer was being misled – or, at best, confused – and that the integrity of malt whisky was being put at risk.

BLENDED SCOTCH WHISKY A stroke of Scottish genius, devised in the Victorian era. Craft producers, mainly in the Highlands and Islands, make small quantities of flavoursome malt whisky. Much larger, more industrial distilleries, mainly in the Midlands and the south, produce large quantities of more neutral grain whiskies to add volume to the malt. The result is a blended Scotch.

GRAIN WHISKY These may be produced from corn (maize), wheat, or raw barley. A small amount of malted barley is required to provide the enzymes needed in fermentation, in a continuous process, in a column-shaped still. Grain whiskies are light in body and flavour, but not neutral, and are matured for a minimum of three years in oak.

SINGLE GRAIN WHISKY There have been attempts to market single grain whisky as a more interesting alternative to vodka, or perhaps as a Scottish "grappa"? Occasional independent bottlings are also of interest to collectors.

FURTHER LABEL TERMS

PEATING When maltsters kilned their grains over open fires, the fuel was whatever could easily be found. In Poland, a style of beer was made from oak-smoked malt. In Franconia, Germany, beechwood was favoured. In Scotland, whisky malt was kilned over peat fires. The peat gave an especially distinct smokiness to Scotch whisky, and has to varying degrees been retained. Serious whisky lovers have come to cherish peatiness, and demand more, as many of the popular malts have become less smoky to appease consumers who fear flavour. Within the industry, the peat-smoke character is measured in parts per million (ppm) of phenol. The most heavily peated spirit currently being distilled is Octomore, at 80 ppm, but this will not be ready to bottle for some years. Neither will Port Charlotte, at 40 ppm (the same level as Laphroaig). Both are being distilled at Bruichladdich. The level for the whisky called simply Bruichladdich is 2–5 ppm. These figures do not tell the whole story, as the smokiness can be accentuated or softened by the design, shape, and configuration of the stills, the woods used in ageing and so on.

Burning at Bowmore

Stoking the firebox: the smoke rises through the mesh floor of the kiln, upon which the grains of sprouting barley are spread. The heat arrests germination, and the smoke imparts flavour.

DOUBLE/TRIPLE DISTILLATION Most Scottish malt whisky is run through a pair of stills, but a handful of distilleries have over the years used a system of three linked stills (*see* Springbank). Triple distillation was once traditional in the Lowlands of Scotland (*see* Auchentoshan). It is also favoured in Ireland. In theory, the more thorough the distillation, the lighter and cleaner the spirit. Triple should be more exhaustive than double. While this is broadly true, the still's influence on flavour is not completely understood.

BOURBON AGEING Why the name bourbon? The French helped the Americans in the War of Independence, and the Americans acknowledged this by naming towns and counties after the French royal family. Bourbon County, in Kentucky, was known for shipping whiskey down the Ohio and Mississippi rivers to New Orleans and other big cities. (Whiskey had been introduced to the United States by Northern Irish immigrants of Scottish origin.)

Local corn is always used to make bourbon, along with rye or wheat, and the bourbon is then matured in a fresh oak barrel. The inside of the barrel is charred to help the whiskey permeate the wood. After only one use in Kentucky, the barrel may be sent to Scotland and used to mature Scottish whisky. It will still retain enough of its typical vanilla-like flavours to impart some of these to the first fill of this whisky; and along with the vanilla, there may be caramel-toffee flavours, dessert apple, and a touch of tannin. There will still be some lively flavour contributuion in a second fill. By the third fill the barrel may be relatively neutral. Some barrels are recharred in Scotland.

SHERRY AGEING The word "sherry" derives from English attempts to pronounce the Spanish place name Jerez. The wine makers of the Jerez area, in the southwest, near Cadiz and Seville, have a long relationship with the British Isles. Large quantities of their fortified Jerez wines were for a long time shipped to Cork, Bristol (the nearest English port), and Leith (the port that adjoins Edinburgh). Instead of being shipped empty back to Spain, the drained butts and hogsheads were snapped up by whisky distillers. Today, this wine is bottled in Spain, and sherry wood is expensive. Nonetheless some distillers feel that its influence is important. They make the investment (*see pp. 70–1*), and are precise in their requirements. Most sherry is made from the Palomino grape. There are several styles – fino: dry, delicate and fresh; manzanilla: a saltier coastal cousin; amontillado: darker and nuttier; palo cortado: aromatic, complex, and cookie-like; oloroso: rich, creamy, and fruity; Pedro Ximénez (made with the grape of the same name, and not the Palomino): intensely raisiny, treacly and dark. *See also* "Cask Strength" (*pp. 16–17*), "Vintage Editions" (*pp. 18–19*); "Single Cask" (*p. 19*), "Unchillfiltered" (*p. 19*); as well as "Regional Variations" (*pp. 54–65*).

The Spanish connection
The tradition of sherry ageing brings an added dimension to Scotch whisky. The diversity of sherry itself is evident in the museum at the Gonzalez Byass bodega, in Jerez.

FLAVOURS

THE INFLUENCE OF THE LANDSCAPE

THE UNIVERSE OF SPIRITS BEGAN to change when the word "designer", having become an adjective, attached itself to the word "vodka". Then, some of the most famous names in the world of distillation became better known for their "ready-to-drink" confections, misleadingly known in the United States as "malternatives". Now a new generation of consumers faces a choice between drinks that come from nowhere, taste of nothing much, and have a logo for a name; and drinks that come from somewhere, have complex aromas and flavours, and may have a name that is hard to pronounce.

Such drinks reflect their place of origin. They have evolved. They have a story to tell. They are good company, and they require something of the drinker in return: that he or she experiences the pleasure of learning to drink. Real, evolved drinks begin as the gift of God. They are grown, whether from grapes, grain, sugar cane, or, for example, the agave plant. They arise from their own *terroir*: geology, soil, vegetation, topography, weather, water, and air. To what extent they are influenced by each of these elements is a matter for debate, often passionate. People care about real drinks.

The most sophisticated of real drinks are the brandies of France and the whiskies of the British Isles. The most complex brandies are the cognacs and armagnacs. The most complex whiskies are those of Scotland and Ireland.

Within these two duopolies, cognac and Scotch are the best known. In Cognac, the regions of production are contiguous, stretch about 144 kilometres (90 miles) from one end to the other, and are all in flat countryside. The whisky distilleries of Scotland are spread over an area of about 448 kilometres (280 miles) from one end of the country to the other, from the Lowlands to the northern Highlands, from mountain to shore, and from the Hebrides in the west to Orkney (and by now Shetland?) in the north. Theirs is surely the greater complexity.

Under the volcano
Scotland's landscape can be silent and still, yet the evidence of eruptions, glaciations, and rocky collisions is everywhere. The dews and frosts, the marine plants and mountain forests – each valley or island has its own flavour. Arran, left, has extinct volcanoes and a newish distillery.

Whisky is a real drink. A single malt is as real as it gets. There are many potential influences on its character, and much dispute as to the relative importance – if any – of each. The Macallan distillery receives what might seem disproportionate attention in the following pages because it takes what might aptly be termed single-minded positions on almost every issue: the variety of barley; the strains of yeast; the size of still; and the provenance of the casks.

On these and other issues ever more research is carried out, but an apparent insight into one stage of the whisky-making process may raise new questions about the next. In production, if a procedure is changed, the result may not be apparent until the whisky is mature, perhaps 10 years hence.

THE WHISKY COUNTRIES

Scotland and Ireland can be cool and rainy, but their climates are temperate. The conditions are very favourable for the growing of barley, though excessive damp and wind can occasionally be a problem.

The windy main island of the Orkney islands still cultivates bere, a precursor to barley, but grown today for local bakers rather than distillers. It was used in whisky making in the past, and its importance was such that a dispute over taxes on bere even threatened the Act of Union in 1707.

Today, just as different wine regions champion their own grapes, so there are debates in Europe as to the merits of "continental" barleys, such as those grown in Moravia, Bohemia, and Bavaria, versus the "maritime" examples of Denmark, Scotland, England, and Ireland.

The blood of …

… John Barleycorn was spilled by Robert Burns, a Lowlander but from the West. This field of barley is in the East, near the Lowland distillery, Glenkinchie.

Supporters of the continental barleys say they provide a sweeter, nuttier flavour. Protagonists for the maritime varieties argue that they have a clean, "sea-breeze" character.

Naturally, the Scots prefer their own barley. Depending upon the harvest, and their own needs, they have on occasion exported, but in other periods they have augmented their own malt with "imports" from England. Their second choice would be Denmark, and then elsewhere. Purists would prefer that the Scots used only their own barley. The Scots could argue that they are simply victims of their own success in selling so much of their whisky.

It is because barley is more resilient that it has a broader belt of cultivation, and can be more easily transported, than the grapes that make wine and brandy. Scotland's main growing regions are on the more sheltered eastern side of the country: on the shores of the Moray firth (The Black Isle and The Laich of Moray), Aberdeenshire, and the Borders. Ireland's are in the southeast, behind an imaginary line on the map, which runs from the border city of Dundalk (with a history of brewing) in County Louth, to the sailing (and gastronomic) resort of Kinsale, County Cork. Both countries might wish for more cultivable land; Scotland is mountainous, and Ireland boggy.

TASTING THE *TERROIR*

Scotland seems like a machine for the making of whisky: a nation on a small island, awaiting the vapours of the sea; providing summits to unlock their precipitation, which then filters through a diversity of rock, via springs and mountain streams, over peat and heather, to the fields of barley and the distilleries.

Scotland's heather-clad hillsides, its peaty moorlands, and its seaweed-fringed islands all contribute to the character of its national drink. To sample some of the more pungent malts is to taste the *terroir*. But to what extent are the aromas and flavours carried by the mountain streams or burns that feed the distilleries? Is the greater influence in the peat that is used to dry the malt? Then there is the question of the atmosphere in the damp, earth-floored warehouses, and its influence on the whisky.

Heather, peat, and seaweed are not unique to Scotland, but the country is unusually rich in all three. Their local variations, their proportion, their juxtaposition, and their relationship with the rest of the landscape are unique. Every landscape is. The colour of a person's hair or eyes, or the shape of a nose or jawline, are not unique, but the face is, and it derives from them all.

On the map, Scotland presents a weatherbeaten face. The outline – the coast – is penetrated by endless inlets from the sea. These inlets are variously known as "sea lochs" or "firths"; the latter word has the same roots as the Norwegian "fjord".

"SCANDINAVIAN SCOTLAND"

In its topography, its use of Viking words, its Protestant rigour (with some ambivalence toward alcohol), Scotland can resemble Norway, the nearest of the Scandinavian countries. Scotland seems to reach northwards, higher into the spirits belt, while its Celtic cousin Ireland (more especially the Republic) appears to lean south, toward the Roman Catholic countries of mainland Europe.

Scotland is bigger in both land area and population than Ireland. It also has 20 or 30 times as many distilleries. At one stage, for a brief period, the numbers of stills in each of the countries were close, but Ireland's industry spent decades in decline before rediscovering itself in recent years. Whichever country "discovered" the barley distillate, and this is contentious, Scotland is today's pre-eminent "Land of Whisky".

Only whisky made there can be called Scotch. For many years, the industry repeated this without making clear its meaning. Were their spokesmen simply repeating an appellation? Or did they mean that no other country could make a comparable product? Scotch whiskies all taste of their homeland to varying degrees, but in many the taste is so subtle as to be scarcely evident, while in others the aromas of peat and seaweed, for example, are wonderfully shocking.

The handful of malt whiskies (as opposed to the "pot-still Irish" type) made at Bushmills and Cooley in Ireland are similar in style to their Scottish counterparts; as are the handful of Japanese malts, though some have distinct local features. But a whisky cannot taste of Scotland if it is made in Ireland or Japan, however similar the *terroir*. The most characterful whiskies taste of the *terroir*, wherever it is. They are real drinks.

ROCK

Geology as a discipline began in Scotland – with the book *Theory of the Earth*, published in 1788. The author, Dr James Hutton, was a Scot, inspired in part by the natural landscape of his homeland. The geology of Scotland is more varied than that of any country of a similar size. Much of this diversity arises from a spectacular collision 400–500 million years ago. The part of the earth's crust that is now Scotland was at that time attached to North America. It was in

Rosebank

Roses once bloomed at Rosebank. Now rosebay willowherb has taken over. The whisky tastes of camomile ... or carboniferous rock.

collision with a European plate that included England, Wales, and Ireland. The fault line where the two plates met was more or less followed a few million years later by Hadrian's Wall, and the border between England and Scotland has rarely strayed more than a few kilometres from this line since. The geological turbulence continued, with everything from volcanoes to glaciers, until 20,000 years ago.

Thus not only did geology begin with Scotland, but Scotland began with geology: with the thrusts, intrusions, eruptions, and glaciations. It came to rest, semantically, as a Gaelic-language landscape, with "corries" (hollows in the mountainside); "lochans" (small lakes) and "lochs" in a wide range of sizes (sometimes stretching for many miles, and possibly with a small opening to the sea); "straths" (broad valleys); and the "glens" (or narrower valleys) that appear on every other label. *This* is the whisky-making machine.

In 1990, geologists Stephen Cribb and Julie Davison made a study of rock formations in Scotland's whisky regions, and compared them with tasting notes in books on the drink, including this one. Their findings suggested that the similar tastes in certain whiskies produced near each other might in part be due to the similar rock from which the water rose. For example, in the Lowlands, the crisp, dry Glenkinchie and Rosebank share the same carboniferous rock. The oldest rock is that which supplies water to the Bowmore and Bruichladdich distilleries on Islay, off the west coast of Scotland; it was formed about 600–800 million years ago, and seems to contribute an iron-like flavour.

For many years, whisky makers always spoke of granite. Being so hard, granite does not donate minerals to the water. Thus hard rock means soft water, and vice versa. Granite is the principal rock of the

41

Grampians, the group of mountains and sub-ranges that dominates the Highlands, and from which the River Spey flows. Every Speyside distiller seemed to claim that he had soft water, "rising from granite and flowing over peat". In looking at the Grampians, the Cribbs' book *Whisky on the Rocks* identified Ben Rinnes and the Conval Hills as sources of the typical Speyside water, feeding distilleries such as Glenfarclas, Aberlour, and Craigellachie. The study went on to point out that the region's geology is diverse, embracing substantial areas of limestone and sandstone. One distillery that has, sensibly, made a virtue of its sandstone water source is Glenmorangie, located in the northern Highlands.

Mineral flavours – and textures – are familiar from bottled waters, and also seem evident in some malt whiskies. Water is used to steep the grain at maltings (though only a handful of these are attached to distilleries). It is employed in the mash tun at every distillery to extract the sugars from the malted barley. It is used to reduce the strength of spirit in the cask to aid maturation. It is also used to reduce mature whisky to bottling strength. For this last stage the local water is influential only in the handful of distilleries that bottle on site, and in those cases, it is very influential indeed.

SNOW

Vodka marketeers love to promote their products with suggestions of snowy purity, whether they are distilled in St Petersburg, Poznan, or in Peoria, Illinois. Some vodkas are distilled in one place and rectified in another. Others have Slavic origins, but are produced under licence in North America or elsewhere.

Snow on the Spey
The river Spey rises south of the Dalwhinnie distillery, one of Scotland's highest. Clearly whisky made from snowmelt, but also with some peaty complexity. Absolut Scotland ...

Snow-melt is more reliably found in Scottish malt whisky. There is typically snow on Scotland's highest mountain, Ben Nevis (measuring 1344 metres or 4410 feet high), for six to seven months of the year, and occasionally for longer: perhaps from September to May, or even all year. The same can be true in the Grampians, though three or four months is more common.

At sea level, especially in the drier east, Scotland may have less than 800 millimetres (32 inches) of rain and snow a year. In the mountains, that figure can more than triple. Once the snow melts, it descends by a variety of routes, filtering through fissures in the rock, emerging from springs, swelling streams or burns, or gushing into rivers like the Spey, Livet, and Fiddich.

High in the hills, distilleries like Dalwhinnie or Braeval might regard their water as snow-melt. By the time it has swollen the Spey, then been tapped by Tamdhu, it is regarded as river water. If it filters through the Conval Hills in search of Glenfiddich, Balvenie, or Kininvie, it emerges as the spring water of Robbie Dubh. Every distillery knows where it collects its water, and protects its source as a critical asset. Distillers know where their water arrives, but it may be impossible to say whence it came, or how long its journey was, except that it was once rain or snow.

WATER

The worry over water concerns not only quality, but also quantity. A great deal is required, not only for the steeps at the maltings and the mash tun at the distillery, but also to cool the condensers or worm tubs, to wash vessels, and to reduce the strength of the spirit in the cask or the mature whisky at bottling.

Unlike brewers of beer, the distillers of whisky do not add or remove salts to change the composition of their water. Not only must water for malting and mashing be available in volume, it must also be consistent in character. If a source threatens to run dry in the summer, the distillery may stop production and devote a few weeks' "silent season" to annual maintenance and vacations. If the water runs unusually slowly, or quickly, it may become muddy or sandy. If the water source is endangered by a project in the next county upstream, that could be a critical problem. And it is certainly critical if the distillery's production is outstripping the water source. Even the most sophisticated of distillery companies has been known to hire a water diviner to find an additional nearby source. Every effort will be made to match the character of the principal water used.

The issue of soft water versus hard goes beyond the flavour of any salts naturally occurring in the water. Calcium, for example, increases the extract of malt sugars in the mash tun, and may also make for a cleaner, drier whisky. Whether it does – whether, indeed, such influences could survive distillation – is hotly debated.

Visitors to distilleries are sometimes invited to sample the water. It can taste intensely peaty. Yet the whisky may be barely peaty at all. This is the case at the famous Speyside distillery, Glen Grant. The explanation would seem to be that the peaty taste does not survive distillation. Speyside is also rich in heather. Is that why its whiskies are so floral? The circumstantial evidence is strong, but some distillers might argue that the flowery character actually results from reactions during maturation.

On the island of Islay, even the tap water can be tinged a peaty brown or ironstone red. Perhaps the water flowed over peat for a longer distance. Did it linger, and take up more peatiness? Or flow faster and dig up its peaty bed? The bed may also have contributed some ironstone, or some green, ferny, vegetal character. This time, the flavours do seem to carry over into the whisky. Perhaps the flavours were absorbed when the peaty water was used to steep the barley at the beginning of the malting process. Unlike the maltings on the mainland, those on Islay highlight the intensity of local peat. It is the use of peat fires in the drying of the grains that imparts the greatest degree of smokiness and "Islay character" to the malt. The peat in the kiln is the smoking gun. The Islay distiller has the soul of an outlaw.

PEAT

Not only is aroma the bigger part of taste – the drinks and foods that arouse the appetite and the imagination are often fragrant – but these same foods are in fact frequently grilled, barbecued, roasted, toasted, or smoked: the breakfast kippers, bacon, toast, and coffee; the steak sizzling on a

Tasting the *terroir*
The basis of terroir *is the earth. Here, it is sliced, and placed on a fire, so that its smoke pervades the malt. Some peat cutting on Islay is still done by hand.*

charcoal grill; the chestnuts roasting on an open fire. Of all the techniques historically used to kiln malt in different parts of Europe, the peat fires of Scotland surely produce the most evocative aromas. While some devotees of single malts have a catholic view, many take sides: will it be the peaty, briney whiskies of the islands and coasts; or the flowery, honeyed, sometimes sherried Speysiders?

The partisans for peat lust for its intensity (and love quoting ppm), but it also imparts a number of complex flavours and aromas. At least 80 aroma compounds have been found in peated malt.

While peatiness excites connoisseurs, it can alienate first-time tasters. When people say they "don't like" Scotch whisky, they often refer to a "funny taste", which turns out to mean peat. To take exception to such a fundamental element of the drink may seem odd, but distinctive, powerful flavours, especially if they are dry, can be challenging. Very hoppy beers are a perfect parallel. At a pinch, heavily oaked wines might also be drawn into the discussion.

In whisky, the dryness of peat provides a foil for the sweetness of barley malt, but that is a bonus, as is peat's rich content of anti-oxidants, the enemy of free radicals.

Peat was used in the first place because it is a convenient and plentiful fuel. Ninety per cent of the world's peat bogs are in temperate-to-cold parts of the northern hemisphere. Two-thirds of Britain's bogland is in Scotland, which in land area is half the size of England. Scotland's northern Highlands has Europe's largest expanse of blanket bogs. These bogs, in the counties of Caithness and Sutherland, are said to set a standard in the worldwide study of the phenomenon.

The peat that seduces whisky lovers is on the distillery islands of Orkney and Islay. In both cases, the sea air and high winds add salty flavours to the peat. The coast of Islay is heavily fringed with seaweed, which adds an iodine, medicinal character to the atmosphere. This, too, penetrates the peat. The Orcadian peat is younger, more heathery, and incorporates a wide range of salt-tolerant maritime plants. In the western islands, especially Islay, the peat is rich in bog myrtle (*Myrica gale*), also known as sweet gale, which has a sweet, cypress-like aroma and bitter flavour. Bog myrtle was one of the flavourings used in beer before the hop plant was adopted, and clearly influences the flavours imparted by the peat.

When peat is being cut by hand, the spade digs out a cube with surfaces as shiny and dark as a bar of "black" chocolate. It sometimes looks as edible as Mississippi mud pie. A closer look at the muddy block sometimes reveals the fossil-like remains of mosses. The principal component is sphagnum, a spongy moss that intertwines with other plants to form a fibrous soil, which, under pressure, will eventually become coal. The peatbogs of Scotland began to grow between 7000 and 3000 years ago, and are up to 7 metres (23 feet) deep.

Ireland is also famously boggy, and no doubt its rural whiskey makers burned peat, but distilling quickly moved to an industrial scale, concentrated in the few big cities, and the lack of peat became a defining characteristic of the "smooth" Irish whiskies. The large, urban distillers used coke to fire smokeless maltings. Having been overtaken in volume long ago by the country next door, the Irish are now rediscovering the merit of variety. A peated single malt called Connemara was launched in 1995–96 by the Cooley distillery, and has gone on to win several judgings.

HEATHER

In the unofficial national anthem, the "Flower of Scotland" is Robert the Bruce; in heraldry, it is the thistle; in the world of drinks, it is surely heather. While the thistle is Scotland (prickly, defensive, and looking for a fight), heather is attractive and lucky. In Scotland, especially Orkney, it was traditionally the flavouring for an ale. When a whisky has a floral aroma, the flower is frequently heather. Often, it is not the flower itself but heather honey.

These characteristics are especially notable on Speyside and Aberdeenshire, where the hills are dense with heather. Glen Elgin and Balvenie are two whiskies with a notably heather-honey character. In

The colour purple
Heather is a distinctive feature of the Scottish landscape. Its colour does not affect the whisky, but the floral and honey aromas often seem to have jumped into the glass.

Aberdeenshire, Glendronach and Glen Garioch have an enjoyable touch of heather, balancing their dry maltiness.

Heather is a significant component of much peat in Scotland. At some distilleries, notably Highland Park, lore has it that sprigs of heather were thrown on to the peat fire in the maltings. Water flows over heather to several distilleries. Besoms, or brooms, made of heather twigs were once commonplace in Scotland, and were typically used to clean wooden washbacks (fermenting vessels). Whether their effect was to sanitize or inadvertently to inoculate with micro-organisms is a piquant question. Wild yeast activity is at its height in summer, when bees are pollinating, and heather is a favourite source of nectar.

The Greek for the word "brush" gives us the botanical name *Calluna vulgaris* for the purple ling heather, which carpets the hillsides from mid-August into September. The brighter, redder bell heather (*Erica cinerea*) and the pinker, cross-leafed variety (*Erica tetralix*) flower about a month earlier. The English name for this group of small evergreen shrubs derives from their liking of heaths, but they also grow in bogs and on mountainsides. All three occur in Scotland, where heather covers between 1.6 and 2 million hectares (4 to 5 million acres).

Some varieties are found throughout northern Europe, others are native to Scotland, which has the greatest abundance of the plants. Scottish settlers introduced heather to North America.

BARLEY

Everyone knows that wines and brandies are made from grapes, but what about beer or whisky? Many consumers are unsure. Beer is often thought, mistakenly, to be made from hops. And whisky?

In explaining, and therefore promoting, its natural qualities, the grape does rather better than the grain. Wine makers often indicate on their labels which varieties of grape they have used. They may do this even if the wine is not a varietal. They might even discuss their choice of grape varieties on a back label or hang tag, and in their public relations and advertising.

Whisky makers do not in general do this. Why not? Are they using poor-quality barley? No. Malting requires barley of good quality. The argument for reticence is threefold: barley's contribution to flavour in whisky is less than it would be in beer, and even less than that of the grapes in wine. Second, perhaps simply as a reflection of the above, the difference between varieties is less obvious when it comes to flavour. Third, perhaps explaining this, the act of distillation removes some characteristics, and others are masked by the flavours gained during maturation. All of this is true up to a point, but what the distiller puts into his vessels must be a factor in the liquid that issues from them.

Almost all whisky distillers buy their barley according to a set of technical criteria (corn size, nitrogen, moisture content, etc.), rather than by variety. Some varieties bred or selected in the period of innovation after the Second World War are still legends. The last of that line, Golden Promise, represented 95 per cent of the harvest at its peak. Its short straw stands up to the wind; it ripens early (in August); and it produces nutty, rich flavours.

As the industry has grown, farmers have switched to varieties that give them more grain per acre, and therefore increase their profitability, while distillers have sought varieties that yield more fermentable sugars. These, however, do not necessarily produce delicious flavours, any more than do bigger, redder strawberries out of season. Nor do the varieties last much more than four or five seasons before being overtaken by something "better".

In 1994, the author was asked by Macallan to taste blindfold two samples of spirit, fresh from the still ("new make"). What was the purpose of the comparison? What was being sought? No explanation was offered. Nor were there any give-away clues such as colour; the spirit had not yet acquired any, not having begun its maturation. One sample seemed rich, malty, sweet, and Macallan-like. It turned out to have been distilled from Golden Promise, a variety that Macallan regards as being an essential component of its malt grist. The other tasted thin, metallic, and dusty. It had been distilled from a more recent, high-yield variety.

At the time, only one or two farmers were still cultivating Golden Promise, but Macallan had set about persuading others. The distillery stands on an estate, and its farm has now been leased and turned over to Golden Promise. A single farm can contribute only a fraction of the barley required, but the gesture is worth much more. Perhaps one day soon whisky lovers will be offered a single estate malt.

SEAWEED

The medicinal note in most Islay malts, especially Laphroaig, surely derives from seaweed, a source of iodine. The sea washes against the walls at all the distilleries, except Bruichladdich, and the coast is enwrapped with seaweed. How do the seaweedy, iron-like aromas get into the spirit? It seems likely that they are carried ashore by the winds and the rain, and permeate the peaty surface of the island. Then, when the rivers and burns flow over the peat to the distilleries, they

Whisky and water
The village and distillery of Bowmore face the sea loch around which Islay wraps itself.
Some of the distillery's warehouses are below sea level. Even on a calm day, the atmosphere
is rich in the aromas of seaweed.

pick up these flavours and impart them in the steep or the mash tun. If the boggy surface is, indeed, impregnated with the seaweedy rain, then a further opportunity will arise when the peat is cut and burned in the distillery's maltings.

The greatest scepticism concerns the belief that the casks in the warehouses "breathe in" the atmosphere. Distillers who use centralized warehouses, away from the distillery, especially favour this argument. Some age on site spirit which is destined to be bottled as single malt, but send to centralized warehouses spirit that is destined for blending.

Seaweed has been described as one of Scotland's most abundant natural resources. The harvesting of seaweed was once a significant industry in Scotland. There is some circumstantial evidence that the practice was introduced by monks on the islands of the west. This is the part of Scotland with the most seaweed. Skye has especially dense kelp forests, sometimes stretching 5 kilometres (3 miles) offshore and more than 20 metres (65 feet) deep. In the islands, kelp was traditionally used as a fertilizer. It was also collected as a source of iodine. More recently, it was used to provide alginates to clarify beer and set jellies and desserts.

The infusion
Like coffee in a filter, the ground grains of malted barley are soaked in warm water, in a vessel with a sieve-like base. The stirring mechanism rotates and can be lowered so that its blades prevent the mixture from solidifying.

FLAVOURS SHAPED AT THE DISTILLERY

In the balance of influences, much more importance has been accorded in recent years to the way in which the distillery works. Twenty-seven malt distilleries, (about a third of the industry's working total) are owned by Diageo, the world's biggest drinks group; and Diageo argues strongly that the most important influences on flavour come from within the distillery itself.

The basic process of making malt whisky is the same throughout Scotland, but there are endless small but significant areas of variation. The degree of peating in the malt is one, similar to the choice of roasts in coffee. Another example is the density (or original gravity) of the malt-and-water mixture that goes into the mash tun (the "coffee filter"). The time the mixture spends in the mash tun, the temperatures to which it is raised, and the duration of each stage, all vary slightly from one distillery to the next. Inside a traditional mash tun is a system of revolving rakes to stir the mixture. In the more modern lauter system, developed in the German brewing industry, a system of knives is used. The German word "lauter" means pure or transparent, and refers to the solution of malt sugars that emerges from the vessel.

As in cooking, every variation affects everything that follows, so that the permutations are infinite. It can be very difficult to determine which aspect of procedure has what effect. Despite that, the industry in general has over the years adopted a rather casual attitude towards yeast's use in fermentation. The view taken was that yeast's influence on flavour would largely be lost in distillation, and that its job was simply to produce as much alcohol as possible.

For years, almost all of Scotland's malt distillers employed the same two yeast cultures. An ale yeast from one of the big brewers was used because it started quickly. Then there was a second pitching with a whisky yeast from Distillers' Company Limited (now long subsumed into a component of Diageo). This had less speed but more staying power. Mergers and changes in ownership resulted in different yeasts coming into the industry. Many distilleries now use only one culture; even Macallan, who insisted on three, have retreated to two.

The action of yeast in fermentation creates flavour compounds called "esters", which are variously fruity, nutty, and spicy. It is difficult to accept that none of these would survive distillation. Diageo believes that the amount of time spent in the fermenter is critical to the individuality of each distillate. The effect of a new yeast culture can be tasted in new make, but the final result will not be determined until the whisky is mature.

Fermentation vessels in Scottish malt distilleries are known as "washbacks". Some are closed vessels made of metal, usually stainless steel. These are easy to clean and relatively safe from contaminants. Despite this, some distilleries prefer wooden washbacks, usually made from larch or Oregon pine. These are open, with a movable lid. Although they are cleaned thoroughly, it is hard to believe that they accommodate no resident microflora. Perhaps these contribute to the house character of some of the more interesting whiskies. Meanwhile, whether the microclimate in and around the distillery has an influence is hotly debated.

Anyone who cooks will know that a recipe, however rigidly followed, will produce different results every time, depending upon the source of heat, the utensils, the cook, and so forth. The design of the stills is a factor increasingly emphasized by Diageo, but even this has an element of location. Some farmhouse distilleries clearly had stills designed to fit their limited space. Elsewhere, several distilleries in the same valley will have the same shape of still (in much the same way that railway stations on the same line may look alike). Obviously, the local coppersmith had his own way of doing things. Distilleries are reluctant to change the shape or size of their stills when wear and tear demands replacement, or when an expansion is planned. The

legend is that if a worn-out still has been dented at some time, the coppersmith will beat a similar blemish into its replacement, in order to ensure that the same whisky emerges.

Illegal distillers used just one small (and therefore portable), copper pot. Since then stills have grown, and are typically run in pairs (or occasionally threesomes), but the principles have not changed. It is clear that design has been largely empirical, with experiments and innovations introduced by individuals. It is often hard to imagine how a bit of extra piping here or there can make a difference. The ratio of surface areas to heat, liquid, vapour, and condensate have infinite effects that are not fully understood.

Water music?

Not a French horn, or any musical instrument, but the unromantically named worm tub. This one is at Edradour. The coil is 24.5 metres (80 feet) long. The diameter starts at 20 cm (8 inches) and finishes at 5 cm (2 inches).

It is argued that in a tall, narrow still, much of the vapour will condense before it can escape. The condensate will fall back into the still and be redistilled. This is known as reflux. The result is a more thorough distillation and a more delicate spirit. Because there is far less reflux in a short, fat still, the spirit will be oilier, creamier, and richer. This is just the simplest example of the shape influencing the character of the whisky.

Stills vary enormously in size and shapes range from "lantern" or "lamp" to "onion" or "pear". Some have a mini-column above the shoulders or, more often, a "boil ball". Others have pipes known as "purifiers" in order to create reflux. The pipe that carries the vapour to the condenser is sometimes at an upward angle, or it can be straight, or point downward. The first will create the most reflux and the last little or none.

The traditional method of condensing is in a worm tub. The vapours pass through a worm-like coil of copper piping in a tub of cold water. This tends to produce a more pungent, characterful spirit, with a heavier, maltier, cereal-grain character.

The more modern system has the opposite relationship between vapour and water. It involves a single large tube, inside which are packed smaller tubes. The small tubes are circulated with cold water,

Still life

The creaminess of Macallan is attributed in part to its short, fat stills. In this picture, the stillman provides a sense of scale. The stills at Glenmorangie are twice as tall, and produce a spirit of legendary delicacy.

while the vapour passes through the large tube. This is called a shell-and-tube condenser. It is more efficient, and is said to produce lighter, grassier, fruitier spirits.

At a time when the industry was moving from worm tubs to shell-and-tube, Diageo made this change at its Dalwhinnie distillery. It was subsequently decided that the spirit had changed character to an unacceptable degree, and the distillery reverted to worm tubs.

One of the most important judgments in influencing flavour is deciding the speed at which the stills are run. Equally important is the decision about when the process has arrived at an acceptable spirit.

In maturation, most distillery managers prefer a stone-built, earth-floored, cool, damp warehouse. Such an atmosphere is felt to encourage the casks to breathe. In this type of structure, known as a dunnage warehouse, the casks are normally stacked only three high, usually with planks between them as supports. The more modern type of warehouse has a concrete floor and fixed racking. As is often the case, the old, inefficient system, more vulnerable to the vagaries of nature, produces the more characterful result.

REGIONAL VARIATIONS

L IKE WINES – AND MANY OTHER DRINKS – the single malts of Scotland usually identify in their labelling not only their country of origin but also the region within it. To know where in Scotland a whisky was produced is to have a very general idea of its likely character. The differences arise from *terroir* and tradition; there are no regional regulations regarding production methods. In their aroma and palate, some whiskies speak of their region more clearly than others, as is the case with wines. Within Bordeaux, a particular Pomerol, for example, might have a richness more reminiscent of Burgundy; similar comparisons can be made in Scotland.

THE LOWLANDS

These are the most accessible whiskies, in both palate and geography, but sadly few in number. From the border town of Carlisle, it is less than 160 kilometres (100 miles) to the southernmost Scottish distillery, Bladnoch, which has been back in production since December 2000, albeit on a limited scale. It is distilling twice a week for half the year. Spirit tasted at 18 months as work in progress was malty, oily, dry, and very flowery. Mature whisky is not expected until 2008–10. Meanwhile, in the shop, distillery rescuer Raymond Armstrong offers a Flora and Fauna edition of Bladnoch, and various independent bottlings produced by former owners Diageo/UDV (*see* Bladnoch).

Only two Lowlanders are in constant production. One of these is Auchentoshan, sometimes billed as "Glasgow's only working distillery". It is on the edge of the city, at Dalmuir, across the Dunbartonshire county line. In Lowland tradition, the whisky is light in both flavour and body, but surprisingly complex and herbal. Auchentoshan is now the sole practitioner of the Lowland tradition of triple distillation. The distillery does not have a visitor centre, but professional tours are possible by arrangement. With its galleried mash house and uncluttered still-house, it is very visitor-friendly.

Maritime malt
Rivetted, not welded, this pot still has a marine appearance befitting its region. Campbeltown's heyday was the era of coastal steamers. Fat stills make oily, muscular whiskies.

The other thriving Lowlander, at the opposite side of the country, is Glenkinchie, "The Edinburgh Malt". This pretty distillery is about 25 kilometres (15 miles) southeast of the city, in the direction of the border. Its spicy whisky has a popular following, and the distillery has a visitor centre.

In the last couple of years, hope has faded for the reopening of the Lowland distilleries Littlemill and Rosebank, although various bottlings of both are still available (*see pp. 393–96 and 333–34*). Rosebank, which triple distilled, was widely regarded as a classic, and its whisky is collectible. Half a dozen further whiskies are still to be found from Lowland distilleries, some of which closed as long ago as the 1970s. There are even new bottlings, such as those from Glen Flagler and Killyloch (*see pp. 267–68*). These may be esoteric malts, but the region will not quibble.

There were never a great many Lowland malts, but to have only three active distilleries is perilously few. The delicacy of the Lowlanders makes its own contribution to the world of single malts. This style can be very attractive, especially to people who find the Highlanders and Islanders too robust.

The Lowlanders' problem has been that the Highlanders and Islanders have the romance. Many consumers like a gentle, sweetish malt such as is typical in the Lowlands, but they want the label to say it came from the Highlands. This is analogous with the wine industry, where consumers who like sweetish Chardonnays nevertheless insist that they are drinking a "dry white".

The notion of the Lowlands as a whisky region would be reinforced if it could annex two distilleries that are barely across the Highland line: Glengoyne and Loch Lomond. The first is very pretty, can be visited, and is barely outside Glasgow. Its malty whisky would be perfectly acceptable as a Lowlander. The second is a more industrial site, but a much more attractive distillery than it once was, and it makes a variety of whiskies. Pressed to "defect", both would probably cling to the Highland designation.

THE HIGHLANDS

The border between the Lowland and Highland distilleries is surprisingly southerly, following old county boundaries, stretching across the country between the rivers Clyde and Tay. Some commentators talk of a "southern Highlands", embracing the Tullibardine distillery, which is currently mothballed, and Deanston, which is fully active. Beyond these two, the spread is clearly eastern.

The border

It is neither the Berlin Wall nor Hadrian's, but it is Border country. The outer wall of a warehouse is turned to brash advertisement at the otherwise discreet Bladnoch distillery. Several distilleries identify themselves with such bold wall paintings.

THE EASTERN HIGHLANDS includes, among others, the newly independent Edradour, the smallest distillery in Scotland. Another tiny, farm-style distillery, Glenturret, now finds itself greeting visitors as "The Famous Grouse Experience". The much larger but handsome Aberfeldy distillery has a similar role as "Dewar's World of Whisky". All of these, together with Blair Athol, are in Perthshire. Any of them could comfortably be visited in a day trip from Edinburgh (about 112 kilometres, or 70 miles, away), and all are on or near the main road north to Speyside. Perhaps for reasons of geology, several distilleries in this region have notably fresh, fruity whiskies. Farther north, in barley-growing Aberdeenshire, some heftier whiskies emerge from handsome distilleries such as Royal Lochnagar, Glen Garioch, and Glendronach, with its coal-fired stills burning once more.

SPEYSIDE is not precisely defined, but it embraces between a half and two-thirds of Scotland's distilleries, including the most widely recognized whisky names. A generous definition of Speyside is assumed in this book. Strictly speaking, the long-gone distilleries of Inverness were regarded as Highlanders, not Speysiders. The same might be argued of Aberdeenshire distilleries like Glendronach, but it is easier for the visitor to regard this stretch of the Highlands as a contiguous region.

Again for the convenience of the visitor, this book divides the region into a series of river valleys. In some of these valleys, there do seem to be similarities between the whiskies of neighbouring distilleries.

The River Spey itself is lined with distilleries on both banks, but a number of tributaries and adjoining rivers frame the region. Speyside's ascendancy rested not only on the Grampian mountain snow-melt and the malting barley of Banff and Moray, but also on the railway era. Trains on a rustic branch alongside the Spey took workers and barley

Scotland

The principal divisions are between the distilleries of the Lowland, the Highlands, and the Islands. Within the Highlands, the valleys of the Spey and adjoining rivers are a distinct region. In the southwest, so is peninsular Campbeltown. Among the islands, Islay is accorded special status.

Distilleries
- ◉ Operating
- ◉ Mothballed/intermittent production
- ● Closed
- ○ Major town or city
- ▲ Height above sea level

0   20   40   60   80   100 Kms
0   10 20 30 40 50 60 Mls

ORKNEY
ISLANDS
Scapa   Highland Park

JOHN O'GROATS

Old Pulteney

Clynelish

*1081m
(3547ft)*

SPEYSIDE
(See page 60/61)

HEBRIDES

NORTHERN
HIGHLANDS

Glen Ord
Glen Albyn
Glen Mhor

Findhorn   *Spey*

Talisker

SKYE

Balmenach   ABERDEEN

Drumguish   *1309m
(4295ft)*   EASTERN

Lochnagar   HIGHLANDS   Glenury
Royal

Glenlochy   Dalwhinnie   Fettercairn

FORT
WILLIAM   Glencadam   Glenesk
1344m (4409ft)   Blair Athol   Lochside
Ben Nevis   Aberfeldy   Edradour   North Port

Tobermory   WESTERN
HIGHLANDS

MULL   Glenturret

Oban   Deanston   MIDLANDS
Tullibardine

Glengoyne
Loch Lomond   Littlemill   Rosebank   EDINBURGH
Inverleven   Saint
Auchentoshan   Magdalene   Glenkinchie
Kinclaith   GLASGOW

Arran   LOWLANDS

*816m
▲(2677ft)*

ISLAY
(See page 62)   CAMPBELTOWN   SCOTLAND

Glen   Springbank   Glen Flagler
Scotia

*843m
(2766ft)*

Ladyburn

Bladnoch   ENGLAND

or malt to the distilleries, and returned with whisky for the main line to Edinburgh, Glasgow, and London. Only vestiges of the Speyside railway survive today, though it is a popular walk. The active line from Aberdeen to Inverness (just over 160 kilometres or 100 miles) follows the main road. The rivers are crossed as follows:

DEVERON: This valley has Glendronach distillery and Glen Deveron. There are five or six distilleries in the general area, but these are quite widely dispersed. Most produce firm, malty whiskies.

ISLA: This has nothing to do with island (it has a different spelling; there's no "y"). Dominican monks brewed here in the 1200s, and there is mention of heather ale in the records. The oldest distillery on Speyside is Strathisla (founded in 1786), showpiece of Chivas Brothers, in the town of Keith in the Isla Valley. There are four or five distilleries in this area, and some of its whiskies have a cedary dryness.

FIDDICH AND DULLAN: These rivers meet at Dufftown, one of the claimants to be the whisky capital of Scotland. There are still six working distilleries in the area, despite the loss of Pittyvaich in 2002. A couple more are currently silent. Some classically rounded, malty Speysiders are produced here, including the secret star, Mortlach.

LIVET: The most famous distillery is called after the river valley itself, and there are three others in the area, all producing light, soft, delicate whiskies. The Livet appellation was once widely copied, but has been increasingly protected. The hill town, Tomintoul, is a base for exploration.

SPEY: Macallan, Aberlour, and Glenfarclas, three of the heavier interpretations of Speyside malts, are all to be found on the most heavily whiskied stretch of the Spey. There are about 12 distilleries, none more than a kilometre from the next, immediately upstream of the village of Craigellachie, home to a famous hotel and whisky bar.

ROTHES BURN: Actually no more than a stream, this river is one of several that reach the Spey at Rothes, another whisky "capital". This one-street town has five distilleries, producing some very nutty whiskies. Speyburn, usually shot through the trees, is the most photographed distillery in Scotland, while Glen Grant has a spectacular "tropical" garden, a coppersmith's, and a "dark grains" plant, which turns residual malt into cattle feed.

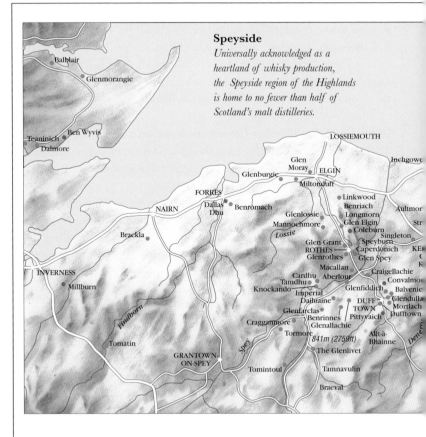

Speyside

Universally acknowledged as a heartland of whisky production, the Speyside region of the Highlands is home to no fewer than half of Scotland's malt distilleries.

LOSSIE: Was it the water that first attracted the Benedictines of Pluscarden to this region? They no longer brew there, but they still have a priory next door to the Miltonduff distillery. Two secret stars, Longmorn and Linkwood, are among the eight distilleries just south of Elgin. The world's most famous whisky shop, Gordon & MacPhail, is in Elgin itself. This sometimes ornate Victorian town is the undisputed commercial capital of Speyside and the county seat of Moray. The Lossie whiskies are sweetish and malty.

FINDHORN: Born-again Benromach is near the town Forres. Production restarted in 1998: the new make tasted creamy and flowery. The museum distillery of Dallas Dhu is nearby, and in the distance is Tomatin.

THE NORTHERN HIGHLANDS is a geographically clear-cut region, which runs from Inverness, straight up the last stretch of the east coast. The region's water commonly runs over sandstone, and there is a gentle maritime influence. There are four or five distilleries in short

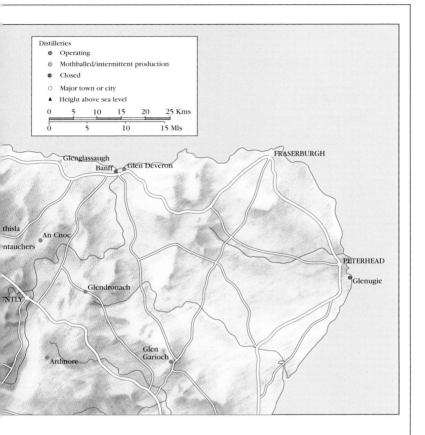

order; including the energetic Glenmorangie and the rich Dalmore. Then there is a gap before the connoisseurs' favourite, Clynelish, and an even bigger gap before the famously salty Old Pulteney in Wick. As its distilleries have become more active, the northern Highlands has gained more recognition as a region. Its whiskies tend toward firm, crisp dryness and a light saltiness.

WESTERN HIGHLANDS The far northwest is the only sizeable stretch of the country with no legal whisky makers. It is just too rugged and rocky. Even the centre cut has only two distilleries. On the foothills of Scotland's (and Britain's) highest mountain, Ben Nevis, the eponymous distillery can be regarded as being "coastal", according to its manager, Colin Ross. Why? Because it is on a sea loch. The Oban distillery certainly does face the sea, and has the flavours to prove it.

The other active mainland distilleries, Loch Lomond and Glengoyne, are so close to Glasgow that they might attract more attention reclassified as Lowlanders. In 2003, Glengoyne was acquired by Ian Macleod Ltd.

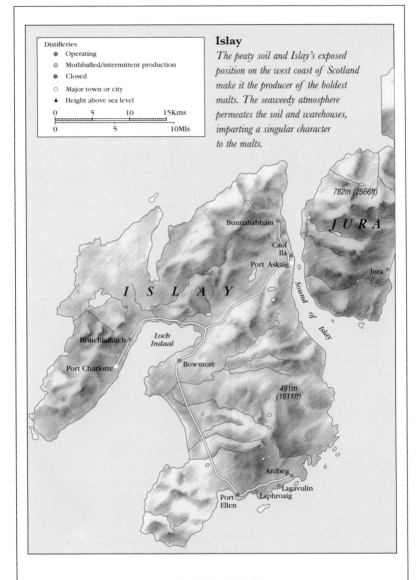

Islay

The peaty soil and Islay's exposed position on the west coast of Scotland make it the producer of the boldest malts. The seaweedy atmosphere permeates the soil and warehouses, imparting a singular character to the malts.

Distilleries
- ● Operating
- ◑ Mothballed/intermittent production
- ● Closed
- ○ Major town or city
- ▲ Height above sea level

0   5   10   15Kms
0   5   10Mls

THE ISLANDS

The greatest whisky island by far is Islay (above), with its seven distilleries. The others have one apiece, except for Orkney, which has two distilleries.

ORKNEY For the moment, Highland Park is Scotland's northernmost distillery. Its whisky is one of the greats, peaty and smoky, but a superb all-rounder. Saltier whiskies from the Scapa distillery have a strong following, but are not in production at the moment.

SHETLAND The first ever legal distillery in Shetland is promised for 2004 – it will be Scotland's most northerly.

SKYE Talisker whisky from Skye is a classic – volcanic, explosive, and peppery. The taste reflects the wild, looming *terroir*.

MULL Tobermory is a restrained islander, but the distillery also produces the peatier, smokier Ledaig. It is to be hoped that Tobermory does not suffer from its parent's acquisition of Bunnahabhain.

JURA The decidedly piney Isle of Jura whisky has appeared in more expressions and has been better promoted since the owning group, Whyte and Mackay, seceded from its American parent, Jim Beam.

ISLAY The 2003 takeover of Bunnahabhain by Burn Stewart makes this distillery look more secure. All seven of the island's workable distilleries are operating, and the Islay Festival in late May is establishing itself as an annual favourite.

ARRAN The newest distillery in Scotland, Arran ran its first spirit in 1995. Its small stills produce a creamy spirit with only faint touches of island character: a touch of flowery pine in the finish.

CAMPBELTOWN

The announcement in 2001 that Springbank's owners planned to restore the Glengyle distillery was quickly followed by the start of work. The distillery, which has been closed for 75 years, is due to reopen in 2004.

The Springbank distillery itself produces three whiskies, using entirely its own malt – the Springbank maltings was restored a decade ago. This distillery has on occasion also assisted with the management of the other Campbeltown distillery, Glen Scotia, which is currently also in production.

Springbank, the independent bottlers Cadenhead, and the Eaglesome shop are all related businesses. The whisky veteran behind them all, Hedley Wright, has been determined to keep Campbeltown on the whisky map. Its remarkable history is evidenced by fragments of about 20 distilleries converted to other uses. There are said to have been 32 distilleries here in 1759. The town's location at the foot of the Kintyre peninsula provides not only a harbour, but also a location surrounded by the sea and often shrouded in mist.

Tun No. 92 9

Rotation No. 0

Bulk Ltrs. 2130/1 2115/2

G/F 12 Y.O. SPECIAL RESERVE

WHAT IS THE PERFECT
AGE?

I N 2000, THE WORLD'S BIGGEST SELLING single malt, the principal version of Glenfiddich, changed its mind about age, for the second time. Like some of its immediate competitors, it had for much of its life carried no age statement. At one stage, it was bottled as an 8-year-old. Now it became a 12-year-old.

In announcing the change, Glenfiddich observed that malt drinkers looked for an age statement as a reassurance of authenticity and quality. This is not true of the more experienced malt drinker, who does not necessarily accept the inference that older is always better.

The extra years worked well for Glenfiddich. The earlier versions were light and pleasantly fruity, but could be a little sharp and thin. The extra years have rounded out the spirit and introduced a touch of the "white chocolate" found in older bottlings.

Glenfiddich, the first malt whisky to be methodically marketed, had possibly become over-familiar. It was seen as an unchallenging whisky, overtaken by more robust neighbours. The 12-year-old was perhaps a response: the whisky catching up with the consumer.

THE IMPOSSIBLE DECISION

Upgrading the age is not easy. Most distilleries have some reserves of maturing whisky that is older than they strictly need, but these stocks would not be sufficient to support such a major change. Had sales been falling sharply, a backlog of stock would have built up, but this was not the case. The decision to increase the age would have required sufficient stock to be laid down 12 years earlier, probably with a view to the change.

The person who makes such decisions has an impossible job. However good their judgment, knowledge, and understanding of the industry; however thorough the company's market research; and however many futurologists it consults, it is simply impossible to predict how much whisky will be required in five, ten or fifteen years. When the time comes, there is always too little or too much. Across the industry this is why distilleries open, close, are mothballed, and so frequently change ownership.

Single but married

Glenfiddich Special Reserve is already 12 years old when it goes into this marrying tun for about four months. The object is to iron out natural differences and ensure a consistent product.

MAKING A VATTING

The components of a bottling may also embrace casks of various sizes and with different histories. Although the contents of the casks will be vatted according to a "recipe", adjustments will have to be made to account for the way in which the whisky has developed during maturation. No two casks, even with the same origin, are alike. Casks from the bottom of the warehouse will have matured at a different rate from those in the airier racks at the top. A warehouse nearer the sea may impart brinier characteristics. Some distilleries have only the classically damp, earth-floored, stone-built warehouses, with casks stacked three high, separated by planks of wood; others have fixed racking, with casks nine high; some have both. All of these factors may affect the distillers' choice of casks for a bottling.

Ages around six, seven, and eight years are commonly used in blends, but they could be used in a vatting for a single malt. If it carries an age statement, regulations demand that it be based on the youngest age, but as "6-year-old" might sound callow, the producer might prefer to manage without an age statement. When Glenfiddich was marketed as an 8-year-old, it probably included whiskies of nine and ten years or more. Now it is a 12-year-old and probably includes whiskies of up to 15 years old. Some of the lighter-bodied malts hit their stride at eight or ten years old, while 12 is so common as to be regarded by consumers in some markets as a standard for mature malt.

DEVELOPING A RANGE

If there were a "best" age for malt whisky, it would be universally adopted. In Italy, where the words "malt whisky" are potent, devotees are delighted with a 5-year-old. In Japan, where age is respected, a 30-year-old is appreciated. In recent years, distillers have offered not only a greater range of ages but also of strengths, types of cask, and finish. These have come to be known as different "expressions" of the same malt. For those consumers bored with consistency, there is the merit of greater individuality in some of the more unusual bottlings, particularly vintages, and especially those at cask strength.

To take Glenfiddich as an example, it also offers: a variation on the 12-year-old (involving casks from Islay); a 15-year-old (Solera Reserve); a 21-year-old (Millennium Reserve, with a variation employing Havana rum barrels); and several dated vintages (of which the 1961 was a single cask). A bottling from a single cask represents a very limited edition, with the merit of its own individuality. Such a bottling is made for malt lovers who wish to explore.

Vintage whiskies

While seeking consistency in its principal product, Glenfiddich offers diversity of character in its vintages. The barley harvest and climate differ slightly each year, but bigger differences develop in the cask.

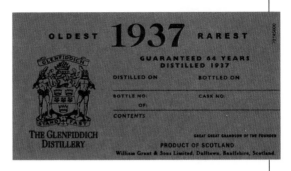

OLDEST **1937** RAREST

GUARANTEED 64 YEARS
DISTILLED 1937

DISTILLED ON   BOTTLED ON

BOTTLE NO: CASK NO:
OF:
CONTENTS

THE GLENFIDDICH
DISTILLERY

GREAT GREAT GRANDSON OF THE FOUNDER
PRODUCT OF SCOTLAND
William Grant & Sons Limited, Dufftown, Banffshire, Scotland.

Glenfiddich's Malt Master, David Stewart, creates daring whiskies that dance on the tongue with balletic elegance. His 12-year-old is a deft transformation, but he might well have preferred to approach the task from a wider angle: retaining some younger malts from the 8-year-old, but increasing the proportion of older malts (or increasing their ages). Young malts can inject liveliness to a vatting, while the older ones add complexity. This might have produced an even more complex whisky. Why did he not follow that course? Because it would have precluded the use of the age statement "12 years old".

Blenders like to use a wide range of ages within a vatting, but are constrained by the marketing men, with their reliance on bold statements of maturity.

In 1991, nine casks of a 50-year-old Glenfiddich were bottled. At such an age, whisky can be excessively woody (smelling like musty furniture in a derelict house), but that depends on the quality of the casks. Glenfiddich's semi-centenarian whisky had been in excellent oak. For its age, the whisky was surprisingly rounded and chocolatey, without excessive oakiness. The bottles were sold in London at around US$5000 (about £3,000) each, but one fetched US$70,000 (about £40,000) in an auction in Milan.

In 2003, for the Islay Festival, the Bunnahabhain distillery bottled seven hogsheads that had been filled in 1963. Evaporation had taken one or two to below 40 per cent alcohol, the legal minimum for whisky. When all had been checked, it was determined that a vatting of the seven would produce a bottling at 42.9 volume.

A whisky can be too woody at 21 years, or it can still be enjoyable at 50, but – like death and taxes – evaporation eventually takes its toll. Unlike a human being, a whisky that has over-stayed its time on earth is sure to meet the angels. Just as humans in ancient cultures revered trees, especially oaks, so *Quercus robur* and *Q. alba* are the greatest influences on the maturation of *aqua vitae*.

THE PERFECT WOOD

D ID THE FLAVOURS IN YOUR GLASS begin a dozen years ago, with the sowing of barley on the Black Isle? Or decades earlier, as a blizzard on the Grampians? If the malt was peated, you could be enjoying a few leaves of bog myrtle that have been waiting 7000 years for your rendezvous. Or did your favourite flavours emerge a century ago on a forest slope in Galicia, Spain? Or perhaps in the Ozark Mountains of Missouri?

The creation of alcoholic drinks in different parts of the world employs in various roles a whole alphabet of trees: for their fruits and berries; to make charcoal, to act as a filter; as a fuel in the kilning of malt; to provide vessels for fermentation or maturation, or simply to act as containers. Various drinks are stored in (or consumed from) cedar, juniper, and chestnut, but the wood most commonly used for all those purposes is oak. Its most attractive property is its pliability. It must bend to make a barrel, and the elegant curves of this traditional vessel strengthen it, just as an arch reinforces a building. Even in the most mechanized distillery, casks are rolled and occasionally dropped or bounced. They must be tough and not split or leak. They contain an increasingly precious product.

United States regulations insist that bourbon is matured in new oak, but the cask may subsequently cross the Atlantic and be filled three or four times with the spirit of Scotland. If each of those fillings is matured for only six or seven years, the cask will have seen two or three decades' service. If a cask is tapped at 25 years, then repeats the performance, it already has half a century under its belt. It must be tough, yet also able to breathe during the maturation of the whisky, and perhaps also have some flavours and aromas to donate.

OAK AND FLAVOUR

Wooden casks were originally regarded simply as containers. Whisky was sold in the cask to inns and country houses, and customers noted that it mellowed in the cellar. Over the years, it has increasingly been recognized that the character of the wood plays a big part in the

Tough but pliable
Oak does not break under torture, but it bends to provide the elegant, strengthening curves of the cask. This cooperage is in Andalusia. Charring to enhance flavour is more typical in Kentucky.

development of the whisky's aromas and flavours, but how big? The perceived importance of wood has greatly increased across the industry in recent years, yet opinions differ more widely than ever.

The issue was not much discussed while former sherry casks were readily available for the maturation of whisky. These casks seem to have been accepted without much question, though they must have imparted a variety of characteristics. Some had been used in fermentation, others in maturation, others for transport. They had contained different styles of sherry – and sometimes other fortified wines.

As sherry fell out of fashion, exports to the United Kingdom diminished. Meanwhile, the dictator Franco died in 1975, Spain became a democracy, and its trade unions insisted that the bottling of wines be carried out by local labour in Spain.

Distilleries anxious to continue sherry ageing now had to work directly with the bodegas in Jerez. Macallan has been the most consistently active proponent of this approach. So through several changes of control at Macallan, its top managers have each year swapped the granite and heather of Speyside for the orange trees and Moorish architecture of Jerez.

WHICH VARIETY OF OAK?

The Macallan is a full-bodied whisky, which as new make is rich in fruity esters reminiscent of flowering currant, apple, citrus, and even tropical fruits such as banana. These flavours are balanced by the tannins and acids found in European oak.

Setting aside those that grow as shrubs and bushes, there are more than half a dozen European species of oak tree. Two have traditionally been used in cooperage. The second choice is usually *Quercus petraea*, known as the sessile oak, for the way the acorns "sit" on the twigs. The first choice is *Quercus robur*, the pendunculate oak. The epithet refers to the way the acorns are suspended on stalks.

The *Q. robur* tolerates a wide range of growing conditions, and is typically found in England, France, and Iberia. In France, where region appellations are used, Limousin and Tronçais oaks are usually of the *Q. robur* variety.

The principal growing area in Spain is the northwest corner of the country, where the coast between the cities of Santander and Corunna faces the Bay of Biscay and the Atlantic. Behind the coast rise stony hills, the valleys between them dappled with oaks. These once fed shipyards making galleons; then Spanish oak was turned into barrels for wine; and now its final destination is Scotland.

The centre of the timber industry is the city of Lugo, in the province of the same name, in the region of Galicia. A sawmill there cuts staves for Macallan. The staves are air-dried for 12 to 15 months simply by being left outdoors. The weather washes out some of the tannins, moderating the intensity of the wood, and the staves then become casks at a cooperage in Jerez. They are filled with newly pressed cloudy grape juice, for between two weeks and six months, and then used a second time, to mature sherry, before being sent to Scotland. The casks are shipped whole, thus maintaining the sherryish character of the wood. This would diminish if they were knocked down into staves.

Iron lady
Torture continues … this machine forces the hoops to hold the staves in position.

Much as it is desired by Macallan, Spanish oak is less well supported in its own country. Spanish wine makers, including those of Jerez, increasingly prefer the sweeter, more vanilla-like character of American oak.

BUTTS, HOGSHEAD, OR BARRELS?

The casks used for the maturation of sherry are known as butts, and typically have a capacity of 500 litres (110 UK gallons or 132 US gallons). There is a beauty and an integrity to such vessels, but their size and weight make them difficult to handle.

The term "hogshead" refers to a traditional cask size of 250 litres (55 UK gallons or 66 US gallons). Sherry hogshead can be found, but the designation is more commonly applied to a Scottish adaptation of an American barrel. In this instance, the barrel is shipped as staves. It is then reassembled with new heads (barrel ends) to increase the size. The new heads also freshen up the wood influence. The term "American oak" is sometimes used to indicate a bourbon barrel, which typically has a capacity of around 200 litres (44 UK gallons or 53 US gallons). Many single malts are vatted from a combination of sherry butts and bourbon barrels, usually with the latter in the majority.

Many producers of lighter-bodied, more delicate-tasting whiskies feel that they express their aromas and flavours more successfully when matured in bourbon barrels. A long-time proponent of this approach is Glenmorangie. Its 10-year-old is wholly aged in bourbon, and this is the initial regime for other expressions, even though many are wood finishes.

The man in charge of distillation and maturation for Glenmorangie, Bill Lumsden, has worked with the Blue Grass Cooperage in Louisville to develop a bourbon barrel that perfectly suits both sides of the Atlantic. More than 360 kilometres (225 miles) southwest and 160 kilometres (100 miles) south of St Louis, Missouri, oak for the casks is grown around Altenburg, a town settled by immigrants from Saxony in Germany. The town sign still uses the word "*Stadt*" for "city".

This is an area of mixed deciduous woodland, with small, privately owned lots. The soils are very well drained. The part of the country has four definite seasons, but the winter cold has enough restraint not to damage the crop. The wood is clean, without knots, and with good pores. This is white oak, *Quercus alba*.

WHAT HAPPENS DURING AGEING

Several processes take place during maturation. While the new distillate may have some harsh, "spirity" flavours, these can be lost by evaporation. With the expansion and contraction of the wood, caused by seasonal changes in temperature, spirit flavours may be exhaled and the natural aromas of the environment taken into the cask: piney, seaweedy, and salty "sea-air" characteristics can all be acquired in this way. Flavours are also imparted by the cask: sherry wood may add the nutty note of the wine; and bourbon barrels can impart caramel flavours, vanillins, and tannins.

Perhaps the most important influence on the flavour is that of a very slow, gentle oxidation of the whisky. While oxygen is regarded as an "enemy" by brewers and some wine makers, because it can cause "stale" flavours, its influence is also a part of the character of other drinks such as Madeira wines. The importance of oxidation in the

Steam heat
*Scalded into submission ...
after these sequences of
tortures, the casks can settle
down to a life of sipping
sherry, then whisky.*

maturation of whisky has been the subject of much recent work by Dr Jim Swan, originally at the Pentlands Scotch Whisky Research Institute, and more recently by his own company. Dr Swan argues that oxidation increases the complexity and intensity of pleasant flavours in whisky, especially fragrant, fruity, spicy, and minty notes.

As in the production of all alcoholic drinks, the flavours emerge from a complex series of actions and reactions. Traces of copper from the stills are the catalyst. They convert oxygen to hydrogen peroxide, which attacks the wood, releasing vanillin. This promotes oxidation, and additionally pulls together the various flavours present. These processes vary according to the region of origin of the wood, and its growth patterns. Vanillin is a component that occurs naturally in oak. As its name suggests, it imparts a vanilla-like flavour.

In Spain, trees from the most mountainous districts of Galicia are more resiny. In the US, growth is mainly in a belt across Ohio, Kentucky, Illinois, Missouri, and Arkansas. The western part of this contiguous region has the poorest soil and the most arid climate, and therefore the trees have to fight to survive. This optimizes spring growth, which has the most open texture and is the most active in the maturation process.

LIGHT, MEDIUM, OR ALLIGATOR?

Bourbon barrels are toasted or charred on the inside to enable the whiskey to permeate the wood. There are stories of this happy discovery having arisen from an accidental fire, but it seems more likely to have emerged from the technique of toasting the wood to make it pliable.

Charring gives the spirit access to positive properties and flavours in the wood, but also enables it better to expel undesirable flavours. American cooperages typically offer three degrees of char: light, medium, and alligator. The latter, the heaviest, leaves the wood looking like a log so heavily burned that it has formed a pattern of squares reminiscent of an alligator's skin.

A sherry butt or bourbon barrel will impart considerable aroma and flavour to its first fill of whisky. "First-fill sherry casks were used in the maturation of this whisky" is the type of claim that appears on the neck label of an especially voluptuous malt. Some distillers feel that the more restrained second fill provides a better balance. A third fill will impart little, but let the character of the spirit speak for itself. If there is a fourth fill, it is likely to go for blending after which, 30 or 40 years on, the inside of the cask might be recharred. The preferred word is "rejuvenated".

OWNERS, DISTILLERS, AND BOTTLERS

IN THE NEXT SECTION IS A REVIEW, in alphabetical order, of every Scottish malt distillery that has ever witnessed its product in a bottle. These are not "brands" (though their names may be registered); they are actual distilleries: premises at which malt is turned into whisky. Among today's distilleries, only the relatively new Kininvie has not seen its product, a deliciously creamy whisky, bottled. Some of the distilleries reviewed have long closed, but bottlings from their stocks are still being made, or were within recent memory – and therefore may still be on the odd shelf.

NAMES OF DISTILLERIES Some distilleries have been known over the years by several different names. They are listed here by the most recent name on the label of the principal bottlings, though reference may be made in the text to earlier names. If you have bought, or are considering buying, a malt that appears not to be in this book, check the index. If it is not listed there, its name is not that of a distillery. Importers, distributors, and supermarkets often buy malt whisky to bottle under invented names (for example, Glen Bagpipe, Loch Sporran). These products are not reviewed. The bottle will probably contain whisky supplied by a reputable distiller who happens to have a surplus, but the source could change at any time. The next bottle under the same name might contain an entirely different whisky.

WHO OWNS THE DISTILLERIES? The biggest changes ever seen in the ownership of distilleries have taken place in the first few years of this millennium. Although the overall effect has been to concentrate control of Scotland's distilleries yet further, it has also shaken loose a handful into various degrees of independence.

Ninety-odd distilleries are working or capable of being put into operation. Ninety per cent of them are owned by groups, about half of which are international drinks companies. Some of the world's biggest corporations own tiny, rustic distilleries.

THE INTERNATIONAL DRINKS COMPANIES

Diageo is the giant of the industry, and the least changed since the 4th edition of this book. It owns four maltings, twenty-seven malt distilleries, and two grain distilleries. Some elements of this business date from the 1700s, but its emergence as a group can be traced to the 1880s, when a portfolio of distilleries was assembled to produce whiskies to create blends. As the Distillers Company Limited (DCL), this group produced almost all the famous names in blended Scotch, and dominated the industry for 100 years. In the 1980s, DCL merged with Bell's to become United Distillers (UD).

The new company acknowledged the growing interest in malts by introducing bottlings from six distilleries, each highlighting a different region. These were dubbed The Classic Malts. The same whiskies have since been offered with wood finishes as The Distillers Edition. Although each malt in these two families has its own label design, the graphic genre is similar. This still left many UD distilleries without a bottled single malt to offer tourists in their region. A range with labels showing local flora and fauna was developed. This was purely for local sale, though it soon became more widely popular. UD then decided to bottle stocks they still held from distilleries that had closed or that had even been demolished. These were identified as The Rare Malts, and marketed at prices that reflected their scarcity value. As stocks diminished, this series then began to call upon rare vintages from distilleries still in operation. This was reflected in an extension of the series as Cask Strength Limited Editions. More recently, some whiskies that were appreciated by connoisseurs but not widely known have been released as Hidden Malts. Small, outstanding batches are bottled each year as Special Releases, though this rubric does not appear on the labels.

UD merged with Britain's other drinks giant, International Distillers and Vintners (IDV), in 1997 and coined the name Diageo, which is intended to speak of the daily pleasures of food and drink. The group owns Tanqueray gin, Smirnoff vodka, Cuervo tequila, Guinness stout, and many other drinks.

Chivas Brothers has 11 distilleries, all on Speyside, including famous names like The Glenlivet. This group began with two brothers from the Highlands and a wine and spirits shop established in Aberdeen in the mid-1800s. The business was acquired as a foothold in Scotland by Seagram, the Canadian whisky distillers. Taking advantage of the shutdown of US distilling during Prohibition, Seagram had become the world's biggest drinks company. It subsequently diversified into the entertainment industry, and withdrew from distilling. In one of the industry's biggest takeovers, its Scottish distilleries were acquired in 2001 by Pernod Ricard. This family-owned business, based on pastis, is now an international drinks company. Its subsidiaries include Irish Distillers Limited and Wild Turkey Kentucky Bourbon.

Allied Distillers also has roots in Canada's sales of whisky to the United States. Its original parent was Hiram Walker, producer of Canadian Club. Among its ten distilleries, Laphroaig, on Islay, is the only one to have been consistently promoted. Its coal-fired Highland distillery, Glendronach, reopened in 2002, and its products are readily available. The other distilleries in the group have bottlings primarily for sale to visitors. These are called Special Distillery Bottlings. Allied's distilleries have over the years produced whisky primarily for the internationally known Ballantine's blends. Allied-Domecq is today's parent, embracing sherry, brandy, and wine.

Three groups have five malt distilleries each:

The Edrington Group produces one of Britain's best selling blends, The Famous Grouse. Its malt distilleries include Macallan and Highland Park. The core of the group was known as Highland Distillers until a complex realignment in 1999/2000, involving several other old-established businesses in the Scottish whisky trade. It has links with Rémy-Cointreau, the French brandy and liqueur company.

Dewar's, the best-selling blend in the US, was owned by United Distillers until the merger that created Diageo. In approving the merger, the European Commission and the US Federal Trade Commission were both concerned about market domination. Diageo already owned Johnnie Walker and J&B. Dewar's principal distillery, Aberfeldy, and three others were sold to Bacardi, the rum producer. Bacardi already owned Glen Deveron, through Martini & Rossi, the vermouth producer.

Inver House has its origins in a long-gone American group, but was given its present shape by a management buy-out. During the 1990s, the company bought distilleries that were silent or surplus to the requirements of their owners. The Scottish management remains, but the company has since 2001 been owned by Pacific Spirits, a family-controlled drinks company in Thailand.

One company has four malt distilleries:

Whyte and Mackay is an old-established name that has been resurrected. The Whyte and Mackay distilleries were for a time owned by Jim Beam, but in 2001 there was a management buy-out, using the name Kyndal. In 2003, the original name was reinstated. The company also owns the Invergordon grain distillery. Some vintage bottlings bear the rubric Stillman's Dram.

Four companies each have a trio of malt distilleries. (The first is an international drinks group; the next three are only involved in whisky distilling):

Burn Stewart is now owned by Angostura Limited. Based in Trinidad, this company produces the well-known cocktail bitters. This piquant product may seem a drop in the ocean of drink, but it has given rise to its own international company, with a portfolio including rums and wines. In 2003, Angostura acquired Burn Stewart, owner of the Tobermory and Deanston distilleries. Later the same year, it added Bunnahabhain.

William Grant & Sons remains a family firm. The original William Grant was a distillery manager before he set up his own. He and his family built the Glenfiddich distillery in 1886, and Balvenie in 1892. Kininvie was added rather more recently, in 1990. William Grant also owns the Girvan grain distillery. The company's growth has been a well-earned reward for its vision in pioneering the marketing of single malts.

Glenmorangie is the biggest selling malt in Scotland and the fourth worldwide. Glenmorangie plc, formerly known as Macdonald & Muir, is still family controlled, but is quoted on the London Stock Exchange. Its distilleries are Glenmorangie, Glen Moray, and Ardbeg. A small stake is held by the company's American distributor, Brown Forman, owner of Jack Daniel's Tennessee whiskey.

Morrison Bowmore was a family business, built around the highly regarded maltings and distillery in the "capital" of Islay. The company also owns Auchentoshan, the last Lowlander to practise triple distillation. The third distillery in the group is Glen Garioch, in the Highlands. The Morrison family had a long co-operation with Suntory before the Japanese giant became the proud owner of this small but well-balanced business.

Two more distilleries are in Japanese ownership:-

Ben Nevis is owned by the Asahi subsidiary Nikka, old-established Japanese whisky distiller and competitor to Suntory.
Tomatin is owned by Takara Shuzo Co. Ltd, producers of the Japanese spirit shochu.

DEGREES OF INDEPENDENCE

Two companies own a couple of malt distilleries each:

Loch Lomond owns the long-established malt distillery of the same name (with additionally a grain distillery on the site), and has now added Glen Scotia. (It also owned Littlemill, but this distillery is no longer operating and has been partially demolished).

Angus Dundee is a small company bottling under the name MacKillop's Choice. In recent reshuffles, it acquired the Tomintoul distillery from Jim Beam and Glencadam from Allied.

Other links between bottlers and distilleries:

Cadenhead has long shared ownership with Springbank.
Scott's Selection is owned by the Christie family, and opened the Speyside (Drumguish) distillery in 1990.
Gordon & MacPhail bought Benromach from UD and reopened it in 1998.
Murray McDavid has some common ownership with Bruichladdich, acquired from Jim Beam in 2000.
Signatory has the same principal as Edradour, acquired in 2003 from Pernod Ricard.
Ian Macleod acquired Glengoyne in 2003.

NATURAL CASK STRENGTH	SINGLE MALT SCOTCH WHISKY FROM BENROMACH DISTILLERY	CASK Nos. 112, 114
1982		REFILL SHERRY HOGSHEADS
		DISTILLED 02/02/82
59.7% VOL	PROPRIETORS: GORDON & MACPHAIL	
70cl	SPECIALLY SELECTED, PRODUCED AND BOTTLED BY GORDON & MACPHAIL ELGIN · SCOTLAND PRODUCT OF SCOTLAND	BOTTLED 24/10/01

Distilleries not linked to other businesses:

Tullibardine (mothballed), part of Jim Beam's sale to Kyndal, sold to a consortium proposing to run the distillery as part of a retail development.
Arran is a new distillery, established in 1995 as an independent business.
Bladnoch was bought by a private individual from UD and restarted production in 2001.
Glenfarclas is the last family-owned single distillery. Licensed as a farm distillery in 1836, it was acquired two years later by John Grant, and is still in the family. (There is no connection with William Grant & Sons or the Glen Grant Distillery.)

THE CONFUSING WORLD OF INDEPENDENT BOTTLERS

Newcomers to the world of single malts are often puzzled by the way in which whisky from the same distillery may appear under several different labels. Equally, whiskies from 20 or 30 different distilleries may all appear under labels which are almost identical. This is because, with three exceptions, distilleries do not carry out their own bottling. The original farm distilleries pre-dated mechanized bottling. They sold their whisky by the cask to wealthy householders, hotels, or licensed grocers or wine and spirit merchants.

Two merchants, dating from the 1800s, kept malts alive after the industry turned its attention almost entirely to blends. (*See* Gordon & MacPhail *and* Cadenhead, *below.*) As the practice of blending grew, the trade of whisky broker emerged. Brokers buy casks of whisky, often speculatively, and supply them to blenders, bottlers, or merchants. A great deal of whisky is in the hands of brokers. With the growing interest in single malts, the availability of this whisky is exciting the interest of a growing number of independent bottlers. As most distilleries still supply the bulk of their output for blending, some do not wish to be concerned with the business of single malt, and are happy to leave it to the independent bottlers.

At the opposite extreme, some famous distilleries have very definite ideas about the way their whisky is presented as a single malt (age, strength, type of cask). Some have controlled stock, and even bought back casks, to prevent independent bottlings. Others have taken legal action. This can be difficult when the brand name is also a place.

The terms "distillery bottling" or "official bottling" are occasionally used in this book. These terms imply a bottling that has been made on behalf of the distillery's owners. Distilleries that are owned by groups will usually have a central bottling line, typically within easy reach of Glasgow and Edinburgh.

Gordon & MacPhail is a family-owned shop in the Speyside heartland at Elgin, but its bottlings reach every corner of the world. Over the decades, it has acquired considerable stocks, which it has matured in its own warehouses. For this reason Gordon & MacPhail's bottlings of a particular malt have a consistency of style, often with a typical sherry-aged character, especially those in the Connoisseurs Choice Range.

Cadenhead has since the 1960s been owned by the proprietors of Springbank, in Campbeltown. The company is happy to buy small quantities of whiskies as they become available, so that bottling runs are short and the age or type of cask used may vary greatly. This makes for a great diversity of interesting bottlings. Cadenhead led the way in not chill filtering.

OTHER INDEPENDENTS

Adelphi Emphasizes cask strength. Tends toward full-flavoured whiskies. Founded in the early 1990s by Jamie Walker, whose forebears owned the Adelphi Distillery (1825–1902) in Glasgow.

Berry Brothers Seek whiskies that are good examples of the distillery's character (*see* Glenrothes).

Blackadder The jocular name is appropriate. Bottlings range from the noble to the downright eccentric. Raw Cask is a sub-range. Whiskies bottled "on lees". Founded in 1995 by whisky writer Robin Tucek.

Coopers Choice Good regional diversity. Part of The Vintage Malt Whisky Company. Founded in 1992 by a former sales director of Morrison Bowmore.

Douglas Laing Likes to offer contrasting expressions from the same distillery. Typically bottles at 50 volume. Independent bottlings (as Old Malt Cask) since 1998, but family has been in the whisky trade since 1949.

Duncan Taylor Shop in Huntly, Aberdeenshire. Bottler since 2002. Ranges include Peerless and Whisky Galore. Large portfolio, based on inventory (some dating from the 1960s). Bequeathed by pioneering American importer, Abe Rosenberg.

Hart Brothers Emphasizes wood finishes and good oak character. Bottling since 1989. Wine background since 1960s.

Ian Macleod Rare malts at unusual ages or with distinctive finishes. Smart packaging. Chieftain's and Dun Bheagan ranges since 2000. Blender and broker since 1930s.

James MacArthur "Small is Beautiful". Low-profile business, started as a hobby in 1982. Selects in the basis of best age for each whisky.

Lombard Sensitive to age. Buys whiskies and continues to mature. Bottling recent, but brokers since late 1960s.

MacKillop's Choice Selections By Lorne MacKillop, Master of Wine. Bottler since 1998.

Murray McDavid Has sought in each bottling (since 1996) "the truest expression of the distillery". The Mission range is selected by Jim McEwan, of Bruichladdich.

Scott's Selection Emphasizes silent stills and rare malts. Started in mid-1990s by blender Rob Scott (now retired). Linked to the warehousing, blending, and bottling business established by George Christie (*see* Drumguish).

Signatory Father of the new wave of bottlers. Established in 1988 and one of the few to have its own bottling line. Signatory pioneered single cask bottlings. Founder Andrew Symington previously worked in hotels.

Wilson & Morgan Has used Marsala barrels. Based in Italy. Bottling since 1992. Importing since 1960s.

Whiskies reviewed include some bottlings for retailers in the UK. These include:
The Whisky Shop (Glasgow and branches), Royal Mile Whiskies (Edinburgh and London),
The Wee Dram (Bakewell, England), The Vintage House and The Whisky Exchange
(both London), and Oddbins (UK chain).

A–Z
OF SINGLE MALTS

Whatever the arguments about their relative prices, no one denies that a Château Latour is more complex than a mass-market table wine. The fine wines of the whisky world are the single malts. Some malts are made to higher standards than others, and some are inherently more distinctive than their neighbours. This cannot be obscured by the producers' blustery arguments about "personal taste". A tasting note cannot be definitive, but it can be a useful guide, and will tell you, for example, if the whisky is a light, dry malt, or if it is rich and sherryish, or peaty and smoky.

The tasting notes start with a comment on the house style – a quick, first, general indication of what to expect from each distillery's products, before looking at the variations that emerge in different ages and bottlings. I also suggest the best moment for each distillery's whiskies (such as before dinner, or with a book at bedtime). These suggestions are meant as an encouragement to try each in a congenial situation. They are not meant to be taken with excessive seriousness.

Tasting note example:

AUCHENTOSHAN 1973, 29-year-old, Sherry Butt No 793, 55.8 vol

COLOUR Pinkish red. Almost rhubarb-like.
NOSE Jammy. Australian Shiraz. Red apples. Peaches.
BODY Textured. Fluffy.
PALATE An extraordinarily fruity whisky, with peach dominant. Peach-stone flavours, too. Underneath all that, it is hard to divine any Auchentoshan character. Severely marked down for those reasons.
FINISH Nutty dryness. With the cheese? After dinner?

SCORE **69**

COLOUR The natural colour of a malt matured in plain wood is a very pale yellow. Darker shades, ranging from amber to ruby to deep brown, can be imparted by sherry wood. Some distilleries use casks

A character-forming home
Skye forms a natural crucible, in which the flavours of a great whisky are fused. Living in the mountains and surrounded by sea, the whisky assumes a gusty salt-and-pepper house character.

that have been treated with concentrated sherry, and this can cause a caramel-like appearance and palate. Some add caramel to balance the colour. I do not suggest that one colour is in itself better than another, though a particular subtle hue can heighten the pleasure of a fine malt. We enjoy food and drink with our eyes as well as our nose and palate.

NOSE Anyone sampling any food or drink experiences much of the flavour through the sense of smell. Whisky is highly aromatic, and the aromas of malts include peat, flowers, honey, toasty maltiness, coastal brine, and seaweed, for example.

BODY Lightness, smoothness, or richness might refresh, soothe, or satisfy. Body and texture (sometimes known as "mouth feel") are distinct features of each malt.

PALATE In the enjoyment of any complex drink, each sip will offer new aspects of the taste. Even one sip will gradually unfold a number of taste characteristics in different parts of the mouth over a period of, say, a minute. This is notably true of single malts. Some present a very extensive development of palate. A taster working with an unfamiliar malt may go back to it several times over a period of days, in search of its full character. I have adopted this technique in my tastings for this book.

FINISH In all types of alcoholic drink, the "finish" is a further stage of the pleasure. In most single malts, it is more than a simple aftertaste, however important that may be. It is a crescendo, followed by a series of echoes. When I leave the bottle, I like to be whistling the tune. When the music of the malt fades, there is recollection in tranquillity.

SCORE The pleasures described above cannot be measured with precision, if at all. The scoring system is intended merely as a guide to the status of the malts. Each tasting note is given a score out of 100. This is inspired by the system of scoring wines devised by the American writer Robert Parker. In this book, a rating in the 50s indicates a malt that in my view lacks balance or character, and which – in fairness – was probably never meant to be bottled as a single. The 60s suggest an enjoyable but unexceptional malt. Anything in the 70s is worth tasting, especially above 75. The 80s are, in my view, distinctive and exceptional. The 90s are the greats.

A modest score should not dissuade anyone from trying a malt. Perhaps I was less than enthusiastic; you might love it.

ABERFELDY

PRODUCER John Dewar & Sons Ltd
REGION Highlands DISTRICT Eastern Highlands
ADDRESS Aberfeldy, Perthshire, PH15 2EB
TEL 01887 822010 WEBSITE www.dewarswow.com
EMAIL worldofwhisky@dewars.com VC (Visitor Centre)

DEWAR'S WORLD OF WHISKY, which opened in 2000, uses aromas, flavours, music, interactive games, and entire room settings to celebrate one of Scotland's great whisky families. The buccaneering style that made Dewar's White Label a bestseller typified the commercial energy that made blended Scotch the world's most popular spirit, and is well captured in some of the early advertising.

The original John Dewar was born on a croft near Aberfeldy in 1806, and was introduced to the wine trade at the age of 22 by a distant cousin. The family blended whisky and in 1896–98 established their own distillery at Aberfeldy. Its job was to provide the heart of the malt whisky content of the Dewar's blends, and it continued to do so in recent years under the ownership of United Distillers. Perhaps it is the Aberfeldy malt that imparts to Dewar's that fresh, lively crispness.

The hard water used at the distillery rises from whinstone flecked with iron and gold, and runs through pine, spruce, birch, and bracken. It is piped from the ruins of Pitilie, an earlier distillery. Aberfeldy still has its pagoda, though malting stopped in 1972. The owners at the time, DCL, were closing distillery maltings in favour of centralized sites. Some of the space liberated at the distilleries was then used to expand still-houses, at a time when production was being increased. The upgraded still-house at Aberfeldy is in the classic design of the period. The stills themselves are tall, with a gentle contour. The distillery also has a small steam locomotive, no longer in operation.

When UD merged with IDV in 1998, it had an embarrassment of distilleries. Then Aberfeldy, Aultmore, Craigellachie, and Royal Brackla were sold to become John Dewar & Sons, under the ownership of Bacardi.

The UD Flora and Fauna 15-year-old has now been replaced by a Dewar's bottling at 12 years old. This younger whisky is lighter in body, fruitier, and in a more refreshing style. The 25-year-old has deeper aromas and flavours, and more of everything.

HOUSE STYLE Oily, cleanly fruity, vigorous. Sociable, with dessert, or book-at-bedtime, depending upon ascending age.

ABERFELDY 12-year-old, 40 vol

COLOUR Warm gold to bronze.

NOSE Lively. Orange zest. A hint of smokiness. Warm.

BODY Light on the tongue. Oily.

PALATE Emphatically clean fruitiness. Tangerines. Trifle sponges.

FINISH Like biting into a kumquat. Dusty. Spicy. Gently warming.

SCORE **76**

ABERFELDY 25-year-old, 40 vol

COLOUR Bronze.

NOSE A hint of sherry. Warm. Malty sweetness.

BODY Syrupy but not cloying.

PALATE Even maltier. Shortbread, topped with
glazed almonds and orange peel.

FINISH More complex. Spicier. Warming. A touch of oily, perfumy peat.

SCORE **77**

SOME INDEPENDENT BOTTLINGS
ABERFELDY 1978, Connoisseurs Choice, 40 vol

COLOUR Full gold.

NOSE More aromatic. Drier. Toasted marshmallows.

BODY Oilier.

PALATE More expressive. Very citrusy. Sweeter. Scenty.
A beautifully complex, elegant whisky.

FINISH Appetizing. Lemony. Very dry.

SCORE **78**

ABERFELDY 1978, Signatory, 43 vol

COLOUR Greeny gold. White wine.

NOSE Lightly dry. Incense. Flowery.

BODY Oily.

PALATE Orangey, but more creamy in style. Less complex.

FINISH Very sweet indeed, though there is a sudden hit of peaty-smoke dryness in the finish. Very long. Sweet enough to try with (or in) trifle.

SCORE 75

NOW HARD TO FIND
ABERFELDY 15-year-old, Flora and Fauna, 43 vol

COLOUR Amber.

NOSE Oil, incense, heather, lightly piney, and peaty (especially after water is added).

BODY Medium, very firm.

PALATE Very full flavours. Light peat, barley. Fresh, clean touches of Seville orange, rounded.

FINISH Sweetness moves to fruitiness, then to firm dryness.

SCORE 77

ABERFELDY 1980, Bottled 1997, Cask Strength Limited Bottling, 62 vol

COLOUR Pale gold.

NOSE Restrained, fragrant, pine and heather. Drier.

BODY Medium, smooth, distinctly oily.

PALATE Creamier, nuttier. Hint of orange toffee. Still lively, but two or three years in the cask has brought more tightly combined flavours.

FINISH Nutty, late pine. Leafy, peppery dryness.

SCORE 77

OTHER VERSIONS OF ABERFELDY

A 14-year-old from Adelphi (bottled 1997) had a deliciously fresh orange toffee character, with a fruity, peppery finish. SCORE 77

A Scott's Selection 1978, at 59.3 vol, was powerfully fruity and piney, with a bitter finish. SCORE 75

ABERLOUR

PRODUCER Chivas Brothers
REGION Highlands DISTRICT Speyside (Strathspey)
ADDRESS Aberlour, Banffshire, AB3 9PJ
TEL 01340 881249 WEBSITE www.aberlour.co.uk VC

Having acquired Chivas in 2002, with its dazzling family of Speyside distilleries (The Glenlivet, Glen Grant, and Longmorn are but three), will French parents Pernod Ricard still love Aberlour? It was their Number One son; now it has siblings. The whisky is well respected in Scotland, but its greatest popularity, based on merit as much as on adoptive parentage, is in France. At the Speyside Festival in May, the distillery has hosted a series of whisky dinners created by spirited writer Martine Nouet.

Aberlour is at least a super-middleweight in body. With medals galore in recent years, it competes as a light-heavyweight, standing up well against bigger names, much as Georges Carpentier did. Aberlour rhymes with "power" in English, but most French-speakers make it sound more like "amour".

The regular range in Scotland and the rest of the United Kingdom comprises the 10-year-old, the a'bunadh, and the 15-year-old sherry wood finish, but there are larger selections in duty-free and in France. The overall range includes a great many minor variations.

Since 2002, visitors to the distillery have been able to hand-fill their own personally labelled bottle of Aberlour, from an identified single cask. A sherry butt and a bourbon barrel, each felt to provide a good example of its style, are set aside for this purpose. As each is exhausted, it is replaced by a similar cask. This personalized whisky is bottled at cask strength.

On the main road (A95) that follows the eastern bank of the Spey, an 1890s lodge signals the distillery, which is hidden a couple of hundred yards into the glen of the river Lour (little more than a burn). The Lour flows into the Spey. The site was known for a well associated with St Drostan, from the epoch of St Columba. The distilling water is soft. It rises from the granite of Ben Rinnes, by way of a spring in the glen of the Allachie, and is piped half a mile to the distillery.

HOUSE STYLE Soft texture, medium to full flavours, nutty, spicy (nutmeg?), sherry-accented. With dessert, or after dinner, depending upon maturity.

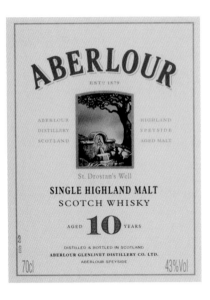

ABERLOUR 10-year-old, Principal Version, 43 vol

COLOUR Amber.

NOSE Malty, spicy, mint toffee.

BODY Remarkably soft and smooth. Medium to full.

PALATE Distinctively clinging mouth feel, with long-lasting flavour development. Both sweetness and spicy, peppery dryness in its malt character. Nutmeg and berry fruit.

FINISH Lingering, smooth, aromatic, clean.

SCORE **83**

ABERLOUR a'bunadh ("The Origin"), No Age Statement, 59.6 vol

A single malt comprising Aberlours from less than 10 to more than 15 years, vatted together. All sherry-ageing, with an emphasis on second-fill dry oloroso. No chill filtration. Mainly in duty-free and British Isles. In Victorian-style bottle.

COLOUR Dark orange.

NOSE Sherry, mint, pralines. Luxurious, powerful.

BODY Full, creamy, textured, layered.

PALATE Rich, luxurious, and creamy, with a hint of mint and cherries behind.

FINISH Nougat, cherry brandy, ginger, faint smoke. Definitely after dinner.

SCORE **86**

ABERLOUR a'bunadh Sterling Silver, 12-year-old, 58.7 vol

COLOUR Darker. Deep, shiny, chestnut.

NOSE Sherry, mint, pralines. Oakier and smokier than
the version above. Sherry. Black chocolate. Oil of peppermint.

BODY Big, firm.

PALATE Drier. Spicier. Ginger-and-plum preserve. More assertive.

FINISH Long. Lots of alcohol, but warming and soothing.
Prunes. Sappy, juicy fresh oak. Cedar. Cigar boxes.

SCORE **87**

ABERLOUR 12-year-old, Sherry-matured, 43 vol

*Matured in first-fill dry oloroso. Originally marketed in France,
but now mainly found in duty-free.*

COLOUR Full amber.

NOSE Nutty, appetizing, relatively fresh, sherry aroma.

BODY Medium, soft.

PALATE Fresh, soft, malty. Soft liquorice, anis, hint of blackcurrant.

FINISH Silky, enwrapping, soothing.

SCORE **84**

ABERLOUR 12-year-old, Double Cask Matured, 40 vol

Vatting of first-fill sherry and unspecified refill casks. Mainly for the French market.

COLOUR Bronze.

NOSE Earthy, fruity. Pears. Apples. Tarte tatin.

BODY Medium, firm.

PALATE Melty pastry. Caramel sauce. Custard (in this instance,
let's call it crème anglaise). Leaves of garden mint.

FINISH More of the mint. Now it has become spearmint.
Ends rather abruptly and sharply.

SCORE **82**

ABERLOUR 16-year-old, Double Cask Matured, 43 vol

Same principle as the above. Also for the French market.

COLOUR Bronze red.

NOSE Seville oranges, lemons. Turkish delight. Rose-water.

BODY Gently rounded.

PALATE Smooth. Spun sugar. Caramel. Tightly combined flavours.
The extra years have made a big difference.

FINISH Cinnamon. Ground nutmeg. Nutty.

SCORE **84**

ABERLOUR Cuvée Marie d'Ecosse, 15-year-old, 43 vol

A marriage of bourbon- and sherry-aged Aberlour, for the French market.

COLOUR Amber.

NOSE Malty and toffeeish, developing flowering currant.

BODY Medium to full. Silky smooth.

PALATE Toffee, liquorice, anise, crème brûlée.

FINISH Late spiciness and ginger. Long, soothing.

SCORE *83*

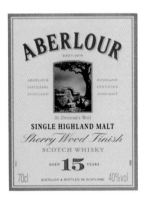

ABERLOUR 15-year-old, Sherry Wood Finish, 40 vol

A marriage of sherry and bourbon. Finished in sherry.

COLOUR Fuller reddish amber.

NOSE Roses, candyfloss (cotton candy), slightly buttery.

BODY Very firm. Smooth.

PALATE Rounded, tightly combined flavours. Beautiful balance of
sherryish nuttiness, anise, and emphatic orange flower.

FINISH Cookies, liquorice toffee. Rootiness, spiciness,
emphatic mint, late dryness.

SCORE *84*

LONG-MATURED EXPRESSIONS IDENTIFIED BY AGE
ABERLOUR 21-year-old, Limited Edition, Cask No 32, 43 vol

Mainly in duty-free and North America.

COLOUR Bright pale orange.

NOSE Sherry, oak, polished leather.

BODY Firm, smooth, lightly creamy.

PALATE Packed with lively flavours: malt, cookies, fruit, mint.

FINISH Spicy, rooty, dry, and very long.

SCORE **85**

ABERLOUR 23-year-old, 40 vol

The intention is to create a position in the regular range for a vatting highlighting the oldest whiskies in the distillery's warehouses. Based on current stocks, this emerges at 23 years.

COLOUR Brassy. Pale for an Aberlour.

NOSE Fresh, pronounced mint toffee.

BODY Creamy. Shortbread.

PALATE Syrupy, fruity. Apricot.

FINISH Slightly tart, sharp. Dryish. Violets.

SCORE **84**

A SELECTION OF VINTAGE-DATED BOTTLINGS
ABERLOUR 1980, 43 vol

Minimum age 22 years, in second-fill casks, mainly bourbon but with some sherry. Mainly for the French market.

COLOUR Iridescent greeny gold.

NOSE Delicately spicy. Develops in the glass. Vanilla. Cedar.

BODY Light but textured.

PALATE A sudden explosion of spicy flavours, especially nutmeg, but also cinnamon and pepper.

FINISH Curiously bittersweet. Briar-like. Very lively.

SCORE **84**

ABERLOUR 30-year-old, Limited Edition, Bottle 852, 43 vol

Mainly in duty-free and North America, but now very hard to find.

COLOUR Amber.

NOSE Polished leather. Tobacco. Cigars.

BODY Firm, smooth.

PALATE Firmly malty, creamy, liquorice, rootiness, hint of smoky peat. Complex and sophisticated. Maturity and finesse.

FINISH Surprisingly fresh oak. Sappiness. Log fires. Warming.

SCORE **85**

ABERLOUR Distiller's Selection, 1988, 40 vol

Mainly for the Spanish market.

COLOUR Amber.

NOSE Soft but expressive. Bourbon oak. Nuts. Fudge. Citrus.

BODY Medium to full. Smooth. Rich.

PALATE A dazzling display of fresh malty flavours. Sweetish, but beautifully balanced. Butterscotch, vanilla, orange and lemon, sambuca.

FINISH Sticky toffee pudding, balanced by a dryness like crystallized ginger.

SCORE **85**

ABERLOUR 1976, 21-year-old, Bottle 921 of 3000, 43 vol

Matured in first-fill bourbon casks.

COLOUR Bright amber.

NOSE Quick, assertive malt honey, then powerful berry fruit at back of nose. Blackberries?

BODY Medium, firm, almost crunchy.

PALATE Dryish, nutty, toffee, fruit, nutmeg. Lacking in roundness.

FINISH Restrained sappy oak. Gingery, warming.

SCORE **83**

ABERLOUR 1964, 25-year-old, Bottle 5664 of 10,000, 43 vol

COLOUR Full amber.

NOSE Richer oak.

BODY Medium to full. Firm, smooth, slippery.

PALATE Firm, smooth. Very good oaky extract. Hint of vanilla creaminess.

FINISH Firm, rounded dryness. Hint of perfuminess.

SCORE **84**

HARD TO FIND

ABERLOUR Antique, No Age Statement, 43 vol

Contains whiskies of 10 to 25 years. Bottled for duty-free stores.

COLOUR Full amber.

NOSE Oloroso sherry, treacle, raisins.

BODY Firmer.

PALATE More dryness, cookie-like malt notes, and spiciness.

FINISH More complex and spicy, with hints of peat. After dinner.

SCORE **84**

ABERLOUR 18-year-old, Sherry Wood Matured, 43 vol
100% sherry-aged. Mainly for the North American market.

COLOUR Bright orangey amber.

NOSE Sherryish but dry and slightly oaky. Burnt sugar.
Spicy, rounded, teasing.

BODY Smooth, nutty.

PALATE Well balanced. Spicy, flowery, nutmeg, nutty, fruity.
Light, delicate flavours for this distillery and age.

FINISH Fresh sherry and oak.

SCORE **84**

ABERLOUR 100° Proof, No Age Statement
(Around 10 years), 57.1 vol
Mainly in duty-free.

COLOUR Bright orangey amber.

NOSE Fresh oak, giving way to light nuttiness and sherry.

BODY Firmer, crisper.

PALATE Dry oiliness. Delicious, soft fruitiness. (Apricots? Cherries?)
Much more spiciness. Some butterscotch, toffee, and cough-candy.
Both robust (tastes relatively young) and complex.

FINISH Big, firm, dry. This version is more of a winter warmer.

SCORE **84**

SOME INDEPENDENT BOTTLINGS

A 12-year-old, at 50 vol, distilled in 1988, in Douglas Laing's Old Malt
Cask series, had the colour of ripe limes; a blossoming fruitiness; a smooth,
sweet, perfumy palate; and a honeyed, distinctively aromatic, soothing
warmth in the finish. SCORE 84

An Aberlour distilled in 1990 was bottled in 2002, at 59.9 vol, by Blackadder,
in its Raw Cask series. It had a slightly darker colour, again with a greenish
tinge. It was very similar, but with a warming finish that was curiously
dry and medicinal. SCORE 79

A 1989 distillate, at 46 vol, bottled at 13 years old by Cadenhead,
had a very pale greenish colour; a lightly syrupy, intensely sweet,
scenty palate; and a soothing, dryish, but more rounded, finish. SCORE 82

A 1970, at 46 vol, from Lombard, had a full gold colour, with a bronze tinge.
The whisky had some more nutty toasty, notes in the palate, and a hint of
peat in the finish. SCORE 85

ALLT-A-BHAINNE

PRODUCER Chivas Brothers
REGION Highlands DISTRICT Speyside (Fiddich)
ADDRESS Glenrinnes, Dufftown, Banffshire, AB55 4DB

A FLURRY OF CONSTRUCTION enlivened Speyside in the mid-1970s, with four or five new distilleries built. It was one of those periods when the industry tries to catch up with underestimated demand. This distillery and the present Braeval were built by Seagrams. Their light, airy architecture is a happy marriage of traditional allusions and modern ideas, but they are lacking in humanity. Both are designed to operate with minimal staff, and their spirit is matured in central warehousing elsewhere.

In Gaelic, Allt-á-Bhainne means "the milk burn", and the distillery lies to the west of the River Fiddich in the foothills of Ben Rinnes, near Dufftown. Its malt whisky is a component of the Chivas blends. There have been no official bottlings, so malt lovers curious to taste the whisky have had to rely on independents. One of them, Cadenhead, has released two different casks from the same year.

HOUSE STYLE Light, slightly vegetal, flowery-spicy. Aperitif.

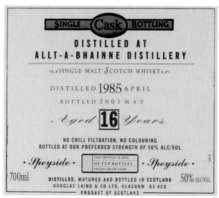

ALLT-A-BHAINNE 16-year-old, The Old Malt Cask, 50 vol

COLOUR	Bright, pale, greeny gold.
NOSE	Hint of peat. Seaweed (the edible kind). Soy sauce. Nutty. Sweaty.
BODY	Light, flabby.
PALATE	Bean curd. Protein-like. Oyster crackers.
FINISH	Sweet. Biscuity.

SCORE 72

ALLT-A-BHAINNE 1992, 9-year-old, Cadenhead, 58.8 vol

COLOUR Pale greeny gold.

NOSE Faint hint of peat. Flowery. Slightly gummy.

BODY Lightly syrupy.

PALATE Intensely sweet. Lemon-sherbet. Surprisingly aggressive. Peppery.

FINISH Liquorice. Fennel. Soothing.

SCORE **73**

ALLT-A-BHAINNE 1992, 9-year-old, Cadenhead, 59.4 vol

COLOUR Very bright greeny gold.

NOSE Heathery. Ferny. Forest floor after rain.

BODY Lightly buttery.

PALATE Fiddlehead ferns with butter.

FINISH Green peppercorns. Quite assertive.

SCORE **75**

ALLT-A-BHAINNE 17-year-old, Sherry Wood, Dun Bheaghan, 43 vol

COLOUR Very bright greeny gold.

NOSE Cleaner. Hint of peat, earthy. Graphite?

BODY Light. Spring water.

PALATE Clean. Sweet. Malty. Marshmallow.

FINISH Minty. Silky.

SCORE **73**

OTHER VERSIONS OF ALLT-Á-BHAINNE

The flowery spiciness of this malt was typified by a 13-year-old bottled by
The Whisky Castle, a shop in Tomintoul, in the late 1990s. SCORE 73
A 12-year-old bottled by James MacArthur in the mid-1990s seemed slightly
bigger, no doubt as a result of the cask used. SCORE 74
A 1980 released by Oddbins in 1992 seemed to have enjoyed sherry, but was
perhaps a little overwhelmed by the sappiness of the oak. SCORE 73

ARDBEG

PRODUCER Glenmorangie plc
REGION Islay DISTRICT South Shore
ADDRESS Port Ellen, Islay, Argyll, PA42 7EA
TEL 01496 302244 WEBSITE www.ardbeg.com
EMAIL oldkiln@ardbeg.com VC

Aready one of the world's great distilleries in the days when single malts were a secret, and revived at a cost of millions (whether euros or dollars), Ardbeg shines ever more brightly. Its reopening was one of the first signs of the Islay revival, of which it has become both a principal element and a beneficiary. Its owners' ambitions for the distillery are being rewarded. So is their faith in young manager Stuart Thomson and his wife Jackie.

Her knowledge and energy "front of house" have consolidated the distillery's popularity with visitors. When Ardbeg reopened, one of the former kilns was turned into a shop, also offering tea, coffee, a dram, and a clootie (dumpling). The Old Kiln is also used by local people: it now serves meals, and has been the western venue for writer Martine Nouet's whisky dinners (*see p. 441*).

Ardbeg aficionados still cling to the hope that the second kiln may one day return to use. The maltings were unusual in that there were no fans, causing the peat smoke to permeate very heavily. This is evident in very old bottlings. The peaty origins of the water are also a big influence in the whisky's earthy, tar-like flavours. Some lovers of Ardbeg believe that an apple-wood, lemon-skin fruitiness derives from a recirculatory system in the spirit still.

The distillery traces its history to 1794. The maltings last worked in 1976–77, though supplies of their malted barley were no doubt eked out a little longer. Ardbeg closed in the early 1980s, but towards the end of that decade began to work again, albeit very sporadically, using malt from Port Ellen. Whisky produced at that time, but released by the new owners, is less tar-like than the old Ardbeg. Such heavily peated whisky as was inherited has been used in some vattings. The distillery is currently buying an especially heavily peated malt, the impact of which will be seen in bottlings in the course of the next six or seven years.

HOUSE STYLE Earthy, very peaty, smoky, salty, robust. A bedtime malt.

ARDBEG 10-year-old, 40 vol

COLOUR Fino sherry.

NOSE Smoke, brine, iodine dryness.

BODY Only medium to full, but very firm. A young light-heavyweight, not musclebound by age. Pound-for-pound, the hardest hitter in the Ardbeg team, though without the power conferred by the old maltings.

PALATE Skips sweetly along at first, then becomes mean and moody. Bottlings a little variable.

FINISH Hefty, lots of iodine.

SCORE **85**

ARDBEG 17-year-old, 40 vol

COLOUR Full, shimmering, greeny gold.

NOSE Assertive, briney, seaweedy, tar-like. Hint of sulphur.

BODY Medium, oily. Very firm.

PALATE Peppery but also sweet. Cereal grains, oil, gorse. Tightly combined flavours. More mature and rounded, but still robust. Very appetizing.

FINISH Oily. Lemon skins. Freshly ground white pepper.

SCORE **86**

ARDBEG 21-year-old, 56.3 vol

Slightly more assertive than an Adelphi bottling reviewed in the fourth edition of this book.

COLOUR Deeper. More refractive and oily. Greeny gold.

NOSE Firm, but aromas more tightly combined. As though the brine and iodine-like seaweed had permeated a stretch of hard, compacted sand.

BODY Firm, unyielding.

PALATE Instant hit of flavours. The maritime character overlaying pepper, lemons, fresh limes, bananas. (After that bracing walk on the beach, an afternoon of snoozy luxury with fruits and pastries?)

FINISH After the snooze, a hot shower with coal-tar soap. That characteristic tar-like smokiness and phenol.

SCORE **87**

ARDBEG 1976, 46 vol

COLOUR Again, that oily green tinge.

NOSE Still showering with coal-tar soap.

BODY Lotion-like.

PALATE Fresh, perfumy, therapeutic.

FINISH Very smoky. Driftwood bonfires. Remarkably late suggestion of sherry.

SCORE **88**

ARDBEG 1977, 46 vol

Very similar, but less rounded in flavours.

COLOUR Slightly more oily than the vintage above.

NOSE Bonfires again. Sappy. Leafy.

BODY More oily. Clings to the tongue.

PALATE Sweet lemons.

FINISH Fragrant smokiness. Lingering warmth.

SCORE **87**

ARDBEG "Lord of the Isles " 25-year-old, 46 vol

"The supreme expression of Ardbeg", according to the label, but where is the smoke and clamour of battle? This whisky is named after the island rulers who fought the Vikings.

COLOUR Full gold.

NOSE Sea air. Distant smoke.

BODY Silky.

PALATE The Ardbeg fruitiness, usually lemony and fragrant, has become more assertive and complex with age. Here, there are flavours reminiscent of candied orange peel and, especially, cherries. Lots of flavour development. Walnuts, almonds. Marzipan. Bittersweet. The roundness of flavours masks the peat.

FINISH Long, haughty. Steely. Not as earthy as might have been hoped.

SCORE **89**

COMMITTEE RESERVE, 55.3 vol

More than 20,000 enthusiasts for Ardbeg have joined this "committee". This bottling, made in 2002, was vatted from whiskies distilled in the 1970s, 80s, and 90s.

COLOUR The Committee's whisky is marginally paler than the Lords'.

NOSE Very fresh. Herbal. Spicy. A suggestion of saffron.

BODY Textured. Tongue-coating.

PALATE Sweet, then sharp. Huge flavour development in the middle, becoming spicy (saffron again, salty, sandy).

FINISH Big, firm, gripping, long. Warming, soothing, appetizing. A *tour de force*.

SCORE **90**

ARDBEG Uigeadail, 54.2 vol

COLOUR Pale gold.

NOSE Intensely smoky. Dry, clean, tangy barbecue smoke.

BODY Light, firm.

PALATE Firm, very smooth, then explodes on the tongue.

FINISH Hot. Alcoholic. A shock to the system.

SCORE **92**

FOUR SINGLE-CASK BOTTLINGS FOR FOREIGN MARKETS

ARDBEG 1976, Cask No 2396, 53.5 vol *(For the Italian market.)*

COLOUR Dark orange satin.

NOSE Dusty. Earthy.

BODY Light to medium. Slightly chewy.

PALATE Chewy sweetness. Earthy. Bitter chocolate.

FINISH Powerful, long, warming. Woody. Menthol. Spearmint.

SCORE **88**

ARDBEG 1976, Cask No 2395, 54.4 vol *(For the Japanese market.)*

COLOUR Greeny orange.

NOSE More oily. Orange essence. Black chocolate. Coffee.

BODY Slightly bigger and smoother.

PALATE Expressive. Delicious. Lightly syrupy. Sweetish. Fruitier.
More obvious orange. Reminiscent of orange-liqueur chocolates.

FINISH Smoky, fragrant dryness. Some late, disappointing woodiness.

SCORE **91**

ARDBEG 1975, Cask No 4701, 54.4 vol *(For the French market.)*

COLOUR Golden plum. Greengage?

NOSE Iced buns. Spiced buns. Malt loaf.

BODY Fondant.

PALATE Ginger cake. Yorkshire Parkin. Treacle toffee.

FINISH Shredded root ginger. Bitter chocolate. Mid-afternoon in the patisserie.

SCORE **89**

ARDBEG 1975, Cask No 4716, 45 vol *(For the German market.)*

COLOUR Golden plum.

NOSE Sweetness and saltiness. Sandy beach. A hint of seaweed.

BODY Firm.

PALATE On the thin side, but firmer and drier than the rest of this group.

FINISH Cedary. Some woody bitterness.

SCORE **87**

THE ARDBEGGEDDON ARDBEG 1972,
29-year-old, Sherry Cask, 48.4 vol

Bottled by Douglas Laing for The Whisky Shop. An outstanding Ardbeg, lyrically, presenting the full range of the distillery's typical flavours.

COLOUR Bright pale gold.

NOSE Rich, soft, oily smokiness. Very appetizing.

BODY Seductively smooth.

PALATE Against a firm, steely background: a dexterous interplay of grassy peatiness; oiliness; just lurking suggestions of lemony fruitiness, sherry, and oak.

FINISH Lively, evocative, maritime flavours. A long walk on a sandy beach, with a vigorous, salty spray.

SCORE **92**

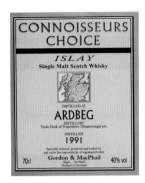

ARDBEG 1991, Connoisseurs Choice, 40 vol

COLOUR Pale, warm gold.

NOSE Light, dry. A hint of peat. Tobacco. Peppermint.

BODY Oily. Creamy.

PALATE Sweet, minty, developing a herbal, spicy dryness.

FINISH A gentle sting. What happened to the heavyweight embrace, the boxer still punching in the clinches?

SCORE **92**

ARDBEG Provenance, Distilled 1974, Bottled 1998, 55.8 vol

An intentional reminder of the old Ardbeg.

COLOUR Full gold to bronze.

NOSE Sea air. Seaweed. Oak, rope, leather.

BODY Rich and creamy, but dry on the tongue.

PALATE Huge flavour development. Malty, toffeeish, sweet, fruity. Barbecue wood. Mustard. Salt.

FINISH Distinctly sappy, smoky, and very warming.

SCORE **93**

ARDMORE

PRODUCER Allied Distillers Ltd
REGION Highlands DISTRICT Speyside (Bogie)
ADDRESS Kennethmont, by Huntly, Aberdeenshire, AB54 4NH
TEL 01464 831213 VC

H AD COAL-FIRED STILLS been disdained in favour of steam in the early days of Ardmore, that might have been seen as progress. To douse the flames as the distillery celebrated its recent centenary seemed perverse indeed. This sizeable distillery is at the eastern fringe of Speyside, where Aberdeenshire barley country begins. Will the switch to steam mean a less caramelish maltiness in Ardmore whisky and the blends of parent Teacher's (so to speak)? Probably.

HOUSE STYLE Malty, creamy, fruity. After dinner.

ARDMORE 12-year-old, Centenary Bottling, 40 vol

More elegant, but less robust, than the regular Gordon & MacPhail 12-year-old bottling.

COLOUR Warm primrose.

NOSE Fresh, clean, sweet. Flowery-fruity. Cream. Sherry trifle.

BODY Light, but very smooth. Slippery smooth.

PALATE Delicate, fruity (raspberry?) flavours reminiscent of blancmange.

FINISH Flowery. Nutty dryness. Toasted almonds.

SCORE **73**

EARLIER VERSIONS OF ARDMORE

The fruity flavours emerge much more strongly – sweet orange, red apple? – in a 21-year-old at 40 vol, also bottled for the centenary. This version is much more robust, complex, and expressive. SCORE 75

ARRAN

PRODUCER Isle of Arran Distillers Ltd
REGION Highlands ISLAND Arran
ADDRESS Lochranza, Isle of Arran, Argyll, KA27 8HJ
TEL 01770 830264 WEBSITE www.arranwhisky.com
E-MAIL arran.distillers@arranwhisky.com VC

SINCE IT OPENED IN 1995, and released its first whisky in 1998, the Isle of Arran distillery has inspired several similar projects elsewhere in Scotland. Until any of them is realized, Arran is still the country's newest distillery.

The island, a favourite with walkers and bird-watchers, is easily accessible. From Glasgow it is a short drive south to the Ayrshire port of Ardrossan, whence a frequent ferry runs to Brodick, on the east of the island. A narrow road then winds its way round the north coast to the distillery, in the village of Lochranza. There is accommodation in Lochranza, and a ferry to Kintyre, for those who wish to visit the Campbeltown distilleries. A couple more ferries extend the trip to Islay and Jura.

Arran has dramatic granite mountains, peaty land, and good water. The island was once known for its whisky, but spent a century and a half without a legal distillery. The inspiration for a new distillery came after a talk given at the Arran Society in 1992. Industry veteran Harold Currie, a retired managing director of Chivas, organized a scheme in which 2000 bonds were sold in exchange for whisky from the new distillery. As Arran has many visitors, the distillery was seen as an additional attraction for tourists. It has a shop and a restaurant with an excellent kitchen.

HOUSE STYLE Creamy, leafy. Restorative or with dessert.
No obvious island character.

ARRAN SINGLE MALT, 43 vol

COLOUR Attractive pale yellow.

NOSE Fresh, creamy, vanilla-like. Flowery.

BODY Creamy.

PALATE Fresh cream. Flowery. Leafy. Vegetal. Angelica.

FINISH Children's sweets. Liquorice. Spicy.

SCORE **73**

ARRAN SINGLE MALT, Nonchillfiltered, 46 vol

COLOUR Bright, pale, greeny gold.

NOSE Distinctly flowery sweetness. Appetizing.

BODY Creamy, dusty, substantial.

PALATE Flowery, almondy, fresh cream.

FINISH Perfumy. Sweet limes. Lightly vegetal dryness.

SCORE **74**

SOME SINGLE CASK ARRANS

ARRAN Single Cask, Cask No 95/173, Sherry Hogshead, 55.3 vol

COLOUR Tamarind.

NOSE Nutty. Dates. Cinnamon.

BODY Syrupy.

PALATE Fruity. Gingery. Sappy. A curious inversion. As though the
whisky (rich and sweet, but without penetrating flavours) provides
the background, while the sherry and wood are the highlights.

FINISH Powerful. Spicy. Developing some oiliness.

SCORE **76**

ARRAN Single Cask, Bottle 332 of 347, Distilled 18 July 1997, Bottled 14 October 2002, 58.6 vol

Exclusively for the wine and spirit merchant Hanseatic, of Bremen.
Matured in sherry. Also reracked to finish in sherry.

COLOUR Full, warm, gold.

NOSE Oily. Marshmallow. Seed cake.

BODY Soft, luxurious.

PALATE Dried fruits. Raisins. Sauternes. Chocolate.

FINISH Firm. Gripping. Winey.

SCORE **77**

AUCHENTOSHAN

PRODUCER Morrison Bowmore Distillers Ltd
REGION Lowlands DISTRICT Western Lowlands
ADDRESS Dalmuir, Clydebank, Dunbartonshire, G81 4SJ
TEL 01389 878561   WEBSITE www.auchentoshan.com VC

THIS IS A CLASSIC LOWLAND DISTILLERY, not only in its location, but also in its adherence to triple distillation. Light-bodied whiskies result; light in flavour, too, but by no means bland. If you fancy single malts, but do not care for intensity, Auchentoshan offers the perfect answer: subtlety. Stan Getz rather than Sonny Rollins; Vivaldi, as opposed to Beethoven.

Auchentoshan ("corner of the field") is pronounced "och'n'tosh'n", as though it were an imprecation. The distillery is at the foot of the Kilpatrick Hills, just outside Glasgow. There are suggestions of a distillery on the site around 1800, but 1825 is the "official" foundation date. The distillery was rebuilt after the Second World War, re-equipped in 1974, and further overhauled ten years later, when it was acquired by Stanley P. Morrison. The acquisition provided a Lowland partner for their Islay and Highland distilleries, Bowmore and Glen Garioch. The company is now called Morrison Bowmore, and is controlled by Suntory. The Japanese cherish the distilleries, and the upkeep is superb. Much has been done to highlight the equipment at Auchentoshan and to show how the whisky is made.

HOUSE STYLE Light, lemon grassy, herbal, oily. Aperitif or restorative.

AUCHENTOSHAN Select, No Age Statement, 40 vol

COLOUR Shimmery gold.

NOSE Appetizing, clean, warm, cereal grain. Cookies fresh from the oven.

BODY Lightly oily.

PALATE Lemon-grass notes. Toasty maltiness –
definite, but light. Cleanly sweet.

FINISH Light, crisp. Hint of lemon-grass spiciness.

SCORE 79

AUCHENTOSHAN 10-year-old, 40 vol

COLOUR Bright yellowy gold.

NOSE A warm embrace, with perfumes of vanilla,
lemon grass, and saddlery.

BODY Light but soft, oily.

PALATE Lemon zest, marshmallow, sweet but not cloying.

FINISH Longer. Lemon grass, faint ginger, vanilla, perfumy. Soft.

SCORE 83

AUCHENTOSHAN Three Wood, No Age Statement, 43 vol

*This whisky has at least ten years in bourbon wood, a good year in oloroso and six months
in the hefty Pedro Ximénez. In addition to offering an unusual array of wood
characteristics, it fills a gap in Auchentoshan's age range.*

COLOUR Orange liqueur.

NOSE Soft. Orange zest, apricot, dates, marshmallow.

BODY Oily. Marshmallow-like.

PALATE Perfumy, lemon grass, cashews. A delicate interplay of flavours, but
the whisky struggles to make itself heard among the woods.
Better with little or no water.

FINISH Long. Creamy. Raisins. Aniseed. Fresh oak. Sappy dryness.

SCORE 85

AUCHENTOSHAN Selected Cask Vatting, 18-year-old, Distilled 1978, 58.8 vol

This superb vatting further fills the previous gap in the age range.

COLOUR Full gold to bronze.

NOSE Linseed, saddlery, fresh leather.

BODY Smooth, layered, soft.

PALATE Linseed, fresh leather, perfumy. A very expressive Auchentoshan.

FINISH Clean, lemony, scenty.

SCORE **87**

AUCHENTOSHAN 21-year-old, 43 vol

COLOUR Full, deep gold.

NOSE Orange zest, date boxes, cedar, oil.

BODY Light to medium, oily, very smooth indeed.

PALATE Oily, citrusy, orange peel, lightly spicy, with lots of flavour development. Full of subtleties. More oak character than previous entry. Fresh, with no obtrusive woodiness.

FINISH Cedar, vanilla, beautifully rounded and aromatic.

SCORE **86**

AUCHENTOSHAN 22-year-old, 43 vol

COLOUR Deep gold to amber.

NOSE Rich fresh leather.

BODY Very firm, smooth, and oily.

PALATE Oily, cedary, spicy. Male cosmetics. If soap were edible.

FINISH Dry, cedary.

SCORE **86**

VINTAGE-DATED AUCHENTOSHANS

Logically, a Lowland whisky is too light in body and flavour to cope with much influence of wood. Despite this, Auchentoshan has retained its character in bottlings at considerable ages, for example, a 22-year-old and a 31-year-old each rated 86 points in the fourth edition of this book. The more recent bottlings, reviewed here, have proven less resilient. The 1973 is the more interesting drink, but says little of whisky, let alone of Auchentoshan. The 1965 is more whiskyish, but less rounded. Both are of more interest to the collector than the taster.

AUCHENTOSHAN 1973, 29-year-old, Sherry Butt No 793, 55.8 vol

COLOUR Pinkish red. Almost rhubarb-like.

NOSE Jammy. Australian Shiraz. Red apples. Peaches.

BODY Textured. Fluffy.

PALATE An extraordinarily fruity whisky, with peach dominant.
Peach-stone flavours, too. Underneath all that, it is hard to divine any
Auchentoshan character. Severely marked down for those reasons.

FINISH Nutty dryness. With the cheese? After dinner?

SCORE **69**

AUCHENTOSHAN 1965, 31-year-old, Cask No 2502, 49.3 vol

COLOUR Old gold.

NOSE Some candy-floss sweetness.

BODY Syrupy, then dusty. Icing sugar. Cocoa powder.

PALATE Spun sugar. Quickly becoming drier. Nutty. Flavours reminiscent
of peanut shells, coconut-fibre matting.

FINISH Dry, musty.

SCORE **72**

SOME INDEPENDENT BOTTLINGS

There was something of a flood of 1992 distillates, bottled at 10 years.
A Cadenhead bottling was creamy tasting but slightly aggressive. SCORE 81

A Murray McDavid edition was fresh with a deliciously clean,
marshmallowy maltiness, and an excellent balance of herbal,
yeasty dryness. SCORE 83

A James MacArthur bottling, at 64.2 vol, combined a flapjack sweetness,
oaty oiliness, and cleansing dryness. SCORE 82

The other three bottlings were at 46 vol. A Whisky Galore edition had a
garden mint aroma and a fresh, floral, apple-blossom palate. SCORE 84

AUCHROISK

PRODUCER Diageo
REGION Highlands DISTRICT Speyside
ADDRESS Auchroisk Distillery Mulben, Banffshire, AB55 6XS
TEL 01542 885000 WEBSITE www.malts.com VC

TOO YOUNG to make promises for eternity, but "Always Auchroisk" might be a wise text for the future. This distillery was established in 1974. Given that a distillery can survive two or three times as long as a human, Auchroisk is barely an adolescent. For several years, it has, in the hope of seducing foreigners, been calling itself The Singleton. That term is sometimes used to indicate a single cask (in this case, a sherry butt). It was therefore thought to be an appropriate substitute for the original Gaelic name, which means "ford on the red stream".

The distillery, between Rothes and Dufftown, is on a ridge by the Mulben Burn, which flows into the Spey. Nearby is a spring called Dorie's Well, which determined the site of the distillery. The soft water and large stills make whisky of a delicacy that deserves a chance to show itself without sherry, and under its own name.

Phonetic guides can always be provided, except that no one agrees. Auch Roysk, says the manager; Ach Rask (or Rusk), insist the locals. There is schism over the "ch" being pronounced as a "th". Can the foreigners cope with this? Funny how the simply delicious Singleton never hooked as many sales worldwide as some unpronounceably complex whiskies from the west.

HOUSE STYLE Very soft. Berry fruits. Aperitif. Or with fruit salad or similar desserts.

AUCHROISK 10-year-old, 43 vol

COLOUR Soft, burnished yellow.

NOSE Pronounced fruitiness. White grapes. Gooseberry. Berry fruits.

BODY Light, soft, seductive.

PALATE Lightly fruity, with a suggestion of figs. Becoming nuttier and drier. Shortbread.

FINISH Faint sun-scorched grass and peat.

SCORE **78**

A 27-year-old independent bottling from Old Malt Cask, 43.8 vol, had a suggestion of bananas and cream toffee. SCORE 77

AULTMORE

PRODUCER John Dewar & Sons Ltd
REGION Highlands DISTRICT Speyside (Isla)
ADDRESS Keith, Banffshire, AB55 6QY
TEL 01542 881800 VC

A FINE MALT IN THE OAKY STYLE that seems to characterize the whiskies made near the river Isla. This distillery, which is just north of Keith, was built in 1896, and reconstructed in 1971. In 1991, United Distillers, its owners at the time, introduced a bottling in their flora and fauna series. They issued a Rare Malts edition in 1996, and a Cask Strength Limited Bottling in 1997–98. These and other past bottlings were reviewed in the fourth edition of this book. In 1998, Aultmore was acquired by Bacardi, but no new bottlings have yet appeared.

HOUSE STYLE Fresh, dry, herbal, spicy, oaky. Reminiscent of a fino sherry, albeit a very big one. Before dinner.

AULTMORE 1989, Signatory, 43 vol

COLOUR Crystal-bright greeny gold.

NOSE Steely. Slightly smoky.

BODY Soft, rounded.

PALATE Lean, sweet and fruity, then nutty. Developing cereal-grain oiliness. Flavours reminiscent of bread and butter pudding.

FINISH Gently spicy.

SCORE 75

AULTMORE 1987, 15-year-old, Whisky Galore, 46 vol

COLOUR White wine.

NOSE Fruity. Flowering currant.

BODY Distinctively firm, smooth, and oily.

PALATE Tightly combined flavours. Spicy, dry, appetizing.

FINISH Gentian bitterness, but gentle.

SCORE 76

BALBLAIR

PRODUCER Inver House Distillers Ltd
REGION Highlands DISTRICT Northern Highlands
ADDRESS Edderton, Tain, Ross-shire, IV19 1LB
EMAIL enquiries@inverhouse.com WEBSITE www.inverhouse.com

THE CHANGE OF CONTROL AT INVER HOUSE in 2001 has thus far had no dramatic effect on the company's portfolio of malt distilleries. They are all relatively small, long established, and generally traditional in design and process. None is a household name, but all are respected distilleries. This one and Speyburn are especially pretty, and are the most popular choices when an art director or photographer want to show a "typical" malt distillery in an attractive location.

The light spiciness and fresh dryness of the northern Highland malts are equally typical in the Balblair whiskies. These characteristics show best in young whiskies. So why the increase in older bottlings? Perhaps that is one small sign of the new broom: tidying the stock in the warehouses. There is a limit to the number of heirlooms that can be accommodated; whiskies can become woody; and evaporation can take them below the minimum permitted alcohol.

They are made using water that has flowed from the piney hillsides of Ben Dearg and over dry, crumbly peat towards the river Carron and the Dornoch firth. A burn near the distillery feeds Balblair, which is amid fields at Edderton, close to the firth and the sea. There is said to have been brewing and distilling in the vicinity in the mid-1700s. Balblair is among Scotland's oldest distilleries. It began in 1790, and the present building dates from the 1870s.

HOUSE STYLE Light, firm, dry. Aperitif when young.
Can be woody when older.

BALBLAIR "Elements", No Age Statement, 40 vol

COLOUR Full gold.

NOSE Sea breezes. Slight salt. Barley-malt sweetness.

BODY Lean but smooth. Textured.

PALATE Teasing, appetizing, balance of slight salt and
shortbread-like fresh malt. Faint hint of raspberries.

FINISH Plum-skin dryness.

SCORE 76

BALBLAIR 10-year-old, 40 vol

COLOUR Shimmery, pale gold.

NOSE Fresh. Salty. Vanilla. A hint of chocolate.

BODY Light on tongue.

PALATE Malty dryness. Shortbread sprinkled with sugar.
Custard. Summer pudding.

FINISH Concentrated fruity dryness. Summer pudding. Comforting.

COMMENT Approachable and well structured, with delicious flavours.

SCORE 77

BALBLAIR 16-year-old, 40 vol

COLOUR Pale amber.

NOSE Nutty. Light, fresh spiciness. Fragrant.

BODY Firm, smooth, textured.

PALATE Smooth and surprisingly satisfying. Again, the saltiness and
shortbread. This time, it is chocolate shortbread. A light whisky but
packed with flavours. Very lively.

FINISH Toffee apples. Cedary dryness.

SCORE 78

BALBLAIR 27-year-old, 46 vol

COLOUR Dark chestnut.

NOSE Cocoa powder. Winey.

BODY Firm, dusty.

PALATE More chocolate, but more bitter. Good quality cooking chocolate.

FINISH Slightly gritty and astringent. Much improved with
a splash of water.

SCORE 77

BALBLAIR 31-year-old, Bottled 2002,
Highland Selection Limited Edition, 55 vol

COLOUR Very bright pale gold.

NOSE Grassy. Sun-dried grass. Dusty. Restrained cedar.

BODY Cedary, but rather woody for most tastes

PALATE Dry. Some spiciness.

FINISH Stern. Unyielding. Dry, but not astringent.

SCORE **76**

A 31-year-old for the French market begins with a more open, malty, fresh brioche character, but quickly retreats into its own thoughts. SCORE 77

BALBLAIR 33-year-old, 54.4 vol

COLOUR Bright gold.

NOSE Peaty, earthy, almost pungent.

BODY Firm, smooth.

PALATE Oily. Seed cake. Banana cake. Spicy.

FINISH Big. Spicy. Lemon grass. Fragrant peat. Long.

COMMENT A whisky that starts life with some restraint has
certainly developed over the years.

SCORE **79**

CASK No 893

ADELPHI DISTILLERY LIMITED

3 GLOUCESTER LANE, EDINBURGH EH3 6ED, SCOTLAND

FROM BALBLAIR, 37 YEARS OLD

54.3%
vol

DISTILLED AT BALBLAIR DISTILLERY 1965
BOTTLED IN SCOTLAND 2002
SELECTED BY ADELPHI DISTILLERY LIMITED

70cl

INDEPENDENT BOTTLING
BALBLAIR 37-year-old, Adelphi, 54.3 vol

COLOUR Apricot.

NOSE Again, cedary.

BODY Drying.

PALATE Cedary, but also spicy and liquorice-like.
The rich spiciness rounds out the flavours.

FINISH Robust.

SCORE **78**

BALMENACH

PRODUCER Inver House Distillers Ltd
REGION Highlands DISTRICT Speyside
ADDRESS Cromdale, Grantown-on-Spey, Morayshire, PH26 3PF
EMAIL enquiries@inverhouse.com WEBSITE www.inverhouse.com

TWO NEW BOTTLINGS in the Highland Selection were a robust reminder of Balmenach just as its owners, Inver House, became part of Khun Charoen's interests. There had been loose talk of Balmenach being regarded by Inver House as a "flagship". Its distillate has the most powerful aromas and flavours among those produced in the group, but Balmenach today seems geographically very remote. In the upper reaches of Speyside, beyond the Livet and Avon, the bowl known as Cromdale ("crooked plain") was once alive with illicit distillers. When Balmenach emerged there as a legal distillery in 1824, it was in the heart of whisky country.

The family that founded Balmenach, in 1824, also produced two appropriately distinguished authors: Sir Compton Mackenzie (*Whisky Galore*) and Sir Robert Bruce Lockhart (*Scotch, in fact and story*, and other books on soldiering, espionage, and travel). Balmenach later had its own spur on the Strathspey railway. The distillery contributed malt whisky to many blends, especially Crabbie's and Johnnie Walker.

In 1991 a bottled single malt was issued at 43 vol in the flora and fauna series. A review appeared in subsequent editions of this book, praising the whisky for its depth of heather-honey flavours, herbal dryness, and sherry (SCORE 77). Two years later, United Distillers announced that Balmenach was to be mothballed. Four years on, it passed to Inver House. In the interim, very flowery expressions of Balmenach were bottled under the name Deerstalker, by Aberfoyle & Knight, of Glasgow (SCORE 79).

HOUSE STYLE Big. Herbal, savoury. Hints of peat.
Distinctive. Teasing. Surprisingly food-friendly.

BALMENACH 27-year-old, Bottled 2001, Highland Selection, 46 vol

NOSE Sweet tropical fruits. Bananas. Plantains being cooked on a barbecue.

PALATE Becoming drier. Vegetal. Yeasty. Perhaps the meal is
in Thailand or China?

FINISH A touch of smokiness. Roasted bell-peppers. Some chilli-like heat.

SCORE **79**

BALMENACH 1972, 28-year-old, Highland Selection, 46 vol

NOSE Sweet at first. Honeydew melons. Then leafy: a suggestion of sorrel.
A hint of grass and peat-smoke.

PALATE Lightly honeyish, becoming creamy. Quite rich, leathery. Some peat.

FINISH Dry, big. Gingery. Black treacle. Smoky, sulphury, heady.

COMMENT A robust malt, but with many subtleties of character.

SCORE **80**

SOME INDEPENDENT BOTTLINGS

BALMENACH 30-year-old, 1972 Port Wood, Released 2002, Hart Brothers, 50.1 vol

NOSE Honey, with a suggestion of chocolate, but also herbal notes.

PALATE Peppery and dry, but also creamy.

FINISH Orangey, zesty. Appetizingly spicy. Cilantro?

COMMENT Very distinctive. Bring on the chicken molé.

SCORE **77**

BALMENACH 1974, Connoisseurs Choice, 40 vol

COLOUR Deep bronze.

NOSE Glazed pastry. Savoury. Gingery.

BODY Softy. Oily.

PALATE Expressive. Spicy. Phenol.

FINISH Smoky, herbal.

SCORE **77**

A 1978 12-year-old Coopers Choice, at 43 vol, from the Vintage Malt
Whisky Company, had some curiously aromatic wood notes. SCORE 74

A 13-year-old, at 60.1 vol, from Adelphi, had an herbal,
aromatic, mint character. SCORE 77

A 1971 30-year-old from Cadenhead had a sweeter,
maltier richness. SCORE 77

THE BALVENIE

PRODUCER William Grant & Sons Ltd
REGION Highlands   DISTRICT Speyside (Dufftown)
ADDRESS Dufftown, Banffshire, AB55 4BB
TEL 01340 820373   WEBSITE www.thebalvenie.com

As seductively honeyed as a speysider can be; ever more aristocratic, in recent years introducing vintages as though they were eligible offspring, The Balvenie is increasingly recognized far from her domain. Her tendency toward voluptuousness, and her ready charm, win friends easily. A dalliance by the sea resulted in the birth, in 2001, of The Balvenie Islay Cask. Fellow Speysiders resented the notion of a whisky from their elevated territory even contemplating the addition of "Islay" to its name. Meanwhile, Islanders complained that The Balvenie was merely courting popularity. There have been no more Islay Casks. It was a holiday romance.

She may be a notably rich spirit, but Bad Penny offers the easiest mnemonic for Balvenie's vowel sounds. The Balvenie distillery was built in 1892 by the Grant family, who had already established Glenfiddich in 1886. It is highly unusual for a distillery to remain in the same ownership throughout its history, but both Glenfiddich and Balvenie have done so, on their original sites, which adjoin one another. One became the world's biggest selling malt and the other the epitome of luxury, but both were established, thriftily, with second-hand stills. Balvenie's are more bulbous, and that feature no doubt contributes to the distinct character of the whisky. The distillery also has its own small floor maltings, using barley from the family farm.

In 1990, Grant's added to the site a third distillery, Kininvie. This also produces a creamy spirit, but Kininvie has not thus far been bottled as a single malt. Adjoining the site is the silent Convalmore distillery, acquired by Grant's in 1992 to augment warehousing capacity.

Grant's site is at Dufftown, where the rivers Fiddich and Dullan meet on their way to the Spey. The Balvenie distillery is near the castle of the same name, which dates at least from the 1200s. The castle was at one stage known as Mortlach and was at another stage occupied by the Duff family, and is now owned by the nation of Scotland.

HOUSE STYLE The most honeyish of malts, with a distinctively orangey note.
Luxurious. After dinner. Ages well.

THE BALVENIE Founder's Reserve, 10-year-old, 40 vol

Matured in 90% American oak and 10% sherry.

COLOUR Bright gold.

NOSE Orange-honey perfume. Musky. Faint hint of peat.

BODY Medium.

PALATE Honeyed sweetness drying to lightly spicy notes. Very lively.
Just a touch of sherry.

FINISH A tingly surge of flavours, with lingering, syrupy honey.

SCORE **85**

THE BALVENIE Double Wood, 12-year-old, 40 vol

First- and second-fill bourbon casks, then six to twelve months in sweet oloroso casks.

COLOUR Amber.

NOSE Sherry and orange skins.

BODY Medium, rich.

PALATE Beautifully combined mellow flavours: nutty, sweet, sherry,
very orangey fruitiness, heather, cinnamon spiciness.

FINISH Long, tingling. Very warming.

SCORE **87**

THE BALVENIE Single Barrel, 15-year-old, 50.4 vol

All first-fill bourbon casks.

COLOUR Pale gold.

NOSE Assertive. Dry, fresh oak. Heather. Rooty. Coconut. Lemon pith.

BODY Firm.

PALATE Lively. Cedar. Orange skins, pineapple-like sweetness and acidity.

FINISH Very dry. Peppery alcohol.

SCORE **85**

THE BALVENIE Islay Cask, 43 vol

Seven years in bourbon barrels, then finished for six months at Balvenie in casks
that had held Islay whisky for six months.

COLOUR Bronze with pinkish tinge.

NOSE Restrained, but distinct, seaweed and salt.

BODY A touch of syrupiness in the middle.

PALATE Honeyed, then some peaty smokiness. The smokiness is enwrapping,
rather than attacking, as it might be in an Islay malt.

FINISH Fragrantly smoky. Orangey flavours emerge. Lively, emphatic finish.
Bonus points for a bold idea.

SCORE **89**

BALVENIE Port Wood, 21-year-old, 40 vol

Primarily matured in bourbon casks, then a short period in first-fill port pipes.

COLOUR Reddish amber.

NOSE Perfumy, fruity. Passion fruit. Raisiny. Nutty dryness. Marzipan.

BODY Rich.

PALATE Very complex. Toffee, creamy, winey, aniseed.

FINISH Long, cedary, dry.

SCORE **88**

BALVENIE Single Barrel, 25-year-old, 46.9 vol

COLOUR Pale, bright, gold.

NOSE Honeyed.

BODY Lightly syrupy.

PALATE Surprisingly peaty, though the characteristic honey is always there.

FINISH Firm. Peaty.

SCORE **86**

BALVENIE 50-year-old, 45.1 vol

For the collector, rather than the taster, whiskies this old once won points simply
for being. As more are released, they have to justify themselves.

COLOUR Mahogany.

NOSE The best feature. Heavy, dark red fruits. Plum strudel, dusted with
cinnamon. Evokes images of cafés in Vienna. Incongruous? Perhaps.
When this was being distilled, the Red Army was leaving.

BODY Light, drying. A curiously inky texture.

PALATE More plums. Passion fruit. Woody tannins. Iron-like flavours weigh
down the palate. Spicy notes try to lift it, but eventually lose the struggle.

FINISH Quite bitter and astringent.

SCORE **85**

SOME VINTAGE BOTTLINGS OF THE BALVENIE
THE BALVENIE 1989, Port Wood, 40 vol
Finished for a year in second-fill port pipes with a view to a more subtle wine character.

COLOUR Warm gold.

NOSE Hint of cream toffee.

BODY Creamy, clinging.

PALATE A suggestion of passion fruit. Orange muscat, "peach stone" nuttiness, then spicy dryness. Port character very restrained.

FINISH Silky.

SCORE **87**

THE BALVENIE Vintage Cask, 1972, 49.4 vol

COLOUR Rich, warm, gold to amber.

NOSE Buttery richness. Butterscotch pudding. Bread and butter pudding. Honey.

BODY Rich, soft, delicious. Astonishingly syrupy smooth.

PALATE Still evoking thoughts of desserts, but the honeyed pastries of the Balkans. Then a suggestion of chocolate powder hints at tiramisu.

FINISH Bitter chocolate. Terry's chocolate oranges. The ultimate dessert whisky. Beautifully composed.

SCORE **92**

THE BALVENIE Vintage Cask, 1970, 44.6 vol

COLOUR Gold.

NOSE Fudge. Honey. A hint of heather. Very soft, floral.

BODY Lightly creamy.

PALATE Intensely sweet and Sauternes-like. Or perhaps orange Muscat? With water yet sweeter and fruitier.

FINISH The sweet components become more like dark, clear, liquid honey. The fruity element becomes more intense and perfumy. All the elements of a classic Balvenie, beautifully presented and combined.

SCORE **91**

THE BALVENIE 1968, Vintage Cask, 50.8 vol

COLOUR Full gold to bronze.

NOSE Clear liquid honey. Heathery.
More perfumy and orangey when water is added.

BODY Fudgey, soft.

PALATE Honeyed. Very pronounced orange zest. Lots of flavour development.
With water. Hazelnut or almond. Some smoke. Slight menthol. Mint.

FINISH Lemony. Dry. Warming. Very long.

SCORE **90**

THE BALVENIE Vintage Cask 1967, 49.7 vol

COLOUR Full gold.

NOSE Very aromatic. Butterscotch, honey. Acacia. Faint peat.

BODY Light syrupy. Slightly drying. Nutty. Chewy.

PALATE Buttery maltiness. Honey. Orange. Linctus-like.
Hint of vanilla. Juicy oak.

FINISH Orange skins. Lemon grass. Lightly peaty balancing dryness.

SCORE **88**

THE BALVENIE Vintage Cask 1966, 42.1 vol

COLOUR Full gold to bronze.

NOSE Very aromatic. Butter, honey, lemon. Grass. Faint peat.

BODY Medium, firm, rounded.

PALATE Buttery maltiness. Honey. Orange. Lemon grass. Juicy oak.
A beautifully balanced classic Speyside whisky.

FINISH Lemon. Grass. Lightly peaty balancing dryness.

SCORE **88**

EARLIER VERSIONS OF THE BALVENIE

A 1964 Vintage, long gone, was similar but nuttier and drier. SCORE 88
A 1951 had a dark brown colour and was full of peat and oak smoke, but
still with some malty smoothness underneath it all. Slightly astringent, but
bonus points for traditional values and distinctiveness. SCORE 88

OTHER VERSIONS OF THE BALVENIE

A rare independent bottling by Signatory in 1990, of a 1974 distillate:
bright full gold; dry, malty shortbread aroma; firm, lightly syrupy
body; honey, cinnamon, and lemon in palate; smooth,
long, rounded, satisfying, warming finish. SCORE 87

BANFF

PRODUCER DCL
REGION Highlands DISTRICT Speyside (Deveron)
SITE OF FORMER DISTILLERY Inverboyndie, on B9139, 1 mile west of Banff

THE HOUSE OF COMMONS was once supplied with whisky from this distillery, near the adjoining towns of Banff and MacDuff. The two face each other across the Deveron, where the river flows into the Moray firth. The county of Banffshire once stretched from the Deveron to the Spey. This eastern flank of Speyside embraced half the region's distilleries. It has fewer today, but it is still barley country, its coastal strip linking the Laich of Moray with Aberdeenshire. The county became Banff and Buchan and is now subsumed into Aberdeenshire.

The distillery, dating from at least 1824, closed in 1983, leaving a substantial amount of stock. Its buildings have gradually been dismantled, though remains loom through the sea mist. They are in a field next to a graveyard. The spirits of Banff are restless judging from the profusion of independent bottlings.

HOUSE STYLE Fragrant. Lemon grass. Sweet. Restorative or after dinner.

BANFF 1980, 21-year-old, Cask No 2914, Signatory Vintage, 43 vol

COLOUR	Vinho verde.
NOSE	Light. Fresh. Grassy.
BODY	Light, creamy, appetizingly dryish.
PALATE	Grassy. Oaty. A suggestion of golden syrup.
FINISH	Kendal mint cake.
COMMENT	A pleasant, easily drinkable malt. Showing few signs of age, good or bad.

SCORE 70

Earlier from Signatory, in its Silent Stills series, a 1978 bottling, at 18 years old and 58.8 vol, was drier and smokier. SCORE 67

BANFF 1978, 22-year-old, Bottled 2002, The Coopers Choice (The Vintage Malt Whisky Company), 56 vol

COLOUR Greeny gold. Lime-tinged.

NOSE Grassy. Aromatic.

BODY Smooth. Creamy.

PALATE Condensed milk. A hint of chocolate. Late flavour development. Becomes very lively.

FINISH Big surge. Lemon zest.

SCORE **69**

BANFF 1976, 25-year-old, James MacArthur's Old Master's, 57.1 vol

COLOUR Full greeny gold.

NOSE Soft. Warm. Burnt grass.

BODY Slippery smooth.

PALATE Peaty, earthy. Chocolate powder. Sweetish. A touch of vanilla. Some syrupiness.

FINISH Long. Warming. Spicy. Minty. Extra strong peppermints.

SCORE **69**

BANFF 24-year-old, Cadenhead, 58.3 vol

COLOUR Bright gold.

NOSE Clean, dry, peat-smoke fragrance. A hint of the sea?

BODY Syrupy.

PALATE Vanilla. Syrupy-sweet flavours. Grassy. Sun-dried grass.

FINISH Lemon grass. Complex spiciness. Gingery, dry. Very long. Real depth and staying power.

SCORE **72**

An earlier 1976, at 21 years and 58.2 vol, from Cadenhead, was peatier and earthier, with more vanilla. Less bright and clean. SCORE 67

BANFF 1976, Connoisseurs Choice, 40 vol

COLOUR Vinho verde.

NOSE Fresh. Grassy. Lemon grass.

BODY Smooth. Creamy.

PALATE Fresh cream. Coconut. Tropical fruits.

FINISH Fruity, aromatic dryness. Perhaps even a hint of phenol.

SCORE **73**

BEN NEVIS

PRODUCER Ben Nevis Distillery Ltd
REGION Highlands DISTRICT West Highlands
ADDRESS Lochy Bridge, Fort William, PH33 6TJ
TEL 01397 702476 VC

MUCH-IMPROVED BOTTLINGS are beginning to emerge as Ben Nevis marks a dozen years under the ownership of the respected Japanese distillers Nikka. The distillery, at Fort William, lies at the foot of Scotland's highest mountain, Ben Nevis (1344m/4409ft). The peak does not have quite the significance of Fuji, but it is a powerful symbol of Scotland.

The distillery was established in 1825 by "Long John" McDonald. The well-known blended Scotch, Long John, was named after him. The distillery, with its curiously anthologous architecture, is in a very visible spot on a road with a heavy tourist traffic, but relatively distant from any other distilleries. Its regional appropriation to the western Highlands is supported by its being close to a sea loch. "We are a coastal distillery" insists manager Colin Ross, standing in front of the mighty mountain.

HOUSE STYLE Fragrant. Robust. Waxy fruitiness. Tropical fruit.
Oily, a touch of smoke. Restorative or book-at-bedtime.

BEN NEVIS 10-year-old, 46 vol

Found at 40 vol or 43 vol in some markets.

COLOUR Warm bronze to amber.

NOSE Perfumy, spicy, soft. Waxed fruit. Kumquats. Hard black chocolate.

BODY Emphatically big, firm, smooth.

PALATE Orange-cream pralines in black chocolate. Belgian toffee wafers.

FINISH Orange zest. Pithy dryness. Touch of cigar smoke.

SCORE **77**

Also at 10 years old, tasted as a work in progress, a single cask, aged entirely in sherry, emerged with orange marmalade colour; flavours of pickled peaches and rum butter; texture as dense as a mince pie; and a long, warming finish.

BEN NEVIS 21-year-old, Limited Edition in Decanter, 60.5 vol

Now hard to find.

COLOUR Bronze to amber.

NOSE Box of black chocolates.

BODY Big, smooth.

PALATE Oilier, juicier, chewier, drier.

FINISH Robust. Oaky spiciness.

SCORE **77**

BEN NEVIS 26-year-old, Distilled 1975, Cask No 945, Bottled 2001, 53.9 vol

COLOUR Bright greeny gold.

NOSE Leafy. Fruity.

BODY Firm. Smooth.

PALATE Fruity, A touch of honey. Dry maltiness. Chocolatey.

FINISH Spiciness. Chillis. Peppery. Rather aggressive.

SCORE **77**

Distilled and bottled in the same years as the previous whisky, cask no 946 emerged at 52.3 vol, slightly richer and sweeter. SCORE 78

An earlier 26-year-old (distilled 1972, bottled 1998), 57.4 vol, had a fuller colour, more sherry character, some smokiness, and a beautiful balance. SCORE 78

BEN NEVIS 1966, Bottled 1998, 51 vol

COLOUR Bright golden yellow.

NOSE Oily.

BODY Very oily.

PALATE Oily, flowery, surprisingly neutral. Disappointing, like some other Ben Nevis distillates from the 1960s.

FINISH Mustardy.

SCORE 62

SOME INDEPENDENT BOTTLINGS

BEN NEVIS 35-year-old, Distilled April 1957, First Sherry Wood, Hart Brothers, 50.1 vol

COLOUR Very attractive reddish amber.

NOSE Tightly combined and balanced, fragrant smoke, oak and hard-toffee maltiness.

PALATE Chewy. Malty honeycomb in dark chocolate. As though the Belgians had upgraded the British Crunchie bar. Tropical fruits.

FINISH Clinging. Bittersweet. Firm. Intense black chocolate, but avoids astringency. An outstanding bottling.

SCORE 82

A Cadenhead bottling of 1986 at 17 years old and 46 vol was oily, feinty, and hot. Rather harsh all round. SCORE 60

A Blackadder bottling of 1984 at 60.8, from cask no. 257, balanced its woodiness with a luscious, sweet, treacle-toffee character. SCORE 76

Cask no 258, at 61.2 vol, had winey, Syrah-like flavours, and hints of raspberry vinegar. Lots of sweetness suggested a dessert whisky, but the idyll was shattered by the intensity of woodiness. SCORE 78

BEN WYVIS

PRODUCER Whyte and Mackay Ltd
REGION Highlands   DISTRICT Northern Highlands
ADDRESS Invergordon Distillers, Cottage Brae,
Invergordon, Ross-shire, IV18 0HP

A NEW ENTRY IN THIS BOOK, yet it finally appears a quarter of a century after the distillery closed. The wait for whisky has been twice as long as the distillery's lifespan. Several distilleries had short lives and subsequently appeared in spirit, but Ben Wyvis is surely the ultimate ghost of the glens. Its name is pronounced with a short "y", as in myth: wyv-iss. It derives from the mountain peak Ben Wyvis (1046 metres or 3432 feet), variously translated into English as "big green slope" or "terrible hill", northwest of Inverness and the Black Isle; the peak is part of the northern Highland range.

The regional designation Ferintosh was used to identify whiskies from the Black Isle and Dingwall, on the Cromarty firth, in the late 1600s and 1700s. The name Ferintosh was later applied for a time to a distillery built as Ben Wyvis in Dingwall in 1879. This first Ben Wyvis closed in 1926. The buildings were later used as whisky warehouses, and some still stand, masquerading as a business park.

The economic recovery after the Second World War led to a boom in the whisky industry in the late 1950s and the 1960s. In 1965, a new Ben Wyvis distillery was built further north on the Cromarty firth, at Invergordon. It shared a site with the Invergordon grain distillery. The intention was that Ben Wyvis would provide malt whisky for the Invergordon blends. The Invergordon company had its own ups and downs, and Ben Wyvis ceased production in 1976.

It is said that one cask of Ben Wyvis was exported to the United States in 1974. There was still some stock of Ben Wyvis when the current century dawned and Invergordon was restructured as Kyndal, two very limited releases have been made. There have also been two bottlings from Signatory. It turns out to have been a highly distinctive malt.

Around the same time, in the opposite corner of Scotland, another half-forgotten distillery was suddenly back in view. Hedley Wright, proprietor of Springbank, announced that he was to reopen Glengyle after 70 years' silence. The stills had long gone, but they have been replaced with those from Ben Wyvis.

HOUSE STYLE Light, dry, herbal, savoury, appetizing.

BEN WYVIS 27-year-old, Distilled 1972, Cask No 745, Bottle No 11 of 187, Cask Strength, 45.9 vol

COLOUR Bright pale gold. Green tinge.

NOSE Very distinctive. Drily flowery. Herbal. Fresh mint. Pesto-like.

BODY Light but textured.

PALATE Herbal. Savoury.

FINISH Soft, buttery. Some mustard.

SCORE **81**

BEN WYVIS 37-year-old, Distilled 17 June 1965, 45.5 vol

COLOUR Full gold. Green tinge.

NOSE More perfumed. Mint. Leafy.

BODY Firmer. Drier.

PALATE Toasted pine nuts. Smoky. Roasted vegetables.

FINISH Very crisp dryness.

SCORE **80**

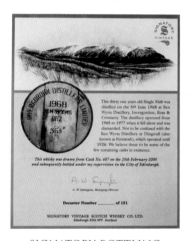

SIGNATORY BOTTLING

BEN WYVIS 31-year-old, Distilled 5 June 1968, Bottled 25 February 2000, Signatory, Cask No 687, 56.5 vol

COLOUR Full gold. Green tinge.

NOSE Slightly more vegetal. Cucumber.

BODY Firm. Smooth.

PALATE Dry, cleansing, appetizing.

FINISH Coriander seeds. Pepper.

SCORE **79**

BENRIACH

PRODUCER Chivas Brothers
REGION Highlands   DISTRICT Speyside (Lossie)
ADDRESS Longmorn, Elgin, Morayshire, IV30 3SJ

TWIN OF THE MUCH LOVED LONGMORN (but not identical). The two occupy adjoining sites. Both distilleries were built in the 1890s, but Benriach was silent from 1900 until it was restored in 1965. Benriach has its own floor maltings. This has not been used since the 1990s, but is beautifully maintained. Benriach is the more agricultural-looking distillery, Longmorn the more elaborate. Benriach has a traditional mash tun. Both distilleries have onion-shaped stills, but Benriach's are steeper. Benriach's whiskies are in general sweeter, those from Longmorn more complex. At older ages, Benriach begins to narrow the gap.

HOUSE STYLE Cookie-like, with touches of butterscotch. Restorative. A mid-afternoon malt?

BENRIACH DISTILLERY
EST.1898
A   SINGLE
PURE HIGHLAND MALT
Scotch Whisky
Benriach Distillery, in the heart of the Highlands, still malts its own barley. The resulting whisky has a unique and attractive delicacy
PRODUCED AND BOTTLED BY THE
BENRIACH
DISTILLERY CO
ELGIN, MORAYSHIRE, SCOTLAND, IV30 3SJ
Distilled and Bottled in Scotland
AGED 10 YEARS

BENRIACH 10-year-old, 43 vol

COLOUR Pale, bright gold.

NOSE Light, clean, honey. Flowery dryness.

BODY Light, smooth, textured.

PALATE Pronounced cereal grain. Oatmeal cookies. Spicy seed cake.

FINISH Cookie-like, butterscotch sweetness. Then drying and thinning to appetizing, lightly honeyish floweriness. Fresh and well defined.

SCORE 72

BENRINNES

PRODUCER Diageo
REGION Highlands DISTRICT Speyside
ADDRESS Aberlour, Banffshire, AB38 9WN
TEL Contact via Dailuaine 01340 872500

As A MOUNTAIN, Ben Rinnes spreads itself to two words and is hard to miss; as a distillery and a whisky, Benrinnes compounds itself so neatly that it is too easily overlooked. It is no novice. Benrinnes may have been founded as early as the 1820s, and was largely rebuilt in the 1950s. The distillery had a long association with the Crawford blends. Its malt whisky did not have official bottling until 1991, in a Flora and Fauna edition. Benrinnes' system of partial triple distillation places it among the handful of quirky, individualistic distilleries in the Diageo group.

HOUSE STYLE Big, creamy, smoky, flavoursome, long.
Restorative or after dinner.

BENRINNES 15-year-old, Flora and Fauna, 43 vol

COLOUR Autumnal reddish brown.

NOSE Heavy, almost creamy. A whiff of sherry, then a firm, smoky, burnt-toffee character.

BODY Medium to full, firm.

PALATE Dry, assertive, rounded. Flavours are gradually unlocked. Hints of liquorice, aniseed, vanilla, bitter chocolate, smokiness.

FINISH Satisfying, soothing. Faintly sweet and smoky.

SCORE 79

BENRINNES 21-year-old, Distilled 1974, Rare Malts, 60.4 vol

COLOUR Bright gold.

NOSE Earthy. Hint of peatiness.

BODY Medium, firm.

PALATE Oily, nutty, toffeeish, creamy. Developing vanilla, orange, lime.

FINISH Delayed, surging finish. Sweetish spicy. Long, lingering, expressive.

SCORE **79**

A 1974, at 22 years old, from Adelphi, was grassy, flowery and fruity. SCORE 78

SOME INDEPENDENT BOTTLINGS
BENRINNES 1989, Signatory, 43 vol

COLOUR Greeny gold. Vinho verde.

NOSE Earthy, dry, and dusty. The aroma in a country store that stocks everything from bacon and cheese to hardware.

BODY Medium, creamy.

PALATE Lightly nutty. Salty. Savoury. Tasty. Distinctive.

FINISH Lemony. Appetizing.

SCORE **78**

An earlier Signatory bottling, a 1982 at 43 vol, had hints of peat and sherry, but beautifully balanced. SCORE 79

BENRINNES 19-year-old, Douglas Laing, 50 vol

COLOUR Pale oak.

NOSE Cedary. Winey. Sherry. Reminiscent of amontillado.

BODY Very creamy. Unusually dense.

PALATE Creamy, earthy, slightly woody. Damson fruitiness.

FINISH Jammy fruitiness eventually blocked by woodiness.

SCORE **76**

BENRINNES 1973, Connoisseurs Choice, 40 vol

COLOUR Deep gold.

NOSE Creamy, toffeeish.

BODY Firm, toasty.

PALATE Gingerbread. Vanilla. Marshmallow. Rose-water.

FINISH Restrained, soothing warmth and balancing dryness. Controlled oakiness. Beautifully composed.

SCORE **78**

BENROMACH

PRODUCER Gordon & MacPhail
REGION Highlands DISTRICT District Speyside (Findhorn)
ADDRESS Invererne Road, Forres, Moray, IV36 3EB
TEL 01309 675968 WEBSITE www.gordonandmacphail.com
EMAIL info@gordonandmacphail.com VC

PRINCE CHARLES IS NO DOUBT among the malt lovers keen to taste this 100-year-old distillery's born-again whisky. Benromach appeared to have died while in the care of United Distillers in the mid-1980s. The distillery, the most immediately visible to travellers approaching Speyside from Inverness, was closed. Sadder still, its valuable copper stills were removed. United did subsequently issue one Rare Malts edition, at 20 years old. Apart from that isolated instance, Benromach was for many years available only in independent bottlings.

A flowery 12-year-old and a more fruity 15-year-old, both popular ages, and each scoring 77, have dried up since the fourth edition of this book. However much inventory a distillery has, its stocks are finite. Devotees mourn, and independent bottlers lose a source. On this occasion, Gordon & MacPhail decided to try and buy the distillery. Having succeeded, they re-equipped it with smaller stills. The idea was to adapt it to present demand, but also to produce a richer spirit. With its new still-house, Benromach was reopened in 1998 – by Prince Charles. The early batches have long passed the three-year transition from spirit to whisky, but will be given a few more summers before they are considered sufficiently mature to release. At that point, there will be a further ascent of the legend. "Bottled by Gordon & MacPhail" is no longer enough. This has already become "by the Proprietors". Eventually, the legend will say: "Distilled and bottled by Gordon & MacPhail."

HOUSE STYLE Assertive, flowery, sometimes creamy. With dessert or after dinner.

BENROMACH Centenary Bottling, 17-year-old, 43 vol

COLOUR Deep, full gold.

NOSE Very flowery, herbal, smoky, complex, long.

BODY Firm, smooth, oily.

PALATE Malty background. Richly sherryish. Peachy.
Flowery. Lively. Complex.

FINISH Nutty, juicy oak, soothing, very long.

SCORE **79**

BENROMACH 18-year-old, 40 vol

COLOUR Full gold.

NOSE Very restrained at first, but gradually becomes very fragrant.
Flowery. Lime blossom. Ground almonds. Sugared almonds.
Mint imperials. Very faint smoke.

BODY Lightly soft, syrupy, flirtatious.

PALATE Perfumy, fragrant. Faint smoke again.

FINISH Very dry but well judged.

SCORE **80**

BENROMACH Cask Strength, 1982, Cask Nos 112 and 114, 59.7 vol

COLOUR Deep, shining gold.

NOSE Fresh air. Ozone. So fresh as to be almost astringent.

BODY Firm, smooth, dryish.

PALATE Oily, liquorice. Treacle toffee. Toasted nuts. Toffee apples.

FINISH Peppermint.

SCORE **77**

An earlier cask strength, at 61 vol, was more rounded, and had a more
obvious contribution from sherry. SCORE 78

BENROMACH 25-year-old, 43 vol

COLOUR Bright gold. Faint green tinge.

NOSE Hint of garden bonfires.

BODY Very light. Spring water. As though the whisky had
attenuated in the bottle.

PALATE Slightly vegetal. Rooty. Chlorophyll. Gin-like.

FINISH Lightly dry. Eccentric, but appetizing.

SCORE **77**

BENROMACH Vintage 1973, 40 vol

COLOUR Full, refractive gold.

NOSE Distinctly sweeter, but also with acidity. Pear syrup. Fresh apples.
Some crème fraîche acidity.

BODY Firm. Dry.

PALATE Apple pie with butterscotch and cream.

FINISH Burnt pie crust. Slight phenol.

SCORE **77**

BENROMACH Port Wood Finish, 19-year-old, 45 vol

COLOUR Attractive orange pink.

NOSE Lightly fruity. Dark, soft fruits as it opens. Nut toffee. A hint of coffee.

BODY Surprisingly light, soft, smooth.

PALATE Sweet. Some fruitiness, but lacks complexity.

FINISH Proposes a seduction, then vanishes. A tease.

SCORE **77**

OTHER VERSIONS OF BENROMACH

The Rare Malts 20-year-old, bottled in 1998 at cask strength,
is creamy, fruity, almondy, and cedary. SCORE 77

A Scott's Selection from the same year, at 52.1 vol,
is very flowery, fruity, and dry. SCORE 77

A Cadenhead 1965, bottled at 28 years old and 47.6 vol,
is heavily sherried and smoky, attenuated with age, but
still with a delicate nuttiness and floweriness. SCORE 77

BLADNOCH

PRODUCER Raymond Armstrong
REGION Lowlands DISTRICT Borders
ADDRESS Bladnoch, Wigtownshire, DG8 9AB
TEL 01988 402605 WEBSITE www.bladnoch.co.uk VC

FINALLY DISTILLING AGAIN, since 2001, and producing a very flowery "new make". Some time before the end of the decade, this spirit should be ready for release as mature whisky. It promises to restore a corner of pride to the Lowlands as malt whisky region. Meanwhile, new proprietor Raymond Armstrong has been buying casks and bottles of Bladnoch whisky from previous owners UDV and from the trade in general, to ensure that he has something to sell in the distillery shop.

Bladnoch is the southernmost working distillery in Scotland. It takes its water from the river Bladnoch, which flows into the Solway Firth, which forms the border with England.

The pretty little distillery, established between 1817 and 1825, was originally attached to a farm, and used local barley. For a time, it triple distilled. It was mothballed in 1993 by its then owner, United Distillers.

The distillery gave rise to the hamlet of Bladnoch. Nearby is Wigtown, noted for its bookshops. A little farther away is Dumfries, where Robbie Burns's house can be visited.

Raymond Armstrong, from Northern Ireland, bought the distillery buildings with a view to converting them into a holiday home, but came to feel they should be returned to their original purpose. He spent two years restoring the distillery to working order. Armstrong, a surveyor and builder, had no connections with the whisky industry, but had family links with Wigtownshire. The area is geographically very close to Northern Ireland.

HOUSE STYLE Grassy, lemony, soft, sometimes with a suggestion of bananas. A classic Lowlander. Perhaps a dessert malt.

BLADNOCH 10-year-old, Flora and Fauna, 43 vol

Launched in UDV period. Becoming hard to find.

COLOUR Amber.

NOSE Hint of sherry, fragrantly fruity, lemony.

BODY Fuller, firm.

PALATE Lots of development from a sherryish start through cereal-grain grassiness to flowery, fruity, lemony notes.

FINISH Again, surprisingly assertive.

 SCORE **85**

BLADNOCH 23-year-old, Rare Malts, Distilled 1977, Bottled 2001, 53.6 vol

COLOUR Pale bright gold.

NOSE Aromatic. Straw, grass, lemon grass.

BODY Light, oily.

PALATE Dry. Bamboo-like woodiness. Some vanilla smoothness.

FINISH Exotic fruits. Chillis. Hot. Needs softening with a good splash of water.

 SCORE **78**

CASKS OF BLADNOCH ACQUIRED BY THE DISTILLERY.

Tasted as works in progress.

1991, Refill Barrel, Cask No 3998, 54.3 vol

COLOUR Vinho verde.

NOSE Floral, vegetal.

BODY Light. Firm.

PALATE Starts very sweet. Then develops coriander-like dryness.

FINISH Hint of liquorice. Cough sweets. Hot. Fisherman's Friend.

1990, Cask Unspecified, 52.9 vol

COLOUR Shimmery. Very pale greeny gold.

NOSE Fresh, light, fruitiness. Passion fruit.

BODY Light, drying.

PALATE Oily. Lemon curd. Lemon zest.

FINISH Zesty. More liquorice.

1988 Refill Hogshead, Cask No 2631, 57.3 vol

COLOUR Gold.

NOSE Morning dew. Wet grass.

BODY Firm. Smooth.

PALATE Lively start. Fruity. Bananas. Grassy coriander, lemons. Cream.

FINISH Leafy. Vegetal.

SOME INDEPENDENT BOTTLINGS

BLADNOCH 1992, James MacArthur, Cask No 720, 57.6 vol

COLOUR Very pale, green-tinged.

NOSE Light, dusty fruitiness.

BODY Oily.

PALATE Zest of lemon. Sweet lime cordial. Leafy dryness.

FINISH A suggestion of old books.

SCORE **78**

BLADNOCH 1990, Signatory, 43 vol

COLOUR Gold. Faint green tinge.

NOSE Warm. Banana-like.

BODY Textured.

PALATE Bananas. Cream, cereal grain. Falls away in middle.

FINISH Late recovery. Some lively acidity.

SCORE **79**

A 1974 from Signatory, at 50.6 vol, had a full gold colour and a generous spoonful of liquorice in the aroma and palate. This expression seemed to have reached its conclusion very quickly, but this proved to be a grandstand finish, exploding with fruitiness and spiciness. SCORE 84

BLADNOCH 1989, 13-year-old, Cadenhead, 54.9 vol

COLOUR Very pale greeny gold.

NOSE Lime peels.

BODY Delicate. Petal-like.

PALATE Slow to open up, but water helps. Chlorophyll. Herbal. Vanilla.

FINISH Drying.

SCORE **79**

BLADNOCH 1988, Connoisseurs Choice, 40 vol

COLOUR Bright, greeny gold.

NOSE Fresh. Green. Grassy. Leafy.

BODY Soft.

PALATE Clean. Perfumy. Rounded. Superbly balanced. Beautifully combined flavours. Banana toffee? Nougat, perhaps.

FINISH Anis.

SCORE **86**

Gordon & MacPhail also released a cask strength
(cask nos 3151 and 3158, 58.8 vol) bottling from the same year.
This had a warm, bronze colour; discreetly suggesting sherry.
The hint was more strongly spelled out in the aroma and palate,
but Bladnoch's typical citrus and banana esters
smile through. SCORE 87

BLADNOCH 1987, Scott's Selection, 58.9 vol

COLOUR Pale vinho verde.

NOSE Heavy tropical flowers. Some fruity acidity.

BODY Firm, rounded.

PALATE Very sweet. Scottish tablet.

FINISH Bittersweet, geranial. Assertive.

SCORE **76**

BLADNOCH Distilled June 1980, Bottled January 1997, Royal Mile Whiskies, 56.6 vol

COLOUR Gold.

NOSE Lightly honeyed.

BODY Light, thin.

PALATE Honey again, developing orange-flower and acacia notes. Pleasant
enough, but neither as complex or as rounded as might have been hoped.

FINISH Seville orange marmalade.

SCORE **77**

BLAIR ATHOL

PRODUCER Diageo
REGION Highlands DISTRICT Eastern Highlands
ADDRESS Pitlochry, Perthshire, PH16 5LY
TEL 01796 482003
WEBSITE www.discovering-distilleries.com/www.malts.com VC

B LAIR IS A SCOTTISH NAME, referring to a tract of flat land, a clearance, a battlefield, or someone who originates from such a place. Blair Castle is the home of the Duke of Atholl. The village of Blair Atholl ends with a double "l", while the distillery prefers to keep it single. The distillery is nearby at the inland resort of Pitlochry, known for its summer theatre. The well-designed, beautifully maintained distillery, overgrown with ivy and Virginia creeper, traces its origins to 1798. It has been sympathetically expanded several times.

Its malt whisky is extensively used in the Bell's blends. The whisky matures quickly, and behaves like a gentleman. It is a sturdy, well-proportioned whisky rather than a big bruiser, but it can take a lot of sherry without becoming showy or belligerent.

HOUSE STYLE Redolent of shortbread and ginger cake. Spicy, nutty.
A mid-afternoon malt?

BLAIR ATHOL 12-year-old, 43 vol

Released in 2000 in the Single Distillery Malt series, a further development of the flora and fauna selections.

COLOUR Attractive dark orange. Satin sheen.

NOSE Rich. Moist, cake-like. Lemon grass. Assam tea. (A hint of peat?)

BODY Silky smooth.

PALATE Spiced cake. Candied lemon-peels. Lots of flavour development.

FINISH Lightly smoky. Rooty. Treacley. Impeccable balance between sweetness and dryness.

SCORE **78**

BLAIR ATHOL 12-year-old, Commemorative Limited Edition, 43 vol

A much more sherryish version.

COLOUR Distinctively deep. Orange liqueur.

NOSE Very complex. Fragrant, candied orange peels, dried fruit, cinnamon.

BODY Medium, silky.

PALATE Walnuts. Sweetish. Cakey. Faint treacle or molasses.

FINISH Very smooth, round, soothing, lightly smoky.
Very sophisticated for its age. Blair Athol matures quickly, gaining perfuminess, sweetness, richness, spiciness, complexity, and length. The sherry helps to emulsify the elements.

SCORE **77**

BLAIR ATHOL 18-year-old, Bicentenary Limited Edition, 56.7 vol

COLOUR Full peachy amber (but less dark than the 12-year-old).

NOSE Very delicate, finessed, orange and cinnamon.

BODY Bigger and firm.

PALATE Dates. Raisins. Dried figs. Moist cake. Butter.

FINISH Toasty. The slightly burnt crust on a cake.

SCORE **78**

BLAIR ATHOL 1981, Bottled 1997, Cask Strength Limited Bottling, 55.5 vol

Now becoming hard to find.

COLOUR Deep, bright orange red.

NOSE Oakier and smokier, but appetizingly so.

BODY Medium, firm, smooth.

PALATE Delicious, clean toffee. Firm, slightly chewy. Pronounced black treacle. Lively. Hints of banana, orange, lemon. Faint fragrant smokiness.

FINISH Ginger, toasty oak.

SCORE **78**

BLAIR ATHOL 25-year-old, Douglas Laing & Co, 49.3 vol

COLOUR Bright pale, greeny gold.

NOSE Candied orange peel. Marzipan. Sponge cake with
fresh fruit.

BODY Clean, syrupy.

PALATE Creamy, perfumy. Fresh citrus. Pineapple.

FINISH Beautifully rounded dryness,

SCORE 78

BLAIR ATHOL 1973, Signatory Cask Strength Series, 55 vol

COLOUR White wine.

NOSE Lightly smoky. Lightly fruity.

BODY Light to medium, textured.

PALATE Lemony, syrupy, lightly smoky.

FINISH After a palate that seems to lack complexity, a very long finish.
Starts flowery and fruity, with suggestions of an almost-ripe pear or
dessert apple. Develops to buttery shortbread. Then a late, surprising
hit of gingery warmth.

SCORE 74

BOWMORE

PRODUCER Morrison Bowmore Distillers Ltd
REGION Islay DISTRICT Lochindaal
ADDRESS Bowmore, Islay, Argyll, PA34 7JS
TEL 01496 810441 WEBSITE www.bowmore.com VC

EVOCATIVE NAMES like Dawn, Dusk, Voyage, and Legend accentuate the dream-like nature of the place. The village of Bowmore is the "capital" of Islay, but barely more than a hamlet, where the river Laggan flows into Lochindaal. On the edge of the boggy moor, the round church looks down the hill to the harbour.

The distillery, founded in 1779, is kept in beautiful condition – but not to be confused with the local school, which has decorative pagodas. In both geography and palate, the whiskies of Bowmore are between the intense malts of the south shore and the gentlest extremes of the north. Their character is not a compromise but an enigma, and tasters have found it difficult to unfold its complexity. The water used rises from iron-tinged rock, and picks up some peat from the earth as it flows by way of the Laggan, through moss, ferns, and rushes, to the distillery. While the peat higher on the island is rooty, that at Bowmore is sandier.

The company has its own maltings, where the peat is crumbled before it is fired to give more smoke than heat. The malt is peated for a shorter time than that used for the more intense Islay whiskies. Up to 30 per cent of the whisky is aged in sherry. The distillery is more exposed to the westerly winds than others, so there may be more ozone in the complex of aromas and flavours.

HOUSE STYLE Smoky, with leafy notes (ferns?) and sea air.
Younger ages before dinner, older after.

EXPRESSIONS WIITH NO AGE STATEMENT
BOWMORE Legend, 40 vol

A light, young version, identified in some markets as an eight-year-old.

COLOUR Full gold.

NOSE Firm, peaty, smoky, very appetizing.

BODY Slightly sharp.

PALATE Very singular flavours, deftly balanced: a touch of iron, leafy, ferny, peaty. Underlying earthy sweetness. A fresh, young whisky, but no obvious spiritiness.

FINISH Sweet, then salty.

SCORE **80**

BOWMORE Surf, 43 vol

COLOUR Bright gold.

NOSE Fresh peat smoke.

BODY Light but smooth.

PALATE Light, dry, some nutty malt. A light, smooth, entry-level Bowmore. Seems very tame at first, with a cookie-like maltiness, but the characteristic ferny lavender, fragrant smoke and sea air gradually emerges.
One of the sweeter Bowmores.

FINISH Sweet smokiness. With water, later saltiness, honey-roast peanuts.

SCORE **78**

BOWMORE Dusk, Bordeaux (Claret) Wine Casked, 50 vol

This is a wine fiinish.

COLOUR Seems fractionally paler than claret finish. Orangey.

NOSE Seems slightly smokier than the version labelled Bowmore Claret. Peaty. Leathery. Deliciously evocative and appetizing.

BODY Chewy.

PALATE Rich, fruity, smoky. Lots of flavour development: fruit, nuts (almonds?), vanilla.

FINISH Toffeeish, oaky, smoky. Long.

SCORE **86**

BOWMORE Dawn, Ruby Port Cask Finished, 51.5 vol

COLOUR Very interesting pinkish amber.

NOSE Sooty smoke.

BODY Soft, textured, lightly toffeeish.

PALATE Smoky and fruity, lively.

FINISH Leafy, peaty. Slightly chewy.

SCORE **83**

BOWMORE Voyage, Port Casked, 56 vol

COLOUR Bright orange.

NOSE Less obviously smoky. More perfumy. Drier.

BODY Less toffeeish than most port finishes.

PALATE Smooth, light on the tongue. Develops some fruitiness.

FINISH More lively. Seems crisp at first, but lingers
very warmly, with late saltiness.

SCORE **84**

BOWMORE Claret, Bordeaux Wine Casked, 56 vol

COLOUR Rich, dark, honey.

NOSE Very big in both departments. Lots of recognizably claret-like
fruit-and-cedar notes – and a powerful response from Bowmore smokiness.

PALATE Bowmore beats Bordeaux.

FINISH Toffeeish (more port-like) fruit fights back convincingly. Oak keeps
the contestants apart. Finally a salty battle is won by the distillery character.

COMMENT The fighter beat the boxer, but it was wonderfully enjoyable.

SCORE **90**

BOWMORE Cask Strength, 56 vol

Vatting of whiskies in mid-teens.

COLOUR Sunny, yellowy gold.

NOSE Sea air. Cereal-grain oiliness. Nutty. Malty sweetness. Syrupy. Scenty.

BODY Medium, substantial, smooth.

PALATE Earthy dryness. Some tasters have found "wet wool". Others find it
carbolic. Lively. Flavours not very well integrated.

FINISH Orange peel. Leafy. Ferns. Peaty.

SCORE **81**

BRACKLA

PRODUCER John Dewar & Sons Ltd
REGION Highlands ISLAND Arran DISTRICT Speyside (Findhorn Valley)
ADDRESS Royal Brackla Distillery Cawdor, Nairn,
Inverness-shire, IV12 5QY TEL 01667 402002 VC

THE FIRST BOTTLING OF BRACKLA under Dewar's ownership was scheduled for 2003–04, but has been subject to delay. The bottling, at 10 years old, will replace a Flora and Fauna at the same age. The latter, and a Rare Malts bottling, were introduced in the 1990s, when Royal Brackla was owned by Diageo/United Distillers. The distillery was extended in the 1970s, and was twice rebuilt in earlier years. In 1835, Brackla became the first distillery to receive the royal warrant. This is granted to companies that supply goods to the royal household. The distillery was founded in 1812, on the estate of Cawdor, not far from Nairn, on the western fringes of Speyside.

HOUSE STYLE Fruity, cleansing, sometimes with a dry, hot finish.
A refresher or a pousse-café.

ROYAL BRACKLA 10-year-old,
Flora and Fauna, 43 vol

COLOUR Pale gold.

NOSE Smoky, slightly sulphurous, burnt, molasses.

BODY Medium, drying on the tongue.

PALATE Starts malty and sweet, becoming robustly fruity,
then spicy notes.

FINISH Cedary, smoky.

SCORE **74**

ROYAL BRACKLA 20-year-old, Bottled 1998, Rare Malts, 59.8 vol

COLOUR Bright gold.

NOSE Flowery, melony, gingery.

BODY Rich, syrupy.

PALATE Very sweet. Honey. Anis.

FINISH Warming. Late angelica, pepper, cedary dryness. Slightly astringent.

SCORE **75**

Vintage 1991
Single Highland Malt Scotch Whisky
Matured in a sherry butt for 10 years
Distilled at Royal Brackla Distillery

70cl   NATURAL COLOUR   43%vol

ROYAL BRACKLA 1991, Distilled 1991, Bottled 2002, Butt No 6367, Signatory, 43 vol

COLOUR Greeny gold.

NOSE Sweet, oaty.

BODY Oaty. Oily. Slightly drying.

PALATE Marshmallow. Cookies. Oatcakes.

FINISH Curiously short. That typical dry, hot, finish.

SCORE **71**

An earlier bottling of a 1979 Brackla from Signatory, at 43 vol,
was fruity and dryish, with a weak finish. SCORE 69

From the same bottler, a 1975 at 58.6 vol was a great deal more impressive,
with an appetizing balance of restrained fruit and big spiciness. SCORE 75

"Green" BRACKLA 1975, 27-year-old, The Whisky Exchange, 59.7 vol

COLOUR Very dark. Somewhere between onyx and ironstone.

NOSE Saddlesoap.

BODY Lightly chewy.

PALATE Butter. Rum butter. Toffee. Rich and enjoyable.

FINISH Warming. Rummy. Gently oaky.

SCORE **77**

BRACKLA 1975, Murray McDavid "Mission" Series, 46 vol

COLOUR Deep gold.

NOSE Candyfloss, peach ice cream.

BODY Very rich and chewy.

PALATE Buttery. Mint humbugs. Liquorice.

FINISH Rooty. Some astringency.

SCORE **78**

An earlier bottling from Murray McDavid, a 1979 at 17 years old
from refill sherry, was drier and fruitier. SCORE 72

ROYAL BRACKLA 1975, 25-year-old,
The Coopers Choice, 43 vol

COLOUR Full gold to bronze.

NOSE Tea-like, perfumey.

BODY Slightly thin. Perfumey. Drying on the tongue.

PALATE Oily. Darjeeling tea. Malty.

FINISH Madeira-like. Tired.

SCORE **69**

An earlier Coopers Choice, a 1984, bottled in 1998 at 13 years old, was the
peatiest among the examples reviewed here. SCORE 76

ROYAL BRACKLA 15-year-old, Cadenhead, 58.2 vol

COLOUR Bright pale gold.

NOSE Lemon grass. Honeydew melon.

BODY Much richer.

PALATE Syrup, vanilla, ginger, then spicy smokiness.

FINISH Deliciously smoky, lively and warming. Quite aggressive.
A muscular malt of a style that is sadly vanishing
from the Highlands. Very enjoyable.

SCORE **77**

ROYAL BRACKLA 1975, Cask No 5467, Adelphi, 59.5 vol

COLOUR Burnished bronze to copper.

NOSE Rich heavy sherry. Butter. Rum. Moist fruitcake.

BODY Firm, smooth.

PALATE Chewy. Mint toffee. Treacle toffee.

FINISH A small explosion of spiciness. Ginger, allspice.
Hot, dry. Very long.

SCORE **78**

BRAEVAL

PRODUCER Chivas Brothers
REGION Highlands DISTRICT Speyside (Livet)
ADDRESS Chapeltown, Ballindalloch, Banffshire, AB37 9JS

Braes of Glenlivet was the distillery's name when the whiskies reviewed here were distilled. This name had the merit of linking this distillery with its famous neighbour and parent – but made it difficult for the owners to dissuade other companies from treating Glenlivet as a region or style. The current name, Braeval, is an even older form. Brae is Scottish Gaelic for a "hillside" or "steep bank". Against a mountain ridge, this distillery is perched on a stream that feeds the River Livet. Despite its romantic name, and handsomely monastic appearance, it is a modern distillery, built between 1973 and 1978. It can be operated by one man, or even from its parent distillery. Braeval's whisky is a component of Chivas Regal, among others.

HOUSE STYLE Light, sweet, honeyish, with a zesty finish. Aperitif.

BRAES OF GLENLIVET 1975, Connoisseurs Choice, 40 vol

COLOUR Very pale greeny gold.

NOSE Fragrant. Vanilla.

BODY Dancing on the tongue.

PALATE Flowery. Herbal. Very appetizing.

FINISH Lightly dry. Zesty.

SCORE **77**

BRUICHLADDICH

PRODUCER The Bruichladdich Distillery Co. Ltd
REGION Islay DISTRICT Loch Indaal
ADDRESS Bruichladdich, Islay, Argyll, PA49 7UN
TEL 01496 850221 WEBSITE www.bruichladdich.com
EMAIL laddie@bruichladdich.com VC

ISLANDERS CARRIED CHILDREN on their shoulders to witness the historic moment. They lined the Islay shore to watch the reopening in 2001 of Bruichladdich, Scotland's most westerly distillery. The single morning plane, bringing more guests, was running late. The people on the shore scanned the skies. They had waited ten years; what was another hour? Lovers of Bruichladdich had come from London, Seattle, and Tokyo. There were tears of joy, a ceilidh, and fireworks at midnight.

The new owners, headed by Mark Reynier, of the London wine merchants La Reserve, bought the distillery with plenty of maturing stock. Like many distilleries, Bruichladdich has a miscellany of former bourbon barrels and sherry butts, some containing their first fill of Scotch whisky, others their second or third. In any distillery, the selection of casks to make a bottling is critical. On the new team at Bruichladdich, this task is in the hands of one of the principals, veteran Islay whisky maker Jim McEwan. In his early vattings, McEwan has juggled casks to shake off the notion that Bruichladdich is almost too mild to be an Islay whisky.

The whisky has long combined light, firm maltiness with suggestions of passion fruit, seaweed, and salt. McEwan has coaxed out more fruitiness and some sweetness, and has given everything more life and definition. The latter qualities are heightened by the use of the distillery's own water in reduction and by the lack of chill filtration. These changes in procedure were made possible by the installation in 2003 of a bottling line. Bruichladdich thus becomes the third distillery to have its own bottling line on site. (The others are Springbank and Glenfiddich/Balvenie.)

The new range began with whiskies at 10, 15, 17, and 20 years old. As these are vatted from stock, their ages will increase over the next decade, until spirit distilled by the new team is ready. An annual vintage is also being released, and a bottling of yet older whiskies under the rubric Legacy. Yet further ranges are planned – under the rubrics Links and Full Strength. At the distillery, visitors who wish to buy a bottle are invited to sample from three current casks. The visitors bottle their own whiskies, under the rubric Valinch. This refers to the oversized pipette that is used in distilleries to remove samples from casks. This device is sometimes known as a "thief".

When Bruichladdich reopened, McEwan immediately reset the stills to produce a spirit to his requirements. This will remain light to medium in its peating. Two new spirits were added, with a heavier peating.

Bruichladdich (pronounced "brook laddie") is on the north shore of Lochindaal. The new owners have promoted the nickname "The Laddie", and introduced labels in a pale seaside blue to match the paintwork at the distillery. The distillery's water rises from iron-tinged stone, and flows lightly over peat. Unlike the other Islay distilleries, Bruichladdich is separated from the sea loch, albeit only by a quiet, coastal road.

The distillery was founded in 1881, rebuilt in 1886 and, despite an extension in 1975, remains little changed. All maturing spirit in its ownership is warehoused on the island, either at Bruichladdich or in the vestiges of the Lochindaal distillery, at Port Charlotte, the nearest village. Some independent bottlers of Bruichladdich have labelled the whisky Lochindaal.

The name Port Charlotte will be used on one of the new heavily peated spirits from Bruichladdich. An even peatier whisky will be called Octomore, after another former distillery at Port Charlotte. Parts of that distillery survive as Octomore Farm, home of Port Charlotte's lighthouse keeper, fire fighter and lifeboatman – who was also one of the pipers on the opening day at Bruichladdich.

HOUSE STYLE Light to medium, very firm, hint of passion fruit, salty, spicy (mace?). Very drinkable. Aperitif.

BRUICHLADDICH 10-year-old, 46 vol

COLOUR Bright greeny gold.

NOSE Fresh, clean. Very soft "sea air". Wild flowers among
the dunes. A picnic at the beach.

BODY Satin.

PALATE Summer fruits. Passion fruit. Zesty, almost
effervescent, Bruichladdich at its fruitiest.

FINISH The flavours meld, with a late frisson of sharpness.

 SCORE **82**

BRUICHLADDICH 15-year-old, 46 vol

COLOUR Bright yellow.

NOSE Sea air. Perfumy. Slightly sharp.

BODY Firm, cracker-like, malt background.

PALATE Starts with a clean, grassy sweetness, then manifests an
astonishingly long, lively series of small explosions. Peppery.

FINISH Underlying iron. Savoury. Appetizing.

 SCORE **80**

BRUICHLADDICH 17-year-old, 46 vol

COLOUR Deep gold, with green tinge.

NOSE Firm, confident, fruity. Passion fruit and sea air.

BODY Firm. Very dry.

PALATE Powerful. Long, sustained development of fruity,
estery flavours.

FINISH Iron. Salt. Muscular. Stimulating.

 SCORE **83**

BRUICHLADDICH 20-year-old, 46 vol

COLOUR Bright solid gold.

NOSE Seafront aromas. Like standing on the jetty at Bruichladdich.

BODY Smooth. Malty. Oily.

PALATE More cereal grain. More fruit. More salt.

FINISH Ironish, but also very flowery; more so than the others in this flight. A well-rounded whisky. Deceptively powerful, with a great depth of character.

SCORE **84**

SOME VINTAGE-DATED BOTTLINGS
BRUICHLADDICH 1984, Vintage, 46 vol

COLOUR Pale gold.

NOSE Very flowery, leafy. Dry earth, sand. Sea air.

BODY Lightly creamy. Drying.

PALATE Salt and pepper.

FINISH Sandy. Cayenne pepper. Very peppery indeed. Try it with a Baltimore crab-feast or New Orleans crawdads.

SCORE **78**

BRUICHLADDICH 1970, Vintage, 44.2 vol

COLOUR Medium to full gold.

NOSE Heavy, blossomy aroma. Fruit trees. Fresh limes.

BODY Oily.

PALATE Gentle, slow start. Leafy, malty. Brooding.

FINISH Surge of spicy, sandy flavours. Very spicy.

SCORE **80**

SOME VALINCH BOTTLINGS
BRUICHLADDICH 1990, Cask No 998, 60.2 vol

COLOUR Gold, green tinge.

NOSE Dry. Slightly peaty.

BODY Marshmallow.

PALATE Bay leaves, peppercorns, ground white pepper.

FINISH Grainy, savoury, dry, hot.

SCORE **78**

BRUICHLADDICH 1966, Legacy, 40.6 vol

COLOUR Full gold. Orange tinge.

NOSE Estery. Apple crumble.

BODY Lean.

PALATE Estery. Calvados. Cider. Some refreshingly fruity acidity.

FINISH Passion fruit.

SCORE **82**

BRUICHLADDICH 1986, Cask No 700, 53.3 vol

COLOUR Full greeny gold.

NOSE Grassy. Dunes. Salty.

BODY Beeswax. Oily.

PALATE More maltiness and especially fruitiness.

FINISH Still hot and dry, but softened by the oiliness of the spirit.

SCORE **78**

BRUICHLADDICH 1983, Fresh Sherry Butt, 58.8 vol

COLOUR Mandarin orange.

NOSE Pralines. Bitter chocolate. Filled with orange cream.

BODY Rich and creamy.

PALATE Sweet. Gingery.

FINISH Very spicy More ginger. Lively.

SCORE **79**

BRUICHLADDICH 1972, Cask No 9, 48.8 vol

COLOUR Very full gold.

NOSE Clean, sweet. Sea breezes.

BODY Smooth, oily.

PALATE Temptingly approachable. Very expressive and full of flavour.
Orange and passion fruit meld with spicy, salty notes.

FINISH Gently dry. Very appetizing.

SCORE **79**

BRUICHLADDICH 1970, Cask No 5079, 48.2 vol

COLOUR Apricot.

NOSE Malty. Dusty. Short pastry.

BODY Syrupy. Juicy.

PALATE Fruity. Delicious. The maltiness and fruitiness of Bruichladdich at its best. Bring on the clootie dumplings.

FINISH Late perfuminess. Fragrant. Resiny.

SCORE **80**

SOME INDEPENDENT BOTTLINGS OF BRUICHLADDICH
BRUICHLADDICH 12-year-old, Royal Mile Whiskies,
Distilled July 1985, Bottled April 1998, 336 Numbered Bottles, 46 vol

COLOUR Very pale, clear, greenish.

NOSE Fruity, vegetal, wild garlic.

BODY Rounded, dry.

PALATE Malty, marshmallow-like. Fruity.

FINISH Dusty. Herbal. Light, balancing bitterness.

SCORE **76**

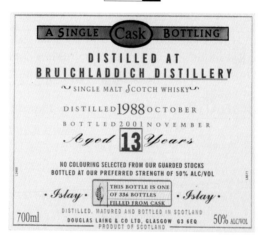

BRUICHLADDICH 13-year-old, Distilled October 1988,
Bottled November 2001, The Old Malt Cask, 50 vol

COLOUR Vinho verde.

NOSE Freshly cut grass.

BODY Syrupy but light.

PALATE Vegetal. Faint peatiness. Ash. Earthy.

FINISH Fruity. Dry.

SCORE **76**

BRUICHLADDICH 13-year-old, Adelphi, 57.9 vol

NOSE Heather. Flowery. Mint. Menthol. Faintly medicinal. Salt.

PALATE Very light but oily. Passion fruit. Grassy.

FINISH Peppermint, drying.

COMMENT Interesting, but not typical.

SCORE **72**

Also from Adelphi: a 1970 vintage at 30 years old and 49.4 vol, released in 2001, had a bright, golden colour; a palate that was fruity, but also full of almondy nuttiness; and a late crescendo of mace-like spiciness. SCORE 80

BRUICHLADDICH 1988, Gordon & MacPhail, Cask Nos 1955 and 1956, Distilled 25 October 1988, Bottled 3 January 2003, Cask Strength, 54.2 vol

COLOUR Bright gold, with a greenish tinge.

NOSE Perfumy. Talc-like.

BODY Slippery-smooth.

PALATE Good malty background. Dry and, by the standards of Bruichladdich, quite a peat accent.

FINISH Sting of peat, then lingering dryness.

SCORE **80**

Also from Gordon & MacPhail, in their Cask Strength series, a 1969 Bruichladdich, bottled in 2003 at 52.5 vol. This is sherry-led expression, but with a beautiful interplay of creamy maltiness and salty flavours. For a picnic by Lochindaal? SCORE 80

An earlier Gordon & MacPhail bottling of a 1969 Bruichladdich, at 54.3, emerged with a classically seaweedy aroma; a malty, cakey palate; and a salty finish; while still having enjoyed a close encounter with sherry. SCORE 81

BRUICHLADDICH 16-year-old, Distilled 1986, Bottled March 2003, Bourbon Hogshead, Cadenhead, 55.9 vol

COLOUR Primrose.

NOSE Salty, sandy.

BODY Slippery-smooth. Seems to slip away.

PALATE Creamy, then fruity, then sandy. Three big hits.
Bruichladdich in assertively unfancy mood.

FINISH Slightly blood-like. One of the hits connected.
It's not real blood, just passion fruit.

SCORE **78**

BRUICHLADDICH 1986, Scott's Selection, 57.2 vol

COLOUR Very pale, bright, vinho verde.

NOSE Leafy, grassy, peaty.

BODY Syrupy, but very light.

PALATE Oaty, dusty, developing some sweetness.

FINISH A touch of lactic acidity. Appetizing and refreshing.

SCORE **77**

BRUICHLADDICH 1970, Raw Cask, 53.8 vol

COLOUR Deep gold. Almost orange marmalade.

NOSE Warm, sweet, fruity.

BODY Densely creamy.

PALATE Sweet. Oily. Slightly perfumey. Smoky. Peaty.

FINISH Some maritime notes.

SCORE **77**

BRUICHLADDICH 26-year-old, Stillman's Dram, 45 vol

COLOUR Full gold to amber.

NOSE Spicy (some tasters have found mace),
fruity, sherry, lightly toasty oak, sea air.

BODY Medium, very smooth.

PALATE Light oak, malt, salt, passion fruit, sherry sweetness.
Flavours tightly locked together.

FINISH Lightly toasty oak, seaweed, salt and pepper.

SCORE **77**

BRUICHLADDICH 33-year-old, Distilled May 1969, Bottled December 2002, Cask No 2329, Duncan Taylor, 48.7 vol

COLOUR Full gold.

NOSE Very perfumey.

BODY Light, lapping on tongue.

PALATE Butter, syrupy but dryish. Fennel. Italian spices.

FINISH Restrained but tasty. Appetizing.

SCORE **79**

OTHER VERSIONS OF BRUICHLADDICH

A 25-year-old (1968), at 53.8 vol, from Cadenhead,
is flowery and complex. SCORE 78

A 1968, at 52.9 vol, in Signatory's 10th anniversary series, is sherryish,
malty, and salty, with a distinct smoky fragrance in the finish. SCORE 79

A 1965, at 53.5, from Gordon & MacPhail, is even
more sherryish, with lots of oak and smoke. SCORE 78

BUNNAHABHAIN

PRODUCER Burn Stewart Distillers plc
REGION Islay   DISTRICT North Shore
ADDRESS Port Askaig, Islay, Argyll, PA46 7RP
TEL 01496 840646   WEBSITE www.blackbottle.com
EMAIL enquiries@burnstewartdistillers.com   VC

A NEW LIFE for the elusive Bunnahabhain set the seal on the Islay revival in the new millennium. Elusive? Bunnahabhain has the most hidden location of the Islay distilleries, the most superficially difficult name (pronounced "boona'hhavn"), and the most delicate whisky. Even its new owners, since 2003, are the smallest group in the industry. Bunnahabhain joins the Tobermory and Deanston distilleries in the Burn Stewart group, well known in the Far East for its Scottish Leader blends. With the acquisition of Bunnahabhain, Burn Stewart also gain the cult blend Black Bottle, which contains malts from all the Islay distilleries. At the time of the takeover, Burn Stewart had recently joined the worldwide group that includes the "super-premium" vodka Belvedere and has as its unlikely flagship Angostura Bitters.

The Bunnahabhain distillery had been well maintained by its previous owners, Edrington, but both production and marketing of its products had been sporadic. Stocks were sinking – not a happy state of affairs for the whisky whose packaging bears the words of the Islay anthem, "Westering Home". Despite its delicacy, Bunnahabhain does have a touch of Islay maritime character.

The distillery, expanded in 1963, was built in 1881. It is set around a courtyard in a remote cove. A kerb has been built to stops visitors' cars from rolling into the sea. A ships' bell, salvaged from a nearby wreck, hangs from the wall. It was at one time used to summon the manager from his home if he were urgently needed. The distillery's water rises through limestone, and because it is piped to the distillery, it does not pick up peat on the way. The stills are large, in the style that the industry refers to as onion-shaped.

HOUSE STYLE Fresh, sweetish, nutty, herbal, salty. Aperitif.

BUNNAHABHAIN 12-year-old, 43 vol

COLOUR Gold.

NOSE Remarkably fresh, sweet, sea-air aroma.

BODY Light to medium, firm.

PALATE Gentle, clean, nutty-malty sweetness.

FINISH Very full flavour development. Refreshing.

SCORE **77**

BUNNAHABHAIN Auld Acquaintance Hogmanay Edition, 1968, Bottle 1 of 2000, 43.8 vol

COLOUR Orange satin, with pinkish tinge.

NOSE A rich, moist Dundee cake. Toasted nuts. Salty. Sea breezes.

BODY Creamy.

PALATE Malted milk. Chocolate. Nonetheless avoids
being cloying. Deftly balanced.

FINISH Dark cocoa powder.

COMMENT A brilliantly sunny winter's day; a long walk by the sea in the
late afternoon; oatcakes and cheese; Dundee cake; a dram at dusk. Still
recognizably Bunnahabhain, but so different. More such essays, please.

SCORE **86**

BUNNAHABHAIN 1968, The Family Silver, 40 vol
Now hard to find.

COLOUR Attractive pale walnut.

NOSE Fragrant sea air and polished wood.

BODY Firm, creamy.

PALATE Depth of flowery nuttiness and creamy flavours.

FINISH Delightful teasing subtlety of nuttiness and gently salty sea air.

SCORE **79**

BUNNAHABHAIN 1966, Cask No 4379, 46.1 vol

COLOUR Blood orange

NOSE Smoky. Fresh sea breezes. Could that be the puffer
leaving for Glasgow?

BODY Rich, creamy.

PALATE Fresh, concentrated flavours. Unusually estery. Ginger-toffee.
Becoming nutty. Very concentrated flavours.

FINISH Dusty. Spice-shop. Long. Warming

SCORE **80**

BUNNAHABHAIN 1963, 750 bottles, 42.9 vol

COLOUR Gold, with a touch of olive.

NOSE Cashew nuts.

BODY Light and satin smooth.

PALATE Gunpowder tea. Ginseng.

FINISH Just enough bitterness to be appetizing. Salty.

SCORE **83**

SOME INDEPENDENT BOTTLINGS
BUNNAHABHAIN 20-year-old, James MacArthur, 57 vol

COLOUR Deep orange satin.

NOSE Mango chutney. Pickled walnuts.

BODY Oily, buttery.

PALATE Toffee. Japanese plum wine.

FINISH Sweetness and bitter coffee. Nice drink. Where's the whisky?

SCORE **71**

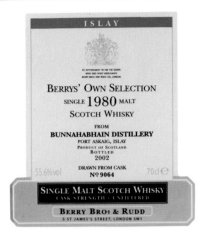

BUNNAHABHAIN 1980, Cask No 9064, Bottled 2002, Unchillfiltered, Berry Brothers and Rudd, 55.6 vol

COLOUR Iridescent greeny gold.

NOSE A walk by the seafront.

BODY Extraordinarily oily.

PALATE Sweet, caramel, shortbread.

FINISH Sudden surge of salt. Slight astringency.

SCORE 79

BUNNAHABHAIN 22-year-old, Distilled 1980, Bottled 2003 Cask No 5899, Dun Bheagan, 58 vol

COLOUR Full, refractive, gold.

NOSE Expressive, full, honeyish.

BODY Light, firm, smooth.

PALATE Rounded. Some vanilla. Honey. Nutty. Salty.

FINISH Spicy. Salty. Long. Appetizing.

SCORE 81

BUNNAHABHAIN 35-year-old, Distilled March 1967, Bottled September 2002, Hart Brothers, Cask Strength, 40.5 vol

COLOUR Deep, iridescent, gold.

NOSE Dried fruits. Caramel. Smoke from an open fire.
Some cellar character.

BODY Surprisingly light.

PALATE Sweetness, saltiness and some oakiness.

FINISH Some musty woodiness.

SCORE 79

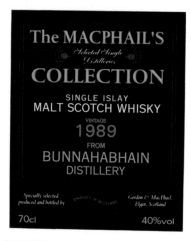

BUNNAHABHAIN 1989, The MacPhail's Selection, 40 vol

COLOUR Full gold.

NOSE Fragrant. New leather upholstery in a luxury car.

BODY Surprisingly light.

PALATE Cream toffee. Shortbread. Afternoon tea.

FINISH Ginger cookies. Spicy.

SCORE **79**

An earlier bottling of a 1989 Bunnahabhain by Gordon &
MacPhail was richer all round: sherryish, gingery, toasty, salty.
A breakfast whisky for the truly decadent. SCORE 80

BUNNAHABHAIN 1982, Distilled 1982, Bottled 2001, Scotts Selection, 52.5 vol

COLOUR White wine.

NOSE Light. Fragrant. Some vanilla. Hint of lemon grass.

BODY Slightly oily but very light.

PALATE Light, sweet, toast.

FINISH Late surge of salt. Quite stinging – and sustained.

SCORE **78**

From the same bottler, a 1981 Bunnahabhain, at 51 vol, is more
flowery and complex. SCORE 80
A 1969, at 40.1 vol, is drier and cedary, but seems to have lost some
dimension with age. SCORE 79

BUNNAHABHAIN 1979, Murray McDavid, Bourbon Barrel, 46 vol

COLOUR Old gold.

NOSE Salt, fresh limes. Citrus peel.

BODY Creamy. Oily.

PALATE Lightly nutty. Clean, grassy, peat.

FINISH Fragrant.

COMMENT Surprising peatiness, but without smokiness.

SCORE **80**

From the same bottler, a 1979 Bunnahabhain from sherry wood
has vibrant flavours of toffee, ginger, and malt, but they are
eventually overpowered by the wood. SCORE 76

BUNNAHABHAIN 36-year-old, Distilled June 1966, Bottled November 2002, Cask No 4872, Duncan Taylor, 40.1 vol

COLOUR Dark gold.

NOSE Fresh. Salty. Harbourfront.

BODY Surprisingly light. Drying.

PALATE Cookie-like. Chocolate digestives? Very subtle flavours,
mellowed by age. Some Maderisation?

FINISH Very late salt, a reminder of the whisky's maritime youth.

SCORE **79**

CAOL ILA

PRODUCER Diageo
REGION Islay   DISTRICT North shore
ADDRESS Port Askaig, Islay, Argyll, PA46 7RL
TEL 01496 302760   Distillery has shop
WEBSITE www.discovering-distilleries.com/www.malts.com

AT THE ISLAY FESTIVAL OF 2002, three stylishly boxed expressions of Caol Ila were released by owners Diageo, as part of a new range with the rubric "Hidden Malts". Public attending the festival were invited to join whisky writers at the tasting. The tools of modern marketing were much in evidence, but so was the patrimony of Islay malt. Manager Billy Stichell, an Ileach, with four generations of family in the industry, provided an accomplished commentary. It was the first time he had spoken in public.

It was further announced at Caol Ila that Hidden Malts would also emanate from another three Diageo distilleries: Clynelish, Glen Elgin, and Glen Ord. For the moment each of them would release only one age.

The launch of Caol Ila in an official bottling, in such a public way, and implicitly as the flagship in the new range, finally confirmed that it was far from hidden. Its malts had become more readily available, and appreciated, in recent years.

The name, pronounced "cull-eela", means "Sound of Islay". The Gaelic word "caol" is more familiar as "kyle". The distillery is in a cove near Port Askaig. The large windows of the still-house overlook the Sound of Islay, across which the ferry chugs to the nearby island of Jura. The best view of the distillery is from the ferry.

Its 1970s façade is beginning to be accepted as a classic of the period, after years of being deemed brutal. Inside, the distillery is both functional and attractive: a copper hood on the lauter tun; brass trim; wash stills like flat onions, spirit stills more pear-shaped; Oregon pine washbacks. Some of the structure dates from 1879, and the distillery was founded in 1846.

Behind the distillery, a hillside covered in fuchsias, foxgloves, and wild roses rises toward the peaty loch where the water gathers. It is quite salty and minerally, having risen from limestone. As a modern, well-engineered distillery, making whisky for several blends, it has over the years used different levels of peating. This is apparent in the independent bottlings.

HOUSE STYLE Oily, olive-like. Junipery, fruity, estery. A wonderful aperitif.

THE HIDDEN MALTS

CAOL ILA 12-year-old, 43 vol

COLOUR Vinho verde.

NOSE Soft. Juniper. Garden mint. Grass. Burnt grass.

BODY Lightly oily. Simultaneously soothing and appetizing.

PALATE Lots of flavour development. Becoming spicy. Vanilla, nutmeg, white mustard. Complex. Flavours combine with great delicacy.

FINISH Very long.

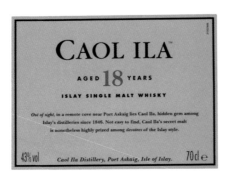

CAOL ILA 18-year-old, 43 vol

COLOUR Fullest of the three. Fino sherry on a sunny day.

NOSE Fragrant. Menthol. Markedly vegetal. Nutty vanilla pod.

BODY Firmer. Much bigger.

PALATE More assertively expressive. Sweeter. Leafy sweetness. Spring greens. Crushed almonds. Rooty, cedary.

FINISH Powerful reverberations of a remarkable whisky.

CAOL ILA Cask Strength, 55 vol

COLOUR Palest of the three, remarkably pale. White wine.

NOSE Intense. Sweetish, smokiness. Coconut. Grapefruit.

PALATE A very lively interplay of flavours, with malty sweetness fruity
esteriness and peppery dryness. Perfumy, with suggestions of thyme.

FINISH The flavours come together in a rousing finale, with the alcohol
providing a back beat.

SOME EARLIER OFFICIAL BOTTLINGS, NOW HARD TO FIND

CAOL ILA 15-year-old, Flora and Fauna, 43 vol

COLOUR Fino sherry, bright.

NOSE Aromatic, complex.

BODY Light, very firm, smooth.

PALATE Rounder, with the flavours more combined.

FINISH Oily and warming enough to keep out the sea.

CAOL ILA 1981, Bottled 1997,
Cask Strength Limited Bottling, 63.8 vol

COLOUR Bright limey yellow.

NOSE Fragrant peat smoke, juniper, seaweed. Very appetizing.

BODY Firm, oily.

PALATE Assertively oily, junipery. Late surge of peaty dryness. Very dry.

FINISH Wonderfully long and warming.

SCORE **82**

CAOL ILA 20-year-old, Bottled 1996, 57.86 vol

150th Anniversary Edition

COLOUR Orange.

NOSE Sweet seaweed. Juniper. Pine nuts.

BODY Medium, smooth, rounded.

PALATE Enormously complex and distinctive. Nutty, appetizingly seaweedy, peppery, salty. Tightly combined flavours. Beautifully balanced.

FINISH Sherry, toasty oak, seaweed, lemon skin, pepper.

SCORE **85**

SOME RARE MALTS
CAOL ILA 20-year-old, Rare Malts, 61.3 vol

Becoming hard to find.

COLOUR Full greeny gold.

NOSE Powerfully aromatic. Roasted peppers. Olives. Salt.

BODY Medium but gentle, oily, soothing.

PALATE Oily. Roasted peppers, olives, lemon juice.

FINISH Dry, junipery, vine leaves, stemmy. Intense, expressive.

SCORE **83**

CAOL ILA 21-year-old, Rare Malts, 61.3 vol

Becoming hard to find.

COLOUR Attractive, subtle pale gold.

NOSE Very fresh. Sea air.

BODY Medium, oily, smooth.

PALATE Astonishingly fresh. More sea air. Almost a sandy taste.

Fresh seaweed. Sweet and dry, olivey. Sustained development of flavours.

FINISH Big, long. Expressive. Smoky fragrance. Appetizing. Oaky dryness.

SCORE **82**

CAOL ILA 23-year-old, Rare Malts, 61.7 vol

Released 2002.

COLOUR Warm gold to pale amber.

NOSE Distinctly peaty. A robust, straight-ahead,

Caol Ila in traditional Islay style.

BODY Firm, dry.

PALATE Peaty, gritty, salty.

FINISH Sweet, smoky. Some underlying estery fruitiness.

SCORE **84**

SOME GORDON & MACPHAIL BOTTLINGS
CAOL ILA 1988, Gordon & MacPhail,
Cask Strength Series, 57.6 vol

COLOUR White wine.

NOSE Hugely peppery.

BODY Lightly syrupy.

PALATE Flowery. Oily, buttery. Then a surge of pepper.

FINISH A smoky explosion.

SCORE **84**

CAOL ILA 1988, Connoisseurs Choice, 40 vol

COLOUR White wine. Very pale.

NOSE White pepper. Juniper.

BODY Light. Soft.

PALATE Vegetal, smoky.

FINISH Delicate leafy, dry.

SCORE **79**

GORDON & MACPHAIL WOOD FINISHES, ALL AT 40 VOL

CAOL ILA 1988, Calvados finish. Pale, shimmery, greeny gold. Fruity, tannic notes in aroma and palate? SCORE 79

CAOL ILA 1988, Claret finish. Warm gold. Starts enticingly, with sweet, creamy flavours, but becomes very astringent. SCORE 77

CAOL ILA 1988, Cognac finish. Quite big-bodied. A heavyweight struggle between the world's two great spirits. The whisky wins, but the Cognac goes the distance and even rallies in the final round. Extraordinarily long.
SCORE 81

CAOL ILA 1990, Vintage Cognac finish. Much smoother proceedings. Restrained, concluding in a gentlemanly draw. A charming after-dinner companion. SCORE 80

CAOL ILA 1990, Port finish. Tell-tale pinkish-bronze colour. Nutty. Port establishes a harmony with the maritime notes of the whisky. SCORE 80

CAOL ILA 1988, Sherry finish. The warm amber colour delivers all it promises. Dried apricots, spices, and lightly salty Islay character. A dryish but deftly balanced whisky. SCORE 79

SOME INDEPENDENT BOTTLINGS OF CAOL ILA

CAOL ILA 1983, 19-year-old, Unchillfiltered, Berry Brothers & Rudd, 46 vol. Pale gold. Textured. Very fruity and spicy. Sweetish and warming. SCORE 77

CAOL ILA, Distilled 1992, Bottled 2000, Black Adder Raw Cask, 58.6 vol. White wine colour. Starts creamy and sweet; becomes appetizingly dry, with suggestions of sea-salt. Well-rounded. SCORE 78. From the same bottler, a 1990, at 58.5, is oilier, drier, and longer. SCORE 79

CAOL ILA 1993, 10-year-old, Cadenhead, 60.8 vol. Bright gold. Fresh sea air on the nose. Lemony fruitiness in the palate. Salty dryness in the finish. SCORE 78

CAOL ILA 1990, 12-year-old, Rum Finish, Chieftain's Choice, 46 vol. Medicinal aroma; sudden rush of peat. Big, fresh flavours. Creamy sweetness in background presumably from rum. SCORE 79

CAOL ILA 1991, 11-year-old, The Coopers Choice, 43 vol. Very pale, greenish. Clean, oily, light, dry. Grassy crispness in the finish. Reminiscent of bison-leaf vodka. SCORE 77

CAOL ILA 1992, 10-year-old Dun Bheagan, 43 vol. Very pale colour. Fresh aroma. Soft, lean malt character. Becoming fruity and junipery. Then crisp, grassy finish. SCORE 77

CAOL ILA 1990, 12-year-old, Duncan Taylor Whisky Galore, 46 vol. Greenish tinge. Quite big bodied. Oily. Mustardy. SCORE 77

CAOL ILA 23-year-old, Kingsbury, 60 vol. Primrose. Oily, waxy, junipery. Hints of blackcurrant. Where is the whiff of the sea? It blows in eventually. SCORE 77

CAOL ILA 1989, Bourbon Cask. Murray MacDavid, 46 vol. Aromatic, nutty. Palate warm, oily, butter. Vanilla. Late, laconic, mustardy finish. SCORE 77 An earlier counterpart, distilled in 1989, had more of the house character, notably a touch of iodine. SCORE 77

CAOL ILA 1991, Port Wood, Signatory, 48 vol. Very pale, white wine. Touch of estery, figgy sweetness. Nuttiness and sandy dryness in the middle. Late fruity (brambles) warmth. SCORE 78. A 1989, at 46 vol, in Signatory's unchillfiltered series, was briney, medicinal and a fine example of the more peated style of Caol Ila. SCORE 83. A 1981 Caol Ila at 58.2 vol had a fuller amber colour and big flavours, with sherry, spices, and oak Finished dry but not astringent. SCORE 82

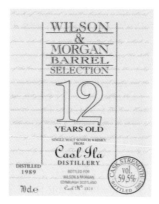

CAOL ILA 1989, 12-year-old, Wilson & Morgan, 59.5 vol. Very pale greenish. Oily, viscous. Cereal-grain notes. Touch of peat. A winter warmer. SCORE 77

CAPERDONICH

PRODUCER Chivas Brothers
REGION Highlands DISTRICT Speyside (Rothes)
ADDRESS Rothes, Morayshire, AB38 7BN

LESSER KNOWN PARTNER to the renowned Glen Grant. The two distilleries, under the same ownership, are across the street from one another in the whisky town of Rothes. This little Speyside town has five distilleries. Caperdonich, founded in 1898, was rebuilt in 1965 and extended in 1967. Its name is said to indicate a "secret source". From the start, it has been a back-up to Glen Grant. When young, the malts of both distilleries are light and fragrant in their bouquet, medium-bodied, and nutty-tasting.

Of the two, Caperdonich is perhaps a dash fruitier and slightly more smoky. It, too, is a component of the Chivas Regal blend. The Chivas group kept a tight control of its malts during the last years of its ownership by Seagram, of Canada. This policy seems to have been maintained since the takeover by Pernod Ricard, of France. There are official bottlings of Glen Grant, but not of Caperdonich. The independent bottlings tend to be very old. The fourth edition of *Malt Whisky Companion* commented "Some malt lovers would dismiss them for an overpowering oakiness; others would love them for their sherry and intensity." In the years since the last edition, the industry has used less peat and been stingier with sherry. Bottlings that have become available since the fourth edition are each two or three decades old, less intense, oaky, and sherryish, with more grainy notes.

HOUSE STYLE Dried fruits, grainy, toasty. Breakfast? After dinner?

CONNOISSEURS CHOICE

SPEYSIDE
Single Malt Scotch Whisky

DISTILLED AT
CAPERDONICH
DISTILLERY
Proprietors: Glenlivet & Glen Grant Distilleries Ltd.

DISTILLED
1980

Specially selected, produced and bottled by
Gordon & MacPhail
Elgin Scotland
Product of Scotland

70cl 40% vol

CAPERDONICH 1980, Gordon & MacPhail, 40 vol

COLOUR Yellow-amber.

NOSE Chocolate-covered dates. Fruity. Cherry brandy.

BODY Firm. Very smooth. Silky.

PALATE Oily. Hazelnut liqueur. Very mild indeed.

FINISH Restrained ginger. Woody dryness, as though the tongue had encountered the stick in a lollipop.

SCORE **74**

CAPERDONICH 1979, Signatory, 43 vol

COLOUR Extraordinarily pale. Almost "white", with a tinge of green.

NOSE Lollipop sticks. A suggestion of vanilla. A hint of raspberry.

BODY Very light but slightly syrupy.

PALATE Toasted marshmallow.

FINISH Very lightly spicy.

SCORE **69**

CAPERDONICH 1970, Duncan Taylor & Co., 51.7 vol

COLOUR Full yellow gold.

NOSE A crusty loaf, fresh from the oven, dusted with flour and sitting on a wooden bread board.

BODY Medium. Chewy. Mozzarella on a pizza.

PALATE Malty. Grainy. Slightly vegetal.

FINISH Mustard cress. Hot.

SCORE **75**

CAPERDONICH 1968, Lombard, 46 vol

COLOUR Gold, with faint green tinge.

NOSE Slightly smoky. Oily. Linseed.

PALATE Bath Oliver biscuits. Some perfumy notes. (Lavender. Potpourri?)

FINISH Dry. Drying. Woody.

SCORE **79**

CARDHU/CARDOW

PRODUCER Diageo
REGION Highlands DISTRICT Speyside
ADDRESS Aberlour, Banffshire, AB38 7RY
TEL 01340 872555 WEBSITE www.discovering-distilleries.com VC

A CONTROVERSIAL CHANGE, seen by some whisky lovers as a threat to the future of single malts, lay behind the adjustment to this distillery's name in 2003.

Such a threat could not issue from a less congruous location. Cardow has several claims to renown. It provided the industry with a dynastic family, the Cummings, and contributed twice to the tradition of strong women running distilleries. Helen Cummings distilled illegally on the family farm. Her daughter-in-law, Elizabeth, developed the legal distillery, which produced malt whisky as a substantial component of the Johnnie Walker blends.

The distillery was founded as Cardow (Gaelic for "black rock", after a nearby point on the river Spey). An alternative spelling, "Cardhu", better reflecting the pronunciation, was adopted when the distillery began to promote a bottled single malt. This mild, easily drinkable whisky was launched to compete with the popular malts in the early days of consumer interest.

It was a modest success in the United Kingdom, but enjoyed far greater sales in new markets for malts, such as France and Spain. In the latter country, the distinction between malts and blends seems to engage the consumer less than the age statement. Cardhu found itself head to head with the blend Chivas Regal, both being 12 years old. The Spaniards' taste for Scotch whisky is so great that the success of Cardhu in that market rendered it the world's fastest growing malt, outstripping the capacity of the distillery. Rather than "rationing" Cardhu, or increasing its price, owners Diageo decided to drop the designation "single" malt and substitute the imprecise "pure". Thus Cardhu was consumed by its own success.

The distillery, having reverted to the name Cardow, continues to produce whisky for bottling as Cardhu, but this is augmented by other Speyside distilleries under the same ownership.

Had Cardhu never been the name of a distillery and a single malt, there would be no cause for concern. Given that Cardhu was a single malt for between 30 and 40 years, and is now merely "pure" (meaning, in this instance, a vatted malt), there is a risk of confusion. The singularity of the name has been compromised, however good the "pure" malt.

How good, in this instance, is the pure malt? It seems a very good match, perhaps fractionally bigger: darker, oilier, nuttier, and drier. Initially, the only other component whisky to have been identified is Glendullan, but there are at least two others.

Diageo concedes the danger of confusion, and has worked hard to steer clear, but does not rule out more such transformations. If a single malt can, without changing its name, become less singular, how long before devotees become sceptics?

Other drinks try to set apart something special: microbrewed beers, real ales, first-growth clarets, Napoleon brandies, … but none is as clearly defined as a single malt. It would be monumentally foolish to squander that advantage. The tasting notes below refer to Cardhu as a single malt.

HOUSE STYLE In the original form: light, smooth, delicate; an easy-drinking malt. Greater ages are richer, more toffeeish, and often work well with desserts.

CARDHU 12-year-old, 40 vol
Was widely distributed, and therefore still to be found,
though it has been replaced by Cardhu Pure Malt.

COLOUR Pale.

NOSE Light, appetizing, hints of greengage, and the gentlest touch of smoke.

BODY Light and smooth.

PALATE Light to medium in flavour, with the emphasis on malty sweetness and vanilla.

FINISH A lingering, syrupy sweetness, but also a rounder dryness with late hints of peat, although again faint.

SCORE 72

CARDHU 1974, Signatory, 54.1 vol

COLOUR Distinctive reddish orange. Reminiscent of blood oranges.

NOSE Very rich and toffeeish.

BODY Syrupy. Soothing.

PALATE Treacle toffee. Underlying fruity complexity. Apricots. Nectarines. Plums.

FINISH Perfumy. Fragrant. Smoky. Slightly bitter.

SCORE **75**

CARDHU 1973, 27-year-old, Cask Strength, Rare Malts, 60.02 vol

COLOUR Full, bright, greeny gold.

NOSE Much more peaty than today's Cardhu. Hint of hessian, peat fire. Oaky.

BODY Big. Very malty. Marshmallow-like.

PALATE Complex. Toasted marshmallows. Very assertive. Softens a little with
late flavour development. Slightly burnt grassiness and fruitiness.
Grated tangerine peel. Lemons. Just a hint of sherbet.

FINISH Firm, very dry, lingering.

SCORE **77**

An earlier Rare Malts bottling of Cardhu (distilled 1973), at 60.5 vol,
has a richer, marshmallow maltiness, a suggestion of crystalized fruit,
and a hint of tangerine in the finish. SCORE 76

CLYNELISH

PRODUCER Diageo
REGION Highlands DISTRICT Northern Highlands
ADDRESS Brora, Sutherland, KW9 6LR
TEL 01408 623003
WEBSITE www.discovering-distilleries.com/www.malts.com VC

CULT STATUS SEEMS TO have been conferred in recent years on the Clynelish distillery and its adjoining predecessor, Brora, which command the middle stretch of the northern Highlands.

The appeal of their malts lies partly in their coastal aromas and flavours. Sceptics may question the brineyness of coastal malts, but some bottlings of Brora and Clynelish make that characteristic hard to deny. They are the most maritime of the East Coast malts, and on the Western mainland are challenged only by Springbank.

For a time, the big flavours of Clynelish and Brora were heightened by the use of well-peated malts. Clynelish cultists are always keen to identify distillates from this period. A similar preoccupation is to distinguish malts made at the Brora distillery from those that were distilled at Clynelish.

The two distilleries stand next door to each other on a landscaped hillside near the fishing and golfing resort of Brora. They overlook the coastal road as it heads toward the northernmost tip of the Scottish mainland.

The older of the two distilleries was built in 1819 by the Duke of Sutherland to use grain grown by his tenants. This distillery was originally known as Clynelish: the first syllable rhymes with "wine", the second with "leash". The name means "slope of the garden". After a century and half, a new Clynelish was built in 1967–68, but demand was sufficient for the two distilleries to operate in tandem for a time. They were initially known as Clynelish 1 and 2. Eventually, the older distillery was renamed Brora. It worked sporadically until 1983.

Brora is a traditional 19th-century distillery, in local stone (now overgrown), with a pagoda. Clynelish's stills greet the world through the floor-to-ceiling windows, in the classic design of the period, with a fountain to soften the façade.

Inside, the still-house has its own peculiarities, in which the deposits in the low wines and feints receivers play a part. The result is an oily, beeswax background flavour – another distinctive feature.

For years, this robustly distinctive malt was available only as a 12-year-old, bearing a charmingly amateurish label, from Ainslie and Heilbron, a DCL subsidiary, whose blends were given brand names of equal charm. The Real McTavish was a good example. Since the United Distillers and Diageo eras, Brora and Clynelish have been positively anthologous. Editions have been issues by Flora and Fauna, The Rare Malts, Cask Strength Limited Editions, Hidden Malts, as well as Special Releases.

HOUSE STYLE Seaweedy, spicy. Mustard-and-oil.
With a roast-beef sandwich.

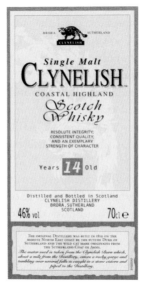

CLYNELISH, 14-year-old, 46 vol, Hidden Malts

Replaces more seaweedy Flora and Fauna edition reviewed in the fourth edition of Malt Whisky Companion.

COLOUR Bright pale orange.

NOSE Fragrant. A stroll in the sand dunes.

BODY Firm, oily and seductively smoky.

PALATE Firm hit of cleansing flavours. Coriander. Orange. Dry. Spicy.
Distinctively mustardy.

FINISH The spiciness becomes yet more perfumy and exotic.
Both satisfying (without being satiating).

SCORE 81

BRORA 1977, 24-year-old, Cask Strength, The Rare Malts, 56.1 vol

COLOUR Very bright primrose. Lime tinge?

NOSE Very flowery. Camomile. Suggestion of sweet lime.

BODY Lightly oily.

PALATE Lively, fruity, refreshing. Distinctive gorse or whin; that coconut flavour. Then fresh lime, then peppery seaweed.

FINISH Sandy, grainy, mustardy. Wasabi?
Does the 18th hole at Brora serve sushi?

SCORE **84**

BRORA 30-year-old, Special Release, Limited Bottling of 3000, 52.4 vol

COLOUR Greeny gold.

NOSE Fruity. Fresh limes. Indian lime pickle.

BODY Light but firm.

PALATE Powerfully peaty, with "island" flavours of spinach-like seaweed, salt and pepper.

FINISH Stingingly mustardy. Joyously extrovert.

SCORE **86**

EARLIER "OFFICIAL" BOTTLINGS

A 1982 Clynelish at 57.7 vol, in the Cask Strength series of Limited Editions, was assertive, seaweedy and slightly metallic. SCORE 81

A 1975 Brora, at 20 years and 59.1 vol, also in the Rare Malts series, had an intensely flowery aroma; a flowery, seaweedy, medicinal palate; and iodine, seaweed and salt in its long, lingering finish. A classic. SCORE 84

A 1977 Brora, at 21 years and 56.9 vol, in the Rare Malts series, had a good maritime character and a distinctively tar-like note. SCORE 85

A 1972 Clynelish, at 22 years and 58.95 vol, in the Rare Malts series, had more spice. Earlier Rare Malts from Brora have included a more flowery 1975. SCORE 84

There was also a wonderfully seaweedy, medicinal 1972. SCORE 86

SOME ADELPHI BOTTLINGS OF CLYNELISH

One independent bottler with a particular enthusiasm for Clynelish is
Adelphi. Here is a selection of recent bottlings, all scoring more than 80.

CLYNELISH 1989, 9-year-old, Cask No 6081, Adelphi, 61.6 vol

COLOUR Very pale gold.

NOSE Very flowery. Soft for a relatively young example.

BODY Light, smooth.

PALATE Flowery. Cress. Pepper. Salt. Delicate interplay of flavours. A lovely,
flowery aperitif.

FINISH Lightly seaweedy. Late sweetness.

SCORE **81**

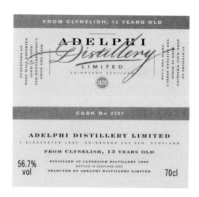

CLYNELISH 1989, 13-year-old, Cask No 3281, Adelphi, 56.7 vol

COLOUR Brassy gold.

NOSE Aromatic: fruity, flowery, vegetal (dock leaves?), appetizing

BODY Dry, biscuity, cracker-like

PALATE Reminiscent of edible seaweed. Interplay of sweetness, spicy
mustard and vegetal dryness.

FINISH Peppery. Very salty Not the most peaty Clynelish, but a lovely
distinctive whisky.

SCORE **82**

A 12-year-old Clynelish from Adelphi, cask no 3280 at 57.2 vol, was
unusually sweet. Syrupy, creamy, peppery, dry (passion-fruit?). It had a long,
peaty glow. Enjoyable, but very restrained for a Clynelish. SCORE 81

A 27-year-old Clynelish from Adelphi, cask no 2569 and at 56.3 vol, had wet
grass, fresh earth, and peat in the aroma. Deliciously smooth. Syrupy without
being cloying. Developing peat. Finish was typically mustardy. SCORE 84

MORE INDEPENDENT BOTTLINGS
OF BRORA AND CLYNELISH

CLYNELISH 1972, 29-year-old, Berry Brothers & Rudd, 43 vol

COLOUR Very clear pale gold or *eau-de-nil*.

NOSE Very fresh. Sliced limes. Lemon zest. Vanilla.

BODY Light and delicate but beautifully rounded.

PALATE Light cereal-grain character. Sliced dessert apple, but very rounded. Hint of lemony acidity.

FINISH Crisp, gingery, refreshing.

SCORE **79**

CLYNELISH 1976, Cask No 6501, Blackadder, Bottled 2002, 59 vol

COLOUR Dark oak.

NOSE Treacle toffee. Mint toffee.

BODY Cough syrup.

PALATE Fig-like. Fig Newtons. Ginger biscuits. Intense.

FINISH Maritime character emerges. Salty. Long. Woody.

SCORE **78**

CLYNELISH 1989, 13-year-old, Cask No 3287,
South African "Sherry" Wood, Chieftain's, 46 vol

COLOUR Full gold. Faint greenish tinge.

NOSE Lemony. Winey acidity.

BODY Rich, smooth.

PALATE Lemony. Oily. Anis. Lively flavours that seem to be trapped in malt like plums in a pancake.

FINISH Lemon curd. Zest of lemon.

SCORE **78**

CLYNELISH 1990, Connoisseurs Choice, 40 vol

COLOUR Attractive warm bronze.

NOSE Harbourfront. Seaweed. Slightly sour.

BODY Firm. Steely. Stern.

PALATE Iron-like flavours. Passion fruit. Gorse. Sea mist.
Flavours tightly combined.

FINISH Salty. Savoury. Appetizing.

SCORE 80

A Clynelish 1989, cask no 3248, at 57.9 vol, from the same merchant, has a considerably fuller colour, more like dark oak. With that hue comes a sherry creaminess, butteriness, and hint of cocoa. Then, through all those flavours, comes the salty tang of the sea. A deft balance of two extremes, and a luxurious nightcap. SCORE 84

BRORA 1982, Connoisseurs Choice, 40 vol

COLOUR Full, bright, yellowy gold.

NOSE Powerful. Gorse in a sea mist.

BODY Very firm.

PALATE Salsify, asparagus, edible cactus, juicy cucumber. Very unusual.
Both refreshing and appetizing, though rather weak in the middle.

FINISH Oily, olivey, peppery.

SCORE 79

THE COOPERS CHOICE
CLYNELISH 1990, 12-year-old, The Coopers Choice, 43 vol

COLOUR Old gold to bronze.

NOSE Dried orange skins.

BODY Dry, toffeeish.

PALATE Orange toffee. Banana toffee. Rather thin and one-dimensional.

FINISH Lemony. Just a suggestion of salt and seaweed.

SCORE **76**

CLYNELISH 1990, 12-year-old, port finish, 46 vol, Coopers Choice.
Fresh sea smells. A walk in the dunes. Creamy. Reminiscent of a mustardy
hollandaise sauce (perhaps served with samphire). Fruity, mustardy,
dry finish is not quite enough of a foil. SCORE 79

CLYNELISH 1983, 16-year-old, 43 vol, Coopers Choice. Very fresh
and aromatic. Pears. Cress. Pepper. Suggestions of olive oil in the
palate. Falls away in the middle. Then develops sweet mustard
notes. The finish is grassy, sandy, peppery, seaweedy. SCORE 80

HART BROTHERS
CLYNELISH, 14-year-old, Cask Strength, Hart Brothers, 53.3 vol

COLOUR Bright, shimmery gold, with faint greenish tinge.

NOSE Vegetal. Seaweedy. A walk on the beach.

BODY Smooth, rounded, promising.

PALATE Clean, sweet. Suggestions of liquorice. Children's sweetshops.
Liquorice allsorts. Develops more adult flavours. Fennel? Celeriac?
Becomes more typically vegetal. Complex. Satisfying.

FINISH Sweet, peppery, lively.

SCORE **81**

KINGSBURY'S
CLYNELISH 1990, Amontillado Sherry Cask, Bottled 2000, Kingsbury's, 54.2 vol

The sherry complements rather than overpowers the classic Clynelish character.

COLOUR Very full gold.

NOSE Very oily. Orange zest. Citrus peels. Lemon

BODY Medium, firm.

PALATE Oily. Lemon. Mustard. Pine nuts. Cream.

FINISH Bitter salad leaves. Powerfully dry.

SCORE **82**

DOUGLAS LAING
BRORA 20-year-old, Single Cask Bottling, 50 vol

COLOUR Bright, greeny gold.

NOSE Curiously cloth-hall aroma, as though the whisky were being nosed among rolls of silk and satin. Or perhaps just among the occupants of sleek evening dresses.

BODY Oily. Slightly buttery.

PALATE Cereal grain. Restrained apple and lemon. Toast.

FINISH Touch of ginger marmalade.

SCORE **79**

Brora 18-year-old, 50 vol. This earlier bottling of Brora from the same house at the same strength, but two years younger, was much peatier, to the point of evoking Islay. It fell away somewhat in the middle, but came back for a stinging, fruity finish. Reminiscent of citron pressé. Very long saltiness. SCORE 82

LOMBARD
CLYNELISH 1982, Lombard, 50 vol

COLOUR Extraordinarily pale. *Eau-de-nil.*

NOSE Peaty.

BODY Oily but light and drying.

PALATE Peaty, grassy, peppery.

FINISH Dry, sharp, penetrating.

SCORE **76**

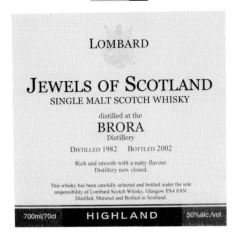

BRORA 1982, Lombard (Jewels of Scotland), 50 vol

COLOUR Greeny gold.

NOSE More maritime, harbourfront character.

BODY Firm, slippery.

PALATE Slightly chewy. Both fruity and vegetal.
Lemons and spinach with Indian spices.

FINISH Spicy, perfumy, rounded.

SCORE **78**

JAMES MACARTHUR
CLYNELISH 10-year-old, James MacArthur, 59.8 vol

COLOUR Attractive greeny primrose.

NOSE Hint of the sea.

BODY Textured.

PALATE Sweet, mustardy, iron iodine salty, very lively.
Lots of flavour development. Light but warm smokiness.

FINISH Salty. Long. Stinging. Very appetizing indeed.

SCORE **83**

CLYNELISH, 1989, Cask No 1122, James MacArthur, 58 vol

COLOUR Pale, greeny gold.

NOSE Hint of the sea.

BODY Medium to full, textured.

PALATE Like biting into crudités. Celery, palm hearts, artichokes, spinach.

FINISH Robust. Salty. Peppery.

SCORE **82**

Another 1989 Clynelish, at a mere 1.1% stronger in alcohol, is milder in flavours, but crisp, clean, and decisive. Sweet, becoming grassy and mustardy, long, and appetizing. SCORE 80

MURRAY MCDAVID
CLYNELISH 1972, Mission Range Series, 46 vol

COLOUR Pale gold. Almost iridescent.

NOSE Very aromatic. Strawberry jam. Marzipan. Almonds.
Spice-shop aromas.

BODY Silky.

PALATE Oily. Very lively. Extraordinarily spicy. Mustard, cumin seeds, coriander seed, cilantro.

FINISH Slightly sour, acid tang. Very appetizing. Perfect with salmon.

SCORE **85**

SIGNATORY
CLYNELISH 1983, Signatory, 43 vol

COLOUR Very pale white wine.

NOSE Light seaweed and sea air.

BODY Lightly silky.

PALATE Light, refreshing, weak in the middle, developing some peppery notes.

FINISH Peppery, light, fruity seaweed, sea salt, pepper.
Very late, mustardy dryness, and heat.

SCORE **78**

BRORA 1982, Cask No 278, Signatory, 58.6 vol

COLOUR Vinho verde.

NOSE Sweet. Vanilla.

BODY Lightly creamy.

PALATE A gentle approach to the sea. Across the grassy dunes
to the sandy, salty shore.

FINISH Intensely vegetal. Juicy. Tasty. Nettle soup with the sting intact.

SCORE 79

BRORA 1981, 21 year-old, Butt No 1422,
Signatory Unchillfiltered Collection, 46 vol

COLOUR Fractionally greener.

NOSE Slight cellar character.

BODY Creamier.

PALATE Creamy. Grassy sweetness. Earthy.

FINISH Late, restrained, maritime notes. Vegetal, seaweed.

SCORE 79

Also from Signatory, a 1989 Clynelish at 56.7 vol, finished in South
African "sherry" casks. Buttery sweetness in the aroma. Palate
suggests banana liqueur. Then smoky, like a pancake that has burned
slightly. Caramel-ish, spicy finish. A very unusual expression of Clynelish.
SCORE 75

THE WHISKY SHOP
BRORA 1972, 30-year-old, Cask Strength, The Whisky Shop, 47.4 vol

COLOUR Dark mahogany.

NOSE A hint of sweetish smoke.

BODY Firm. Smooth.

PALATE Chewy. Dry. Treacle toffee. Prunes encased in chocolate.
Some fruity-vegetal Brora character squeaks through.

FINISH Cigar boxes. Woody. For those who like woody whiskies.
Or for collectors.

SCORE 79

AN CNOC

PRODUCER Inver House Distillers Ltd
REGION Highlands   DISTRICT Speyside (Isla/Deveron)
ADDRESS Knock by Huntly, Aberdeenshire, AB5 5LJ
WEBSITE www.inverhouse.com   EMAIL enquiries@inverhouse.com

AN CNOC IS SCOTTISH GAELIC for "the hill", and the most distinctively simple among a confusing variety of styles used on labels. The full name of the distillery, in Gaelic, is Cnoc Dubh ("black hill"). In English, this is rendered as "Knockdhu", not to be confused with another wholly unrelated distillery, Knockando ("little black hill"). There was probably no thought of confusion when these two distilleries were established, both in the 1890s, as their original purpose was to produce whisky for blending, rather than as single malt.

Knockdhu was built in 1894 to supply malt for the Haig blends, and closed in 1983. Only after its acquisition by its present owners, and its reopening, did official bottlings, albeit on a small scale, begin to be issued in the 1990s.

HOUSE STYLE Creamy and fruity. A dessert malt?

AN CNOC 12-year-old, 40 vol

COLOUR Pale gold.

NOSE Very aromatic, smooth, fruity. Pineapple?

BODY Light but very smooth.

PALATE Smooth, creamy vanilla notes. Very soft note of fruit.
Very drinkable and enjoyable.

FINISH Creamy, oaty. Sweet herbs.

SCORE **75**

AN CNOC 13-year-old, Limited Edition,
Highland Selection, 46 vol

COLOUR Pale, shimmery gold.

NOSE Light, dry. Slight burnt grass. Then lemon grass
and mint.

BODY Light but smooth, with some chalkiness.

PALATE Lightly syrupy, herbal, minty, rummy. Flavours that one expects
from a bigger, darker whisky. Slightly odd, but enjoyable. Given the
monosyllabic name, could be a flavoured spirit from a little known, newly
independent republic in Central Asia.

FINISH Hint of cloves. Warming. Soothing. Very long.

SCORE **76**

CNOC DHU/KNOCKDHU 21-year-old, Limited Edition, 57.5 vol

This was a limited release, now hard to find. Superseded by the 23-year-old.

COLOUR Fractionally fuller gold.

NOSE Appetizingly perfumy. Marshmallow maltiness, restrained fruit,
grass, and peat-smoke fragrance. Beautifully balanced.

FINISH Fruit zest. Spicy. Smoky fragrance.

SCORE **77**

KNOCKDHU 23-year-old, Limited Edition, 57.4 vol

COLOUR Refractive, greeny gold.

NOSE Softly sweet lemon grass. Hint of fragrant smoke. Marshmallow.

BODY Smooth. Cinder toffee.

PALATE Toffeeish. Textured. Full of flavour. Clotted cream. Dessert apples.
Sweet without being cloying. Delicious.

FINISH Lemony. Rounded. The lightest touch of peat.

SCORE **78**

AN CNOC 1975, 26-year-old, Highland Selection, Unchillfiltered, 48.2 vol

COLOUR Fractionally paler.

NOSE Again, soft and sweet. Perhaps slightly more flowery and perfumy.
Very attractive indeed.

BODY Fuller. Beautifully rounded. Very smooth.

PALATE The typical lemon grass arrives late. Sweet grass. Meadow flowers.

FINISH Lingering sweetness, balanced by grassy dryness. Sun-dried grass?
And a late surge of spiciness.

SCORE **79**

KNOCKDHU 1989, 12-year-old, Cask No 286, Adelphi, 56.6 vol

COLOUR Deep gold to bronze.

NOSE Mint toffee.

BODY Medium. Very smooth.

PALATE Butterscotch sauce. Oat cookies with raisins.
Ginger snaps. Delicious.

FINISH Long, warming. Serve it with dessert. No, pour it
over the ice cream.

SCORE **77**

COLEBURN

PRODUCER Diageo
REGION Highlands DISTRICT Speyside (Lossie)
ADDRESS Longmorn by Elgin, Moray, IV38 8GN

T HE USHER'S WHISKIES, pioneer blends, once relied heavily upon
malt from this distillery. Coleburn was built in the booming 1890s.
It closed in the grim 1980s, the year before its owners DCL were
subsumed into United Distillers, which in turn became part of Diageo.
The Coleburn distillery still stands, but has not been licensed since
1992, and is unlikely to work again. There have been sporadic
proposals to redevelop the site for other uses. Its whisky, always
intended for blending, was never destined for solo stardom. A
valedictory Rare Malts vintage was as enjoyable as any Coleburn to
have been bottled in recent decades.

HOUSE STYLE Dry, fruity. Aperitif.

COLEBURN 21, The Rare Malts, 59.4 vol

COLOUR Bright primrose.

NOSE Flowery, dry. Zest of lemon. Resiny. Leafy. Hint of peat.

BODY Lightly viscous. Oily.

PALATE Peppery. Oil of peppermint. Mint toffee.

FINISH Ginger. Spicy. Medicinal. Warming. Soothing.

SCORE **73**

CONVALMORE

PRODUCER William Grant & Sons Ltd
REGION Highlands DISTRICT Speyside (Dufftown)
ADDRESS Dufftown, Banffshire, AB55 4BD

A RARE MALT OF Convalmore from Diageo in 2003 was something of a surprise – and a very pleasant one, given the quality of the whisky. The pagodas of Dufftown make an impressive congregation of landmarks, and Convalmore's is one of the most strikingly visible. Sadly, the distillery no longer operates.

For much of its life, Convalmore contributed malt whisky to the Buchanan/Black & White blends. The distillery was built in the 1870s; seriously damaged by fire, and rebuilt in 1910; modernized in 1964–65, but mothballed a couple of decades later by its owners at the time, DCL. Their successors, Diageo, still have the right to issue bottlings of Convalmore whisky from stock. In 1992, the premises were acquired by William Grant & Sons, owners of nearby Glenfiddich and Balvenie, but purely as warehousing.

HOUSE STYLE Malty, syrupy, fruity, biggish.
After dinner.

CONVALMORE 1981, Signatory, 43 vol

COLOUR *Eau-de-nil.*

NOSE Aromatic. Perfumy. Lavender. Wild mint.

BODY Very silky.

PALATE Fleshy. Musky. White rum. Cocoa butter. Pralines.
Mint chocolates.

FINISH Fresh, clean, stinging.

SCORE **71**

CONVALMORE 24-year-old, Distilled 1978, Rare Malt, 59.4 vol

COLOUR Shimmery pale gold.

NOSE Gently sweet. Oily cereal character. A fresh day on Speyside,
with a little smoke wafting quickly past.

BODY Medium. Creamy. Syrupy.

PALATE Chocolate cream in a cookie sandwich. Becoming less
chocolatey, more biscuity and drier.

FINISH Fruity. Lemon pith. Slightly woody. Alcoholic. Warming.
Long. Powerful.

SCORE **79**

CONVALMORE 1977, 21-year-old, Cadenhead, 64.4 vol

COLOUR Old gold. Dusty, full gold.

NOSE Oily. Passion fruit. Iron-ish, but sweet.

BODY Drying on the tongue. Clinging syrupiness.

PALATE Gritty. Dry. Sherbety. Peppery.

FINISH Big, long, rummy, warming syrupiness. After dinner.

SCORE **75**

CONVALMORE 1960, Gordon & MacPhail, 40 vol

Released in 1999 as part of a new Rare Old series.

COLOUR Rich, lemony gold.

NOSE Aromatic. Oily. Very "clean" smoke.

BODY Medium. Oily. Clean.

PALATE Begins with a good malt background. Distinctly oily.
Again, lightly smoky.

FINISH Light malt. Hint of honey. Yet more oiliness. Hint of sulphur.
Clean peatiness. Warming. Long.

SCORE **70**

CRAGGANMORE

PRODUCER Diageo
REGION Highlands   DISTRICT Speyside
ADDRESS Ballindalloch, Banffshire, AB37 9AB   TEL 01479 8747000
WEBSITE www.discovering-distilleries.com/www.malts.com

A WONDERFULLY COMPLEX SPECIAL RELEASE in 2003 demonstrated what a great malt this is. Cragganmore, one of Diageo's six "Classic Malts", is still less widely known than might be expected. The distillery, founded in 1869–70, is very pretty, hidden in a hollow high on the Spey. Its water, from nearby springs, is relatively hard, and its spirit stills have an unusual, flat-topped shape. These two elements may be factors in the complexity of the malt. The usual version, from refill sherry casks, some more sherried independent bottlings, and the port finish, are each in their own ways almost equal delights. Cragganmore is a component of Old Parr.

HOUSE STYLE Austere, stonily dry, aromatic. After dinner.

CRAGGANMORE 12-year-old, 40 vol

COLOUR Golden.

NOSE The most complex aroma of any malt. Its bouquet is astonishingly fragrant and delicate, with sweetish notes of cut grass and herbs (thyme perhaps?).

BODY Light to medium, but very firm and smooth.

PALATE Delicate, clean, restrained, with a huge range of herbal, flowery notes.

FINISH Long.

SCORE **90**

CRAGGANMORE 1984, Double Matured, 40 vol

Finished in ruby port.

COLOUR Pale amber.

NOSE Heather honey. Scented. Beeswax. Hessian.

BODY Firm, smooth. Fuller.

PALATE Flowery. Orange blossom. Sweet oranges. Cherries. Port.

FINISH Flowery, balancing dryness. Warming. Soothing.
Connoisseurs might miss the austerity of the original – or enjoy
the added layer of fruity, winey sweetness.

SCORE **90**

CRAGGANMORE 1973, 29-year-old,
Special Release Issued 2003, 52.5 vol

COLOUR Gold, with a faint green tinge.

NOSE Fragrant, grassy, herbal, with both dryness and sweetness.

BODY Soft, slightly oily, dry.

PALATE Dry notes like bison grass, thyme and pepper, but also sweeter
flavours like liquorice and orange blossom.

FINISH Long, dry, flowery, cleansing.

SCORE **92**

SOME INDEPENDENT BOTTLINGS OF CRAGGANMORE:

Murray McDavid's bottling of a cask from 1990 at 46 vol is pale straw
in colour. A subtle refined nose hinting at berry fruits, mandarin, dried
apple, white pepper and a grassy note. Medium weight. The palate
is slightly flat. SCORE 80.

A 1989 bottling from Blackadder at 59.6 vol is light gold in colour; water
brings out slightly grubby wood. The palate and body shows a light
whisky which has had little interaction with the cask. SCORE 70

Signatory's 1989, 55.7 vol, is light gold with a nose of powdered almond,
sultana, and suggestions of weight; the palate is soft and sweet with good
character, but lacks the depth of the official bottlings. SCORE 83

CRAIGELLACHIE

PRODUCER John Dewar & Sons Ltd
REGION Highlands DISTRICT Speyside
ADDRESS Craigellachie, Banffshire, AB38 9ST
TEL 01340 881212

FOR ITS 2003/04 selection, the Craigellachie Hotel, with its renowned whisky bar, went for the first time to the local distillery. The whisky of Craigellachie had a very low profile under the ownership of Diageo; perhaps it will rediscover itself under Dewar's. The distillery was founded in 1891 and remodelled in 1965.

The village of Craigellachie – between Dufftown, Aberlour, and Rothes – is at the very heart of Speyside distillery country. It also has the Speyside Cooperage. Here, the Fiddich meets the Spey, and the latter is crossed by a bridge, designed by the great Scottish engineer Thomas Telford. Craigellachie is pronounced "Craig-ella-ki" – the "i" is short.

HOUSE STYLE Sweet, malty-nutty, fruity. After dinner.

CRAIGELLACHIE 14-year-old, Flora and Fauna, 43 vol

COLOUR Old gold.

NOSE Fragrant. Lightly smoky. Plenty of sweet, crushed-barley maltiness.

BODY Medium.

PALATE Starts sweet, slightly syrupy, and malty, then becomes nutty, developing a very fruity, Seville-orange character.

FINISH Orangey, lightly smoky, aromatic, warming.

SCORE 75

CRAIGELLACHIE 1982, 2003 Single Cask Bottling for the Craigellachie Hotel, 60 vol

COLOUR Pale, bright gold. Almost iridescent.

NOSE Very evocative. Warm. Fresh earthiness. The forest floor. Wild mushrooms. Chanterelle vol-au-vents. Pastry fresh out of the oven. Shortbread.

BODY Firm. Smooth. Lightly syrupy.

PALATE Creamy. Slight accent towards maltiness, but very well balanced. Starts sweet, but develops some fruity acidity. Apricots. Fruit pies. Apple, especially. Flavours tightly bound together.

FINISH Soothing warmth.

SCORE **78**

CRAIGELLACHIE 13-year-old, Adelphi, Cask No 3783, 59.2 vol

COLOUR Bright gold.

NOSE Sweet, malty, nutty, buttery.

BODY Medium but rich.

PALATE Creamy, nutty. Lacks complexity, but delicious.

FINISH Light, clean fruitiness. Orange zest. Quick.

SCORE **75**

A 40 vol from the same year, bottled by Gordon & MacPhail, was superbly balanced, with a more peaty smokiness and the faintest suggestion of sherry. SCORE 78

CRAIGELLACHIE 1981, Signatory, 43 vol

COLOUR White wine.

NOSE Fragrant. Restrained dessert apples, grass, and fragrant smokiness.

BODY Oily.

PALATE Cereal-grain oiliness. Very oily. Perfumy. Soapy.

FINISH Flowery. Dessert apples again.

SCORE **75**

OTHER VERSIONS OF CRAIGELLACHIE

A 1973 22-year-old Rare Malts edition, at cask strength, begins with crushed barley, moving to fudgey nuttiness and peanut brittle. SCORE 77

DAILUAINE

PRODUCER Diageo
REGION Highlands DISTRICT Speyside
ADDRESS Carron, Aberlour, Banffshire, AB38 7RE
TEL 01340 872500

BETWEEN THE MOUNTAIN BEN RINNES and the river Spey, at the hamlet of Carron, not far from Aberlour, the Dailuaine ("Dal-oo-ayn") distillery is hidden in a hollow. The name means "green vale", and that accurately describes the setting. It was founded in 1852, and has been rebuilt several times since.

It is one of several distilleries along the Spey valley that once had its own railway halt for workers and visitors – and as a means of shipping in barley or malt and despatching the whisky. A small part of the Speyside line still runs trains for hobbyists and visitors, at the Aviemore ski resort, and Dailuaine's own shunting locomotive has appeared there under steam, but is now preserved at Aberfeldy, a distillery formerly in the same group. Most of the route from the mountains to the sea is now preserved for walkers, as the Speyside Way. Dailuaine's whisky has long been a component of the Johnnie Walker blends. It was made available as a single malt in the Flora and Fauna series in 1991, and later in a Cask Strength Limited Edition.

HOUSE STYLE Firmly malty, fruity, fragrant.
After dinner.

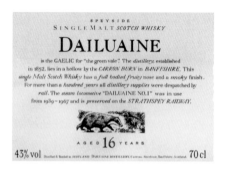

DAILUAINE 16-year-old, Flora and Fauna, 43 vol

COLOUR Emphatically reddish amber.

NOSE Sherryish but dry, perfumy.

BODY Medium to full, smooth.

PALATE Sherryish, with barley-sugar maltiness, but balanced by
a dry cedar or oak background.

FINISH Sherryish, smooth, very warming, long.

SCORE **76**

DAILUAINE 1980, Bottled 1997,
Cask Strength Limited Edition, 63 vol

COLOUR Bright deep orange. Very distinctive.

NOSE Lightly smoky. Orange marmalade. Sherry. Oak.

BODY Medium to full. Smooth.

PALATE Sherryish. Firm maltiness. Surge of peat smoke. Oak.

FINISH Oaky, dry, earthy, peppery.

SCORE **77**

DAILUAINE 1973, 22-year-old, Rare Malts, 60.92 vol

COLOUR Full gold.

NOSE Distinctly peaty.

BODY Light to medium. Very smooth.

PALATE Long-lasting flavours. Tightly combined barley-sugar sweetness
and flowery dryness. Less sherried and big than the above, but with
more distillery character.

FINISH Fruity, perfumy. Violets?

SCORE **77**

SOME INDEPENDENT BOTTLINGS OF DAILUAINE

A 22-year-old Adelphi bottling at 55.2 vol, cask no 4151, has a nose of
Olde English marmalade, ripe fruit, vanilla oak cream, and menthol;
sweet soft body and a palate that delivers soft vanilla fruits, blackberry,
grilled nut fruit. A gentle giant. SCORE 80

The 21-year-old (1979 distillation, 43 vol) from Cooper's Choice
has a perfumed nose akin to geranium and with water soft cooked fruits;
the body is quite light and the palate has grassy notes mixed with soft
creaminess. SCORE 75

A 1975 Connoisseurs Choice from Gordon and MacPhail at 40 vol is
malty and rich with more European oak influence: leather, nut,
stewed orange. A heavier-bodied dram with an oozy, soft depth.
Plenty of chocolate in here. Deep. SCORE 77

DALLAS DHU

PRODUCER DCL
REGION Highlands DISTRICT Speyside (Findhorn)
ADDRESS Forres, Morayshire, IV36 2RR
TEL 01309 676548 VC

T HE NAME MEANS "black water valley". This Dallas accommodates a hamlet rather smaller than its indirect descendant in Texas (named after US Vice-president George Mifflin Dallas, who seems to have been of Scottish origin). The Dallas Dhu distillery was established in 1899. Despite a fire in 1939, it does not appear to have changed greatly. Latterly, its whisky appeared in the Benmore blends and vattings, and as Dallas Mhor single malt.

The distillery closed in 1983 and reopened to the public in 1988, under the aegis of Scotland's Historic Buildings and Monument Directorate. There are no plans to restart production, but the later batches continue to appear in independent bottlings.

HOUSE STYLE Silky, honeyish, sometimes chocolatey. After dinner.

DALLAS DHU 1980, Gordon & MacPhail, 40 vol

COLOUR Gold.

NOSE Some oak. Cox s apple. Heavy perfumed greenhouse
aromas: tomato, flowers. Spice.

BODY Round and soft.

PALATE Ripe fruits, lush and sweet.

FINISH Spices.

SCORE 83

DALLAS DHU 1979, Murray McDavid Mission Range, 46 vol

COLOUR Rich gold.

NOSE Soft orchard fruit. Fruitcake, dried peach. Elegant and soft.

BODY Silky and chewy.

PALATE Sweet, complex, long, and elegant. Orange, date, juicy fruits. toffee.

FINISH Nutmeg.

SCORE **83**

DALLAS DHU 1978, Signatory, 43 vol

COLOUR Amber.

NOSE Dried sweet fruits. Caramelized fruits, toffee, date. Rich, voluptuous.

BODY Soft and rich.

PALATE Thick. Apricot, dried mango, singed notes. Great balance.

FINISH Light spice.

SCORE **80**

DALLAS DHU 21-year-old, Distilled 1975, Rare Malts, 61.9 vol

COLOUR Old gold.

NOSE Orange blossom. Honey. Musk. Heathery. Peat smoke.

BODY Smooth, light on the tongue, syrupy.

PALATE Orange zest, crème brûlée, burnt sugar.

FINISH Slightly chewy, treacle toffee. Late warmth. Long.

SCORE **81**

DALLAS DHU 1978, Signatory, 59.7 vol

COLOUR Bright greeny gold.

NOSE Quick hit of intense syrupy fruit.
Becoming more floral, perfumy and soapy.

BODY Syrupy.

PALATE Very appetizingly, pleasantly grassy and smoky. Creamy in the
middle, with a suggestion of white chocolate. Then smoky again.

FINISH Quite hot. Ginger cookies.

SCORE **75**

DALLAS DHU 1970, 32-year-old, Coopers Choice, 46 vol

COLOUR Old Gold to dull bronze. Quite full.

NOSE Soft. Malty. Buttery. Cinnamon.

BODY Light. Firm. Textured. Chewy.

PALATE Sticky toffee pudding.

FINISH Powerful. Fruity. Warming.

SCORE **80**

THE DALMORE

PRODUCER Whyte and MacKay Ltd
REGION Highlands DISTRICT Northern Highlands
ADDRESS Alness, Morayshire, IV17 0UT
TEL 01349 882362 WEBSITE www.dalmoredistillery.co.uk

A RECORD PRICE FOR A BOTTLE OF WHISKY was established in 2002, when a Dalmore 62-year-old single malt was sold at auction to an anonymous bidder for just over £25,000/$38,000. Records are made to be broken, but this was a timely boost to the distillery, not long returned to Scottish ownership. The record-breaking sale took place at McTear's, the Glasgow auction house. The whisky was vatted from vintages of 1868, 1878, 1926, and 1939. Over the years, it had been racked several times, latterly in an oloroso sherry butt from Gonzalez Byass.

The man who makes the vattings and blendings for Whyte and Mackay, Richard Patterson, is one of the industry's extroverts. He may well have celebrated with a cigar. One of his creations is Dalmore The Cigar Malt, a rich whisky intended to accompany a fine Havana. It is easy to imagine the finest cigars being smoked in the oak-panelled offices at Dalmore. The panels previously graced a shooting lodge.

Dalmore, said to have been founded in 1839, was once owned by a distinguished local family, the Mackenzies, friends of James Whyte and Charles Mackay, who created a famous name in blended Scotch. Latterly, the proprietor was Jim Beam, of Kentucky. The management buy-out of Jim Beam's Scottish distilleries led to the restoration of the Whyte and Mackay name.

Dalmore has an unusual still-house. The wash stills have a conical upper chamber and the spirit stills are cooled with a water jacket – another distinctive feature. There are two pairs of stills, identical in shape but different sizes. The warehouses are by the waters of the Cromarty Firth. About 85 per cent of the whisky is matured in bourbon casks, mainly first-fill, the rest in sweet oloroso and amontillado, but it is all married in sherry butts.

HOUSE STYLE Rich, flavourful, orange marmalade. After dinner.

THE DALMORE 12-year-old, 40 vol

COLOUR An attractive amber hue.

NOSE Arousing, with rum butter, malt loaf, and soda bread.

BODY Medium. Silky smooth.

PALATE Gradual flavour development. Malty sweetness,
orange jelly beans, spiciness (anise?), perfuminess, heather,
light peat Even a faint, salty tang of the sea.

FINISH Toasty. Grainy, Long

SCORE **79**

THE DALMORE "Black Isle", 12-year old, 43 vol

COLOUR Slightly darker and redder. Copper.

NOSE More obvious sherry. Apricot jam. Morello cherries. Pipe tobacco.

BODY Velvety.

PALATE Seville oranges. Candied orange peels in mincemeat. Mince pies.

FINISH Rooty. Liquorice. Lingering.

SCORE **80**

THE DALMORE Cigar Malt, 40 vol

*A marriage of Dalmore whiskies between ten and 20 years old,
mainly in the-mid teens.*

COLOUR Dark orange.

NOSE A soft smokiness. Suggestions of black chocolate and orange creams.

BODY Firm.

PALATE Rich, rounded. A hint of rum butter, then dryish and firm.
Hard caramel toffee. Hint of burnt sugar. Faint smoke. Never cloying.
With the cigar, a complement rather than a contrast.

FINISH Light, smoky, wood bark, ground almonds, dryness. Scores points
for originality and for balance.

SCORE **81**

THE DALMORE 1978, 21-year-old, 43 vol

COLOUR	Pale orange.

NOSE Soft, perfumy, fruity.

Body Silky.

PALATE A distinctly finessed and elegant interpretation. Very well combined, complex flavours. Orange, chocolate, flowers, late spices, hint of smoke.

FINISH Light touch of citrus. Whiff of smoke.

SCORE *81*

THREE BOTTLINGS FOR JAPAN

A 1980, at 22 years old and 60.8 vol (cask no 158), has suggestions of pastry, apple pie (a little too long in the oven) and a dousing with calvados. SCORE 79

A 1979, at 23 years and 54.8 vol (cask no 595) has more fruit – albeit rather tannic apples. SCORE 80

A 1974, at 28 years old, and 57.9 vol (cask no 5883) has a smoother start and a much more mature middle palate, with typically rich, spicy, Dalmore flavours, but ends abruptly and rather woodily. SCORE 81

THE DALMORE 30-year-old Stillman's Dram, 45 vol

Releases under this rubric vary in age and style.

COLOUR Tangerine

NOSE Musky. Curaçao orange peels. Tomatoes in a hothouse. Geraniums.

BODY Lightly creamy.

PALATE Very sustained flavour development. Very spicy.
Christmas spices. Nutmeg, cinnamon.

FINISH Dusted pastry. Salt.

SCORE *81*

THE DALMORE 30-year-old Special Cask Finish
(Gonzalez Byass), 42 vol

COLOUR Full amber. Tawny.

NOSE Clotted cream stirred with honey, poured over nectarines.

BODY As sensuous as a massage.

PALATE Sweet, creamy, caramelized flavours. Crème brûlée.

FINISH Biscuity, with dark flavours. Like tiramisu with lots of
espresso and no vanilla sugar.

SCORE **82**

THE DALMORE 50-year-old, 52.6 vol

*Occasional bottlings. Some have contained proportions of far older whiskies, dating to
1868. The enjoyment is in the pleasure of tasting history. A whisky of this age has more
memory than muscle. (Available at the Sheraton Hotel, Edinburgh.)*

COLOUR Chestnut.

NOSE Astonishingly, the fruit is still discernible. Perfumy, polished oak.
Quickly moving to surprisingly fresh smokiness and oakiness.

BODY Has lost some fullness with age, but still some substance.

PALATE Orange, lemon pith, flowering currant, sap, oak, smoke.

FINISH Caramelized charred oak.

SCORE **85**

THE DALMORE 62-year-old, 40.5 vol

COLOUR Dark oak.

NOSE Hickory smoke. Mesquite. Or perhaps apple wood.
Very appetizing.

BODY Beeswax oiliness.

PALATE Orange. Mint. Menthol. Pipe tobacco. The big Dalmore
flavours have settled down in harmonious maturity.

FINISH Mild. Surprising lack of woody astringency.
There is even some sweetness.

SCORE **86**

DALWHINNIE

PRODUCER Diageo
REGION Highlands   DISTRICT Speyside
ADDRESS Dalwhinnie, Inverness-shire, PH19 1AB
TEL 01540 672219   VC
WEBSITE www.discovering-distilleries.com/www.malts.com

O NE OF THE HIGHEST DISTILLERIES in Scotland, at 326 metres (1,073 feet), Dalwhinnie has the Monadhlaith Mountains to one side, and the Forest of Atholl, the Cairngorms, and the Grampians to the other. Its name is Gaelic for "meeting place". The village of the same name stands at the junction of old cattle-droving routes from the west and north down to the central Lowlands. Much whisky smuggling went on along this route. The distillery was called Strathspey when it opened in 1897. It is near the upper reaches of the Spey, although Dalwhinnie represents the Highlands in Diageo's Classic Malts range.

HOUSE STYLE Lightly peaty. Cut grass and heather honey. Clear flavours against a very clean background. Aperitif.

DALWHINNIE 15-year-old, 43 vol

COLOUR Bright gold.
NOSE Very aromatic, dry, faintly phenolic, lightly peaty.
BODY Firm, slightly oily.
PALATE Remarkably smooth, long-lasting flavour development. Aromatic, heather-honey notes give way to cut-grass, malty sweetness, which intensifies to a sudden burst of peat.
FINISH A long crescendo.

SCORE 76

DALWHINNIE 15-year-old,
Friends of the Classic Malts Bottling, 56.9 vol

COLOUR Light gold.

NOSE Hard to get much on nose: sulphur, guava, coconut cream. Alcohol.

BODY Light and delicate.

PALATE Delicate, but better weight than the nose suggests. Tropical fruit.
More about feel than aroma.

FINISH Crisp. Oaky.

SCORE **70**

DALWHINNIE 1980, Double Matured, 43 vol
Oloroso finish.

COLOUR Sunny gold to bronze.

NOSE Oloroso, liquorice, rooty, grassy.

BODY Firm, rounded.

PALATE Very sweet, toffeeish start. Honey. Lemons. Long flavour
development to peatiness, cut grass, vanilla, and fresh oak. Beautiful
interplay and balance. The sherry sweetness seems, by contrast, to
accentuate the usually light peatiness of Dalwhinnie.

FINISH Very long. Cut grass, peat, smoke, oak.

SCORE **79**

DALWHINNIE 1973, 29-year-old, Special Release of 2003, 57.8 vol

COLOUR Restrained, warm gold.

NOSE Appetizingly fruity. Lemon grass. Orange juice on breakfast pancakes.

BODY Smooth. Textured.

PALATE Bursts with fruitiness. Apples, bananas?
Against cereal-grain background.

FINISH Refreshing. Lively. Scenty.

SCORE **78**

DALWHINNIE 1966, 36-year-old, Limited Bottling of 1500,
Bottled 2002, 47.2 vol

COLOUR Full gold. Hint of bronze.

NOSE Aromatic. Oily. Restrained peat. Some grassy, moorland aromas.

BODY Very light. As fresh as spring water.

PALATE Clean, very firm maltiness. Honey-glazed biscuits.
Pronounced vanilla. Slowly developing lively, appetizing moorland grass
and faint smokiness.

FINISH Very long and warming.

SCORE **79**

DEANSTON

PRODUCER Burn Stewart Distillers plc
REGION Highlands DISTRICT Eastern Highlands
ADDRESS Deanston, near Doune, Perthshire, FK16 6AG
TEL 01786 841422 WEBSITE www.burnstewartdistillers.com
enquiries@burnstewartdistillers.com

THE TOWN OF DOUNE was known in the 17th century for the manufacture of pistols, some of which may have seen service on the Spanish main. Now the old empire strikes back. The Trinidadian drinks company, Angostura, has acquired Burn Stewart, owners of the town's Deanston distillery. That enterprise itself has an interesting history. It is housed in a cotton mill, designed in 1785 by Richard Arkwright and extended in 1836. The mill was driven by the waters of the river Teith. The supply of good water apparently contributed to the decision to turn the building into a distillery at a time when the whisky industry was doing very well.

It opened as the Deanston distillery in 1965–66, with the vaulted weaving shed serving as a warehouse. The distillery prospered during the 1970s, but closed during the difficult mid-1980s. At the time it was owned by Invergordon. With the growth of interest in single malts in the late 1980s and early 1990s, Deanston was bought by the blenders, Burn Stewart, and more versions of this pleasant whisky became available.

HOUSE STYLE Light, slightly oily, nutty, accented toward a notably clean, malty sweetness. Restorative.

DEANSTON 6-year-old, 40 vol

Mainly for the French market.

COLOUR Light gold.

NOSE Lightly perfumed, grass, cream, muesli, slightly nutty.

BODY Soft and light.

PALATE Cereal-like with a soft mid-palate and a malty note. Slightly hard.

FINISH Green grape. Immaturity still there.

SCORE **70**

DEANSTON 12-year-old, 40 vol

COLOUR Very pale, greeny gold. Fino sherry.

NOSE Linseed oil.

BODY Light, smooth, soothing.

PALATE Malty, drying in finish. Reminiscent of a lightly nutty, dry sherry.

FINISH Again, very light, but a touch of nuttiness. In character, less of a
Highland malt than a very good Lowlander.

SCORE **70**

DEANSTON 17-year-old, 40 vol

COLOUR Markedly fuller. Bright bronze.

NOSE Linseed oil, grass, cereal grain, barley sugar.

BODY Light to medium.

PALATE Cereal grain, more emphatically nutty. Slightly creamy.

FINISH Nutty, appetizing.

SCORE **71**

DEANSTON 21-year-old, Limited Edition Decanter, 43 vol

COLOUR Copper.

NOSE Shows good maturity. Cashew, fruitcake, basil, coconut, box tree.

BODY Soft and gentle.

PALATE Oaky, light orange notes, clean juicy malt. Slight bitter note.

FINISH Dry, spicy, short.

SCORE **75**

DEANSTON 1992, Signatory, 46 vol

COLOUR Rich gold.

NOSE Sweet, clotted cream, estery. Privet, dry oak.

BODY Fir and dry.

PALATE Cashew nut, strawberry, becoming very dry. Dry oak and dry malt.

FINISH Nutty.

SCORE **67**

DRUMGUISH

PRODUCER Speyside Distillers Co. Ltd
REGION Highlands DISTRICT Speyside
ADDRESS Tromie Mills, Glentromie, Kingussie, PH21 1HS
TEL 01540 661060
WEBSITE www.speysidedistillers.co.uk VC By appointment

O NE OF THE NEWEST DISTILLERIES in Scotland, having made its
first spirit in 1991, and now beginning to develop a portfolio of
more mature whiskies. The handsome, gabled stone building
intentionally looks a hundred years old. Its opening was the realization
of a dream for its owner, George Christie, who had planned it for three
or four decades, his progress on the project ebbing and flowing with
the fortunes of the industry. One of his earlier essays was a vatted malt,
popular in the United States, under the name Glentromie.

Christie's distillery is at Drumguish, where the tiny river Tromie
flows into the highest reaches of the Spey. His company, Speyside,
takes its name not only from its location, but also from a distillery by
that name that operated in nearby Kingussie between 1895 and 1910.

HOUSE STYLE Oily, nutty, lightly peaty. Aperitif.

DRUMGUISH No Age Statement, 40 vol

COLOUR Full gold.

NOSE Flowery. Jasmine. Passion fruit.

BODY Medium, soft.

PALATE Cashew nuts and a sweetish dried-grass note that recalls great
Scotch whiskies of the past. Cookies. Toasted marshmallows.

FINISH Faintly kirsch-like, dry fruitiness. A bit abrupt.

SCORE **73**

SPEYSIDE 10-year-old, 43 vol

COLOUR Golden satin.

NOSE Pronounced oily nuttiness.

BODY Very light and soft.

PALATE Sweet, buttery, rich. Some cream toffee, cookies, and caramel.

FINISH Lightly dry. Leafy. Grain mustard. long

SCORE **75**

DUFFTOWN

PRODUCER Diageo
REGION Highlands DISTRICT Speyside (Dufftown)
ADDRESS Dufftown, Keith, Banffshire, AB55 4BR
TEL 01340 822100 WEBSITE www.malts.com

THE EARL OF FIFE, James Duff, laid out this handsome, hilly little town of stone buildings in 1817. The town's name is pronounced "duff-ton". Dufftown lies at the confluence of the rivers Fiddich and Dullan on their way to the Spey. There are six active malt distilleries in the town; a further two survive as buildings but are highly unlikely ever to operate again. A ninth, Pittyvaich, has recently been bulldozed.

Only one of the distilleries appropriates Dufftown as its name. This distillery and Pittyvaich, its erstwhile next-door neighbour, were both owned by Bell's until that company was acquired by United Distillers, now Diageo. Dufftown's stone-built premises were a meal mill until 1896, but they have since sprouted a pagoda, and were twice expanded in the 1970s. They now comprise one of Diageo's larger distilleries, but most of its output goes into Bell's, the biggest selling blend in the UK.

HOUSE STYLE Aromatic, dry, malty. Aperitif.

DUFFTOWN 15-year-old, Flora and Fauna, 43 vol

COLOUR Pale golden.
NOSE Assertively aromatic.
BODY Lightly syrupy.
PALATE Malty, on the dry side, becoming flowery.
FINISH Lingers, but very light.

SCORE **71**

DUFFTOWN 1979, Bottled 1997, Refill Sherry, Murray McDavid, 46 vol

COLOUR Full amber.

NOSE Toast. Marmaladey sherry.

BODY Medium, firm, oily.

PALATE Butter, honey, oranges. Toasty and grainy. Sesame-seed bagels.

FINISH Smoky. Slightly burnt and astringent.

A version distilled and bottled in those years, but with more sherry, at 57.1 vol, from Cadenhead, had an attractive, dark orange colour; a big aroma of oak, toast, orange, and cinnamon; a syrupy body; and a very fruity palate; finishing with dry malt and lots of sappy oak. SCORE 72

DUFFTOWN 1976, 20-year-old, Cask Strength, Rare Malts

Tasted as a work in progress.

COLOUR White wine.

NOSE Heather honey. Very honeyish.

BODY Medium, firm.

PALATE Lively, fruity, perfumy. Flapjacks. Shortbread. Fudge.

FINISH Ginger cookies. Sweetish smokiness.

DUFFTOWN 1975, 21-year-old, Cask Strength, Rare Malts, 54.8 vol

COLOUR Vinho verde.

NOSE Honey. Honeydew melon. Glace cherries. Waxy. Lipstick.

BODY Creamy, firm.

PALATE Remarkably fudgey. Treacle toffee.

FINISH Very gingery. Sweet, "leafy bonfires" smokiness.

EDRADOUR

PRODUCER Signatory Vintage Scotch Whisky Co. Ltd
REGION Highlands   DISTRICT Eastern Highlands
ADDRESS Pitlochry, Perthshire, PH16 5JP   TEL 01796 472095
WEBSITE www.edradour.co.uk   EMAIL info@edradour.fsbusiness.co.uk   VC

T HE COUNTRY'S SMALLEST DISTILLERY was returned to Scottish –
and independent – ownership in 2002. Edradour is a working
commercial distillery on a farmhouse scale, using very old, open
equipment, the function of which is easy to understand – a bonus for
the visitor. It is near the inland resort of Pitlochry, and within easy
reach of Edinburgh and Glasgow. The change in the ownership of
Edradour was greeted with widespread goodwill.

With the much bigger Speyside distillery, Aberlour, it had for some
years been a Scottish outpost of Pernod Ricard. With the acquisition
of Chivas Brothers' ten distilleries, the French found their hands full.
They had looked after Edradour well, but such a small distillery might
benefit from ownership by an individual. It was sold to Andrew
Symington, the enterprising founder of the independent bottler
Signatory. The creation of a new range is still in its early stages, with
the assistance of Iain Henderson, renowned manager of Laphroaig
until his reluctant retirement.

Edradour likes to trace its history back to the beginning of legal
whisky production in the Highlands in 1825, although the present
distillery is believed to have been founded in 1837. The distillery, at the
hamlet of Balnauld, above Pitlochry, is secreted by the hills.

HOUSE STYLE Spicy. Minty. Creamy. After dinner.

EDRADOUR 10-year-old, 40 vol

COLOUR Dark gold to pale amber.

NOSE Minty. Leafy.

BODY On the thin side. Firm.

PALATE Syrupy. Smoky.

FINISH Barbecue. Charcoal.

SCORE **79**

EDRADOUR 1991, 11-year-old, "Straight from the Cask", 60.2 vol

COLOUR Mahogany, with pink highlights.

NOSE Applewood. The embers of a fire.

BODY Syrupy.

PALATE Lots of sherry. Raisins. Nutty. Almonds.

FINISH Cloves. Peppermint. Medicinal. Hot.

SCORE **80**

EDRADOUR Cask Strength, 58 vol

COLOUR Dark amber.

NOSE Perfumy. Cherry blossom. Toffee.

BODY Fudgey creaminess.

PALATE Lovely balance of creaminess and toasty dryness.

FINISH Very spicy ginger marmalade and burnt toast.

SCORE **81**

EDRADOUR 1992, Unchillfiltered, 48 vol

COLOUR Bright gold. Paradoxically, the brightest of the flight.

NOSE Leafy. Vegetal.

Body Soft, smooth.

PALATE Creamy. Vanilla. Pepper.

FINISH Gentle. Soothing.

SCORE **81**

EDRADOUR 1976, Signatory Cask Strength Series, 54 vol

COLOUR Full gold to bronze.

NOSE Garden mint, grass, and peat.

BODY Decidedly creamy.

PALATE Very creamy-tasting. Slightly buttery.

FINISH Late, lively, spiciness.

SCORE **81**

FETTERCAIRN

PRODUCER Whyte and Mackay Ltd
REGION Highlands DISTRICT Eastern Highlands
ADDRESS Distillery Road, Fettercairn, near Laurencekirk,
Kincardineshire, AB30 1YE TEL 01561 340244 VC

THE ESTATE OF THE GLADSTONE FAMILY, who provided Queen Victoria with a famous Prime Minister, accommodates Old Fettercairn. This pretty, cream-painted distillery is amid farmers' fields on the edge of the village of attractive Georgian cottages from which it takes its name. The distillery was founded in 1824, and that date is now incorporated in the names of the whiskies. A malt called Fettercairn 1824, at 12 years old, is being introduced to replace the 10-year-old below. This new version will probably emerge with a similar score. Tasted as a work in progress, it seemed slightly paler in colour, with a Riesling aroma and a syrupy, spicy, palate.

HOUSE STYLE Lightly earthy, nutty. Easy drinking or aperitif.

OLD FETTERCAIRN 10-year-old, 40 vol

COLOUR Full gold.

NOSE Fresh, wet earth. Recent bottlings seem to have more (positive) wood extract. Freshly cut wood. Resiny. Distant sherry note. Scottish tablet. Honey.

BODY Smooth and light.

PALATE Clean and crisp. Toffee notes. Soft spiciness.

FINISH Dry, nutty, slight bitterness.

SCORE **77**

OLD FETTERCAIRN 30-year-old, Stillman's Dram, 45 vol

This replaces the 26-year-old Stillman's Dram.

COLOUR Bright, shimmering gold.

NOSE Creamy sherry. Toffee, raisins. Elegant sweetness.

BODY Medium, silky.

PALATE Sherry sweetness, then an outburst of spices.
Cinnamon, ginger. Dry hazelnut.

FINISH Dry, warm, and lingering.

SCORE **78**

OLD FETTERCAIRN 1972, 30-year-old, Cask No 2895, 53.6 vol

Mainly for Japan.

COLOUR Bright gold.

NOSE Malty and fruity. Stewed apples, vanilla. Hint of peat.

BODY Light to medium.

PALATE Smooth and surprisingly fresh. Cedary.
Delicate fudgey touch. Toasted almonds.

FINISH Dry, lingering, gently spicy.

SCORE **79**

OLD FETTERCAIRN 1973, 29-year-old, Cask No 1966, 54.3 vol

Mainly for Japan.

COLOUR Deep gold.

NOSE Sherry. Sultanas, dried apricots. Spices. Touch of burnt wood.

BODY Medium.

PALATE Assertively spicy (fresh ginger), almost tangy ,
with an oaky background.

FINISH Dry, warm and tingling.

SCORE **77**

OLD FETTERCAIRN 1966, 49.6 vol

COLOUR Autumn gold (or blazing gold ?).

NOSE Superb. Opulent sherry. Rich fruit. Flowery.
Toffeeish. Cedary, peppery. Beeswax.

BODY Light, silky.

PALATE At first, the promise of the aroma is not fulfilled. The palate
seems sweetly mellow and soft, but to the point of seeming tired.
Then the fruit and oak elegantly combine.

FINISH Warm, then quickly fading away. Soft spices in aftertaste.

SCORE **79**

GLEN ALBYN

PRODUCER DCL
REGION Highlands   DISTRICT Speyside (Inverness)
SITE OF FORMER DISTILLERY Telford Street, Inverness,
Inverness-shire, IV3 5LD

A COMPUTER SUPERSTORE AND a home-improvement store now stand on the site in Inverness once occupied by Glen Albyn, a distillery for 140 years, founded by a Provost (Mayor) of the city (generally regarded as the capital of the Highlands). Before the distillery, there was a brewery on the site. There is still a small pub, The Caley. The site is alongside one of Scotland's great feats of engineering, the Caledonian Canal, the dream of James Watt and Thomas Telford. The canal links the North Sea with the Atlantic by joining Loch Ness with a series of further lochs in the Great Glen (also known in parts as Glen Albyn or Glen Mor, More, or Mhor). There is an unconnected Glen Albyn pub in the centre of Inverness. Albyn is a variation on Albion or Alba, old names applied to Scotland, especially the Highlands.

The shopping strip from nowhere (or everywhere?) has not yet buried the individuality, the sensuous pleasure, and the Scottish pride afforded by a local distillery. There is still whisky, but for how long?

HOUSE STYLE Light. Fruity, nutty, dry. Aperitif.

GLEN ALBYN 26-year-old, Distilled 1975, Rare Malts, 54.8 vol

COLOUR Full primrose.

NOSE Very aromatic. Soapy. Linen. Suede

BODY Light but firm. Slippery.

PALATE Lightly buttery. Briefly syrupy. Malty. Smooth. Dry. Slightly musty.

FINISH Bitter. Brimstone. Quite explosive.

SCORE **70**

GLEN ALBYN 1974, 28 year-old, Coopers Choice, 46 vol

COLOUR Deep amber.

NOSE Sherry. Burnt wood. Dry hay. Fresh hazelnuts. Cloves.

BODY Light.

PALATE Cedary. A touch of harshness. Hint of cold smoke.
Seems to want a cigar.

FINISH Dry, nutty, quite lingering.

SCORE **70**

GLEN ALBYN 1974, Gordon & MacPhail, 40 vol

COLOUR Lemony gold.

NOSE Citrusy, herbal. Beeswax.

BODY Light, silky.

PALATE A warm roundness. Beautifully balanced. Creamy maltiness.

FINISH Soft, elegant, and almondy.

SCORE **74**

GLEN ALBYN 1974, Signatory, 58 vol

COLOUR Lemony gold.

NOSE Fragrant. Tangy. Earthy (wet soil after rain). Almond milk.

BODY Light.

PALATE Warm and fizzy. Open spiciness. Restrained nuttiness.

FINISH Dry, oaky, slightly astringent.

SCORE **70**

GLEN ALBYN 34 year-old, Douglas Laing, The Old Malt Cask, 47 vol

COLOUR Amber.

NOSE Sherry. Candied chestnut. Creamy fudge. Hint of cherry.

BODY Light to medium.

PALATE Smooth and soft. Dried fruit. Biting spices.

FINISH Soft and gentle but elusive.

SCORE **71**

GLEN DEVERON

PRODUCER John Dewar & Sons Ltd
REGION Highlands DISTRICT Speyside (Deveron)
ADDRESS Macduff Distillery, Banff, Banffshire, AB45 3JT
TEL 01261 812612

A WELL-KEPT, smart premises that at first sight clearly accommodates some kind of agricultural industry, though not obviously a malt distillery. Glen Deveron was built during the optimistic 1960s, when distillers could not keep up with demand. This distillery has a more workaday appearance than some of the architectural landmarks built by the whisky industry around that time. Its clean, uncluttered interior has in general been mirrored in the character of its whiskies. They, too, have been clean and uncluttered – whiskies that tasted of malt. They still do, but a newish 10-year-old, now the principal product, has a strong wood influence too.

The distillery is at the point where the glen of the Deveron reaches the sea, at the old fishing town and former spa of Macduff. (Both the distillery and its whiskies are sometimes known by the name Macduff.) On the other side of the river is the town of Banff. At a stretch, this is the western edge of Speyside. Not only is it a fringe location geographically – Glen Deveron was for years somewhat lonely as the sole distillery of the William Lawson company. The distillery's output has largely gone into the Lawson blends. Now Lawson, through the international Martini & Rossi group, is part of Bacardi, which also owns Dewars. Perhaps when Bacardi eventually settles into the whisky business, Glen Deveron will be accorded a higher profile.

HOUSE STYLE Malty. Sweet limes in older versions. Restorative or after dinner.

GLEN DEVERON 10-year-old, 1992, 40 vol

COLOUR Deep gold.

NOSE Freshly cut wood. Cedar-like. Surprisingly assertive.

BODY Light to medium. Notably smooth.

PALATE Malted milk. Condensed milk. Fig toffee. Butterscotch.
Thick yogurt. Slightly sour. Lemony

FINISH Crisp. Cinder toffee.

SCORE **72**

GLEN DEVERON 12-year-old, 40 vol

This version is now very hard to find.

COLOUR Gold.

NOSE Faint hints of sherry. Rich, sweet, fresh maltiness.

BODY Light to medium, but notably smooth.

PALATE Full, very clean, delicious maltiness.

FINISH Malty dryness. Quick but pleasantly warming.

SCORE **75**

A very malty 15-year-old, with a good balance of oak,
is also hard to find. SCORE 76

INDEPENDENT BOTTLINGS (AS MACDUFF)
MACDUFF 1988, Gordon & MacPhail, 40 vol

COLOUR Greeny gold.

NOSE Fragrant and lively. Fresh lime juice.

BODY Smoothly flowing.

PALATE Sweet barley sugar. Citrusy, lime-like freshness. Hint of honey.

FINISH Mellow, pleasantly warm.

SCORE **73**

MACDUFF 1969, Duncan Taylor, 40.3 vol

COLOUR Bright, greeny gold.

NOSE Complex. Malty and citrusy. Toffee. Restrained sherry notes.

BODY Dense, velvety.

PALATE Mellow, soothing. Fulfilling maltiness. A nutty touch.

FINISH Lingering but in a whispering tone.

SCORE **74**

GLEN ELGIN

PRODUCER Diageo
REGION Highlands DISTRICT Speyside (Lossie)
ADDRESS Longmorn, Elgin, Morayshire, IV30 3SL
TEL 01343 862000

A "HIDDEN MALTS" BOTTLING, at 12 years old, is a welcome response to those who have urged that this classic Speyside whisky be more readily available as a single. There had previously been a version at around the same level of maturity, but without an age statement. This had been marketed mainly in Japan. The newer expression seems more flowery and complex, while the previous version was more winey.

The distillery itself has never been hidden, but it was for some years heavily branded with the name White Horse, in recognition of its contribution to that blend. The Glen Elgin distillery is very visible on one of the main roads into the town whose name it bears. Although it is just over a hundred years old, its façade dates from 1964, and reflects the classic DCL still-house design of the period.

Where the River Lossie approaches the town of Elgin, there are no fewer than eight distilleries within a few miles. Elgin is also worth a visit for Gordon & MacPhail's whisky shop as well as 13th-century cathedral ruins.

HOUSE STYLE Honey and tangerines. Restorative or after dinner.

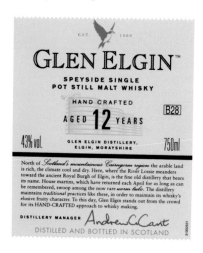

GLEN ELGIN 12 year-old, Hidden Malts, 43 vol

COLOUR Deep gold.

NOSE Fruity and flowery. Heather honey. Pears poached in spices.
Hint of coffee beans.

BODY Light but firm.

PALATE Fresh and crisp, flowery, and gingery. A touch of mandarin.

FINISH Dry and spicy.

SCORE **77**

GLEN ELGIN Centenary, 19-year-old, 60 vol

Bottle 297 of 750 to commemorate the first distillation on 1 May 1900.

COLOUR Pale amber, pinkish tinge.

NOSE Flowery heather honey, with spicy, cedary, oaky notes.

BODY Textured.

PALATE Warm honey. Seville orange. Toasted nuts.
Beautifully rounded. Elegant.

FINISH Fragrant. Long and creamy. Delicate smokiness.

SCORE **82**

GLEN ELGIN 32-year-old, Distilled 1971,
Special Release 2003, 42.3 vol

COLOUR Full gold.

NOSE Fragrant. Cedary. Honeyed. Seductive.

BODY Soft, rich, tongue-coating.

PALATE Clean, sweet. A hint of Seville orange. Intense heather honey.
Cereal grain. Crunchy. A lovely whisky.

FINISH Gently drying. Shortbread.

SCORE **81**

GLEN ELGIN 1968, Gordon & MacPhail, 40 vol

COLOUR Deep old gold.

NOSE Distinctively sherry. Exotic wood. Rich sweetness.
Candied orange. Crème brûlée.

BODY Medium, velvety.

PALATE Lusciously smooth. Oak and fruit elegantly mingled.
A touch of cinnamon.

FINISH Dry but rich and long. Hint of bitter chocolate.

SCORE **77**

GLEN FLAGLER

PRODUCER Inver House Distillers Ltd
REGION Lowlands DISTRICT Central Lowlands
ADDRESS Towers Road, Moffat, Airdrie, Lanarkshire, ML6 8PL
WEBSITE www.inverhouse.com EMAIL enquiries@inverhouse.com

A SECOND MANIFESTATION of these ghostly spirits has occurred in the new millennium. This is officially their last appearance, but do ghosts respect such sanctions?

Two malt whiskies were produced, under the names Glen Flagler and Killyloch, in different sets of stills – and a grain whisky called Garnheath in a third – at a complex at Moffat, near Airdrie, from 1965. These were some of the shortest lived distilleries in the history of Scotch whisky. The modern complex, in former paper mills, was intended to support the Inver House blends, then owned by Publicker, of Philadelphia, but was hit by one of the industry's cyclical downturns. Killyloch ceased production in the early 1970s, Glen Flagler and Garnheath in the mid-1980s, and the distilleries were dismantled. The warehouses were retained, and a management buy-out created Inver House (*see p. 76*), now Thai-owned.

Glen Flagler was briefly marketed as a single malt. Both it and Killyloch later manifested themselves as vatted malts. In the 1990s, when they seemed to have been lost for ever, the independent bottler Signatory located very small stocks of both malts, and issued them as singles. They were reviewed in the fourth edition of this book.

In 2003, there were official bottlings of both. These were from the last five casks of Glen Flagler (yielding 931 bottles) held by Inver House and the last six casks of Killyloch (371 bottles). The collectibility of these bottles is indicated by the asking price, retail: £425/$680 and £899/$1500 respectively.

HOUSE STYLE Glen Flagler is a spicy, perfumy restorative or aperitif – or, the 1973 edition, with cheese? Killyloch is grainier and sweeter, with dessert. Both have Lowland characters, though these are more obvious in Killyloch.

GLEN FLAGLER 1973, Bottled 2003, 46 vol

COLOUR Old gold.

NOSE Pronounced aroma of new leather. Floral.

BODY Light, slippery.

PALATE Oily, creamy. Smoked cheese.
Drier and more intense than the earlier bottling.

FINISH Dry. Strong, muscular.

SCORE **70**

GLEN FLAGLER 24-year-old, Distilled 1972, Bottled 1997, 52 vol

COLOUR Bright yellow.

NOSE Grassy. Linseed. Young leather.

BODY Medium, firm. Soapy dryness.

PALATE Lemony, oily, peaty.

FINISH Dry. Late, warming, pepperiness.

SCORE **70**

KILLYLOCH 1967, Bottled 2003, 40 vol

COLOUR Lemony yellow.

NOSE Very aromatic. Sourness remarkably like fresh lemon juice.

BODY Light but smooth.

PALATE Lemon sweets. Sherbet. Sweet vanilla. Sharper and
less creamy than the earlier bottling.

FINISH Spicy dryness. Crisp. Refreshing. A lamented Lowlander.

SCORE **68**

GLEN GARIOCH

PRODUCER Morrison Bowmore Distillers Ltd
REGION Highlands DISTRICT Eastern Highlands
ADDRESS Old Meldrum, Inverurie, Aberdeenshire, AB51 0ES
TEL 01651 873450 WEBSITE www.glengarioch.com

HOPES THAT GLENGARIOCH would reopen its maltings were kindled when the distillery was refurbished five or six years ago. They have thus far not materialized, but should not be abandoned. The proprietors have highlighted traditional aspects of both their other distilleries, and have a good story to tell at Glen Garioch.

First, there is the distillery's antiquity. An announcement in *The Aberdeen Journal* in 1785 refers to a licensed distillery on the same site. This makes it Scotland's oldest licence holder. Then there is location. The glen grows some of Scotland's finest barley – and here is one of the few distilleries with its own malting floors. Finally, there is the question of peat. When the distillery was acquired by its present owners, in 1970, their maltster, trained on Islay, was relatively heavy-handed with the peat. The result was a whisky with the "old-fashioned", smoky flavour that the Highland/Speyside region had largely forgotten. The revival of smoky Highlander could be popular at a time when the island whiskies seem to have seized the initiative.

Production stopped in 1995, but distillation restarted in 1997. The building's stonework, decorated with a clock that might grace a municipal building, faces on to the small town of Old Meldrum, on the road from Aberdeen to Banff.

HOUSE STYLE Lightly peaty, flowery, fragrant, spicy.
Aperitif in younger ages. Digestif when older.

GLEN GARIOCH Highland Tradition, 40 vol

COLOUR Gold.

NOSE Attractive, malty. Fresh, mandarin zest. Simple but charming.

BODY Light

PALATE Fresh and direct. Lively summer fruits. Malty.

FINISH Short but refreshing.

SCORE **75**

GLEN GARIOCH 8-year-old, 40 vol

COLOUR Full gold.

NOSE Autumn leaves, grass, hint of peat.

BODY Medium, smooth.

PALATE Malty start, buttery, but very clean. Then flapjack, nutty, lively flavours.

FINISH Late surge of ginger, honey, and heather.

SCORE **76**

GLEN GARIOCH 10-year-old, 40 vol

COLOUR Gold.

NOSE Aromatic and citric. Lemon icing, tinned peach, bran.
New carpets. Drier with water.

BODY Rounded but crisp.

PALATE Cereal with a creamy note playing off the firm maltiness.

FINISH Nutty. Short.

SCORE **75**

GLEN GARIOCH 12 year-old, 40 vol *(Mainly for Asian markets.)*

COLOUR Bronze.

NOSE Fragrant, leafy peatiness. Touch of dry oloroso?

BODY Medium, firm.

PALATE Interlocked heather-honey sweetness and peat-smoky dryness.

FINISH Echoes of both elements. Quick and warming.

SCORE **77**

GLEN GARIOCH 15-year-old, 43 vol

COLOUR Full gold.

NOSE Good whiff of earthy peat, oily smoke. Very aromatic.

BODY Medium, rich.

PALATE Very gradual development from malty, liquorice-like, rooty notes
through heathery, flowery, perfumy smokiness. Full of character.

FINISH Very long, spicy, warming.

SCORE **79**

GLEN GARIOCH 12-year-old, 40 vol

Special bottling for National Trust of Scotland.

COLOUR Rich gold

NOSE Tea bread, raisins, maltings, some sweetness. Chocolate.

BODY Medium.

PALATE Bran provides a crisp frame.
Dried fruits with some richness. Lunchtime.

FINISH Hay loft.

SCORE **75**

GLEN GARIOCH 21-year-old, 43 vol

*The most recent bottlings have more peat, oak, and sherry than
earlier versions at this age. A superb Highland malt.*

COLOUR Burnished amber.

NOSE Leathery, leafy, peaty, smoky, phenolic.

BODY Medium to full.

PALATE Sweet, juicy oak. Butter. Nutty, treacly, gingery cake.

FINISH Big and very smoky, but smooth. Lots of lingering toffee
and fruit. Currants. Flowering currant.

SCORE **81**

GLEN GARIOCH 18-year-old, Selected Cask Vatting, 59.4 vol

COLOUR Deep, warm gold.

NOSE Fresh, floral, fragrant, gentle. Peat-tinged.

BODY Surprisingly rich.

PALATE Rich, sweet, clean, syrupy maltiness.

FINISH Very long. Treacle toffee. Gingery spiciness. Rooty dryness.
Very warming. Extremely late echo of phenolic peat.

SCORE **80**

GLEN GARIOCH 27-year-old, Selected Cask Vatting, 49.6 vol

This bottling is now hard to find.

COLOUR Bright amber.

NOSE Softly peaty, still with a hint of phenol.

BODY Medium.

PALATE Interplay of malty sweetness and dryness.

FINISH Spicy. Pepper and earthy saltiness.

SCORE **80**

GLEN GARIOCH 1986, Individual Cask Bottling,
Cask No 3065, 250 Bottles Only, 54.4 vol

COLOUR Reddish.

NOSE Fig roll, black banana. Clove, boot polish, oloroso.
With water an artificial lavender note.

BODY Rich and rounded.

PALATE Rich, sweet perfumed and resinous.
The lavender perfume unbalances things.

FINISH Lightly smoky.

SCORE **70**

GLEN GARIOCH 29-year-old, Individual Cask Bottling, Distilled April 1968, Cask No 626, Hogshead, 56.6 vol

Strictly for the lover of long-matured, oaky whiskies.

COLOUR Very dark orange to chestnut.

NOSE Charred oak. Phenol. Earthy saltiness again.

BODY Big, firm.

PALATE Black-treacle toffee, developing late mint notes. Extra-strong peppermints. Very drying on the tongue.

FINISH Extraordinarily long. Cough sweets.

SCORE **81**

GLEN GARIOCH 200th Anniversary Limited Edition, 43 vol

Distilled in 1961, when Glen Garioch was scarcely peated, and when the stills were heated by coal rather than steam. Matured in first-fill American oak.

COLOUR Bright, deep gold.

NOSE Astonishingly fresh for a whisky of such age. Remarkably minty.

BODY Medium, firm, rounded.

PALATE Freshly soft and clean. Almost menthol-like, developing to a leafier, garden-mint note. Some tasters have found flavours reminiscent of star-fruit. Dryish, against a lightly syrupy malt background.

FINISH Long, minty, warming. Dryish hints of vanilla pod. Remarkably gentle.

SCORE **81**

INDEPENDENT BOTTLINGS

Cadenhead bottles an 11-year-old, distilled 1990, at 56.6 vol. Straw coloured with a nose as soft as American cream soda, it develops an attractive floral quality with water. The palate is summery, light and soft with clover honey sweetening the maltiness. SCORE 76. A 16-year-old single cask no 1585, at 51.9 vol, exclusive to The Whisky Exchange, has an aroma reminiscent of Darjeeling tea; treacle toffee in the palate and liquorice in the finish. SCORE 80

GLEN GRANT

PRODUCER Chivas Brothers
REGION Highlands   DISTRICT Speyside (Rothes)
ADDRESS Rothes, Morayshire, AB38 7BS   TEL 01340 832118   VC

A CHIC SUCCESS IN ITALY, and a Victorian classic in Scotland. Glen Grant was the lone single malt in many a bar from Glasgow to Genoa in the days when this form of whisky was scarcely known outside the Highlands. The distillery, founded in 1840 by John and James Grant, quickly gained a reputation for the quality of its whisky. James Grant, who was a prominent local politician, played a big part in bringing railways to the area, and they in turn distributed his product. The turreted and gabled offices in the "Scottish baronial" style, and the distillery, are set around a small courtyard. James Grant's son, a military major, brought plants from his travels in India and Africa, and created a garden in the glen behind the distillery. In 1995, the garden was restored and is open to visitors.

For the greater part of its history, and until the last couple of decades, Glen Grant has won its renown as a single malt in versions bottled by merchants. Older vintages can still be found bearing in small type the name of bottlers Gordon & MacPhail. Much the same classic label is now used under the name Glen Grant Distillery. Since 1977, the enterprise has been owned by Chivas. The whisky has long been a contributor to Chivas Regal, and is highly regarded by most blenders.

Glen Grant itself remains among the world's big-selling whiskies, but much of its volume is in the younger ages, especially in the important Italian market, where it has been marketed at five years. The version with no age statement, which is the principal Glen Grant in Britain, contains malt less than 10 years old.

HOUSE STYLE Herbal, with notes of hazelnut. In younger ages,
an aperitif; with sherry age, after dinner.

GLEN GRANT 5-year-old, 40 vol

COLOUR Very pale, white wine.

NOSE Light, dry fruitiness, spirity.

BODY Light, slightly sticky, almost resiny.

PALATE Spirity. Pear brandy.

FINISH Fruity, quick.

SCORE **65**

GLEN GRANT No Age Statement, 40 vol

COLOUR Gold.

NOSE Fruity, flowery, nutty, faintly spirity.

BODY Light but firm.

PALATE Dry, slightly astringent at first, becoming soft and nutty.

FINISH Herbal.

SCORE **74**

GLEN GRANT 10-year-old, 43 vol

COLOUR Full gold.

NOSE Still dry, but much softer, with some sweetness.

BODY Light to medium, with no obvious intervention of sherry.

PALATE Lightly sweet start, quickly becoming nutty and very dry.

FINISH Very dry, with herbal notes.

SCORE **76**

GLEN GRANT 15-year-old, Gordon & MacPhail, 40 vol

COLOUR Medium amber.

NOSE Some sherry.

BODY Light to medium.

PALATE Sherryish, soft and nutty, dry.

FINISH Mellow, warming.

SCORE **80**

GLEN GRANT 21-year-old, Gordon & MacPhail, 40 vol

Take it slowly, and appreciate the subtlety and development.

COLOUR Full amber red.

NOSE Lots of sherry.

BODY Medium, soft.

PALATE Sherryish sweetness at first, then malt and grassy-peaty notes, finally the nutty Glen Grant dryness.

FINISH Lingering, flowery.

SCORE *81*

GLEN GRANT 25-year-old, Gordon & MacPhail, 40 vol

Not so much chess as wrist wrestling, with the sherry coming out on top. A robust version.

COLOUR Dark.

NOSE Lots of sherry.

BODY Medium, firm.

PALATE Dry oloroso character at first, then nutty dryness. A lot of depth.

FINISH Deep, flowery, peaty.

SCORE *81*

GOOD TO GO, AT 50-PLUS

The Grants of Rothes and the Urquharts of Elgin were both
Victorian entrepreneurs in the durable Scottish mould. Some equally
durable Glen Grants slumber among the 7000 casks in the warehouse
of the Urquhart's little shop, Gordon & MacPhail. On the facing
page is a trio that got away ... went on the bottle. Each is more
than 50 years old.

GLEN GRANT 1950, Gordon & MacPhail, 40 vol

COLOUR Gold with copper glints.

NOSE Very perfumed. Violet, rhubarb, nutty, stewed fruit.
Complex slightly faded.

BODY Delicate, a lacy texture.

PALATE Ethereal. Oak, resin, sandalwood. Nutmeg, lanolin.
Soft smoke in background.

FINISH Lightly smoky.

SCORE **83**

GLEN GRANT 1952, Gordon & MacPhail, 40 vol

COLOUR Gold.

NOSE Gentle, sweet, and fragrant. Herbal, green fern,
light smoke, beechnut, smoky.

BODY Soft, rounded, and gentle.

PALATE Autumn bonfires, nuts, a rich complex body. Heather. Rooty. Old.

FINISH Smoke. Still sweet.

SCORE **86**

GLEN GRANT 1953, Gordon & MacPhail, 45 vol

COLOUR Mahogany with dull yellow/green rim.

NOSE Chicory coffee, acorn, walnut, chestnut paste.

BODY Tight and firm.

PALATE Dry, tannic, black tobacco, bitter chocolate. Very dry.

FINISH Espresso. Bitter.

SCORE **73**

GLEN KEITH

PRODUCER Chivas Brothers
REGION Highlands   DISTRICT Speyside (Strathisla)
ADDRESS Station Road, Keith, Banffshire, AB55 3BS

CHIVAS OWNS TWO DISTILLERIES next door to one another in the town of Keith, on the River Isla. One simply takes the name of the district, Strathisla; the other is Glen Keith, which was built on the site of a corn mill in 1957–60. It was one of the first of a new generation of malt distilleries at that time, and was intended as a showpiece for a blend called Passport. The branding on the building has the feel of a late 1950s time warp.

Glen Keith had the first gas-fired still in Scotland, and pioneered the use of computers in the industry. Some 1960s' distillates were bottled by Gordon & MacPhail in the 1980s. A less chewy official bottling, initially with a 1983 vintage date, made its debut in 1993–94. The whisky is now simply identified as being 10 years old.

HOUSE STYLE Gingery, rooty, tart. Before dinner.

GLEN KEITH 10-year-old, 43 vol

COLOUR Solid gold.

NOSE Flower petals. Lemon grass. Rooty. Ginger. Cedar. Oak.

BODY Medium.

PALATE Sweet, chewy, ginger cake.

FINISH Very late, fruity tartness.

SCORE 73

GLEN MHOR

PRODUCER DCL
REGION Highlands DISTRICT Speyside (Inverness)
SITE OF FORMER DISTILLERY Telford Street, Inverness, Inverness-shire, IV3 5LU

Purists pronounce it the Gaelic way, "Glen Vawr", to rhyme with "law". The distillery, built in 1892 in Inverness and demolished in 1986, was one of several at which the poet, novelist, and pioneering whisky writer, Neil Gunn, worked as an exciseman. In his book, *Scotch Missed*, Brian Townsend writes that Gunn was inspired by Glen Mhor to let slip his observation that "until a man has had the luck to chance upon a perfectly matured malt, he does not really know what whisky is". Even in Gunn's day, Glen Mhor could be found as a single malt, and casks still find their way into independent bottlings.

HOUSE STYLE Aromatic, treacly. Quite sweet. With dessert or after dinner.

GLEN MHOR, 22-year-old, Distilled 1979, Bottled 2001, Rare Malts, 61 vol

COLOUR Shimmery old gold.

NOSE Surprisingly fresh, minty, and herbal.

BODY Lightly syrupy. Texture reminiscent of whipped cream. Rose-water, sherbet. Meringue on a shortbread base.

FINISH Distinctly leafy and grassy.

SCORE 78

SOME INDEPENDENT BOTTLINGS

GLEN MHOR 1979, Gordon & MacPhail, "Cask" Series, 66.7 vol

COLOUR Deep gold to peach.

NOSE Liquorice. Rooty. Grassy.

BODY Rich.

PALATE Liquorice, treacle toffee, madeira.

FINISH Winey acidity. Hessian. Light oak. Toast. Spicy warmth.

SCORE **77**

GLEN MHOR Vintage 1977, Signatory, Cask No 1546, 43 vol

COLOUR Greeny gold.

NOSE Soft liquorice. Waxy.

BODY Light but smooth, and oily.

PALATE Liquorice. Fruit gums. Lemon jelly. Quite sweet.

FINISH Limes. Chilli.

SCORE **72**

GLEN MHOR 20-year-old, Distilled 1976, Cadenhead, 57.9 vol

COLOUR Primrose.

NOSE Light lipstick.

BODY Light to medium. Syrupy.

PALATE Sugary. Lemony. Flowery, perfumy, lemon character.

FINISH Sherbety. Spicy, becoming drier. Warming.

Wins points for balance, especially in that late dryness.

SCORE **74**

GLEN MHOR 21-year-old, Distilled 1976, Hart Brothers, 43 vol

COLOUR Pale greeny gold.

NOSE Fruit gums. Lemon. Lime. Developing to lemon grass.

BODY Syrupy but gritty (like a golden, sweet molasses).

PALATE Sugary. Lemony. Then a lemon-pith dryness.

FINISH Sugar. Strong peppermint sweets. Mint imperials.

Warming. Long. Digestif.

SCORE **73**

GLEN MORAY

PRODUCER Glenmorangie plc
REGION Highlands   DISTRICT Speyside (Lossie)
ADDRESS Bruceland Road, Elgin, Morayshire, IV30 1YE   TEL 01343 542577
WEBSITE www.glenmoray.com   EMAIL tdavidson@glenmorangieplc.co.uk

THE GRAPEY NOTE that some devotees find in Glen Moray is a house characteristic. It preceded the distillery's enthusiasm for wine finishes, most recently Vallée du Rhône. The earlier Chardonnay and Chenin Blanc finishes, launched in 1999, seemed to be aimed at ladies who lunch. The use of whites was an innovation in the industry. Glen Moray shares owners with the more northerly Glenmorangie distillery, which pioneered the notion of "wine" finishes but with reds, port, and madeira.

The two distilleries' similar names pre-date their common ownership. It is a second coincidence that both were formerly breweries. Glen Moray was converted into a distillery in 1897, acquired by its present owners in the 1920s, and extended in 1958. Its whiskies are admired, but have never enjoyed great glamour. Now they sport a change of orientation: skirts instead of kilts – the distillery previously favoured gift tins decorated with the liveries of Highland regiments. The smartly kept distillery is in boggy land near the river Lossie, just outside Elgin.

HOUSE STYLE Grassy, with barley notes. Aperitif.

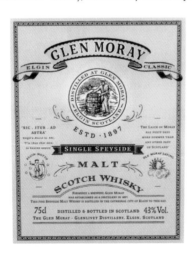

GLEN MORAY 8-year-old, 43 vol

Mainly available in Italy.

COLOUR Very pale, satiny gold.

NOSE Fresh but soft. Sweet, with a late, oily hint of peat.

BODY Very light, but smooth and oily.

PALATE Very light indeed. Oily. Gin-like.

FINISH Light touch of cereal-grain firmness. Late, very light, smoky warmth.

SCORE **71**

GLEN MORAY Single Speyside Malt, No Age Statement, 40 vol

Six to ten years in bourbon casks, then "mellowed" in Chardonnay.

COLOUR Very pale gold.

NOSE Fresh, scented, fruity. Like an unpeeled dessert grape.
Perhaps a suggestion of banana. Very light hint of the sea.

BODY Very soft, textured.

PALATE Watermelon. Banana. White chocolate. Lightly creamy. Shortbread.

FINISH Grape skins. Apple cores. Hay. Cereal grains.
Lightly dry and very crisp.

SCORE **78**

GLEN MORAY 12-year-old, "Mellowed" in Chenin Blanc, 40 vol

COLOUR Softer, more yellowy.

NOSE Pears. Walnuts. Fresh oak.

BODY Smooth, oily. Beeswax. Honeyed.

PALATE Pears in cream. Late, lively, peachy fruitiness. Garden mint.

FINISH Raisiny. Also resiny. Fresh oak. Soothing warmth.

SCORE **76**

GLEN MORAY 16-year-old, "Mellowed" in Chenin Blanc, 40 vol

COLOUR Old gold.

NOSE Very aromatic. Hint of cloves. Apples. Tannin.

BODY Smooth and very firm.

PALATE More assertive. Toffee, apple, oak.

FINISH Long. Hints of peat. Grassy. Leafy. Resiny. Peppery.

SCORE **76**

GLEN MORAY 1981, Single Sherry Butt, Cask No 3661, 57.7 vol

COLOUR Chestnut.

NOSE Honeydew melon. A hint of garden mint. Milk pudding. Caramel. Cedar.

PALATE Creamy. Spicy. Sultanas. Plum cake. Nougat. Some toffeeish chewiness. Rich but mature.

FINISH Slightly burnt. Slightly rooty and woody.

SCORE **82**

GLEN MORAY 1976, Vallée du Rhône, 46 vol

COLOUR Pinky sunset.

NOSE Soft and ripe. Bruised plum, caramelized fruit, dried orange peel, vanilla.

PALATE Slick and soft, plum cake and crackerbread. Orange peel.

FINISH Winey, soft.

SCORE **75**

GLEN MORAY DISTILLERY Manager's Choice 1974, 53.2 vol

COLOUR Old gold.

NOSE Perfumed candles. Wax. Smoke. Joss sticks. Spicy.

BODY Oily, Creamy, malty.

PALATE Drying.

FINISH Slightly sharp. Provocative.

SCORE **77**

SOME VINTAGE EDITIONS OF GLEN MORAY
GLEN MORAY 1974, Port Wood Aged, Limited Edition, Bottled 1997

COLOUR Full gold.

NOSE Lovely, perfumy complexity.

BODY Far richer than other versions.

PALATE Oily cereal grain. Honey-roast nuts.

FINISH Perfumy again. Sugared almonds. An after-dinner malt of extraordinary delicacy. Beautiful balance of distillery character and port.

SCORE **80**

GLEN MORAY 1973, 43 vol

COLOUR Pale gold, with a tinge of green.

NOSE Very sweet, but still extremely clean.

BODY Very smooth indeed.

PALATE Very complex, with lots of development of sweet (barley, malt and chocolate), delicately spicy notes.

FINISH Light sweetness and light peatiness. Long and lingering, with surges of flavour.

SCORE **78**

GLEN MORAY 1966, 43 vol

COLOUR Solid amber.

NOSE Nutty, juicy, oaky but fresh.

BODY Smooth, soft.

PALATE Nutty dryness, malty sweetness, and a hint of grassy peatiness, beautifully balanced and rounded. A confident, elegant malt.

FINISH Sweetness and dryness, with the latter eventually winning. Touches of sappy oakiness. A curiously spicy lift at the very end.

SCORE **80**

GLEN MORAY 1959, Bottled 1999, 48.4 vol

COLOUR Full amber.

NOSE Rich fruitcake steeped in sherry.

BODY Very creamy indeed.

PALATE Rich. Fruitcake. The dryness of burnt currants. Intensely nutty, almondy, marzipan development.

FINISH Light, nutty dryness. Chewy. Long. Developing a touch of charred oak.

SCORE **79**

GLEN ORD

PRODUCER Diageo
REGION Highlands DISTRICT Northern Highlands
ADDRESS Muir of Ord, Ross-shire, IV6 7UJ TEL 01463 872004
WEBSITE www.discovering-distilleries.com/www.malts.com VC

THE LAUNCH IN 2003 of a 12-year-old "Hidden Malt" from Glen Ord was very welcome, but begged a question. Why was it hidden in the first place? Why has this distillery been obliged to play hide-and-seek over the years? Under different managements, its whisky has occupied endless different positions in the marketing portfolio. It has even sported different names: Glenordie, Ordie, Ord, Muir of Ord.

It is at a village called Muir of Ord ("the moor by the hill"), just to the west and north of Inverness. This is the region where Ferintosh, the first famous whisky, was made (*see also* Ben Wyvis). Glen Ord also has a maltings (of the drum type). The distillery and maltings look over the barley-growing country of the Black Isle.

HOUSE STYLE Flavoursome, rose-like, spicy (cinnamon?),
and malty, with a dry finish. After dinner.

GLEN ORD 12-year-old, Hidden Malt, 43 vol

COLOUR	Full gold.

NOSE Fresh. Turned earth, daffodil. Resiny. Sultana, malt. Hint of sulphur.

BODY Medium, firm.

PALATE Dry grass, warm cinnamon, then toffee. Good punch.

FINISH Malt and oak.

SCORE 78

GLEN ORD 1974, 23-year-old, Rare Malts, 60.8 vol

COLOUR Very pale primrose.

NOSE Very fresh, assertive. Leafy, lightly peaty. Fragrant smoke.

BODY Big, soft, slightly syrupy.

PALATE Nutty malt, raisins, ginger, lemon peel, roses.

FINISH Spicy, flowery, peaty.

SCORE **78**

GLEN ORD 28-year-old, Distilled 1975,
Special Release 2003, 58.3 vol

COLOUR Primrose.

NOSE The slightest hint of smokiness. Crusty bread baking.
Sweeter than ordinary bread; brioche, perhaps.

BODY Medium.

PALATE Assertive. Honeyed. Expressive. Spicy. Unusually lively.

FINISH Extraordinary explosion of sweet-and-sour flavours. Spicy. Vanilla.
Flowery. Leafy. Lemon juice.

SCORE **82**

GLEN ORD 1983, Signatory, 58.3 vol

COLOUR Gold.

NOSE Attractive. Meadow grass. Fresh malt. Stewed orange, vanilla.
Toasty wood, cedar.

BODY Silky. Liqueur-like.

PALATE French patisserie. Red fruits. Oranges.

FINISH Grassy.

SCORE **80**

GLEN SCOTIA

PRODUCER Loch Lomond Distillery Co. Ltd
REGION Campbeltown
ADDRESS 12 High Street, Campbeltown, Argyll, PA28 6DS
TEL 01586 552288 *Visits by appointment only*
EMAIL mail@lochlomonddistillery.com

LOVERS OF CAMPBELTOWN MALTS will be pleased to learn that a new bottling of Glen Scotia is envisaged around the middle of this decade, but that is not yet certain. If it materializes, it is likely to be an eight-year-old.

Glen Scotia has been in full production since 1999, after being acquired by the Loch Lomond company. Production had been very sporadic for more than a decade before that. The only official bottling for some years has been a 14-year-old, and there are still stocks available. By now, much of the vatting must comprise older whiskies. This would account for a slightly rounder, less fresh character. Glen Scotia, founded around 1832, is known for more than one manifestation of spirit: it is said to be haunted by the ghost of a former proprietor who drowned himself in Campbeltown Loch.

HOUSE STYLE Fresh, salty. Aperitif, or with salty foods.

GLEN SCOTIA 14-year-old, 40 vol

COLOUR Full, refractive gold.

NOSE Aromatic, waxy, piney.

BODY Seems light on the tongue, then quickly becomes oily and smooth.

PALATE Dry maltiness, coconut, saltiness. Very appetite-arousing.

FINISH Long and robust.

SCORE 86

INDEPENDENT BOTTLINGS

*Glen Scotia is hard to find, and good casks even more elusive,
judging from the quality of independent bottlings.*

GLEN SCOTIA 1991, Lombard Brands, 50 vol

COLOUR White.

NOSE Harsh, vegetal, sulphury.

BODY Thin.

PALATE Hot with raw edges. Lacks maturity.

FINISH Short.

SCORE **60**

GLEN SCOTIA 1990, Gordon & MacPhail, 40 vol

COLOUR Gold.

NOSE A little metallic. Stewed fruit.

BODY Dry. Drying.

PALATE Malty. Falls apart in the mouth.

FINISH Short.

SCORE **67**

GLEN SCOTIA 1990, Signatory, 43 vol

COLOUR Pale gold.

NOSE A touch of smoke. Intense and zesty.

BODY Light. Dry.

PALATE A raw edge. Lacks substance.

FINISH Short, dry.

SCORE **70**

GLEN SPEY

PRODUCER Diageo
REGION Highlands DISTRICT Speyside (Rothes)
ADDRESS Rothes, Aberlour, Banffshire, AB38 7AU
TEL 01340 882000

A FLORA AND FAUNA BOTTLING launched in 2002 renders this distillery slightly more visible. It is in the heart of Speyside, but not on the river. Glen Spey, dating from the 1880s, is in Rothes. Much of its whisky is destined for the house blend of an aristocratic wine and spirits merchant in St James's, London. (It is coincidence that neighbour Glenrothes follows a parallel path). In the case of Glen Spey, the merchant is Justerini & Brooks, whose house blend is J&B.

Giacomo Justerini was an Italian, from Bologna. He emigrated to Britain in pursuit of an opera singer, Margherita Bellion, in 1749. The romance does not seem to have come to fruition, but Justerini meanwhile worked in Britain as a maker of liqueurs. By 1779, he was already selling Scotch whisky. Brooks was a later partner in the firm. The business was for a time part of Gilbeys, at which point there was for a time a nutty, grassy eight-year-old Glen Spey.

HOUSE STYLE Light, grassy, nutty. Aperitif.

SPEYSIDE
SINGLE MALT
SCOTCH WHISKY

The Scots Pines beside *the ruins of*
ROTHES CASTLE, provide an *ideal habitat*
for the *GOLDCREST*, *Britain's smallest bird*,
and overlook the

GLEN SPEY

distillery. Founded in 1885, *the distillery was*
originally part of the *Mills of Rothes*. Water
from the DOONIE BURN is used to produce
this *smooth, warming single MALT SCOTCH*
WHISKY. A slight sense of *wood smoke* on
the nose is rewarded with a *spicy, dry* finish.

AGED 12 YEARS

43% vol   Distilled & Bottled in *SCOTLAND*
GLEN SPEY DISTILLERY Rothes, Aberlour, Banffshire, Scotland   70cl

GLEN SPEY 12 year-old, Flora and Fauna, 43 vol

COLOUR Full gold.

NOSE Cookie-like maltiness (rich tea biscuit), dusty floor.
Kumquat. Leafy. Garden mint.

BODY Medium. Oily.

PALATE Vivacious. Starts intensely sweet, with light citrus notes,
then becomes dramatically drier.

FINISH Crisp. Lemon zest. Pith.

SCORE **75**

GLEN SPEY 19-year-old, Cadenhead, 57 vol

COLOUR Light gold.

NOSE Very light. Some lime leaf, dry grass, oak, green walnut.

BODY Thin.

PALATE Light residual sweetness but overall dry.

FINISH Cayenne and citrus.

SCORE **70**

GLEN SPEY 1974, 26-year-old, Cask No 792, Signatory, 50.4 vol

COLOUR Straw.

NOSE Corn husks, cream light and grassy. Touch of mint.

BODY Fluffy.

PALATE Tiger nuts, apple sponge, cream, green grapes.

FINISH Sweet and light.

SCORE **75**

GLENALLACHIE

PRODUCER Chivas Brothers
REGION Highlands DISTRICT Speyside
ADDRESS Aberlour, Banffshire, AB38 9LR

TRUE WHISKY LOVERS LIKE TO SAMPLE EVERYTHING, and Glenallachie (pronounced "glen-alec-y") is certainly worth tasting. Although it has only a modest reputation, it is a good example of a subtle, delicate, flowery Speyside malt.

The distillery was built in 1967 primarily to contribute malt to the Mackinlay blends. It was temporarily closed in the late 1980s, then acquired and reopened by Campbell Distillers at the end of the decade.

A dam and a small waterfall soften the exterior of the functional, modern distillery building. It takes its water from a spring on Ben Rinnes, just over the hill from its senior partner, Aberlour. Despite their proximity, their water is different, and so is their whisky: Glenallachie lighter, more acidic, drier, more delicate; Aberlour richer, more luscious, sweeter, maltier.

HOUSE STYLE Clean, subtle, delicate. Aperitif.

GLENALLACHIE 12-year-old, 40 vol

A Mackinlay bottling that is now difficult to find. A graceful pre-dinner companion.

COLOUR Very pale.

NOSE Hint of peat. Fragrant. Lightly malty.

BODY Light but firm.

PALATE Beautifully clean, smooth, and delicate.

FINISH Starts sweet and develops towards a long, perfumy finish.

SCORE 76

GLENBURGIE

PRODUCER Allied Distillers Ltd
REGION Highlands DISTRICT Speyside (Findhorn)
ADDRESS Forres, Morayshire, IV36 0QX TEL 01343 850258

A RARE RELEASE OF GLENBURGIE as a single malt came in 2002, when proprietors Allied launched their range of Special Distillery Bottlings. These 15-year-olds are primarily for sale at the group's distilleries, but will no doubt find their way farther afield. This example is a long overdue reminder of an enjoyable malt.

A noted admirer of Glenburgie's herbal, fruity whisky was writer Maurice Walsh, whose story *The Quiet Man* was made into a movie starring John Wayne and Maureen O'Hara. Like Robert Burns and Neil Gunn, writer Walsh had a "day job" as an exciseman, in his case at Glenburgie. A less romantic, more technical claim to the noteworthiness of this distillery is its second malt whisky.

The distillery traces its history to 1810, and on its present site to 1829. It is in the watershed of the Findhorn, at Alves, between Forres and Elgin. Glenburgie was extended after the Second World War, at a time when many whiskies were in short supply. At that time, some Allied distilleries were being given additional stills of a different design, to extend their range. These "Lomond" stills, with a column-shaped neck, produced an oilier, fruitier malt. The whisky from Glenburgie's Lomond stills was named after Willie Craig, one of the company's senior managers. Those stills were removed in the early 1980s, but Glencraig can still be found in independent bottlings.

HOUSE STYLE Oily, fruity, herbal. Aperitif.

GLENBURGIE 15 year-old, 46 vol

COLOUR Bright gold.

NOSE Attractive sweetness, fragrant. Praline,
touch of orange peel.

BODY Medium, firm.

PALATE Round, velvety. Assertive. Fruity, toffeeish.

FINISH Dry, leafy. Hint of liquorice.

SCORE **76**

SOME INDEPENDENT BOTTLINGS OF GLENBURGIE
GLENBURGIE 12 year-old, Douglas Laing,
The Old Malt Cask, 50 vol

COLOUR Pale gold.

NOSE Oaky, gingery. Fresh oak, lemon zest.

BODY Oily, medium.

PALATE Smooth, clinging. Fruity. Touch of cinnamon. Walnut.

FINISH Dry, lingering.

SCORE **72**

GLENBURGIE 10-year-old, 40 vol, Gordon & MacPhail

COLOUR Full gold.

NOSE   Touch of sour cream.

BODY Light and smooth.

PALATE Sweet and soft. Buttery fudge.
Fermentation flavours.

FINISH Quick, sweet then oaky.

SCORE **67**

GLENBURGIE 1967, Signatory, 53 vol

COLOUR Bright, sparkling gold.

NOSE Quite complex. Malty and fruity. Beeswax. Citrus touch.

BODY Velvety, oily, firm.

PALATE Rich. Developing fruit and cream. Coating.
Tangy without water.

FINISH Spicy followed by a soothing sweetness.

SCORE **74**

GLENBURGIE 1966, Duncan Taylor, 40.7 vol

COLOUR Light gold.

NOSE Complex, charming. Flowery, honey. Pipe tobacco.
Hint of smoke. Liquorice.

BODY Round, oily.

PALATE Delicate smoothness. Juicy fruitiness, kiwi, pears.
A touch of smoke. Lighthearted sherry.

FINISH Sensuous, lasting. Slow fade to soft spiciness.

SCORE **76**

SOME INDEPENDENT BOTTLINGS OF GLENCRAIG
GLENCRAIG 1981, 21 year-old, Cadenhead, 56.2 vol

COLOUR Full gold.

NOSE Intense. Definitely sherry. Resiny. Strong coffee. Cloves.

BODY Firm, oily.

PALATE Powerful. Smooth to start then develops lively spiciness.

FINISH Very warm, with a slight bitter touch. Seems everlasting.

SCORE **68**

GLENCRAIG 1975, Gordon & MacPhail, 40 vol

COLOUR Deep gold.

NOSE Aromatic elegancy. Leafy. Rich fruit. Apricot. Almonds.

BODY Very oily, round.

PALATE Appetizing spiciness. Rich. Dried fruit. Toffee. Nourishing.

FINISH Warming and fulfilling.

SCORE **73**

GLENCADAM

PRODUCER Angus Dundee Distillers plc
REGION Highlands DISTRICT Eastern Highlands
ADDRESS Brechin, Angus, DD9 7PA TEL 01356 622217

WHEN MERCHANT AND INDEPENDENT bottler Angus Dundee acquired its first distillery, Tomintoul, there were no dramatic changes. The same may be true of this one, its second acquisition. Glencadam's previous owners, Allied, have not aggressively promoted their distilleries, either, though the 15-year-old Glencadam reviewed below was from their series of Special Distillery Bottlings.

Glencadam is a notably creamy malt. Appropriately, much of the distillery's output has over the years gone into "Cream of the Barley", originally blended in Dundee, but popular in Belfast.

The neat little distillery, at Brechin, was founded in 1825 and modernized in 1959. The very soft water is piped an astonishing 48 km (30 miles) from Loch Lee, at the head of Glen Esk. With neighbour North Port now gone, Glencadam is a lonely survivor on this stretch of coastline.

HOUSE STYLE Creamy, with a suggestion of berry fruits.
With dessert, or after dinner.

GLENCADAM 15-year-old, 46 vol

COLOUR Old gold.

NOSE Perfumy. Floral, elegant. Ripe summer fruit. Plum pudding, peach melba.

BODY Full, silky.

PALATE Smooth, mouth-coating. So creamy. Strawberry yogurt.
Rounded and appealing.

FINISH A little shy but sweet and satisfying.

SCORE **73**

GLENDRONACH

PRODUCER Allied Distillers Ltd
REGION Highlands DISTRICT Speyside (Deveron)
ADDRESS Forgue, by Huntly, Aberdeenshire, AB5 6DB
TEL 01466 730202 VC

THE BEST NEWS for malt lovers in 2002 was the restarting of production at Glendronach, after six years' silence. At the same time, the distillery's owners took a new interest in making its products available, with plans for a new bottling at 12 years old. This new version will have a light touch of sherry, rounded with a reracking in bourbon barrels. Over the years, Glendronach 12 has appeared in a confusion of styles. At one stage, there was a welcome choice between "The Original" (second-fill, mainly bourbon) and a version labelled "100 per cent matured in sherry casks". These two were then replaced by "Traditional", which attempted to marry their virtues. Stock problems led to this being replaced by a 15-year-old, which is itself now becoming hard to find.

The whiskies are greatly appreciated by malt lovers, but much affection is also felt for the place. Deep in Aberdeenshire's fertile barley-growing country, the glen of the Dronac Burn almost hides the cluster of buildings, but a pagoda is hard to conceal. The floor maltings have not restarted, but there have been suggestions that they might. A flourish of tradition that has been rekindled is the use of coal-fired, direct-flame stills. While steam heats more evenly, flame creates hot spots, which can promote a caramel-ish, toffee-like maltiness.

The distillery has its own small mansion house, flower beds and kitchen garden, as though it were a small estate. (Domaine Dronac?)

The fifth Duke of Gordon, the man behind the legalization of distilling in the Highlands in the 1820s, is credited with having encouraged local farmers to establish this distillery. It was later run by a member of the William Grant (Glenfiddich) family, and in 1960 was acquired to help provide the malty background to the well-known blend Teacher's, now owned by Allied. Teacher's own principal distillery was Ardmore. As that is nearby in Aberdeenshire, and was also coal-fired until recently.

HOUSE STYLE Smooth, big, with a teasing sweet-and-dry maltiness.
Sherry-friendly. After dinner.

GLENDRONACH 15-year-old, 40 vol

100% sherry maturation; being phased out.

COLOUR Full amber.

NOSE Sweet, raisiny sherry, balanced by polished oak
and sweetish, fragrant peat smoke.

BODY Rich and smooth.

PALATE Oaky. Dry maltiness. Crunchy toffee. Buttery.

FINISH Liquorice-toffee, sherry notes.

SCORE **79**

GLENDRONACH 18-year-old, 43 vol

There has also been a peatier limited edition at 19 years old.

COLOUR A bright, extremely deep amber.

NOSE Very heavily sherried. Burnt-toffee dryness. Hint of smoke.

BODY Smooth, slightly drying.

PALATE Starts with burnt-toffee dryness, moves to malty sweetness,
then to sherry.

FINISH Long, smooth, warming, with some toffeeish dryness.

SCORE **78**

GLENDRONACH 1968 Vintage, 43 vol

100% matured in sherry casks; very limited availability.

COLOUR Chestnut.

NOSE Mince pies, doused in spirit and served with black coffee.

BODY Firm. Drying.

PALATE Crème de menthe. Cedary notes. Charred oak. Sappy. Woody.

FINISH Long, warming.

SCORE **78**

INDEPENDENT BOTTLINGS OF GLENDRONACH

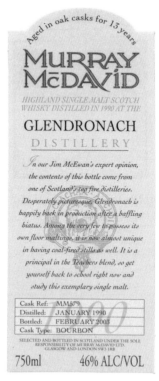

Aged in oak casks for 13 years

MURRAY McDAVID

HIGHLAND SINGLE MALT SCOTCH
WHISKY DISTILLED IN 1990 AT THE

GLENDRONACH

DISTILLERY

*In our Jim McEwan's expert opinion,
the contents of this bottle come from
one of Scotland's top five distilleries.
Desperately picturesque, Glendronach is
happily back in production after a baffling
hiatus. Among the very few to possess its
own floor maltings, it is now almost unique
in having coal-fired stills as well. It is a
principal in the Teachers blend, so get
yourself back to school right now and
study this exemplary single malt.*

Cask Ref:	MM579
Distilled:	JANUARY 1990
Bottled:	FEBRUARY 2003
Cask Type:	BOURBON

SELECTED AND BOTTLED IN SCOTLAND UNDER THE SOLE
RESPONSIBILITY OF MURRAY McDAVID LTD.
GLASGOW AND LONDON SW3 1RB

750ml   46% ALC/VOL

GLENDRONACH 1990, Murray McDavid, 46 vol

COLOUR Chardonnay-like.

NOSE Creamy malt. Minty leaves. Hint of burnt wood. Cloves.

BODY Full, almost viscous.

PALATE Sweet nuttiness. Leafy. Roasted nuts.

FINISH Dry, nutty.

SCORE **72**

GLENDRONACH 1976, Signatory, 51.7 vol

COLOUR Full gold.

NOSE Sherry. Rich dried fruit, raisins, bananas and dates.
Orange chocolate. Nutmeg.

BODY Syrupy.

PALATE Round and creamy. Opulent display of fruit and spices.

FINISH Warm, tasty, drying out on oak.

SCORE **74**

GLENDULLAN

PRODUCER Diageo
REGION Highland   DISTRICT Speyside (Dufftown)
ADDRESS Dufftown, Banffshire, AB55 4DJ
TEL 01340 822100

Now a contributor to the vatted adaptation of Cardhu, and traditionally to the blend Old Parr, which is popular in Japan. As a single malt, Glendullan has in recent years been offered in a flora and fauna edition, and no fewer than four Rare Malts versions.

This distillery, established in 1897–98, has had its moments of glory, notably the supply of its whisky in the early 1900s to King Edward VII, an honour that was for some years proclaimed on its casks. Today, Glendullan has the highest volume production among Diageo's distilleries, despite a name so unjustly close to "dull one". The reference is to the river Dullan, on which Dufftown stands.

HOUSE STYLE Perfumy, fruity, dry, chilli-like, oily, big. Put it in a hip flask.

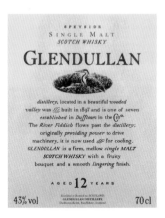

GLENDULLAN 12-year-old, Flora and Fauna, 43 vol

COLOUR Almost white, with just a tinge of gold.

NOSE Light, dry maltiness. Hint of fruit.

BODY A hard edge, then silky.

PALATE Dry start, becoming buttery, malty, nutty, perfumy, and lightly fruity.

FINISH Extraordinarily perfumy and long.

SCORE **75**

GLENESK/HILLSIDE

PRODUCER DCL
REGION Highlands DISTRICT Eastern Highlands
SITE OF FORMER DISTILLERY Kinnaber Road, Hillside, Montrose,
Angus, DD10 9EP

At THE MOUTH OF THE South Esk river, at Montrose, lies Glenesk. Over the years, a confusion of names have been used for this establishment, employing various prefixes to the word Esk. At times it has also been known as Hillside. It began as a flax mill, converted in 1897 to become a malt distillery. At one later stage it made only grain whisky. Its career was intermittent, even by the standards of a cyclical industry.

From the mid-1960s to the mid-1980s, it was again a significant malt distillery, contributing to the famous blend VAT 69, made by William Sanderson, part of DCL and later United Distilleries. There were for a short time William Sanderson bottlings of Glenesk Single Malt at 12 years old, but these are now very hard to find. They had a distinctly aromatic, clean, dry, fresh maltiness. In recent years, there have been several bottlings under the Hillside name in the Rare Malts series. The distillery closed in 1985. Its relatively modern maltings on an adjacent site was sold, but still operates.

HOUSE STYLE Fresh, clean, dry. Aperitif.

HILLSIDE 25-year-old, Distilled 1969, Rare Malts, 61.9 vol

COLOUR Bright, pale greeny gold.

NOSE Vanilla.

BODY Light, firm.

PALATE Sweetish start. Then dry maltiness. Dried apricot and dried banana.

FINISH Slightly resiny, herbal, and salty. Crisp. Fresh.

SCORE 69

GLENFARCLAS

PRODUCER J. & G. Grant
REGION Highlands   DISTRICT Speyside
ADDRESS Ballindalloch, Banffshire, AB37 9BD   TEL 01807 500257
WEBSITE www.glenfarclas.co.uk   EMAIL enquiries@glenfarclas.co.uk   VC

WITH A SIXTH GENERATION of the family now active in the business, prospects look good for this most independent of distilleries. Glenfarclas whiskies are in the top flight among Speysiders, though they are not as widely known as some similar examples from this region. From the river Spey, it is about a mile to Glenfarclas ("valley of the green grass"). The distillery is near the village of Marypark. Behind it, heather-covered hills rise towards Ben Rinnes, from which the distillery's water flows. Barley is grown in the surrounding area.

The distillery belongs to a private, family-owned company, J. & G. Grant. The family is not connected (except perhaps distantly) to any of the other whisky-making Grants, and does not own any other distilleries or bottlers. Glenfarclas traces its history to 1836, and has been in the family since 1865. Although some of the buildings date from that period, and the reception room has panelling from an ocean liner, the equipment is modern, and its stills are the biggest in Speyside.

HOUSE STYLE Big, complex, malty, sherryish. After dinner.

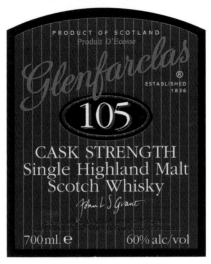

GLENFARCLAS 105, No Age Statement, 60 vol

*Known as 105°, and 8 to 10 years old. A very youthful version for such a
big malt, but it wins points for firm-muscled individuality.*

COLOUR Full gold to bronze.

NOSE Robust: butterscotch and raisins.

BODY Full, heavy.

PALATE Very sweet, rich nectar, with some honeyish dryness.

FINISH Long, and warmed by the high proof. Rounded.

SCORE **88**

GLENFARCLAS 10-year-old, 40 vol

Elegant and quite dry for a Glenfarclas.

COLOUR Full gold.

NOSE Big, with some sherry sweetness and nuttiness,
but also smokiness at the back of the nose.

BODY Characteristically firm.

PALATE Crisp and dry at first, with the flavour filling out as it develops.

FINISH Sweet and long.

SCORE **86**

GLENFARCLAS 12-year-old, 43 vol

For many devotees, the most familiar face of Glenfarclas.

COLOUR Bronze.

NOSE Drier, with a quick, big attack.

BODY Firm, slightly oily.

PALATE Plenty of flavour, with notes of peat smoke.

FINISH Long, with oaky notes, even at this relatively young age.

SCORE **87**

GLENFARCLAS 15-year-old, 46 vol

*Many enthusiasts feel that this age most deftly demonstrates the complexity
of this malt. Certainly the best-balanced Glenfarclas.*

COLOUR Amber.

NOSE Plenty of sherry, oak, maltiness, and a hint of smokiness –
all the elements of a lovely, mixed bouquet.

BODY Firm, rounded.

PALATE Assertive, again with all the elements beautifully melded.

FINISH Long and smooth.

SCORE **88**

GLENFARCLAS 17-year-old, 43 vol

Mainly available in the Far East.

COLOUR Full amber.

NOSE Fuller sherry. Light, fragrant smokiness. Clean oak.

BODY Firm, rounded.

PALATE Firm at first, then a surge of buttery notes in the middle, moving to fruity dryness.

FINISH Touch of almonds and bitter chocolate.

SCORE **88**

GLENFARCLAS 21-year-old, 43 vol

COLOUR Amber.

NOSE More sherry. Butter. Sultana-like fruitiness. Sweet lemon juice on a pancake. Greater smokiness, as well as a dash of oak. All slowly emerges as distinct notes.

BODY Big, firm.

PALATE Immense flavour development. Raisiny, spicy, gingery.

FINISH Remarkably long, with lots of sherry, becoming sweetish and perfumy.

SCORE **89**

GLENFARCLAS 25-year-old, 43 vol

More of everything. Perhaps a touch woody for purists, but a remorselessly serious after-dinner malt for others.

COLOUR Dark amber.

NOSE Pungent, sappy.

BODY Big, with some dryness of texture.

PALATE The flavours are so tightly interlocked at first that the whisky appears reluctant to give up its secrets. Very slow, insistent flavour development. All the components gradually emerge, but in a drier mood.

FINISH Long, oaky, sappy. Extra points out of respect for idiosyncratic age.

SCORE **88**

GLENFARCLAS 30-year-old, 43 vol

COLOUR Refractive, bright amber.

NOSE Oaky, slightly woody.

BODY Very firm.

PALATE Nutty and oaky.

FINISH Oaky, sappy, peaty.

SCORE **87**

GLENFARCLAS 40-year-old, Millennium Edition, 54.7 vol

COLOUR Deep amber, with a yellowy suggestion of a gibbous moon.

NOSE Oaky.

BODY Medium to full. Very firm.

PALATE Oaky start, with nutty maltiness and raisiny sweetness fighting through. Tightly locked flavours open with a dash of water.

FINISH Peat. Log fires. Oak.

SCORE **87**

GLENFARCLAS 8-year-old, 40 vol

Exclusive to Dutch market.

COLOUR Amber.

NOSE Good weight. Malt, butterscotch, rich fruit and nut. Lightly honeyed. Attractive.

BODY Light. Slightly rigid.

PALATE Tongue-coating. Nutty and has the distillery's rich mouth feel. Young.

FINISH A little hard.

SCORE **78**

GLENFARCLAS 8-year-old, 40 vol

Exclusive to Swiss/Austrian market.

COLOUR Rich amber.

NOSE Dry. Bracken, balsa wood, peanut. Little honey. Young.

BODY Light to medium. Firm.

PALATE Clean, nutty maltiness. Ripe fruits in centre. Good feel.

FINISH Hard and young.

SCORE **80**

GLENFARCLAS 1990, Family Malt Collection, 43 vol

Exclusive to Spanish market.

COLOUR Copper.

NOSE Dense and thick. Syrup, membrillo, red fruit, runny toffee, orange.
Bracken-like maltiness.

BODY Full, soft, and rich.

PALATE Sweet and chewy. Toffee, walnut, soft fruit. Dries towards finish.
Great balance.

FINISH Nut, cedar.

SCORE **83**

GLENFARCLAS 1979, Port Vintage, 40 vol

COLOUR Gold.

NOSE Malt mixed with crème de framboise, floral notes,
and fruitcake.

BODY Sweet and full-bodied.

PALATE Honey glazes the tongue. Hint of smoke, yellow wine gums,
hazelnut. Exotic.

FINISH Long, fragrant.

SCORE **83**

SOME OTHER EXCLUSIVE BOTTLINGS

A bottling of 1990 at 46 vol, exclusive to Bernard Massard of
Luxembourg, has a copper colour; a nose of bung cloth, treacle toffee;
raisins and dates on the palate; and a slightly tannic finish. SCORE 80
A cask from the same year, 1990, was also bottled for
Mähler-Besse in Bordeaux at 46 vol. Amber hued with a
roasted meat/figgy nose; the full-bodied palate shows damson,
raisin, and clove and cedar on the finish. SCORE 80

The distillery has also bottled a series exclusively
for Hanseatische of Bremen:

A 1989 at 43 vol from first-fill oloroso has an earthy, fungal nose;
the palate shows treacle, dusty tannins, and a firm structure;
the finish is figgy. SCORE 78

A 1986 at 43 vol from a fino cask shows lifted, crisp notes on the nose
reminiscent of olive, planed wood, and lime. A medium-bodied example
with a palate that has dry coriander, malt, and a sweet centre;
the finish hints at flowers. SCORE 83

A 1983 at 43 vol had an aroma of wholemeal flour with hints of hazelnut
and chamois leather. The lightest of the range, the palate was sweet with
touches of almond with charred notes behind. Intriguing. SCORE 80

A 1959 at 46 vol (The Historic Reserve No.1), which was distilled on
Christmas Day of that year, has a nose, appropriately enough, reminiscent
of Christmas cake: raisin, sultana, treacle. There is also violet, apple and a
hint of rancio. Medium-bodied with a soft mouth feel; there are notes of
bitter chocolate on the palate as well. Complex. SCORE 90

GLENFIDDICH

PRODUCER William Grant & Sons Ltd
REGION Highlands DISTRICT Speyside (Dufftown)
ADDRESS Dufftown, Banffshire, AB55 4DH
TEL 01340 820373 VC WEBSITE www.glenfiddich.com

As BOLD AND ADVENTUROUS as ever, the stag has been raising its antlers in the glen of the river Fiddich. Not only has the world's biggest selling single malt whisky increased the age of its principal expression (*see pp. 67–69*), it has also introduced controversial innovations like Havana Reserve and Caoran.

The Glenfiddich distillery lies on the small river whose name it bears, in Dufftown. The name Fiddich indicates that the river runs through the valley of the deer. Hence the company's stag emblem.

This justifiably famous distillery was founded in 1886–87, and is still controlled by the original family. As a relatively small enterprise, it faced intense competition from bigger companies during the economic boom after the Second World War. Rather than relying on supplying whisky to blenders owned by the giants, it decided in 1963 to widen the availability of its whisky as a bottled single malt. An industry dominated at the time by blended Scotches regarded this as foolishness. The widely held view was that single malts were too intense, flavoursome, or complex for the English and other foreigners.

This independent spirit was an example without which few of its rivals would have been emboldened to offer themselves as bottled single malts. Devotees of the genre owe a debt of gratitude to Glenfiddich. The early start laid the foundations for the success of Glenfiddich. Its fortunes were no doubt further assisted by its being, among malts, very easily drinkable.

Devotees of malts who are ready for a greater challenge will find much more complexity in the longer matured versions, including the one that is aged for 15 years then vatted in a solera system.

The Glenfiddich distillery is full of character. Much of the original structure, in honey-and-grey stone, remains beautifully maintained, and the style has been followed in considerable new construction. Glenfiddich also led the way in the industry by being the first to have a visitor centre. Some may be argue that this is for tourists rather than purists, but no visitor to this part of the Highlands should miss it.

A truly traditional element is the use of coal firing in one of the two still-houses. The stills are small, and the whisky is principally aged in "plain oak" (refill bourbon), although about 10 per cent goes into sherry casks. Whisky aged in different woods is married in plain oak.

Adjoining the Glenfiddich site, William Grant also owns The Balvenie (established 1892), with a small floor maltings, and the newish (1990) Kininvie malt distilleries. Kininvie is little more than a basic still-house. Its rich, creamy malt goes into the Grant's blends, but has not been bottled as a single. Elsewhere in Scotland, it has the Girvan grain distillery (*see* Ladyburn).

HOUSE STYLE When young, a dry, fruity aperitif;
when more mature, a raisiny, chocolatey after-dinner malt.

GLENFIDDICH Special Reserve, 12-year-old, 40 vol

COLOUR Slightly fuller gold than it used to be. Faint green tinge.

NOSE Fresh but sweet, appetizing, fruity, pear-like, juicy grass.

BODY Lean. Smooth. Oily maltiness.

PALATE Malty sweetness. White chocolate. Good flavour
development. Toasted hazelnuts.

FINISH Fragrant suggestion of peat smoke.

SCORE 77

GLENFIDDICH Caoran Reserve, 12-year-old, 40 vol

Caoran refers in Gaelic to the embers of a peat fire. A very gently smoky,
dryish background is achieved by the use of casks that previously
contained whisky from the peaty island of Islay.

COLOUR Deep gold.

NOSE Treacle toffee slightly burned. Sweet, cedary logs on a slow fire.

BODY Light to medium. Oily. Scented.

PALATE White chocolate. Cassata ice cream. Strega.

FINISH Thick chocolate wafers. Dark caramel. Gently warming alcohol.

SCORE **82**

GLENFIDDICH Solera Reserve, 15-year-old, 40 vol

COLOUR Bright gold.

NOSE Chocolate. Toast. Hint of peat.

BODY Light but very smooth indeed.

PALATE Suave. Silky. White chocolate. Pears in cream. Cardamom.

FINISH Cream. Hint of ginger.

SCORE **81**

GLENFIDDICH 15-year-old, Cask Strength, 51 vol

Especially available in duty-free.

COLOUR Full gold.

NOSE Soft, light peat smoke.

BODY Smooth, lightly creamy.

PALATE Smooth. Hazelnut. Light cream. Dry maltiness.

FINISH Tasty, appetizing. Grassy notes and peat smoke.

SCORE **80**

GLENFIDDICH Ancient Reserve, 18-year-old, 40 vol

A proportion of the whisky in this version is older than the age on the label, with a slight accent toward first-fill sherry (butts, rather than hogsheads, and made from Spanish oak rather than American), and earth-floored, traditional warehouses.

COLOUR Old gold.

NOSE Richer.

BODY Softer.

PALATE More mellow and rounded, soft, and restrained.
Scores points for sophistication and sherry character.

FINISH Nutty. A flowery hint of peat.

SCORE **78**

GLENFIDDICH Havana Reserve, 40 vol

To be renamed Gran Reserva.

COLOUR Apricot.

NOSE Toasty. Biscuity. Petit fours. The aroma when
a box of chocolates is opened.

BODY Soft. Lightly creamy.

PALATE Vanilla flan. Sweet Cuban coffee.

FINISH Juicy. A hint of dried tropical fruits.

SCORE **86**

GLENFIDDICH 30-year-old, 43 vol

COLOUR Full gold, fractionally darker still.

NOSE Notes of sherry, fruit, chocolate, and ginger.

BODY Soft, full, some viscosity.

PALATE More sherry, raisins, chocolate, ginger. Luxurious.

FINISH Unhurried, with chocolatey notes and gingery dryness.

SCORE **86**

GLENFIDDICH Rare Collection, 40-year-old, 43.6 vol

COLOUR Deep, greeny gold. Ripening plum.

NOSE Deliciously appetizing. A real depth of honey aromas, which seem to emerge in layers, as though each were extracted from a different flower. Then beeswax. Finally, a balancing flowery dryness and faint burnt-heather smokiness.

BODY Lean but silky smooth.

PALATE Very slow, sustained emergence of flavours. Firm, dryish, restrained, honey, becoming scenty. Gradually giving way to biscuity maltiness. A hint of bitter chocolate. Finally a surge of soft, oily smokiness, with some peaty dryness.

FINISH Hint of anis. Satisfying. Long.

GLENFIDDICH 1937, Vintage, 64-year-old, 44 vol

COLOUR Beautiful. Like a green fruit that has ripened to pink, then bronze.

NOSE Huge bouquet. Newly dug peat. Burnt heather. Dried flowers. Old books. Leather. Oak.

PALATE Smooth, silky. Wraps round the tongue. Sweet. Perfumy. Toffee in icing sugar. Then treacle toffee. Crème brûlée. Toasted almonds.

FINISH Long and warming, but very woody.

SOME VINTAGE GLENFIDDICHS

1974 In the aroma: pastry out of a hot oven. Fresh pears in butterscotch sauce. The palate suggests milk chocolate first, then dark. Chocolate limes, then mint crèmes. The finish is liqueur-ish but also slightly sharp. SCORE 83

1973 Soft, "box of chocolates" aroma. Silky smooth body. Palate suggests chocolate-coated dates. Balancing, cocoa-powder bitterness in finish. SCORE 87

1967 Touch of sweetness in the aroma. Coconut ice? Nougat? Garden mint in the palate. Slightly gritty. Moroccan mint tea. SCORE 82

1965 Aroma of chocolate soufflé. Syrup-sweet in the mid-palate. Remarkably chocolatey in the finish. Like eating that soufflé. SCORE 86

1961, 43.2 vol Gentle fragrance of pine needles, cypress, box trees, grass, peat, very faint smokiness. Palate has bitter chocolate, orange zest and lemon fudge. Very deftly balanced. SCORE 92

GLENFIDDICH Classic, No Age Statement, 43 vol

This version is no longer bottled, but may still be found.

COLOUR	Pale gold.
NOSE	Softer. Dry maltiness, pear skins, slight sherry, and faint smokiness.
BODY	Firm, smooth.
PALATE	Smooth. Dry maltiness balanced by restrained sweetness, with slight smokiness. Flavours tightly combined.
FINISH	Smooth, dry.

SCORE 76

GLENGLASSAUGH

PRODUCER The Edrington Group
REGION Highlands DISTRICT Speyside (Deveron)
ADDRESS Portsoy, Banffshire, AB45 2SQ

THE "FAMILY SILVER" bottling from the owners, Highland Distillers (now Edrington), was a welcome morsel from Glenglassaugh. This distillery, founded in 1875 and completely rebuilt in 1959–60, has been mothballed since 1986, and shows no sign of being reopened.

The whisky has contributed to highly regarded blends such as The Famous Grouse, Cutty Sark, and Laing's, but its distinctiveness has always seemed a mixed blessing. "Sackcloth … hessian," proclaimed one taster, admiring the distinctive aroma of this malt. "Flax, perhaps?" says another admirer. Maybe it is the aroma of seaside sand dunes covered with rough grass and gorse. This is a coastal malt, produced near Portsoy, between the mouths of the rivers Spey and the Deveron.

HOUSE STYLE Grassy maltiness. Restorative or refresher.

GLENGLASSAUGH 1973 Vintage Reserve, The Family Silver, 40 vol

Now hard to find and of interest to collectors.

COLOUR Deep, old gold.

NOSE Fresh, starched linen. Sea air.

BODY Light to medium. Firm, smooth.

PALATE Smooth, grassy. Slightly leathery and oily.

FINISH Linseed. Soothing. Warming.

SCORE **78**

GLENGLASSAUGH, No Age Statement, 40 vol

This version, bottled by Highland Distillers, is labelled
12-year-old in some markets. It is now hard to find.

COLOUR Gold.

NOSE Fresh linen.

BODY Light, but firm and smooth.

PALATE Grassy, sweetish.

FINISH Gentle, drying slightly.

SCORE **76**

GLENGLASSAUGH 1986, MacPhail's Collection, 40 vol

COLOUR Bright lemony yellow.

NOSE Light. Perfumy. Lemon. Gorse.

BODY Light. Silky smooth.

PALATE Clean. Oily. Hint of cedar. Very slight rooty liquorice.

FINISH Gentle, warming. Slight lemon zest.

SCORE **76**

GLENGLASSAUGH 1974, Scott's Selection, 56.9 vol

COLOUR Deep old gold.

NOSE Cream. Gorse. Oily. Salty.

BODY Viscous.

PALATE Dry, oily. Sherbety.

FINISH Lemony. Hot lemon juice. Warming.

SCORE **77**

GLENGOYNE

PRODUCER Ian Macleod Distillers Ltd
REGION Highlands   DISTRICT Highlands (Southwest)
ADDRESS Dumgoyne (by Glasgow), Stirlingshire, G63 9LV
TEL 01360 550254 WEBSITE www.glengoyne.com
EMAIL reception@glengoyne.com   VC

NEW OWNERS ARE REDISCOVERING GLENGOYNE. It has never been an especially well known distillery, but it has one of the prettiest locations (complete with waterfall), and it is only a dozen miles from the centre of Glasgow. Future marketing is likely to give more emphasis to the claim that Glengoyne is the local whisky of Glasgow, and distillery tours will be promoted as an essential feature of a visit to the city. The distillery is said to have been established in 1833.

It is now felt the previous emphasis on the use of unpeated malt could have been construed as a negative claim, and perhaps too technical to appeal to the lay consumer. Nor is it unique to Glengoyne. If this theme is continued in future advertising, it may be presented in a more positive context: that the lack of peat unmasks the true taste of the malt. Glengoyne does have a clean, creamy malt accent.

HOUSE STYLE Easily drinkable, but full of malty flavour.
Restorative, with dessert, or after dinner.

GLENGOYNE 10-year-old, 40 vol

COLOUR Yellowy gold.

NOSE A fresh but very soft, warm fruitiness (Cox's apples?), with rich malty dryness, very light sherry, and a touch of juicy oak.

BODY Light to medium. Smooth, rounded.

PALATE Clean, grassy, fruity, with more apple notes. Tasty, very pleasant.

FINISH Still sweet, but drying slightly. Clean, appetizing.

SCORE 74

A Glengoyne 12-year-old, at 43 vol, now hard to find is very similar to the 10-year-old. A dash more of everything. SCORE 75

GLENGOYNE 16-year-old, Scottish Oak Finish, 53.5 vol

COLOUR Slightly dull gold.

NOSE Very Aromatic. Smells like a freshly cut tree. Resiny. Lemon skins.

BODY Oily, creamy.

PALATE Toffeeish. Paw-paw. Vanilla Pods. Cinnamon.

FINISH Like biting into a tree bark. Hot, Spicy, flavours. Cloves?

SCORE 80

GLENGOYNE 17-year-old, 43 vol

COLOUR Full gold, with an orange tinge.

NOSE Warm, dry. Maltiness and fruitiness. Palo cortado sherry. Cedar and fresh oak.

BODY Medium, very firm and smooth.

PALATE Deep, rich flavours. Malt, clean fruitiness (hints of apple), nuttiness, cedar, more oak. Really hitting its stride as a mature, sophisticated whisky.

FINISH Long and allusively sherryish.

SCORE 78

GLENGOYNE 21-year-old, 43 vol

A very well balanced edition.

COLOUR Full gold, with a darker orange tinge.

NOSE Fragrant. Hints of apple, oak, and earth.

BODY Firm, smooth.

PALATE Very firm maltiness. Dry creaminess. Clean fruit (hints of orange) and oak.

FINISH Cream. Vanilla pods. Cinnamon.

SCORE 79

GLENGOYNE 30-year-old, 50 vol

An interestingly oaky interpretation.

COLOUR Deep, shining gold to bronze.

NOSE Polished oak.

BODY Medium to full. Rounded.

PALATE Soft, complex. Hints of apple and orange.
Dryish spiciness.

FINISH Firm dry. Hint of charred oak.

SCORE **79**

GLENGOYNE Millennium, 50 vol

A delicious example of maltiness in a whisky. Comprises Glengoynes
of more than 30 years old.

COLOUR Very full gold, with orange tinge.

NOSE Very aromatic, appetizing, and softly spicy.

BODY Creamy.

PALATE Very malty. Long and unfolding. Clean. Sweet start.
Creamy flavours, becoming cookie-like and nutty.

FINISH Chewy, malty. Very soft, restrained, dessert apple.

SCORE **80**

SOME VINTAGE-DATED EDITIONS OF GLENGOYNE

(Released each August, at about 25 years old and cask strength.)

1972, 57.8 vol: amber colour; arousing interplay of sherry, resiny, and grassy maltiness in the aroma; rich, creamy, and nutty, with charred oak and earth in the finish. SCORE 79

1970, 48.5 vol: full gold; fresh aroma, with hint of charred oak; light body, with surprisingly fresh, creamy flavours. SCORE 78
An earlier release of a 1970, identified as a Golden Promise varietal grown in Northumberland, was fractionally richer, maltier, and less dry. SCORE 79

1969, bottled unfiltered at 47 vol: deep gold; polished oak aroma; firm, creamy, oily; more oiliness in the creamy flavour, with a hint of fruity dryness in the finish. SCORE 77

1968 (labelled as being from a single day's distillation, matured only in sherry casks) at 50.3 vol: gold with orange tinge; oak and sherry in the beautifully balanced aroma; exceptionally smooth; chewy maltiness, sherry, ginger, and juicy oak. SCORE 79

Winter 1967 Christmas Day Reserve, 43 vol: gold; very fresh, fragrant aroma, with hint of honeysuckle and clean apple; sweet, creamy, condensed milk in the palate; very sweet, fresh dessert apple, tangerines, and nuts in the finish; beautifully rounded. SCORE 80

SOME SINGLE-CASK BOTTLINGS OF GLENGOYNE

1972, cask no 583, at 55.9 vol: reddish, with buttery notes of zesty lemon, orange, and bitter chocolate. SCORE 78. Cask no 1428, at 60.3 vol: paler, bronze, oily, very sweet; fruity, apples, cloves. SCORE 78

1971, cask no 4855, at 56.2 vol: dark-orange colour, juicy oak, and sherry in the aroma; more sherry and creamy malt in the palate; oily. SCORE 78
Cask no 4678, at 57 vol: dark copper, nutty oloroso, orangey fruit, then resiny dryness. SCORE 78

1970, cask no 1186, at 51.5 vol: dark-walnut colour; oaky, and nutty sherry in the aroma; very rich sherry flavours; late malty liquorice and estery spiciness. SCORE 77. Cask no 3854, at 53.4 vol: pale-walnut colour, polished-oak aroma; sweet apple and butter, almonds. SCORE 76. Cask no 4606, at 54.7 vol: sunny gold; very fruity, apple-like aroma; sweet apple flavours; crisp finish. SCORE 76. Cask no 4605, at 56 vol: golden, grassy, earthy (peaty?) aroma, apple-like, honeyish, very drying in the finish. SCORE 76

1969, cask no 4464, at 54.4 vol: chestnut colour; sappy, resiny aroma; barley-sugar maltiness; brandy butter; oak finish. SCORE 77
Cask no 3525, at 51.6 vol: reddish copper; oaky aroma; resiny, very sweet; wine gums; slight charred oak in the finish. SCORE 76

1968, cask no 4617, at 52 vol: deep yellowy gold; clean, soft, perfumy maltiness; hints of apple and vanilla. SCORE 78

SHERRY VARIATIONS OF GLENGOYNE

The following very limited editions, bottled in the upper 50s by volume, offered a treat for lovers of very heavily sherried whiskies, but the weight of the wine seriously challenged the Glengoyne malt character.

A 1989 matured in a fino cask and bottled in 1998 had a dark walnut colour; a polished oak aroma; a big body; a fat, buttery palate; and a nutty dryness, developing some spiciness in the finish. SCORE 78

A 1985 from palo cortado, bottled in 1997, was dark and reddish, also buttery, but more honeyish and medicinal (cough sweets). SCORE 77

Another 1985, from old amontillado, had similar characteristics but was notably spicier, with ginger and especially cinnamon. SCORE 77

GLENKINCHIE

PRODUCER Diageo
REGION Lowlands DISTRICT Eastern Lowlands
ADDRESS Pencaitland, Tranent, East Lothian, EH34 5ET
TEL 01875 342005
WEBSITE www.discovering-distilleries.com/www.malts.com VC

ACCORDING TO ITS LABEL, "The Edinburgh Malt". This is an eminently visitable distillery, about 25 kilometres (15 miles) from the capital, and near the village of Pencaitland. It traces its origins to at least the 1820s and 1830s, to a farm in barley-growing country in the glen of the Kinchie burn. This rises in the green Lammermuir hills, which provide medium-hard water, and flows toward the small coastal resorts where the Firth of Forth meets the sea.

In the 1940s and 1950s, the distillery manager bred prize-winning cattle, feeding them on the spent grain. Delphiniums and roses grow outside the manager's office, and the distillery has its own bowling green. The buildings resemble those of a Borders woollen mill. For much of the distillery's history, the whisky was largely used in the Haig blends. In 1988–89, it was launched as a single in the Classic Malts range, and in 1997 an amontillado finish was added. In the same year a new visitor centre was opened. Among the exhibits is a 75-year-old model of the distillery which was built by the firm of Basset-Lowke, better known for their miniature steam engines.

HOUSE STYLE Flowery start, complex flavours, and a dry finish.
A restorative, especially after a walk in the hills.

GLENKINCHIE 10-year-old, 43 vol

COLOUR Gold.

NOSE Softly aromatic. Lemon grass. Sweet lemons. Melons.

BODY Light but rounded.

PALATE Soft, spicy. Cinnamon and demerara, then gingery dryness.
An extraordinary interplay.

FINISH Fragrant, spicy, oaky dryness.

SCORE **76**

GLENKINCHIE 12-year-old, Friends of Classic Malts, 58.7 vol

COLOUR Bright gold.

NOSE Grass. Straw. Marshmallow. Lime jelly.

BODY Lightly creamy.

PALATE Smooth. Crème brûlée.

FINISH Finely grated lemon peel. Lemon grass. Root ginger.
Nutmeg. Spicy. Big. Long. Dryish.

SCORE **80**

GLENKINCHIE 1986, Distillers Edition, Double Matured, 43 vol

Finished in amontillado sherry.

COLOUR Full gold.

NOSE Lightly floral aroma of polished oak. Sweet lemon. Spices.

BODY Well-rounded.

PALATE The amontillado seems to heighten the interplay between sweetness
and dryness. First comes brown sugar and butter, then suddenly
dry nuttiness and surprising saltiness.

FINISH Sweet, astonishingly long, and soothing.

SCORE **79**

THE GLENLIVET

PRODUCER Chivas Brothers
REGION Highlands DISTRICT Speyside (Livet)
ADDRESS Ballindalloch, Banffshire, AB37 9DB
TEL 01340 821720 WEBSITE www.theglenlivet.com VC

THE GLITTERING PRIZE IN the great whisky takeover of 2001 was this distillery, in the most famous glen in Scotland: that of the small river Livet, which flows into the Spey. Among the distilling districts, the glen of the Livet is the one most deeply set into the mountains. Its water frequently flows underground for many miles. The mountain setting also provides the weather that whisky makers like. When distilling is in progress, the condensers work most effectively if cooled by very cold water, and in a climate to match. The malt whiskies made in the area are on the lighter side, very clean, flowery, subtle, and elegant.

The Livet's fame also has historical origins, in the period when different legislation and duties were applied to distilling in the Lowlands and Highlands. The Lowland distillers, nearer to the big cities, were treated as a legitimate industry; the more distant, thinly populated Highlands were perceived as having illegal distillers and smugglers in every glen. The glen of the Livet was a famous nest of illicit distillation. After legalization in 1824, the legendary spirit "from Glenlivet" was greatly in demand among merchants in the cities to the south.

Distillers absurdly far from the glen have used the geographical allusion, as if it were a synonym for Speyside in general, but this practice is now in decline as the greater interest in single malts focuses attention on the issue of origin. The distillery at the highest elevation in the glen (and perhaps in Scotland) is the one now known as Braeval. Until recently, it was known as Braes of Glenlivet, and it produces a honeyish, zesty whisky. Slightly lower is Tamnavulin, which has a notably light-bodied malt (though Tomintoul's, just across the hills in adjoining Avon valley, is lighter in palate). See entries for each.

Only one distillery in the area is permitted to call itself The Glenlivet. This is the distillery that was the first to become legal, and it now has an international reputation. The definite article is restricted even further in that it appears on only the official bottlings from the owning company of The Glenlivet distillery, Chivas. These carry the legend "Distilled by George & J. G. Smith" in small type at the bottom of the label, referring to the father and son who established the original business.

The Gaelic word "gobha", pronounced "gow" (as in typically Scottish names like McGowan) translates to Smith. It has been argued that the Gow family had supported Bonnie Prince Charlie and later found it politic to change their name to Smith, but this is open to question.

When the legalization of distillers was proposed by the Duke of Gordon, one of his tenants, George Smith, already an illicit whisky maker, was the first to apply for a licence. His son, John Gordon Smith, assisted and succeeded him. After distilling on two sites nearby, in 1858 the Smiths moved to the present location, Minmore, near the confluence of the Livet and Avon. The distillery stands at a point where the grassy valley is already beginning to steepen towards the mountains.

In 1880, the exclusive designation "The Glenlivet" was granted in a test case. The company remained independent until 1953, when it came under the same ownership as Glen Grant. In the 1960s, considerable quantities of the whisky were acquired by Gordon & MacPhail, leading to subsequent bottlings by them. These very old and sometimes vintage-dated versions are identified as George and J. G. Smith's Glenlivet Whisky.

The Glenlivet, Glen Grant, and Longmorn, and the blenders Chivas, were acquired by the North American and worldwide drinks group Seagram in 1977, since when the official bottlings have been energetically promoted.

By virtue of it being the biggest selling single malt in the large American market, The Glenlivet might be deemed commonplace, but it is a whisky of structure and complexity. It is distilled from water with a dash of hardness, and the peating of the malt is on the light side. About a third of the casks used have at some stage held sherry, though the proportion of first fill is considerably smaller than that.

HOUSE STYLE Flowery, fruity, peachy. Aperitif.

THE GLENLIVET 12-year-old, 40 vol

COLOUR Pale gold.

NOSE Remarkably flowery, clean and soft.

BODY Light to medium, firm, smooth.

PALATE Flowery, peachy, notes of vanilla, delicate balance.

FINISH Restrained, long, gently warming.

SCORE **85**

THE GLENLIVET 12-year-old, French Oak Finish, 40 vol

COLOUR Warm gold to bronze.

NOSE Lots of flowery, fruity, fresh apple. Oak extract.

BODY Soft. Rounded.

PALATE Firm, rich rounded. Desert apples, blackcurrants, peaches, honey.

FINISH Crisp, clean oakiness.

SCORE **87**

THE GLENLIVET 12-year-old, American Oak Finish, 40 vol

COLOUR Deep, refractive yellow.

NOSE The typically peachy bouquet seems to be accentuated.

BODY Firm. Medium to full. Very smooth.

PALATE Rich and fruity, with more peat smoke than usual. Cooked peaches.

FINISH Creamy tastes. Vanilla. Some burnt-grass bitterness.

SCORE **85**

THE GLENLIVET 15-year-old, 43 vol

Mainly in duty-free / travel retail.

COLOUR Old gold.

NOSE Nutty, aromatic. Oak, dried apple / apple skin, freesia, hot sawdust.

BODY Light-bodied, good grip.

PALATE Clean and nutty with a floral lift.

FINISH Hint of smoke.

SCORE **80**

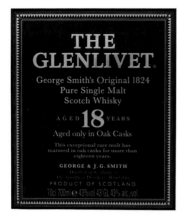 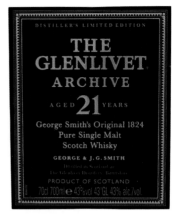

THE GLENLIVET 18-year-old, 43 vol

COLOUR Deep gold to amber.

NOSE Elements beautifully combined. Depth of flowery aromas.
Very light touch of fresh peatiness. Some sweetness and a
hint of sherryish oak. Lightly appetizing.

BODY Firm, smooth.

PALATE Flowery and sweet at first, then developing peach-stone nuttiness.

FINISH Dry, appetizing. Very long, with interplay
of sweet and bitter flavours.

SCORE **87**

THE GLENLIVET Archive, 21-year-old, 43 vol

COLOUR Full gold to bronze.

NOSE Lively. Fruity. Peaty.

BODY Very firm and smooth.

PALATE Light, clean, cereal grain maltiness. Developing toastier, nuttier
flavours. Orange oil. Some macaroon-like sweetness, too.

FINISH Sweet grass. Smoky fragrance.

SCORE **85**

CELLAR NOTES

The first range of vintage-dated Glenlivets was drawn from batches distilled
in the early 1970s, and was released in the late 1990s. These were from years
with very limited stocks, which are now exhausted. The bottlings were
reviewed in the previous edition of this book, and are now hard to find.
They are collector's items. Special editions are now released under the rubric
The Cellar Collection.

THE GLENLIVET 30-year-old, The Cellar Collection, American Oak Finish, 48 vol

COLOUR Attractive pinkish bronze.

NOSE Peach cobbler, being cooked. Warm aroma. Fruity and sweet, with a suggestion of burnt pastry.

BODY Big, smooth, beautifully rounded.

PALATE Like biting into a really good praline. Black chocolate on the outside; fudge, syrupy alcohol, and raisins on the inside.

FINISH Crunchy. Belgian wafers.

SCORE **88**

THE GLENLIVET 1967, The Cellar Collection, Bottled 2000, 46 vol

COLOUR Apricot.

NOSE Sweetly flowery. Hay. Hint of peat. Polished oak.

BODY Firm, textured, lively.

PALATE Sweet peaches, marshmallow, biscuity malt. Shortbread.

FINISH Spicy (cinnamon), appetizing. Very long.

SCORE **90**

THE GLENLIVET 1959, The Cellar Collection, Limited Edition, 41.7 vol

COLOUR Full gold. Peachy.

NOSE Well-done toast, buttered. With apricot jam.

BODY Light to medium. Oily. Creamy.

PALATE Thick-cut marmalade. Orange oil.

FINISH Perfumy. Delicious.

SCORE **85**

THE GLENLIVET 1983, The Cellar Collection, French Oak Finish, 46 vol

COLOUR Distinctively deep, bright orange.

NOSE Lots of floral, tannic oak extract. Heady. Hypnotic.

PALATE Peaches, honey, anis.

FINISH Crisp, dry oakiness.

SCORE **85**

FROM PARADISE

The shrewd shopkeepers at Gordon & MacPhail were as keen on The Glenlivet half a century ago as they were on Glen Grant. They made some excellent purchases, in astonishing quantities, and are said to have had more Glenlivet maturing in their cellars than the distillery itself had laid down. If the three below were cognacs, they would be in the inner cellar that the French call Paradise.

THE GLENLIVET 1943, Gordon & MacPhail, 40 vol

COLOUR Old gold, shading to copper.

NOSE Astonishingly fresh. Fruity. Wonderfully fresh peatiness.

BODY Creamy.

PALATE Astonishingly fresh maltiness. Like Horlicks (malted milk). Moving to cream toffee. Mint toffee.

FINISH Sherry, a hint of spice, menthol? and cedary oakiness. Only faint hint of age. Avoids usual faults.

SCORE **90**

Gordon & MacPhail's bottling of a cask from 1955 at 40 vol has a complex, perfumed nose quality alongside a slightly oily texture. It is complex and spicy, with notes of old leather, chocolate, potpourri; the palate is firm and concentrated. SCORE 83

Gordon & MacPhail has also bottled a 1951 at 40 vol. Full gold in colour; the nose reminds you of Turkish Delight, cut flowers, and brazil nut. A gentle, sweet whisky with delicate wisps of smoke adding to the floral complexity. SCORE 85

GLENLOCHY

PRODUCER DCL/UDV
REGION Highlands DISTRICT Western Highlands
SITE OF FORMER DISTILLERY North Road, Fort William,
Inverness-shire, PH33 6TQ

THE LOCHY IS A RIVER that flows through the town of Fort William, at the foot of the mountain Ben Nevis. In addition to the Ben Nevis malt distillery, which is still very much in operation, Fort William for many years had another, called Glenlochy. This was built in 1898–1900, and changed little over the decades. It passed to DCL in 1953, lost its railway spur in the 1970s, and was closed in 1983. The very impressive pagoda still stands, and can be seen from the train. The equipment has gone, and the premises are now used as offices by unrelated businesses.

One sophisticated and geographically precise taster was reminded of Lebanese hashish by a Scotch Malt Whisky Society bottling of Glenlochy in the mid-1990s. The smokiness is less obvious in some recent bottlings, in which the wood seems tired but more oxidation and ester notes emerge. In 1995, United Distillers released a Rare Malts edition, with a similar bottling the following year.

HOUSE STYLE Peaty, fruity, creamy. With dessert or a book at bedtime.

GLENLOCHY 25-year-old, Distilled 1969, Bottled 1995, Rare Malts, 62.2 vol

COLOUR Old gold.

NOSE Charred oak and roasted chestnuts.

BODY Firm, smooth, oily.

PALATE Marron glacé and clotted cream.

FINISH Dry, big. Lemon zest and pepper.

SCORE **71**

SOME INDEPENDENT BOTTLINGS:

Douglas Laing has a 26-year-old, at 50 vol, on its books. Very light on the nose with hints of peat smoke, demerara sugar, banana, and nut. The palate has wisps of flavour floating through. SCORE 70

Signatory has bottled a 1974 vintage, at 53.3 vol, which shows more distillery character: light smoke, ripe fruits, syrup, and toasty oak. A sweet palate with light, attractive flavours. SCORE 70

A 1965 from Gordon & MacPhail, at 40 vol, is gold in colour; the nose is filled with polished oak, blackberry, caramelized fruit, raisin, and a slight antiseptic note; the palate is nutty and – as with the other examples – all the action is concentrated in the centre of the mouth. SCORE 70

GLENLOCHY 1977, Connoisseurs Choice, 40 vol

COLOUR Full gold to peach.

NOSE Vanilla-flavoured tobacco.

BODY Light, firm, smooth, oily.

PALATE Vanilla, coconut, white chocolate.

FINISH Light lemon zest. Cedar.

SCORE **70**

GLENLOCHY 20-year-old, Distilled 1977, Bottled 1998, Individual Cask, Cadenhead, 55.8 vol

COLOUR Full gold.

NOSE Attractive, perfumy sweetness. Malty. Slight sweet smoke.

BODY Much fuller. Soft.

PALATE Marshmallowy maltiness, but falls away in middle.

FINISH Lemony, grassy, peaty. Long, soothing peatiness.

SCORE **70**

GLENLOSSIE

PRODUCER Diageo
REGION Highlands DISTRICT Speyside (Lossie)
ADDRESS By Elgin, Morayshire, IV30 3SF
TEL 01343 862000

RESPECTED IN THE INDUSTRY (its whisky was once an important element in Haig blends), this distillery has a much lower profile among lovers of malts. A Flora and Fauna edition introduced in the early 1990s has made more connoisseurs aware of it, and there have since been bottlings from Signatory and Hart.

The distillery, in the valley of the Lossie, south of Elgin, was built in 1876, reconstructed 20 years later, and extended in 1962. Next door is the Mannochmore distillery, built in 1971.

HOUSE STYLE Flowery, clean, grassy, malty. Aperitif.

GLENLOSSIE 10-year-old, Flora and Fauna, 43 vol

COLOUR Fino sherry.

NOSE Fresh. Grass, heather, sandalwood.

BODY Light to medium. Soft, smooth.

PALATE Malty, dryish at first, then a range of sweeter, perfumy, spicy notes.

FINISH Spicy.

SCORE 76

SOME INDEPENDENT BOTTLINGS:

Coopers Choice has bottled a 22-year-old at 43 vol. The nose is dry, oaty and biscuity with a rounded malty core; a direct rounded dram with a lightly chewy palate and a finish of dry grass. SCORE 75

Gordon & MacPhail has released a 1975 at 40 vol, as part of its Connoisseurs Choice range. Rich amber in colour the nose is reminiscent of stewed tea and Seville orange, but with light floral notes. European oak leads a softness to the body balancing out what is a pretty crunchy dram with a dry, grassy finish. SCORE 75

A 1961 from Gordon & MacPhail, at 40 vol, has retained a youthful lift on the nose: nutmeg, orange, florist shop; medium-bodied with fine tannins, the palate has a mature, rich feel that has been slightly dulled by time. SCORE 73

GLENLOSSIE Vintage 1981, Sherry Cask Edition, Butt No 1680, Bottle 588 of 595, Bottled 1998, Signatory, 43 vol

COLOUR Gold.

NOSE Very light sherry. Sweet maltiness. Cereal grains. Grass. Sandalwood.

BODY Lightly creamy. Smooth.

PALATE Notably clean maltiness, again with an interplay of dryness and sweetness. Some honeyish, creamy, buttery notes.

FINISH Fudge, then very late, gentle touch of grass, peat, and sandalwood.

SCORE 77

GLENLOSSIE 16-year-old, Distilled 1981, Hart Brothers, 43 vol

COLOUR Gold.

NOSE Malt. Cereal grains. Hint of peat.

BODY Slightly lighter and firmer.

PALATE Nutty sweetness, with a hint of sherry and some butteriness.

FINISH Fresh, grassy peatiness.

SCORE 77

GLENLOSSIE 1974, Connoisseurs Choice, 40 vol

COLOUR Full gold to amber.

NOSE Very attractive interplay of sherry, malt, and floweriness.

BODY Firm, smooth, rounded.

PALATE Fresh. Dryish sherry. Clean maltiness and light touch of butter.

FINISH Nutty sherry and a hint of fresh peatiness.

SCORE 77

EARLIER BOTTLINGS OF GLENLOSSIE

A Gordon & MacPhail 1971, at 40 vol, was sherryish, but still with plenty of distillery character. SCORE 76

A Scotch Malt Whisky Society 1981, at 55.3 vol, was somewhere between the two. SCORE 76

GLENMORANGIE

PRODUCER Glenmorangie plc
REGION Highlands DISTRICT Northern Highlands
ADDRESS Tain, Ross-shire, IV19 1PZ
TEL 01862 892477 WEBSITE www.glenmorangie.com
EMAIL visitors@glenmorangieplc.co.uk VC

STILL THE BIGGEST SELLING MALT WHISKY in Scotland; still dividing opinion by its devotion to wood finishes (which offend some whisky conservatives); still, as a company, much respected and admired.

Glenmorangie pioneered "official" cask-strength bottlings at the beginning of the 1990s. In the middle of that decade, it began introducing wood finishes, from sherry variations such as fino to madeira, port, and French wines. More recently, it has introduced into some vattings of virgin American oak.

The company selects its own trees in the Ozark mountains of Missouri, has its wood seasoned by air drying (rather than kilning), and loans its casks for four years to the Jack Daniel's distillery in Lynchburg, Tennessee. A similar arrangement existed with Heaven Hill, in Bardstown, Kentucky, until the Bourbon distillery lost substantial amounts of wood in a fire. The wood policies at Glenmorangie are some of the most highly developed in the industry. It is significant that the man who developed them, Bill Lumsden, is styled Head of Distilleries and Maturation.

For all its achievements, Glenmorangie is one of the smaller companies in the industry. The distillery is near the pretty sandstone town of Tain (pop. 4000). The town and distillery are on the coast about 65 kilometres (40 miles) north of Inverness. From the A9 road, the short private drive passes between an assortment of trees and a dam shaped like a millpond. Beyond can be seen the waters of the Dornoch firth.

The distilling water rises on sandstone hills and flows over heather and clover, before emerging in a sandy pond about half a mile from the distillery. The sandstone surely contributes to the whisky's firmness of body, the flowers perhaps to its famously scenty character. (A French perfume house identified 26 aromas, from almond, bergamot, and cinnamon to verbena, vanilla, and wild mint. More recently, a New York fragrance company managed only 22).

HOUSE STYLE Creamy, leafy. Restorative or with dessert.
No obvious island character.

REGULAR BOTTLINGS, WITH AGE STATEMENTS

GLENMORANGIE 10-year-old, 40 vol

The principal version.

COLOUR Pale gold.

NOSE Spicy (cinnamon, walnut, sandalwood?), with some flowery sweetness. Fresh. A whiff of the sea. Enticing.

BODY On the light side of medium, but with some viscosity.

PALATE Spicy, flowery, and malty-sweet tones that are creamy, almost buttery. A suggestion of bananas?

FINISH Long and rounded.

SCORE **80**

GLENMORANGIE 15-year-old, 43 vol

Finished in virgin oak.

COLOUR Deep gold.

NOSE Fresh sea air. More breezy.

BODY Smooth, slightly syrupy.

PALATE Lovely balance of sweet creaminess and herbal notes.

FINISH Appetizingly spicy. Clean hit of salt.

SCORE **81**

GLENMORANGIE 18-year-old, 43 vol

COLOUR Full reddish amber.

NOSE Vanilla, mint, walnuts, sappy, oaky.

BODY Medium, smooth, fleshier.

PALATE Cookie-like and sweet at first, more walnuts, then the whole potpourri of spiciness.

FINISH Aromatic, nutty, lightly oaky.

SCORE **81**

GLENMORANGIE 25-year-old, 43 vol

Mainly for the Asian/Pacific market.

COLOUR Dark polished oak.

NOSE An old shop, with fittings in polished oak, leather, and brass.

BODY Big. Slippery.

PALATE Cakey. Oily. Beeswax. A handsome whisky.

FINISH Late, gingery spiciness.

SCORE **80**

OTHER REGULARLY AVAILABLE EXPRESSIONS

GLENMORANGIE Cellar 13, 43 vol

Among the distillery's 14 cellars, this one is nearest to the sea.
The whiskies in this bottling are in the range of 10 to 12 years and more,
all matured in first-fill bourbon barrels.

COLOUR Primrose.

NOSE Soft, with fresh sandalwood, vanilla, and wild mint.

BODY Light to medium. Very smooth.

PALATE Notably soft and malty sweet, with butterscotch, vanilla, and honey.

FINISH Buttercups. Juicy, then late, emphatic saltiness. Very long indeed.

SCORE **81**

GLENMORANGIE Traditional, 100° proof, 57.2 vol

In the same style as the two above, but without chill filtering and at cask strength (in the
British version of the old proof system, 100° equalled 56.6–57.1 vol).

COLOUR Primrose, slightly oily.

NOSE Very aromatic and spicy.

BODY Smooth, firm, slightly gritty.

PALATE Richer, more substantial. Fuller flavours. Sandy-salty notes.

FINISH Robust. Intensely salty. Very long. Soothing.

SCORE **83**

SOME VINTAGE-DATED LIMITED BOTTLINGS
GLENMORANGIE 1979, Bottled 1995, 40 vol

COLOUR Lemony gold.

NOSE Light, fragrant, hint of peat. Faint smoke. Very appetizing.

BODY Surprisingly rich.

PALATE Beautifully balanced. Malty, with some butteriness, moving to spice and salt. Very lively flavours.

FINISH Gentle, soothing.

SCORE **84**

GLENMORANGIE 1977, 21-year-old, 43 vol

COLOUR Bright, greeny gold.

NOSE A hit of oaky vanilla and spice, then grassy peat, and finally a surprisingly emphatic whiff of sea air.

BODY Light but smooth and firm. Slightly oily.

PALATE Sweet and juicy. The fresh oak character combines with the typical walnut, but somewhat overpowers the usual spiciness.

FINISH That very slight peat again, its quick, smoky, fragrant dryness adding an appetizing full-point.

SCORE **84**

GLENMORANGIE 1975, Vintage, 54.2 vol

COLOUR Full amber.

NOSE Scottish tablet. Fudge, in a gift box.

BODY Light, firm, slippery.

PALATE Firm maltiness. A very malty expression. Then big flavour development. The maltiness becomes buttery, then lemon and burnt toast. This is a confident, cerebral whisky.

FINISH Perfectly pitched balancing dryness. Just when it all seems over, a burst of late spiciness and saltiness.

SCORE **85**

GLENMORANGIE 1972, Cask No 1740, (Bottle 066, 1993), 46 vol

COLOUR Very full gold.

NOSE Lightly peaty, flowery, then very spicy. Lots of cinnamon.

BODY Light to medium but smooth and textured.

PALATE Very nutty. Grassy. Dry. Full of fresh flavours.

FINISH Peaty. Grassy. Garden mint. Salty. Slightly sandy or stony. Lightly dry. Crisp, cracker-like.

SCORE **85**

GLENMORANGIE 1971, 43 vol

COLOUR Amber.

NOSE Soft, complex, citrus and spices.

BODY Rich.

PALATE Soft. Treacly malt. Liquorice. Aniseed. Spices.

FINISH Rooty. Lemony. Salty. Warming. Soothing.

SCORE **86**

WOOD FINISHES REGULARLY AVAILABLE

PORT WOOD FINISH

GLENMORANGIE

SINGLE HIGHLAND MALT SCOTCH WHISKY

Handcrafted by the Sixteen Men of Tain

The GLENMORANGIE

DISTILLERY COY, TAIN, ROSS-SHIRE

BOTTLED IN SCOTLAND

GLENMORANGIE Port Wood Finish, 43 vol

No age statement, but typically 12 years in bourbon wood and up to two in port pipes.
Similar regimes for the other wood finishes.

COLOUR Orange, with pinkish blush.

NOSE Pronouncedly fruity and winey.

BODY Very soft indeed, and smooth.

PALATE The port seems to bring out butterscotch notes. It also adds sweeter, winey notes, and melds beautifully with the spiciness of Glenmorangie.

FINISH Soothing, soporific, relaxing. In no hurry to go.

SCORE **87**

GLENMORANGIE Madeira Wood Finish, 43 vol

COLOUR Deep, lemony gold.

NOSE Sweet. Very spicy. Cakey.

BODY Soft, but becoming almost grainy as it dries on the tongue.

PALATE Unusually buttery. Barley-sugar sweetness at first: toffeeish, chewy, cakey. Then nutty and seed-like as it dries. Cinnamon and spices. A teasing interplay of the madeira and the distillery character.

FINISH Short and sweet. Some rummy warmth.

SCORE **86**

GLENMORANGIE Sherry Wood Finish, 43 vol

The sherry is dry oloroso.

COLOUR Darkish gold.

NOSE Nutty. Dry. Faint peat. Sea air.

BODY Soft and curvaceous.

PALATE Voluptuous. Long, sustained development of barley-sugar sweetness, almost overpowers the distillery character.

FINISH Liquorice. Rooty. Late, restrained saltiness.

SCORE **85**

GLENMORANGIE Burgundy Wood Finish, 43 vol

COLOUR Warm bronze.

NOSE Toasty.

BODY Big. Soft. Syrupy.

PALATE Sweetish. Very fruity. Winey. Easily drinkable.

FINISH Lurking behind, and emerging gradually, restrained, balancing, dryness of toast and oak.

SCORE **83**

LIMITED EDITION WOOD FINISHES

(Or, where indicated, wholly matured in the wood shown.)

GLENMORANGIE Tain L'Hermitage (Rhône Wine), Released 1995, 43 vol

COLOUR Distinctively elegant orange.

NOSE Very fruity and sweet.

BODY Creamy.

PALATE Very clean toffee and vanilla, developing to nuttiness and remarkably dry fruitiness. Great length.

FINISH Astonishingly lean and winey. Full of fruity, winey, spicy flavours. Very lively.

SCORE **88**

GLENMORANGIE Claret Wood Finish, Released 1997, 43 vol

COLOUR Orangey amber.

NOSE Fragrant. A hint of the sea. Cedary.

BODY Firm, tongue-coating.

PALATE Dry, cedary start. Boxed dates. Becoming slightly raisiny. Long development of more spicy notes.

FINISH Dry, with a slightly cookie-like, coconut, sweetness and fruity perfuminess.

SCORE **87**

GLENMORANGIE Fino Sherry Finish, Released 1999, 43 vol

Thirteen years in bourbon barrels; two in fino butts.

COLOUR Pale, refractive, greeny gold.

NOSE Gentle sea fragrance. Delicate. Very appetizing.

BODY Light, firm, smooth.

PALATE Very delicate and teasing. Lightly toasty. Cinnamon toast. Faintly rhubarby fruitiness and wineyness. Tinge of sourish acidity.

FINISH The coastal whisky and near-coastal sherry combine in a clinching hug of saltiness and oakiness. A wonderfully stylish whisky.

SCORE **89**

GLENMORANGIE Cognac Matured, Released 1999, 43 vol

COLOUR Lemon beginning to ripen.

BODY Light but firm. Textured.

NOSE Perfumy, lemony, clean, crisp.

PALATE Hint of soft, dusty lemon, then lots of typical Glenmorangie spiciness.

FINISH Hint of icing sugar, then very light and dry. Slightly weak.

SCORE **82**

GLENMORANGIE Côte de Nuits, Released 2000, 43 vol

COLOUR Apricot to pale orange.

NOSE Sandalwood. Candied plums.

BODY Slightly chewy. Nougat.

PALATE Dry, penetrating. Dried raisins. Prunes. A touch of iron tonic. An astonishing interplay of flavours.

FINISH Firm. Extraordinarily long. Almonds. Marzipan. Scores for delicacy, balance, and especially complexity.

SCORE **91**

GLENMORANGIE Côte de Beaune, Released 2001, 46 vol

NOSE Sweetish, creamy, herbal, winey.

BODY Smooth, sweet.

PALATE Soft berry fruits. Prunes. Lots of flavour development. Becoming spicy, with cinnamon and later ginger.

FINISH Figs in cream. Green peppercorns. Very long.

SCORE **87**

GLENMORANGIE Sauternes Wood Finish, Released 2002, 46 vol

COLOUR Yellow-green plum.

NOSE Creamy. Heavy. Tropical garden.

BODY Lightly textured.

PALATE Delicate. Lemon blossom. Orange flower water. Musk.

FINISH Slightly almondy bitterness. Sexy.

SCORE **88**

GLENMORANGIE Madeira Matured, Cask No 3078, 56.6 vol

COLOUR Dark walnut.

NOSE Rich, buttery. Yee, madeira.

BODY Softly sweet, but quickly drying.

PALATE Luscious and toffeeish, then sudden explosion of sand, salt, and oak.

FINISH Stinging saltiness.

SCORE **87**

GLENMORANGIE Rum Wood, Introduced 2002, 45.9 vol

Mainly for the French market.

COLOUR Shimmery, greeny gold.

NOSE Hessian, sackcloth. Sacks of dried fruits.

BODY Silky.

PALATE Dried citrus peel. Curaçao. Citrus zest.

FINISH Gentle. Playful.

SCORE **83**

GLENMORANGIE Malaga Wood Finish, 43 vol

COLOUR Deepish greeny gold.

NOSE Distinctive, complex, rich, sweet, winey.

BODY Quite rich and toffeeish.

PALATE Cedary. Very nutty indeed. The more raisiny notes of malaga seem
to play hide-and-seek in the background. Creamy.

FINISH The characteristic Glenmorangie salt comes through very late.

SCORE **85**

OTHER LIMITED EDITIONS

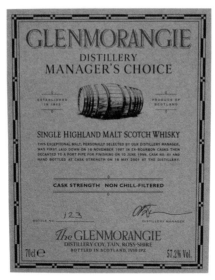

GLENMORANGIE Manager's Choice 2001, Port Wood, Cask Strength, Nonchillfiltered, 57.2 vol

COLOUR Bronze. Rosé tinge.

NOSE "Rough", fresh, fruity. Brought to mind fruit skins
and almondy cherry pits.

BODY Big, smooth.

PALATE Fruity, earthy. Becoming marshmallow-like and malty.
Very port-tasting and curiously unrefined. Scores for robustness and
joie-de-vivre, rather than elegance or sophistication.

FINISH Sandalwood, walnut, salt. All the Glenmorangie flavours come
powering through.

SCORE 86

GLENMORANGIE Manager's Choice 2000, 53.2 vol

COLOUR Gold.

NOSE Fragrant. Pronounced sandalwood.

BODY Relatively big.

PALATE Starts sweet. Unfolds through a long development of flavours,
with suggestions of anis and liquorice. Becomes rooty and slightly bitter.
Impeccably assembled.

FINISH Firm resolution of flavours.

SCORE 83

GLENMORANGIE, Missouri Cask Reserve, Distilled 1991, Released 2002, 55.7 vol

COLOUR Dark, burnished orange. (Or even tamarind?)

NOSE Assam tea. Juicy.

BODY Soft.

PALATE Restrained. Very slow development of flavours. Underlying vanilla sweetness. Creamy. Leafy, herbal, spicy top notes.

FINISH Late surge of warmth. Big and robust all round.

SCORE **84**

GLENMORANGIE Three Cask, 40 vol

Plain charred oak, bourbon, and rioja. Introduced 2001, for the British supermarket Sainsbury's.

COLOUR Soft, warm gold.

NOSE Blackberry pie dusted with icing sugar.

BODY Biting into fruit.

PALATE Scented, dryish. More rioja and less vanilla than might be expected. Some tannins. Dessert apples. Scores points for eccentricity, but the whisky character is masked or muddled.

FINISH Blackberry juice, with some acidity and bitterness.

SCORE **79**

COLLECTABLE GLENMORANGIE

Over the years, Glenmorangie has produced a wealth of special editions. Below are some examples; all are now very hard to find.

The Native Ross-shire GLENMORANGIE 10-year-old, 57.6 vol

COLOUR Bright, pale gold.

NOSE Fragrant, salty.

BODY Medium, smooth.

PALATE Malty-sweet start, then butterscotch, walnut, sandalwood.

FINISH Robust, spicy.

SCORE **80**

GLENMORANGIE Millennium Malt, 12-year-old, 40 vol

The earlier of two millennium bottlings, from first-fill bourbon barrels.

COLOUR Full gold.

NOSE Lightly oaky. Hint of brown sugar.

BODY Slightly syrupy.

PALATE Similar to the Cellar 13, but perhaps more buttery.

FINISH Light, refreshing. An almost spritzy, crunchy, toasty dryness.

SCORE **80**

GLENMORANGIE Elegance, 21-year-old, 43 vol

Presented in a Caithness Glass decanter in the shape of Glenmorangie's stills.

COLOUR Greeny gold.

NOSE Soft. Earthy. Lightly oaky. A hint of peat.

BODY Soft. Very oily.

PALATE More oak and vanilla. Sweet, juicy, and oily, then a surprisingly fresh surge of peatiness.

FINISH Peaty, grassy, salty, warming. Very soothing.

SCORE *82*

GLENMORANGIE 21-year-old, 43 vol

Sesquicentennial bottling. Issued in 1993 to mark the company's 150th anniversary. This version, in a hand-thrown stoneware "lemonade" bottle, is now hard to find.

COLOUR Deep gold, oily, almost mustardy.

NOSE Intensely spicy.

BODY Medium, fleshy.

PALATE Toffeeish, very satisfying, with walnut, then big development of spices. Lemon grass and pronounced peat.

FINISH Juicy oakiness.

SCORE *85*

GLENMORANGIE Original, 24-year-old, 43 vol

An "extra special" millennium edition, dating from the time when the distillery operated its own maltings.

COLOUR Walnut.

NOSE Very distinctive, clean, oaky peatiness. This character is in the background throughout.

BODY Medium. Very firm. Rounded.

PALATE Flowery. Fudgey. Toffeeish. Nutty. Very soft, restrained spiciness. Then toasty and peaty.

FINISH Firm, clean (almost crisp) peatiness. Then long, very soft, spicy and remarkably warming.

SCORE *86*

GLENROTHES

PRODUCER The Edrington Group
REGION Highlands DISTRICT Speyside (Rothes)
ADDRESS Burnside Street, Rothes, Aberlour, AB38 7AA

THE MOST ARISTOCRATIC of London's wine and spirit merchants, Berry Brothers & Rudd, have in recent years showcased Glenrothes (rendered variously as one or two words) as their house malt. These are the principal bottlings of Glenrothes, and they are always vintage dated, with a partially "handwritten" label. The vintages described below have been released since the fourth edition of this book.

In 2002, the company also introduced its own range of bottlings from other distilleries, under the rubric "Berrys' Own Selection". This reflects the new appreciation of Scotland's finest whiskies. It also represents a return to tradition. Once, many respected wine merchants in England as well as Scotland offered their own bottlings of single malts, as well as combining them in house blends. Glenrothes' quietly noble whisky has traditionally been a component of Berrys' internationally known Cutty Sark, and a favourite among blenders. The distillery, established in 1878, is one of five in the small town of Rothes.

The firm of Berrys' began in the 1690s, selling tea, groceries, and wine. Cutty Sark was launched in the 1920s. It is named after the famously fast tea clipper Cutty Sark, which was built in Scotland. Both Glenrothes and Cutty Sark are sold, not only in Berrys' 1730s premises in stately St James's, London, but also in the company's stores at London's Heathrow airport (terminals 3 and 4).

HOUSE STYLE Perfumy, sweet, spicy-fruity, complex. After dinner.

GLENROTHES 1989, 43 vol

COLOUR Old gold.

NOSE A subtle suggestion of soft liquorice, as in Pontefract cakes.

BODY Generous. Supple.

PALATE The liquorice more emphatic now. Spanish root. Develops juicy, mouthwatering flavours. Aniseed. Coconut.

FINISH Soothing, relaxing.

SCORE **82**

GLENROTHES 1973, 43 vol

COLOUR Amber.

NOSE More fine and long. Heather and sweet fruits, spice, floral, apple, prune, nutmeg.

BODY Gentle, subtle yet rich.

PALATE Layers of orange. Vanilla, spice, and raisin flowing together. Fine tannins.

FINISH Nutty. Everlasting. Quintessential Glenrothes.

SCORE **90**

GLENROTHES 1971, 41 vol

COLOUR Copper with a greeny rim.

NOSE Sweet tobacco, liquorice, chewy fruit. Berry fruits, allspice.

BODY Generous, soft. Rich, old, and elegant.

PALATE Cedar, anis, cough sweet. Gently warming.

FINISH Long, complex, sophisticated.

SCORE **87**

GLENROTHES 1967, Berrys' Own Selection, 46.3 vol

COLOUR Old gold.

NOSE Lean, light. Mushroom, dry wood, cooked fruits. Fine ash.

BODY Big, soft.

PALATE Complex. Lots of flavour development. Flowers and spices galore.

FINISH Long, floral.

SCORE **85**

GLENROTHES 1966, Berrys' Own Selection, 52.8 vol

COLOUR Mahogany.

NOSE Dark, woody, fig, and walnut. Madeira cake. Coffee bean.

BODY Dry. Drying.

PALATE Slightly tannic. Good balance between savoury notes and dried fruits.

FINISH Long, drying.

SCORE **82**

SOME INDEPENDENT BOTTLINGS

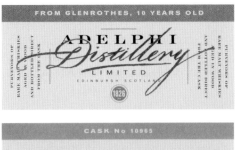

A 10-year-old from Adelphi, at 57.1 vol, is fresh and mouth-filling, with citrus, coconut, and sweet oak. SCORE 89

A 1990 from Signatory, at 46 vol, is rich, like dried fruits, cherries, and bran coated with buttery toffee. Peanut brittle. Luxurious and elegant. SCORE 85

A 1987, MacKillop's Choice, had a juniper note, cereal grains, hard cookies, or crackers.
A madeira finish from the same year had a dusty note, with some charred oak. Both tasted as work in progress.

A 1985, Coopers Choice, at 56 vol, is lean and lemony, with suggestions of desiccated coconut and hazelnut. SCORE 78 A 1975 from the same bottler has concentrated flavours: rose-like, walnuts, earthy, leafy bonfires. SCORE 87

A 1968 from Duncan Taylor, at 57 vol, is plummy, ripe, and full-bodied. Classic Glenrothes. SCORE 85

A 25-year-old from Old Malt Cask, at 50 vol, shows its age. Tartness in the aroma. A little flat and numb in the palate. Sweet but short in the finish. SCORE 70

A 33-year-old, from Hart Brothers, at 46.8 vol, has fondant icing, sweet almonds, vanilla, and wood. SCORE 77

A 1961 from Gordon & MacPhail is fragrant with a hint of camp fires. The palate is slightly faded, but with a discreet, sweet charm. SCORE 79

GLENTAUCHERS

PRODUCER Allied Distillers Ltd
REGION Highlands DISTRICT Speyside
ADDRESS Mulben, Keith, Banffshire, AB5 2YL
TEL 01542 860272

A SPECIAL DISTILLERY BOTTLING launched in 2000 is the most recent official expression from Glentauchers. This is one of a handful of bottlings in recent years. Glentauchers was founded in 1898 and rebuilt in 1965. With no visitor centre and few bottlings, it has not had the attention it merits. With Auchroisk ("The Singleton") as a neighbour, it is in the countryside near the village of Mulben, between the distilling towns of Rothes and Keith.

HOUSE STYLE Clovey dryness and malty sweetness. Soothing at its best.

GLENTAUCHERS 15-year-old, 46 vol

COLOUR Amber.
BODY Light and dry.
NOSE Polished oak, in a long corridor. Gloss paint.
PALATE Apple cake. Raisins. Cloves.
FINISH Short.

SCORE **68**

GLENTAUCHERS 1990, Gordon & MacPhail, 40 vol

COLOUR Amber.
NOSE Fat. Full cream milk. Hazelnut and chocolate spread.
BODY Light and dry.
PALATE Fruity and flowery. A touch of heather. Doesn't deliver promise on nose.
FINISH Short.

SCORE **72**

GLENTURRET

PRODUCER The Edrington Group
REGION Highlands DISTRICT Eastern Highlands
ADDRESS Crieff, Perthshire, PH7 4HA TEL 01764 656565
WEBSITE www.famousgrouse.co.uk VC

A DISTILLERY OR an "experience"? Glenturret is certainly a distillery: the most visitable; one of the smallest; and a claimant to being Scotland's oldest, tucked in a pretty glen just an hour by road from Edinburgh or Glasgow. These attributes proved irresistible to its owners The Edrington Group, who have made it their principal visitor centre. As their biggest selling product is The Famous Grouse, this blend has been linked to the distillery.

A visit to Glenturret is now marketed as The Famous Grouse Experience. The visitor is presented with a very imaginative and entertaining range of experiences, by way of a variety of hi-tech means, though this sits oddly in the location: one of the most rustic and traditional distilleries. A proportion of Glenturret is said to be included in the "recipe" for The Famous Grouse. Given the size of the distillery and the sales of Grouse, it must be a very a small amount. Glenturret's new role has led to a rationalization in the number of bottlings, which was very extensive and idiosyncratic.

Glenturret also has a restaurant providing Scottish dishes (no reservations necessary for lunch; dinner for groups only). Although its world-famous cat Towser is now hunting mice in the heavens, he is remembered in a statue. There is no monument to his alleged 28,899 victims (who documented them so precisely on behalf of the Guinness Book of Records?). Given the amount of mouse-tempting grain on the premises, most distilleries employ a cat. Towser's successor is called Amber.

The distillery is on the banks of the River Turret, near Crieff, in Perthshire. There are records of whisky making in the neighbourhood at least as early as 1717, and some of the buildings on the present site date from 1775. The distillery itself was dismantled in the 1920s, then revived in 1959 by a noted whisky enthusiast, James Fairlie. It was acquired in 1981 by Cointreau, the French liqueur company, and became part of Highland Distillers (now Edrington) in 1990.

HOUSE STYLE Dry, nutty, fresh, flowery. Young as an aperitif; older after dinner.

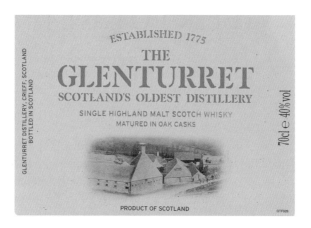

GLENTURRET 10-year-old, 40 vol

COLOUR Pale greeny gold.

NOSE Nasturtiums. Heavy. Sweet.

BODY Light. Seems to vanish.

PALATE Chlorodyne. Cough sweets. Toffee

FINISH Minty. Soothing.

SCORE **76**

GLENTURRET 1987, 54.8 vol

COLOUR Pale gold.

NOSE Beautiful. Vanilla, freesia, fresh malt.

BODY Light.

PALATE Sweet and malty. Tangerine, cut flowers, great balance.
Wood comes through on back palate.

FINISH Clean, nutty.

SCORE **85**

THE GLENTURRET 1980, Limited Edition, 55.2 vol

COLOUR Full gold.

NOSE Coconut oil.

BODY Marshmallow maltiness.

PALATE Nutty. Condensed milk. Cinder toffee.

FINISH Gentle, long, warming. Some soft, restrained, peaty notes.

SCORE **85**

GLENTURRET 1977, 53.2 vol

COLOUR Straw.

NOSE Barley sugar, lemon, bran, floral, pineapple, cooking apple, honeysuckle, becoming buttery in time.

BODY Soft, gentle.

PALATE Honeyed. Stewed orange, liqueur-like. Well balanced.

FINISH Soft, long, drying.

SCORE **86**

THE GLENTURRET 1972, Limited Edition of 522 Bottles

COLOUR Warm gold.

NOSE Peachy, fruity. Coconut oil. Slight cereal-grain oiliness.

BODY Light but creamy.

PALATE Grassy, sweet graininess, maltiness. Flapjack.

FINISH Powerful and soothing. Spiciness and smokiness.

SCORE **83**

SOME INDEPENDENT BOTTLINGS

A 10-year-old from Hart Bros, at 55.5 per cent, is lightly floral, with a nutty maltiness and balancing oak. Slighty tight, but attractive. SCORE 76

A 1990 from Gordon & MacPhail, at 40 per cent, has the aroma of cut flowers, and layers of flavours: raisins, cream, juicy malt, bread and butter pudding, becoming crisp in the finish. SCORE 79

A 1990 Port Finish from Chieftain's Choice, at 12 years and 43 vol, is winey, with suggestions of rose-hips, strawberries, and some oaky dryness. SCORE 70

A 1986 from James MacArthur, at 51.3 vol, has aromas of fresh wood, sap, and wort. It hits its stride more comfortably in mid-palate, with grassy, nutty flavours, but stumbles in an abrupt, hard finish. SCORE 65

A 17-year-old from Wilson & Morgan, at 59.1 per cent, has a whiff of beechwood smoke. It is toasty, with suggestions of malted milk and Terry's chocolate oranges. SCORE 82

A 1985 from Signatory, at 57.1 per cent, was the most substantial in this flight. Pillow-like. Perfect balance between dessert apple fruitiness, light malted milk creaminess, and orange-blossom floweriness. SCORE 89

GLENUGIE

PRODUCER Whitbread/Long John
REGION Highlands DISTRICT Eastern Highlands
SITE OF FORMER DISTILLERY Peterhead, Aberdeenshire, AB42 0XY

T HE CENTRAL STRETCH OF the East Coast has lost all its distilleries. This one was close to the remnants of a fishing village near Peterhead, where the river Ugie reaches the sea. The site incorporates the stump of a windmill. There had been distilling there since the 1830s, and the surviving buildings date from the 1870s.

The Whitbread brewing company, owners since the 1970s, gradually withdrew from the production of spirits during the 1980s, when the whisky industry was suffering one of its cyclical downturns. Industrial premises in Aberdeenshire were being snapped up by small engineering firms servicing the oil boom, and that was Glenugie's fate in 1982–83. Its whisky-making equipment was removed. There is still some stock to be found, and bottlings are still being made, though fewer than three or four years ago.

HOUSE STYLE Flowery, resiny. Can be medicinal. Book-at-bedtime.

Vintage 1976
Single Highland Malt Scotch Whisky
Matured in an oak cask for 25 years
Distilled at Glenugie Distillery
on 27.4.76   Bottled 18.7.2001
Cask No. 2699   Bottle No.   of 272
This whisky has been selected, produced and bottled in Scotland for and under the sole responsibility of Signatory Vintage Scotch Whisky Co. Ltd.
Edinburgh EH6 8PJ, Scotland
70cl   NATURAL COLOUR   51.8%vol

GLENUGIE 1976, Signatory, 51.8 vol

COLOUR Gold.

NOSE Light. Green grass, mandarin.

BODY Sharply fresh.

PALATE Assertive. Cinnamon, nutmeg, vanilla pod.

FINISH Lively. Long.

SCORE **74**

GLENURY ROYAL

PRODUCER DCL
REGION Highlands DISTRICT Eastern Highlands
SITE OF FORMER DISTILLERY Stonehaven, Kincardineshire, AB3 2PY

Has any valedictory bottling ever had the impact of Glenury's 50-year-old, issued as a special release in 2003? This voluptuous malt bore a recommended price tag of almost £1,000/$1,600 a bottle.

Glenury Royal was on the east coast, south of Aberdeen, and close to the fishing port of Stonehaven. The distillery's name derived from the glen that runs through the Ury district. The water for the whisky came from the Cowie, a river known for salmon and trout. The distillery was founded in 1825, partly to provide a market for barley in a period of agricultural depression. Founder Captain Robert Barclay was an athlete, known for an odd achievement: he was the first man to walk 1,000 miles in as many hours without a break. He was also a local Member of Parliament. Barclay had a friend at court to whom he referred coyly as "Mrs Windsor", and through whose influence he was given permission by King William IV to call his whisky "Royal". It was an excellent malt, judging from recent bottlings. The distillery was mothballed in 1985, and the site was later sold for a housing development.

HOUSE STYLE Aromatic, spicy, fruity. Book-at-bedtime.

GLENURY 1953, 50-year-old, 42.8 vol

COLOUR Dark orange.

NOSE Smoke. The burnt skin of chestnuts roasting.

BODY Rich, smooth, luxurious.

PALATE A whole box of liqueur chocolates concentrated into my tasting glass Dark chocolate, variously filled with coffee and cherry liqueurs Perhaps even peppermint.

FINISH Sappy, oaky dryness.

SCORE 89

GLENURY ROYAL 21-year-old, Old Malt Cask, 50 vol

COLOUR Amber.

NOSE More wood on show. Soft and generous: hessian, peanut skin, chocolate spread.

BODY Firm, dry.

PALATE Excellent concentration. Baked apple. Spicy oak. Complex.

FINISH Long and nutty.

SCORE **81**

GLENURY-ROYAL 1972, Gordon & MacPhail, 40 vol

COLOUR Amber.

NOSE Mellow and mature. Honey and chestnut, plum, autumnal. Hard toffee, black cherry.

BODY Long, elegant, and chewy.

PALATE The fruit sits heavily on the palate. Perfect balance. Coffee.

FINISH Long and attractive.

SCORE **84**

GLENURY ROYAL 23-year-old, Distilled 1971, Rare Malts, 61.3 vol

COLOUR Deep, reddish amber.

NOSE Peat, sherry, and polished oak.

BODY Medium, firm, smooth.

PALATE Smooth, tightly combined flavours, beautifully rounded. Treacle toffee, nuts, cedary notes.

FINISH Very long. Starts oaky, then an explosion of long, warming smokiness. A superb example of a Highland malt, hitting as an oak-fisted heavyweight.

SCORE **80**

GLENURY ROYAL 28-year-old, Distilled 1970, Rare Malts, 58.4 vol

COLOUR Shining gold.

NOSE Nutty, almondy, oloroso sherry.

BODY Very firm, rounded. Less sherryish muscle, more of an elegant middleweight.

PALATE Honey, lemons, pistachio nuts, angelica, garden mint.

FINISH Like biting into a green leaf. Tree-bark woodiness. Cinnamon. Fragrant. Long.

SCORE **79**

HIGHLAND PARK

PRODUCER The Edrington Group
REGION Highlands ISLAND Orkney
ADDRESS Kirkwall, Orkney, KW15 1SU TEL 01856 874619 VC
WEBSITE www.highlandpark.co.uk

THIS GREAT ORCADIAN DISTILLERY is now the only islander in The Edrington Group, with the sale of Bunnahabhain, on Islay. Presumably the idea was to concentrate on Highland Park as the group's island malt, and pitch the distinctiveness of Orkney against fashionable Islay. Devotees might expect a clamour of new bottlings from Highland Park: labelled to emphasize the distinctly young, heathery nature of Orkney's peat; the simple beauty of the maltings at the distillery; the big, bulbous stills; the winds that blow salt on to the shore. So far, nothing much has happened, but no doubt it will.

Highland Park is the greatest all-rounder in the world of malt whisky. It is definitely in an island style, but combining all the elements of a classic single malt: smokiness (with its own heather-honey accent), maltiness, smoothness, roundness, fullness of flavour, and length of finish.

Subject to ambitious plans for the Shetland islands, Highland Park is the northernmost of Scotland's distilleries. It dates from at least 1798.

HOUSE STYLE Smoky and full-flavoured. At 18 or 25 years old, with dessert or a cigar. The yet older vintages with a book at bedtime.

HIGHLAND PARK 12-year-old, 40 vol

COLOUR Amber.

NOSE Smoky, "garden bonfire" sweetness, heathery, malty, hint of sherry.

BODY Medium, exceptionally smooth.

PALATE Succulent, with smoky dryness, heather-honey sweetness, and maltiness.

FINISH Teasing, heathery, delicious.

SCORE **90**

HIGHLAND PARK 15-year-old, 40 vol

COLOUR Amber.

NOSE Thick and sweet. Botrytis. Squashed apricot, over-ripe pear. Toasted almond, beech nut.

BODY Chewy.

PALATE Great balance between caramelized fruit, honey, and heathery smoke. Mouth-filling. Fudge. Malt.

FINISH Treacle toffee.

SCORE **87**

HIGHLAND PARK 18-year-old, 43 vol

COLOUR Refractive, pale gold.

NOSE Warm, notably flowery. Heather honey, fresh oak, sap, peat, smoky fragrance. Very aromatic and appetizing.

BODY Remarkably smooth, firm, rounded.

PALATE Lightly salty. Leafy (vine leaves?), pine nuts. Lots of flavour development: nuts, honey, cinnamon, dryish ginger.

FINISH Spicy, very dry, oaky, smoky, hot.

SCORE **92**

HIGHLAND PARK 24-year-old, Distilled 1967, 43 vol

Now very hard to find.

COLOUR Amber.

NOSE Honey, with smooth background smokiness.

BODY Full.

PALATE Starts with smooth honey, becoming deeper in flavour, developing to a smooth, perfumy smokiness.

FINISH Smooth, honeyish, with light fruitiness. Soothing.

SCORE **93**

HIGHLAND PARK 25-year-old, 50.7 vol

COLOUR Amber to copper.

NOSE Immense complexity. Rum and raisin, Christmas spices, dried heather, light smoke.

BODY Layered.

PALATE Mature, with perfect poise. Chocolate, nutty oak. Fine tannins. Light smoke.

FINISH Long and subtle, with bitter orange and scenty lemon.

SCORE **95**

HIGHLAND PARK 25-year-old, 53.5 vol

An earlier bottling.

COLOUR Apricot.

NOSE Full, rounded. Fudge, white chocolate, oloroso sherry, honey, melon, lemon. Fruity.

BODY Firm, rounded.

PALATE More honey, slightly chewy. Nutty toffee. Nougat. Pistachio nuts. Turkish delight. Cedar.

FINISH Lemon, honey, roses. Fragrant, smooth. Balancing dryness.

SCORE **93**

HIGHLAND PARK 1977, Bicentenary Vintage Reserve, 43 vol

COLOUR Pale walnut.

NOSE Polished oak. Leather upholstery.

BODY Firm satin richness.

PALATE Minty. Creamy. Freshly peeled satsumas. Orange peels. Dark cherry flavours. Very bitter black chocolate. Astonishing complexity and length. Great power. Long development of drier flavours.

FINISH Violets. Lingering flowery, scented flavours.

SCORE **94**

IMPERIAL

PRODUCER Allied Distillers Ltd
REGION Highlands DISTRICT Speyside
ADDRESS Carron, Morayshire, AB34 7QP

MALT LOVERS THIRSTING FOR THIS underrated and rarely bottled Speysider have in recent years been permitted a 15-year-old Special Distillery bottling from proprietors Allied.

The Imperial distillery is in Carron, just across the river from Dailuaine, with which it was historically linked. It was founded in 1897 and extended in 1965. It closed in 1985, but was reopened by Allied in 1989, then mothballed in 1998. Imperial's unusually large stills make it hard to use flexibly. "You either make a lot of Imperial or none at all," commented one observer.

HOUSE STYLE Big and (often sweetly) smoky. After dinner or at bedtime.

IMPERIAL 15-year-old, Special Distillery Bottlings, 46 vol

COLOUR	Golden satin. Slight haze.
NOSE	Lemon meringue pie. Key lime pie. Not only the fruit filling but also the pastry. Slightly floury, dusty. Some cellar character.
BODY	Thin but smooth. Falls away somewhat.
PALATE	Lemon skins. Some sweet lemon, becoming quite intense, then drying. Rounds out with a little water.
FINISH	Gently dry. Slight hint of smoky dryness.

SCORE **71**

INCHGOWER

PRODUCER Diageo
REGION Highlands DISTRICT Speyside
ADDRESS Buckie, Banffshire, AB56 2AB   TEL 01542 836700

TASTES MORE LIKE A COASTAL MALT than a Speysider. It is both, the distillery being on the coast near the fishing town of Buckie, but not far from the mouth of the river Spey. To the palate expecting a more flowery, elegant Speyside style, this can seem assertive, or even astringent, in its saltiness. With familiarity, that can become addictive. The Inchgower distillery was built in 1871, and expanded in 1966. Its whisky is an important element in the Bell's blend.

HOUSE STYLE Dry, salty. Restorative or aperitif.

INCHGOWER 14-year-old, Flora and Fauna, 43 vol

COLOUR Pale gold.

NOSE An almost chocolatey spiciness, then sweet notes like edible seaweed, and finally a whiff of saltier sea character. Overall, dry and complex.

BODY Light to medium. Smooth.

PALATE Starts sweet and malty, with lots of flavour developing, eventually becoming drier and salty.

FINISH Very salty, lingering appetizingly on the tongue.

SCORE **76**

OTHER VERSIONS OF INCHGOWER

A Rare Malts 1974, at cask strength, had sea air in the nose; salted cashew, and edible-seaweed flavours. SCORE 79. A 19-year-old from Cadenhead , at 46 vol, is chocolatey, nutty (roast chestnuts), smoke, oak, and resin. SCORE 78.

INVERLEVEN

PRODUCER Allied Distillers Ltd
REGION Lowlands DISTRICT Western Lowlands
ADDRESS 2 Glasgow Road, Dumbarton, Dunbartonshire, G82 1ND

A LANDMARK VANISHED when Ballantine's distillery complex at Dumbarton was demolished in 2002. The towering 1930s building had stood like a castle at the point where the river Leven flows into the Clyde estuary. For many years, this complex operated not only a column still making grain whisky, but also two pot-still houses to produce malt whisky for the Ballantine blends. One of the malt distilleries, called Inverleven, had conventional stills. The other produced a heavier, Lomond-still whisky. The malt stills had ceased operation in 1991–92, two more Lowlanders ceding superiority to the Highlands and Islands.

HOUSE STYLE Perfumy, fruity, oily. With a summer salad when young; with nuts at Christmas when older.

INVERLEVEN 15-year-old, Cadenhead, 58.1 vol

COLOUR Straw.

NOSE Tough and hard. Empire biscuits, twine. Seems young.

BODY Light.

PALATE Summery, elderflower. Despite 15 years,
the whisky tastes a little immature.

FINISH Sweet.

SCORE 72

INVERLEVEN 1986, Gordon & MacPhail, 40 vol

COLOUR Straw.

NOSE Seems artificially sweet. Angelica, boot polish, green plum.

BODY Flat.

PALATE Some malt but insubstantial. Stalky. Slightly woody.

FINISH Dry and hard.

SCORE **69**

INVERLEVEN 1985, Gordon & MacPhail, 40 vol

COLOUR White wine.

NOSE Freshly cut, ripe, sweet pears. Scented, summery.

BODY Lightly creamy.

PALATE Cream flavour. Nectarine, melon, pear. Soft, stalky woodiness.

FINISH Refreshing.

SCORE **71**

A 1979 edition from the same bottler was slightly less fruity and drier. SCORE 71

DUMBARTON (Inverleven Stills), 1969, 27-year-old, Cadenhead, 51.4 vol

COLOUR Bright orangey amber.

NOSE Distinctly clean, peaty smokiness, with surprisingly fresh, orangey notes.

BODY Firmly creamy.

PALATE Juicy, fruity. Orange cream. Nutty, stalky dryness. Slightly woody, but an unusual and very pleasant malt.

FINISH Grassy. Fragrant, smoky dryness.

SCORE **71**

A 1966 (bottled 1984) from Cadenhead was similar but more
cedary and spicy. SCORE 67
A 21-year-old from the same bottler was very gingery and orangey. SCORE 69

JURA

PRODUCER Whyte and Mackay Ltd
REGION Highlands ISLAND Jura
ADDRESS Craighouse, Jura, Argyll, PA60 7XT
TEL 01496 820240 WEBSITE www.isleofjura.com VC

E VERY VISITOR TO ISLAY also makes the crossing to Jura. The two are
so close that they tend to be seen as one. While Islay has seven
working distilleries, Jura has just the one. While Islay has some very
assertive whiskies, Jura's is delicate – but gains power with age. Under
new ownership, the distillery has been more active in introducing new
products and marketing them with some vigour.

Two extraordinarily young bottlings, at three and four years old, were
made for the Japanese market. Both showed considerable potential.
The younger was clean, malty, and assertive, with good maritime
flavours. The marginally less young version was more earthy, flowery,
and fruity. In the British market, "Superstition" is a sweeter, richer,
mature whisky, but seems a little confected, like its marketing story.

The first distillery on the site seems to have been founded around
1810, and rebuilt in 1876. Although a couple of buildings dating back
to its early days are still in use, the present distillery was built during
the late 1950s and early 1960s, and enlarged in the 1970s.

The name Jura derives from the Norse word for deer. These
outnumber people, on an island 55 by 11 kilometres (34 by 7 miles).
Jura has about 225 human inhabitants, among whom its most famous
was George Orwell. He went there to find a healthy, peaceful place in
which to write the novel *1984*. There is a whisky named after him in
the Jura range.

HOUSE STYLE Piney, lightly oily, soft, salty. Aperitif.

ISLE OF JURA Superstition, No Age Statement, 45 vol

COLOUR Bronze satin.

NOSE Very light peat smoke, but also some sherryish sweetness. Sweet hay.

BODY Smooth. Waxy.

PALATE Piney, honeyish. Developing sweet creaminess. Opens very slowly.

FINISH Salty, with a surprising sting.

SCORE **80**

ISLE OF JURA 10-year-old, 40 vol

COLOUR Bright gold.

NOSE Oily, lightly piney, earthy, salty, dry.

BODY Light, slightly oily, soft.

PALATE Sweetish; slowly developing a slight island dryness and saltiness.

FINISH A little malty sweetness and some saltiness.

SCORE **72**

ISLE OF JURA Legacy 10-year-old, 40 vol

The vatting for this version additionally contains substantially older malts.

COLOUR Amber.

NOSE Nutty and malty with a slight metallic note.
Turf and flour sacks, rising dough.

PALATE Firm, sweet bracken. Fresh and clean. Lunchtime.

FINISH Squeeze of fruit juice, then malt.

SCORE **70**

ISLE OF JURA, 16-year-old, 40 vol

COLOUR Full gold to bronze.

NOSE Freshly chopped pine trees. Ferns. Forest floor.

BODY Light, firm, oily-creamy. Dryish.

PALATE Ground coriander. Orange. Rhubarb jam. Buttered scones.

FINISH Salty.

SCORE **77**

ISLE OF JURA Orwell, 42 vol

COLOUR Gold.

NOSE Quite woody and prickly to start. Heather moor, marine. Mossy.

BODY Dry.

PALATE Broad with light smoke all the way playing against central
tangerine-flavoured sweetness. Some complexity.

FINISH Nutty.

SCORE **78**

ISLE OF JURA 21-year-old, 43 vol

COLOUR Pale orange.

NOSE Cedary. Then surprisingly fruity and tropical.
Tinned pineapple, cooked peach, papaya, melon.

BODY Luscious.

PALATE Oak. Fruitiness becomes more orangey. Sweet tobacco.

FINISH Soft fruit. Refreshing acidity.

SCORE **80**

ISLE OF JURA 27-year-old, Stillman's Dram, 45 vol

COLOUR Amber.

NOSE Mature, wood-derived aromas: porcini mushroom, autumnal,
bracken, old spice cupboard. Light balsamic note. Old but balanced.

BODY Dryish.

PALATE Quite perfumed. Candied peel.

FINISH Nutty, angelica.

SCORE **80**

ISLE OF JURA 33-year-old, 55.6 vol

COLOUR Copper, dull rim.

NOSE Wet clay. Tunisian spices.

BODY Chewy.

PALATE Still sweet after all this time. Tobacco leaf, black cherry.

FINISH Long. Chocolatey.

SCORE **80**

ISLE OF JURA 36-year-old, 63.7 vol

COLOUR Old gold.

NOSE Mature. Smoked meat.

BODY Chewy.

PALATE Rich and sweet with a heathery, peppery note.
Though faded, has reminders of smoky power.

FINISH Sweet malt and smoke.

SCORE **80**

SOME INDEPENDENT BOTTLINGS OF JURA

A 6-year-old from Adelphi, at 60.5 vol, is slightly prickly on the nose,
with pulpy fruits in the palate, and some nutty dryness. Young, but well
balanced. SCORE 71

A 1989 from Gordon & MacPhail, at 40 vol, is sweet and simple,
with a crisp finish. SCORE 70

KINCLAITH

PRODUCER Whitbread/Long John
REGION Lowlands DISTRICT Western Lowlands
SITE OF FORMER DISTILLERY Moffat Street, Glasgow, G5 0ND

T HERE WAS ONCE QUITE A SCATTER of malt distilleries in Glasgow. The last was Kinclaith, built in 1957, as part of the complex already housing the Strathclyde grain distillery. The original owner was the American company Schenley, through its subsidiaries Seager Evans and Long John. During the 1960s, when the bulk of Kinclaith production was presumably going into the Long John blends, some trickled out to independent bottlers. Long John was sold to Whitbread in 1975, and Kinclaith was dismantled. In the 1980s, the bottlers Cadenhead released a typically gingery but quite smoky 20-year-old. Gordon & MacPhail has bottled one or two versions from successive years. Recently, Signatory issued the bottling described below.

HOUSE STYLE Light, melony. Aperitif.

KINCLAITH 1975, Signatory, 52.3 vol

COLOUR	Amber.
NOSE	All wood derived. Pine, hickory, bracken.
BODY	Lightly chewy.
PALATE	Gentle and oaky. Soft fruits. Melon. Vanilla. Good length.
FINISH	Dry, nutty.

SCORE 72

KINCLAITH 1967, Connoisseurs Choice, 40 vol

COLOUR	Amber.
NOSE	Smoky, some sherry, faintly sulphury.
BODY	Light, delicate.
PALATE	Light, soft, restrained fruitiness. Melon?
FINISH	Soothing, tasty. Melon. Sherry.

SCORE 68

KNOCKANDO

PRODUCER Diageo
REGION Highlands DISTRICT Speyside
ADDRESS Knockando, Aberlour, Banffshire, AB38 7RT
TEL 01340 882000

MORE WAS HEARD OF this elegant whisky – in Britain, at least – when it was the most promoted malt in the portfolio of IDV, before the merger that created Diageo in 1997.

Knockando is among a small group of malts that are especially influential in the J&B (Justerini & Brooks) blends (*see* Glen Spey, The Singleton/Auchroisk, *and* Strathmill). Knockando is a sophisticated malt, and its labelling policy is somewhat elaborate. In the US, where some consumers believe the guarantee "12-year-old" essential to identify a premium malt, this phrase is used, along with the year of distillation, on the label of the principal version. In Britain, the malt is marketed under its season of distillation. The notion is that the malt is bottled when it is mature, rather than at a specific age.

One season does not differ dramatically from another, though there are very subtle differences. At older ages, the whisky gains greatly in complexity and sherry character.

The water with which the whisky is made rises from granite and flows over peat. The distillery's name, pronounced "knock-AN-do" (or 'du) sounds allusively comical to English speakers, but translates perfectly sensibly as "a little black hill". Knockando is hidden in a fold in the hills overlooking the river Spey at a fine spot for salmon fishing. The distillery was established in 1898.

HOUSE STYLE Elegant, with suggestions of berry fruits. Aperitif.

KNOCKANDO 1989, 43 vol

COLOUR Bright gold.

NOSE Faint, grassy, sweetish, peat. Lemon grass. Marshmallow. Shortbread.

BODY Light but smooth.

PALATE Soft. Creamy. Faintly honeyed. Raspberries. Lemon zest.

FINISH Nutty, toffeeish dryness. Gently appetizing.

SCORE **76**

KNOCKANDO 18-year-old, 1980, 43 vol

Available mainly in the US.

COLOUR Medium gold.

NOSE More shortbread. Almonds. Nice balance of late lemon.

BODY Creamier. Rounder. Very smooth indeed.

PALATE Nuttier, spicier, drier. Tightly combined flavours.

FINISH Late fruit, lemon grass, and light peat. Very appetizing.

SCORE **78**

KNOCKANDO Slow Matured, Distilled 1980, Bottled 1998, 43 vol

Available mainly in France.

COLOUR Bright, medium gold.

NOSE Seems faintly peatier than the version above.

BODY Fractionally oilier?

PALATE Possibly more lemon and raspberry fruitiness.

FINISH Crisp. Shortbread. Late warmth.

SCORE **78**

KNOCKANDO Extra Old, Distilled 1977, Bottled 1999, 43 vol

COLOUR Medium to full gold.

NOSE Soft. Complex. Freshly oaky. Lightly sherryish. Creamy. Faintly smoky.

BODY Smooth. Textured.

PALATE Nutty. Tightly combined flavours gradually unfold. Late fruit.
Raspberries. Strawberries.

FINISH Late, nutty dryness. Satisfying. Soothing.

SCORE **79**

KNOCKANDO Master Reserve 1977, Bottled 1999, 43 vol

COLOUR Full gold.

NOSE Very complex and elegant.

BODY Surprisingly full.

PALATE A more sherried version. Delicious interplay of lively flavours:
cream, fruit, and nut.

FINISH Aniseedy sherry. Warming. Dryish.

SCORE **80**

KNOCKANDO Single Cask, 21-year-old, 43 vol

COLOUR Full gold to pale amber.

NOSE Rich for a relatively light malt. Sherryish. Raisiny.

BODY Full. Smooth. Rounded.

PALATE Yet more sherried. Rich, nutty flavours. Lots of flavour development,
with gradual dryness and faint smokiness. Remarkably appetizing.

FINISH Aniseedy sherry. Nutty. Faint, fragrant smokiness. Soothing.

SCORE **81**

EARLIER VERSIONS OF KNOCKANDO

A 1976 edition called Special Selection, bottled 1992, was notably
raspberryish and on the dry side. SCORE 77

An Extra Old Reserve from 1968, bottled 1992, had more
assertiveness and depth. SCORE 79

Independent bottlings are very rare indeed. A 1980 bottled by
Cadenhead at 12 years old and 58 vol was flowery, honeyish,
and sugar-sweet. SCORE 69

LADYBURN

PRODUCER William Grant & Sons Ltd
REGION Lowlands DISTRICT Western Lowlands
ADDRESS Girvan, Ayrshire, KA26 9PT

MUCH EXCITEMENT AMONG MALT LOVERS who attended the release of an "official" bottling of this rare malt in 2000. As is often the case with old malts, it turned out to be rather woody, but it was much appreciated by collectors. Very old casks do occasionally turn up in the corner of a warehouse, and it is better that they be bottled than remain, becoming woodier and eventually evaporating below the legal minimum alcohol content.

Ladyburn operated for only about a dozen years in the 1960s and 1970s. It was a Lowland malt distillery on the same site as the Girvan grain distillery. Like the Girvan whisky, the Ladyburn was a component of the Grant's blend, no doubt along with Glenfiddich and Balvenie.

No doubt the Girvan and Ladyburn distilleries were built to make Grant's as self-sufficient as possible. Grant's had become something of a maverick when it began seriously to market Glenfiddich as a single malt. Its worry was that it might in future have difficulty in obtaining whiskies from other distilleries for use in its blends. That prospect was disarmed by the success of Glenfiddich.

HOUSE STYLE Aromatic, fruity and dry. Aperitif.

LADYBURN 1973, 50.4 vol

COLOUR Full, greeny gold.

NOSE Powerfully earthy-fruity aroma. Fruit skins. Fruit in boxes at a market.

BODY Smooth and syrupy.

PALATE Sweet. Peach, orangey.

FINISH Assertive. Dry. Peach stones. Rind-like. Woody.

SCORE 60

LAGAVULIN

PRODUCER Diageo
REGION Islay DISTRICT South Shore
ADDRESS Port Ellen, Islay, Argyll, PA42 7DZ TEL 01496 302730
WEBSITE www.discovering-distilleries.com/www.malts.com

RECENT SHORTAGES OF LAGAVULIN date back to a period 16 years ago when the distillery was closed for some time for repairs and renewal. In those days, Lagavulin worked only two days a week. Today, it cannot produce enough to meet anticipated demand. Until the shortage, it was the best selling Islay malt, having overtaken its neighbour Laphroaig. Consideration has been given to adding a pair of stills, but it is felt that might "damage the integrity" of the beautifully kept distillery.

Lagavulin has the driest and most sustained attack of any readily available whisky, though in recent years it has seemed less brutal than it once was.

The launch in 1997–98 of a version identified as being finished in Pedro Ximénez sherry casks excited great interest. How would this famously robust whisky live with the most hefty of sherries? Would each cancel out the other, so that the punch was finally restrained? Or would the two combine to produce a superpower? Neither is quite the case. The two elements are like heavyweights punching in a clinch.

The distillery's water arrives by way of a fast-flowing stream that no doubt picks up plenty of peat on the way there. The maturation warehouses are battered by the sea, and they have their own jetty.

Lagavulin (pronounced "lagga-voolin") means "the hollow where the mill is". There are reputed to have been ten illicit stills on this bay in the mid-1700s. Lagavulin traces its history to 1816.

HOUSE STYLE Dry, smoky, complex. Restorative or nightcap.

LAGAVULIN 12-year-old, Cask Strength, Special Release 2003, 57.8 vol

COLOUR Unusually pale. Vinho verde.

NOSE Delightfully gentle smokiness, but very restrained for Lagavulin. Some floweriness.

BODY Very light.

PALATE Marshmallow. Digestive biscuits. Assam tea.

FINISH Smoky. Some of the peatiness that might be expected in Lagavulin. Slightly fruity. Warming. Firm. Long.

SCORE **91**

LAGAVULIN 16-year-old, 43 vol

COLOUR Full amber.

NOSE Sea spray, peat smoke. Stings the back of the nose.

BODY Full, smooth, very firm.

PALATE Peaty dryness like gunpowder tea. As the palate develops, oily, grassy, and, in particular, salty notes emerge.

FINISH Peat fire. Warming. A bear hug.

SCORE **95**

LAGAVULIN 1979, Double Matured, Distillers Edition, 43 vol

Finished in Pedro Ximénez sherry casks.

COLOUR Orange sandstone.

NOSE Fresh attack, with hits of peat, tar, sulphur, and salt, soothed with beeswax.

BODY Full. Syrupy.

PALATE Rich and extremely sweet, then smoky, becoming medicinal, and eventually seaweedy.

FINISH Pepper, salt, sand. What it loses in distillery character, it gains in a different dimension of distinctiveness.

SCORE **95**

LAGAVULIN 1979, Murray McDavid Mission Range, 46 vol

COLOUR Pale straw.

NOSE Phenolic. Smoked fish. Hot stones on the beach. Bog myrtle.

BODY Soft.

PALATE Fragrant smoke all the way. Soot. Sweet spot in the centre keeps it balanced.

FINISH Enveloping smoke.

SCORE **88**

LAPHROAIG

PRODUCER Allied Distillers Ltd
REGION Islay DISTRICT South Shore
ADDRESS Port Ellen, Islay, Argyll, PA42 7DU
TEL 01496 302418 WEBSITE www.laphroaig.com VC

THIS IS THE MOST MEDICINAL of malts. "Love it or hate it," said one of Laphroaig's advertising slogans (borrowed, without attribution, from a distinguished writer on whisky). Like hospital gauze? Reminiscent of mouthwash or antiseptic? Phenolic? That is the whole point: the iodine-like, seaweed character of Islay.

The famous Laphroaig attack has diminished a little in recent years, unmasking more of the sweetness of the malt, but it is still an extremely characterful whisky, with a distinctively oily body. Laphroaig has its own peat beds on Islay, its own dam on the Kilbride river, a floor maltings at the distillery, and relatively small stills. Its maturation warehouses face directly on to the sea.

The distillery was built in the 1820s by the Johnston family, whose name is still on the label. In 1847 the founder died after falling into a vat of partially made whisky. In the late 1950s and early 1960s, the distillery was owned by a woman, Miss Bessie Williamson – a glamourous lady, judging from a photograph on the wall. The romance of the place extends to occasional weddings at the distillery, part of which serves as the village hall.

HOUSE STYLE Medicinal. Nightcap.

LAPHROAIG 10-year-old

The stronger is slightly richer. Versions have been marketed at 40 and 43 vol.

COLOUR Full, refractive gold.

NOSE Medicinal, phenolic, seaweedy, with a hint of estery (gooseberry?) sweetness.

BODY Medium, oily.

PALATE Seaweedy, salty, oily.

FINISH Round and very dry.

SCORE **86**

LAPHROAIG 10-year-old, Cask Strength, 57.3 vol

COLOUR Very full gold.

NOSE Drier, with "tarred rope" phenol.

BODY Medium, with some syrupy viscosity.

PALATE Seaweedy. Both salty and sweet. Tar-like.

FINISH Medicinal. Tar, phenol, peat, earth. A wonderfully complex whisky.

SCORE **88**

LAPHROAIG 15-year-old, 43 vol

COLOUR Pale amber.

NOSE Phenol, tar, sulphur.

BODY Medium to full, with a soothing oiliness.

PALATE A deceptive moment of sweetness and grassiness, then an explosion of sulphur, burning peat, and Islay intensity.

FINISH Round, dry, long, warming.

SCORE **89**

LAPHROAIG 1976, 43 vol

COLOUR Pale amber.

NOSE Powerful tar aromas.

BODY Medium to full. Firm and smooth.

PALATE Coal-tar soap. Lively embrace of dryness and scenty sweetness.

FINISH Warming, soothing, soporific, long.

SCORE **89**

LAPHROAIG 30-year-old, Bottled November 1997, 43 vol

Bottled from 123 sherry butts branded with the legend SS Great Auk, believed to be the ship in which they came from Jerez over three decades ago.

COLOUR Dark orange.

NOSE Soft. Polished oak. Fragrant smoke. Roses. Lemony notes.

BODY Full, creamy.

PALATE Astonishingly fresh. Toasted almonds. Edible seaweed. Briar. Smoke.

FINISH Musky. Bittersweet. Beautifully balanced for such a great age.

SCORE **90**

LAPHROAIG 40-year-old, 42.3 vol

COLOUR Old gold.

NOSE Heather and sage. Very subtle smoke in background.

BODY Soft.

PALATE Concentrated flavours. Less iodine than usual. More pepper. Unusual, but very lively and appetizing, flowery notes.

FINISH Very smoky. Complex.

SCORE **88**

LAPHROAIG 1988, Murray McDavid, Bourbon Cask, 46 vol

COLOUR Straw.

NOSE Growly and powerful. Phenolic. Tar and medicine. Engine room.

BODY Biscuity.

PALATE Immediate tarry, oily smokiness. Dry and powerful but has good weight in the middle of the mouth.

FINISH Medicinal, smouldering.

SCORE **86**

LINKWOOD

PRODUCER Diageo
REGION Highlands ISLAND Speyside (Lossie)
ADDRESS Elgin, Morayshire, IV30 3RD TEL 01343 862000

A SECRET NATURE RESERVE or a distillery? Linkwood's appropriately flowery Speyside whisky is increasingly appreciated, judging from the profusion of independent bottlings.

The dam that provides the cooling water is a port of call to tufted ducks and goldeneyes – and a seasonal home to wagtails, oyster catchers, mute swans, and otters. In the 4 hectares (10 acres) of the site, nettles attract red admiral and small tortoiseshell butterflies; cuckoo flowers entice the orange tip variety; bluebells seduce bees.

The distillery was founded in 1821. The older of its two still-houses, in the original buildings, continues to be used for a few months each year. It produces a slightly heavier spirit than the larger still-house built in the 1960s and extended in the 1970s.

HOUSE STYLE Floral. Rose-water? Cherries? Delicious with a slice of fruitcake.

LINKWOOD 12-year-old, Flora and Fauna, 43 vol

COLOUR Full primrose.

NOSE Remarkably flowery and petal-like. Buttercups. Grass. Fragrant.

BODY Medium, rounded, slightly syrupy.

PALATE Starts slowly, and has a long, sustained development to marzipan, roses, and fresh sweetness. One to savour.

FINISH Perfumy, dryish. Lemon zest.

SCORE *82*

 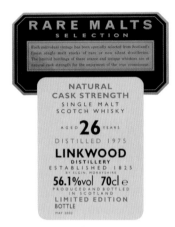

LINKWOOD 1983, Bottled 1997, Cask Strength, Limited Bottling, 59.8 vol

COLOUR Bright gold.

NOSE Turkish delight. Pistachio nuts. Cherries. Fudge.

BODY Medium to full. Rich.

PALATE Fudgey, nutty, moving to flowery dryness.

FINISH Flowery. Lemony. Back to the richness of earlier years, though not quite the complexity.

SCORE *83*

LINKWOOD 1975 26-year-old, Rare Malt, 56.1 vol

A lovely whisky, as Linkwoods so often are.

COLOUR Bright pale gold.

NOSE Like walking on a peaty moorland on a breezy day. Fresh, fragrant.

BODY Light to medium. Syrupy.

PALATE Starts with a faintly smoky sweetness, like the surface of a crème brûlée. Moves into a syrupy, treacle-tart sweetness.

FINISH Intensity of sweet, floral spiciness. Warming. Extraordinary length.

SCORE *84*

LINKWOOD 1974, 22-year-old, Cask Strength, Rare Malts

Tasted as a work in progress.

COLOUR Full gold.

NOSE Rose-water. Flowers. Some peat.

BODY Soft.

PALATE Sugared almonds. Cream toffee. Condensed milk. Indian desserts.

FINISH Almondy. Firm. Sustained. Long.

A 1972 version from Rare Malts, bottled in 1995, was bigger, with a more oaky, cedary aroma, a raisiny palate, and a big finish that suggested sugared almonds and parma violets. SCORE 84

SOME INDEPENDENT BOTTLINGS OF LINKWOOD

A 10-year-old from Dun Bheagan, at 43 vol, has delicate nutmeg, baked apple, and caramelized fruits. Quite oaky for a youngster. SCORE 78

A 10-year-old from James MacArthur, at 59.8 vol, has the mood of spring, with green apple and grass. Still young and a little tight. SCORE 75

A 12-year-old, from Cooper's Choice, at 43 vol, is attractive and summery. Apple pie crust, orchard fruits. Complex, with spicy oak. The perfect pre-lunch malt. SCORE 85

A 14-year-old, distilled in 1984, from Cadenhead, at 58.6 vol, seems still to be maturing. Hard in mid-palate, with curiously unripe grapey notes. SCORE 65

A 15-year-old, from, Duncan Taylor, at 46 vol, is very fruity and flowery: Semillon, dessert apple, blackberry, elderflower. Pastry. Late summer on the lawn. SCORE 82

A 1989 Raw Cask, from Blackadder, at 59.2 vol, has the aroma of autumn fruits, some cellar notes (bung cloth), sherry, and wood that is a little too dominant. SCORE 70

A 1989 from Gordon & MacPhail, at 61 vol, is a classic Linkwood. The aroma is fresh and clean, with a wisp of smoke; the palate fresh, fruity, and lightly chewy; the whole precisely framed in oak. SCORE 83

A 1972, at 40 vol, from the same bottler, is mature and rounded, deliciously reminiscent of tarte tatin. SCORE 85

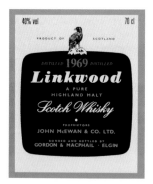

A 1969 is more savoury, with pine, basil, and allspice. SCORE 78
A 1954 retains its equilibrium remarkably for its great age. Still sweet and fruity, with good tannins. Whisky-soaked oak. SCORE 83

A 1989 from Murray McDavid, at 46 vol, has an emphatic influence of American oak. Sweet and fresh vanilla. Creamy. Demerara sugar. Dried pear, dessert apple. Very light smoke. Appetizing. SCORE 82

A 1988 from Signatory, at 43 vol, is unusually leathery and tar-like, in both aroma and palate. SCORE 68

LITTLEMILL

PRODUCER Loch Lomond Distillery Co. Ltd
REGION Lowlands DISTRICT Western Lowlands
ADDRESS Bowling, Dunbartonshire, G60 5BG
TEL 01389 752781 EMAIL mail@lochlomonddistillery.com

Plans to restart production at Littlemill as a tourist attraction were finally abandoned, with regret, in 2003 by Loch Lomond, owners of the silent distillery since its previous proprietors went into liquidation 10 years ago.

Also in 2003, The Whisky Exchange issued a bottling of a 1967 experimental malt called Dunglas: one last fleeting manifestation from a ghost distillery. Dunglas was produced in Littlemill's pot stills, but with the intervention of a rectifier. It was intended for blending. The name was intended to have a double "s", but was mis-spelled in the cask documents.

Until the 1930s, Littlemill followed the Lowland practice of triple distillation. The surviving buildings date from at least 1817, but appear to be older. Littlemill was long believed to date from 1772, but more recent evidence suggests that it was already distilling in 1750. It is thus one of the several claimants, each with a slightly different justification, to being the oldest distillery in Scotland.

HOUSE STYLE Marshmallow-soft. A restorative, or perhaps with dessert.

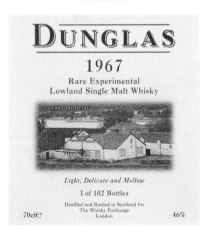

LITTLEMILL 8-year-old, 43 vol

COLOUR Very pale white wine.

NOSE Oily. Marshmallow? Perhaps toasted marshmallows.

BODY Light, soft.

PALATE Malty sweet, yet not overbearing. Marshmallow again, perhaps powdery icing sugar? More recent bottlings slightly less rounded than in the past, and a little more spirity.

FINISH Slight dryness. Coconut?

SCORE **81**

DUNGLAS 1967, The Whisky Exchange, 46 vol

NOSE Perfumy. Crème caramel. Crème brûlée. Then slightly acidic.

PALATE A hint of black chocolate. Dry. Cider apples. Cedary. Slightly woody. Astringent.

FINISH Slightly bitter.

SCORE **73**

SOME INDEPENDENT BOTTLINGS OF LITTLEMILL

LITTLEMILL 1990, 11-year-old, Cadenhead, 60.6 vol

COLOUR Pale, bright, greeny gold.

NOSE Light, lemony.

BODY Creamy. Condensed milk.

PALATE Gentle start. Flowery. Drying.

FINISH Surprisingly hot.

SCORE **77**

LITTLEMILL 1984, 18-year-old, Chieftains Choice, Rum Finish, 46 vol

COLOUR Bright gold.

NOSE Tropical fruits. Pineapple.

BODY Syrupy.

PALATE Cream soda. Coconut.

FINISH A splash of orange.

SCORE **78**

LOCH LOMOND

PRODUCER Loch Lomond Distillery Co. Ltd
REGION Highlands DISTRICT Western Highlands
ADDRESS Lomond Estate, Alexandria, Dunbartonshire, G83 0TL
TEL 01389 752781 WEBSITE www. lochlomonddistillery.com
EMAIL mail@lochlomonddistillery.com

A TRANSFORMATION IS GRADUALLY being wrought at this extraordinary establishment. The building's industrial past (as Britain's oldest car factory and a calico dyeworks) is no longer evident. It has been smartly restyled as a very functional, if complex, distillery. It has three pairs of pot stills, but with a visible difference. Two of the pairs are fitted with rectification columns. They are similar to the Lomond stills (the name is a coincidence) once used by neighbours Ballantine. By being operated in different ways, these stills can produce at least half a dozen different malts. Some of these malts are bottled as singles, but the distillery was designed to produce the components for its own blends. Loch Lomond also has a five-column continuous still.

The distillery is on an industrial estate by the river Leven, which links the Clyde and Loch Lomond. The name Loch Lomond is used on a single malt and a "single blend" (i.e. the grain and malts come from the one distillery). Other malts, such as Inchmurrin, are named after islands in the loch and other places of local interest.

Four of the malts are not usually bottled as singles. These include Glen Douglas, and the progressively more heavily peated Craiglodge, Inchmoan, and Croftengea. With the growing interest in peaty malts, the last may be bottled soon. Tasted as a work in progress, at seven years old, it had a sweet, oily, smoky aroma; a bonfire-like palate; with suggestions of fruit wood, briar, and oak smoke; and a lingering length.

Loch Lomond's unusual pattern of business dates from its acquisition in 1987 by a whisky wholesaler called Glen Catrine. This grew out of a chain of shops, which had their beginning in a licensed grocers. The Loch Lomond distillery, previously owned by the American company, Barton Brands, was established in the mid-1960s.

HOUSE STYLE Loch Lomond: Nutty. Restorative.
Inchmurrin: Fruity. Aperitif. Old Rhosdhu: Piney. Soothing.

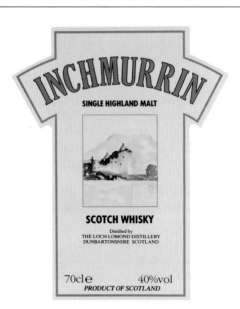

INCHMURRIN 10-year-old, 40 vol

COLOUR Pale apricot.

NOSE Tropical fruit. Watermelons. Orange flower water.

BODY Pleasantly oily.

PALATE Very light-tasting at first, but with some flavour development. Honeydew melon with ginger.

FINISH Spicy, warming, long, soothing.

SCORE **70**

INCHMURRIN 29-year-old, Cadenhead, 54.4 vol

COLOUR Full gold.

NOSE Green malt, reeds, hot sawdust.

BODY Slightly tar-like.

PALATE Assertively nutty. Hazelnut. Hawthorn. Ferns.

FINISH Quite hot.

SCORE **72**

INCHMURRIN 1973, Gordon & MacPhail, 40 vol

COLOUR Bright, reflective, pale, greeny gold.

NOSE Fresh. Fruity. Banana. Lemon zest.

BODY Creamy.

PALATE Flowery. Perfumy. Gin-like.

FINISH Spicy. Hint of clove. Some astringency.

SCORE **71**

LOCH LOMOND, No Age Statement, 40 vol

COLOUR Bright gold.

NOSE Freshly made toast. Brandy snaps.

BODY Candyfloss (cotton candy).

PALATE Powdered sugar. Turkish delight. Pistachio nuts. Banana.

FINISH Light but long. Lemony balancing dryness.

SCORE **70**

LOCH LOMOND 1966, 44 vol

COLOUR Golden.

NOSE Sandalwood, warm hay.

BODY Light, thin.

PALATE Green. Pistachio nuts. Sugared almonds. Intense sweetness.

FINISH Gritty. Abrasive.

SCORE **66**

OLD RHOSDHU, No Age Statement, 40 vol

Minimum 5 years old.

COLOUR Amber.

NOSE Scented. A luxurious malt to drink in the bath.

BODY Light to medium. Soft, oily.

PALATE Dry, perfumy, spicy. Powerful flavours.

FINISH Wintergreen? Perhaps not the bath – the sauna.

SCORE **65**

LOCHNAGAR

PRODUCER Diageo
REGION Highlands DISTRICT Eastern Highlands
ADDRESS Crathie, Ballater, Aberdeenshire, AB35 5TB
TEL 01339 742705
WEBSITE www.discovering-distilleries.com/www.malts.com VC

QUEEN VICTORIA'S FAVOURITE DISTILLERY was once on the tourist route, but has recently been used by Diageo as a place in which to educate its own staff and customers on the subject of malt whisky. The process of making whisky can best be understood in a small, traditional distillery, and Lochnagar qualifies on both counts. It is Diageo's smallest. It is also very pretty – and makes delicious whisky.

The distillery is at the foot of the mountain of Lochnagar, near the river Dee, not far from Aberdeen. A man believed originally to have been an illicit whisky maker established the first legal Lochnagar distillery in 1826, and the present premises were built in 1845. Three years later, the royal family acquired nearby Balmoral as their Scottish country home. The then owner, John Begg, wrote a note inviting Prince Albert to visit. The Prince and Queen Victoria arrived the very next day. Soon afterwards, the distillery began to supply the Queen, and became known as Royal Lochnagar. Her Majesty is said to have laced her claret with the whisky, perhaps anticipating wood finishes. There is no claret finish at Lochnagar as yet. The 12-year-old is aged in second-fill casks, while the Selected Reserve has 50 per cent sherry.

HOUSE STYLE Malty, fruity, spicy, cake-like. After dinner.

ROYAL LOCHNAGAR 12-year-old, 40 vol

COLOUR Full gold.

NOSE Big, with some smokiness.

BODY Medium to full. Smooth.

PALATE Light smokiness, restrained fruitiness, and malty sweetness.

FINISH Again, dry smokiness and malty sweetness. The first impression is of dryness, then comes the sweet, malty counterpoint.

SCORE **80**

ROYAL LOCHNAGAR Selected Reserve, No Age Statement, 43 vol

COLOUR Amber red.

NOSE Very sherryish indeed. Spices, ginger cake.

BODY Big, smooth.

PALATE Lots of sherry, malty sweetness, spiced bread, ginger cake. Obviously contains some very well matured whisky.

FINISH Smoky.

SCORE **83**

ROYAL LOCHNAGAR 23-year-old, Rare Malts, Distilled 1973, 59.7 vol

COLOUR Bright gold.

NOSE Sweet, syrupy, parkin-like.

BODY Medium. Very soft.

PALATE Very appetizing, fresh, clean sweetness. Very good flavour development.

FINISH Marzipan and nutty dryness.

SCORE **81**

ROYAL LOCHNAGAR Rare Malts, 24-year-old, Distilled 1972, 55.7 vol

COLOUR Full, bright gold.

NOSE Fresh soda bread. Yeasty.

BODY Light to medium. Smooth.

PALATE Appetizing, spicy ginger cake. Lots of flavour development and complexity.

FINISH Cake dusted with cinnamon, nutmeg. Satisfying. Very long indeed.

SCORE **81**

LOCHSIDE

PRODUCER Macnab Distilleries
REGION Highlands DISTRICT Eastern Highlands
SITE OF FORMER DISTILLERY Montrose, Angus, DD10 9AD

ONCE THE FAMOUS James Deuchar Brewery, Lochside, in Montrose, then became a distillery from 1957 to 1992. It has since been demolished. Its whisky was the heart of a blend called Macnab's, which was sold in the Spanish market by Distilieras y Crienza, a subsidiary of Domecq sherry. The latter company was acquired by Allied Distillers.

HOUSE STYLE Fruity, dry, gentle. Aperitif.

LOCHSIDE 10-year-old, 40 vol

Now hard to find.

COLOUR Gold.

NOSE Some flowering currant.

BODY Light to medium, soft, smooth.

PALATE Malty start, but not especially sweet. Lots of flavour development.

FRUITY (Blackcurrant?). Becoming dry.

FINISH Gentle, not very long.

SCORE **74**

OTHER VERSIONS OF LOCHSIDE

A 1981 from Murray McDavid, at 46 vol, has a clean, oaty aroma; a juicy palate; and a finish reminiscent of cake icing. SCORE 75

A Lochside from the same year, at 50 vol, by Lombard, has the aroma of the malt barn; lemon curd in the palate; and raspberries in the finish. SCORE 70

A 35-year-old from Old Malt Cask, at 50 vol, has maderization in the aroma; a toasty palate; and crusty bread in the finish. SCORE 75

LONGMORN

PRODUCER Chivas Brothers
REGION Highlands DISTRICT Speyside (Lossie)
ADDRESS Elgin, Morayshire, IV30 3SJ TEL 01542 783042

IT IS TO BE HOPED that the new owners make this distillery's whisky more readily available. Longmorn is one of the finest Speyside malts, cherished by connoisseurs but not widely known. It is admired for its complexity, its combination of smoothness and fullness of character, and from its big bouquet to its long finish. It is noted for its cereal-grain maltiness, beeswax flavours, and estery fruitiness.

The distillery was built in 1894–95, and has a disused waterwheel and a workable steam engine. Much of the equipment is very traditional, and imposing in its size and beautiful condition, including the Steel's mash mixer and some very impressive spirit safes. Alongside the distillery is the disused Longmorn railway halt.

HOUSE STYLE Tongue-coating, malty, complex. Versatile, delightful before dinner, and especially good with dessert.

LONGMORN 12-year-old, 40 vol

COLOUR Full, bright gold.

NOSE Complex, firm.

BODY Firm, smooth, gentle.

PALATE Deliciously fresh, cereal-grain maltiness. Slow, long flavour development, evolving towards a clean, flowery fruitiness.

FINISH Clean, smooth, appetizing.

SCORE 85

LONGMORN 15-year-old, 45 vol

COLOUR Full gold.

NOSE Big, slightly oily, barley malt, flowery-fruity notes.

BODY Smooth, rounded, medium to big.

PALATE Very emphatic, fresh, clean, cereal-grain maltiness.
Suggestions of plum skins.

FINISH Tangerines, nuts. Then peppery. Appetizing. Very long.

SCORE **87**

SOME INDEPENDENT BOTTLINGS OF LONGMORN

A 1990, at 12 years old and 46 vol, from Duncan Taylor, seems a little
immature. It has a grapefruity aroma; lively, almost fizzy, palate;
and marshmallow finish. SCORE 71

A 1969 from the same bottler, at 40.1 vol, is plump, juicy, and fruity,
reminiscent of mangoes and cling peaches. SCORE 80

A delicious 25-year-old, from Gordon & MacPhail, at 40 vol, has a full
bronze colour; mead-like aromas; strawberry jam in the palate;
and marrons glace and cedar in the finish. SCORE 89

In contrast, a 1973, at 55.7 vol, from the same bottler, starts well, with rich
treacle, but dries into cigar ash. SCORE 66

A 1970, at 40 vol, is back to raspberries, with oranges and cloves.
Complex, beautifully balanced, full of life. SCORE 85

A 1973 from Blackadder, at 56.9 vol, is dull, woody and dusty. SCORE 59

A 1972, cask no 1099 from MacKillop's Choice, was tasted as a work in
progress. It was rich and concentrated, with flavours reminiscent of cocoa butter.

A 1968 sherry cask, no 910, was very sweet and charred-tasting. More sherry
than whisky. A 1967, cask no 3345, was well-structured, resiny, with honey
and kumquats A 1966, cask no 611, was faded, sooty, and flat.

A 1971 from Scott's Selection, at 57.8 vol, is tired: tannic, bitter and
chicory-like. For the drinker who likes pickled walnuts and extremely
bitter chocolate. SCORE 62

THE MACALLAN

PRODUCER The Edrington Group
REGION Highlands DISTRICT Speyside
ADDRESS Aberlour, Banffshire, AB38 9RX
TEL 01340 872280 WEBSITE www.themacallan.com VC

As BRONZED AND MUSCULAR as a practitioner of the noble art, Macallan is Speyside's best known heavyweight – and constantly embracing a new challenge. In one such engagement, Macallan has over the years collected, and bought at auction, bottles of its own whisky from the 1800s.

An 1874 Macallan, bought by the company for £4000/$6000, inspired a bold attempt to replicate its character by making a vatting from stocks. The key seemed to be an accent toward fino sherry wood, rather than the dry oloroso currently preferred. There was sufficient fino wood in Macallan's warehouses, and a credible replica of the 1874 was produced. This appeared at the time to be a unique exercise, but a further three replica whiskies have been created since (see pp. 352–54).

It is not necessary to make replicas of Macallans from the early to mid-1900s, as sufficient casks were laid down. Some of these whiskies, designated by the company as Exceptional Single Casks, have been released, one at a time, in recent years.

From the 1920s, it seemed to have become pricey to lay down generous quantities. Most of the whisky was still in cask, but some had been bottled, to prevent evaporation taking it below the minimum legal strength. One hogshead yielded only 40 bottles; the most generous butt provided 548.

It was decided to create an offering of very old whiskies. What constitutes "very old"? The definition was set at more than 30 years old, i.e. distilled no later than 1972. Not all years were represented in the warehouses, but the chronology was surprisingly thorough. Master distiller David Robertson and whisky maker Bob Dalgarno nosed nearly 600 casks, selecting one or two from each year for vintage bottlings. Where there was no stock for a year, Macallan bought back casks, and even cases of bottles, from the trade and collectors. The range launched in 2003, has the rubric "Fine and Rare", with its own style of bottles, and labels highlighting vintage dates. This packaging was also applied to bottles drawn from stock, or bought back; they were all rebottled. All of the whiskies were hand bottled at the distillery, at cask strength. Prices range from £20,000/$33,000 for the most expensive bottle to £65/$110 for the cheapest miniature. The initial offering amounts to 10,000 bottles, valued at just under £14 million/$23 million. The whiskies can be bought, or a catalogue obtained, from specialist retailers; through Macallan's website or at the distillery gift shop. There are even some bars selling these whiskies, inevitably at very high prices.

"Rather than dribbling out occasional vintages, we wanted to make a full range available," explained David Robertson. "If someone is celebrating an important birthday, for example, they might like a gift of whisky from the year they were born. Most distilleries don't have the breadth of stock to do this. We can."

To collectors, no name has the magic of Macallan. The name derives from the Macallan church, now a ruin, on the Easter Elchies estate, which is on a cliff overlooking Telford's bridge over the Spey, at Craigellachie. Immediately across the river is Aberlour.

A farmer on the hillside is believed to have made whisky from his own barley in the 1700s. Macallan became a legal distillery as soon as that was possible, in 1824. In 1998, the estate farm was put back into service to grow Golden Promise barley, albeit a token amount in relation to Macallan's requirements. The manor house from the early days has been restored as a venue for the entertaining of visitors.

Macallan has long been a renowned contributor to blends, notably including The Famous Grouse. In 1968–69, the company decided that single malts would also be an important element of the future.

The character of Macallan has traditionally begun with Golden Promise barley, but this Scottish variety is becoming hard to find. Cultivation has drastically diminished because Golden Promise offers a relatively ungenerous yield of grain to farmers. Its yield to distillers in terms of spirit is also on the low side, but the nutty, oily, silky flavours produced are delicious (*see* "Barley", *pp. 47–48*). Until about 1994, Macallan used only Golden Promise. Since then, there has been the odd year when a good harvest and reduced production of whisky has made this possible, but at other times its share of the grist has dropped to 30 or 25 per cent, and even approached 20. More common varieties such as Chariot or Optic have provided the greater share.

Some distillers do not concern themselves with barley varieties, but simply set out a technical specification of performance. Many take the same view of yeasts, and in recent years some have switched from using two strains to one. These arguments seem to ignore a fundamental point: what the consumer gets out of the glass must depend upon what the producer puts in. Macallan has in recent years used four yeasts, and currently employs two of them. The company believes that this particular combination enhances its fruity, spicy aromas and flavours.

Macallan's oily, creamy richness is enhanced by the use of especially small stills. When the company has expanded output to cope with demand, it has added more stills, rather than building bigger ones. The number grew from six to 21 between 1965 and 1975. The wash stills are heated by gas burners. This use of direct flame can impart a caramelization of the malt which steam heat does not. Macallan also believes it takes the narrowest cut in the industry.

When Macallan decided to market a single malt, the principals made tastings from stock and decided that their whisky tasted best from dry oloroso butts.

Meanwhile, faced with the high cost of obtaining the casks, Macallan has been carrying out exhaustive research to establish exactly what are the influences on flavour. Given that an oak tree takes 100 years to reach maturity, and the whisky another ten or a dozen, progress is slow.

The European oak variety *Quercus robur* is rich in tannins, and imparts both the full colour and the resiny, spicy (clove, cinnamon, nutmeg) fragrances and flavours that are typical of Macallan.

Macallan's current view is that the reaction between wood and sherry is also of great importance. This appears to wash out the harshest tannins and help release a rich, rounded spiciness. This is felt to be far more significant than any aromas and flavours imparted by the sherry itself. One rather extreme piece of research suggested that barely a third of aromas and flavours originated from the spirit, almost 60 per cent from the oak, and less than 10 per cent from the sherry.

The current regime is that the butts are first filled with mosto (grape juice) for three months' primary fermentation. They then have two years with maturing sherry in a bodega. They are then shipped to Scotland. Between 70 and 80 per cent of Macallan is matured in first-fill butts, the remainder in second-fill. In the principal versions of The Macallan first and second fill is vatted in broadly those proportions.

HOUSE STYLE Big, oaky, resiny sherried, flowery-fruity. Spicy.
Very long. After dinner.

THE MACALLAN Distiller's Choice, No Age Statement, 40 vol
Mainly for the Japanese market.

COLOUR Bronze. Paler than most Macallans.

NOSE Especially fragrant.

BODY Medium. Very smooth.

PALATE Lightly buttery and malty. Lively, youthful flavours.
Emphasis on classic Speyside floweriness rather than sherry.

FINISH Highlights the crisp dryness of Macallan.

SCORE **81**

THE MACALLAN 10-year-old, 40 vol
Mainly for the UK market.

COLOUR Amber.

NOSE Sherry. Butterscotch. Honeyish malt character.
Depth of aromas even at this young age.

BODY Full, without being syrupy.

PALATE Lots of sherry, without being rich. Plenty of malt.
Sweetish. Rounded.

FINISH Satisfying, malty, gingery, becoming dry, with a hint of smoke.

SCORE **87**

THE MACALLAN 12-year-old, 43 vol
Mainly for export markets.

COLOUR Amber.

NOSE Sherry, honey, flowery notes.

BODY Full, smooth.

PALATE The first hints of flowering currant. Altogether more expressive.

FINISH Slightly more rounded.

SCORE **91**

THE MACALLAN 15-year-old, 43 vol

Now hard to find.

COLOUR Medium amber.

NOSE This age best expresses the estery fruitiness of Macallan.

BODY Full, very smooth.

PALATE Toffeeish. Gently fruity and spicy.
Hints of peat. A little lacking in dimension.

FINISH Grassy. Lightly peaty.

SCORE **92**

THE MACALLAN 25-year-old, 43 vol

COLOUR Full amber red.

NOSE At this age, a definite smokiness manifests itself, and
embraces all the other aromas that have appeared earlier.

BODY Full, firm, round.

PALATE The smokiness greatly enhances the complexity.

FINISH Dry, complex, very long.

SCORE **95**

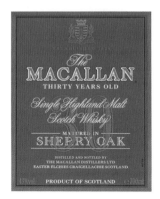

THE MACALLAN 30-year-old, 43 vol

COLOUR Full orange.

NOSE This age best highlights the resiny contributions of the oak itself.
Reminiscent of polished oak. The faintly piney, floral aromas of
furniture polish. The waxed skin of fresh tangerines. Orange zest.

BODY Medium to full.

PALATE Despite its great age, no aggressive oakiness or overbearing
sherry. Tightly combined flavours. Its great appeal is its mellow
maturity. Complex. Just a whiff of smoke.

FINISH Dry, warming, soothing, but disappears too quickly.

SCORE **95**

MACALLAN 18-YEAR-OLDS

Most years, The Macallan has released an 18-year-old, at 43 vol, in which some malt lovers find the most robust interplay of the estery whisky and the dry oloroso maturation. These are vatted to offer continuity of character, but inevitably they vary slightly. The following five bottlings at 18 years old are each given their own score. This is a new feature in the fifth edition of this book. In the fourth edition, when this year-by-year review of the 18-year-olds was introduced, an overall score of 94 was given for the category.

1984 Attractive, deep tawny colour. Appetizing, yet rich, oaky, raisiny aroma. Slippery body. Flavours establish a grip nonetheless, and pace themselves. Perfumy notes. Chocolate fudge. Malty middle. Clean, crisp, gingery spiciness in finish. SCORE 94

1983 Fractionally darker and more reddish. More sappy aroma. More immediately gingery and spicy. Drier. More resiny. Harder edge. Arguably harsher, more robust. SCORE 93

1982 Deep, dark orange. Fruity, toffeeish aroma. Sweetish. More toffee and chocolate in palate. Beeswax. Leafy. Cilantro? Chilli-pepper finish. SCORE 94

1981 Bright, deep amber. Palest colour in this flight. Aromas and flavours so melded as to be hard to unpick. Smooth, urbane. Like a person who answers questions with dismissive brevity to imply a loftier knowledge. The whisky eventually admits to some spiciness and a pleasantly oaky dryness in the finish. SCORE 93

1980 Deep bronze. Fullest colour in this flight. Perfumy, spicy aroma, with cinnamon accent. Oily. Smooth. Toffeeish. Becoming spicy. SCORE 92

COLLECTABLE

1978 Solid orange-amber colour; big bouquet, with some peat;
medium to full, soft body; beautifully rounded and complete, with
a nutty-sweet sherry accent; firm, smooth, dry, warming finish.

1977 Darker and redder; sherry and restrained fruit on the
nose; buttery malt character; sweeter, more sherryish finish.

1976 Bright, full, orange colour; peaty, oaky aroma; firm and
smooth; lively flavours of grass, peat, and oak.

1975 More orangey colour; spicy lemon grass and peat in the aroma;
fresh, juicy calvados and flowering currant in the palate; fresh, oaky finish.

1974 Reddish tinge; beautifully balanced peat and malt in the
aroma; malty, sherryish sweetness becoming estery and
perfumy; sweetness and spice in the finish.

1973 Bright, full amber; very perfumy aroma; very full flavours;
sappy oak and vanilla spiciness in a slow, long finish.

1972 Deep orange; oak and peat aroma; very smooth; good balance
between peat and syrupy malt; drying, with some astringency, in finish.

1971 Shimmery orange; soft, inviting aroma;
oily, perfumy; sherry sweetness.

1970 Full amber orange; assertive sherry aroma; notably
complex; long, vanilla-and-oak finish.

1969 Amber, but paler than usual; peat and malt in the aroma;
nutty, sweetish, syrupy; some peat in finish. A restrained edition.

1968 Apricot colour; fudgey, nutty aroma; light on the tongue;
slightly syrupy; toffeeish, gently spicy finish.

1967 Tawny colour; very spicy, almost minty aroma; very
smooth; buttery malt character; melony finish, with grassy peat.

1966 Bottled "early". This year's edition was a 17-year-old
(and labelled as such, of course). Tawny colour; peaty and spicy
aroma; oily, nutty, smooth; very restrained peat in the finish.

1965 Tawny red; nutty, sherry aroma; aniseed, liquorice; spicy, oily finish.

1964 Medium orange colour; good balance of peat and malt
in the aroma; lightly fruity palate, falling away in the middle;
with nutty, sherry sweetness in the finish.

1963 Refractive orange colour; lightly oaky aroma; light,
sweet, and sherryish, with a cedary finish.

GRAN RESERVA

This rubric indicates 18-year-old whiskies matured
in first-fill sherry casks, at 40 vol.

1982

COLOUR Chestnut.

NOSE Oaky and phenolic, but appetizingly so. A suggestion of cloves.

BODY Big, firm, smooth.

PALATE Extraordinarily powerful flavours. Initially more reminiscent
of port than sherry. Then a suggestion of Pedro Ximénez. Tar-like,
but less smoky than sweet. Cough medicine. Liquorice.

FINISH Soothing. Warming. Long.

SCORE **95**

1981

COLOUR Mahogany red.

NOSE Freshly cut wood. Sawmill aromas.

BODY Viscous, but lighter in body.

PALATE Similar but slightly lighter, and less complex in flavours.

FINISH Dry. Very slightly woody and astringent.

SCORE **94**

1979 Bottled 1997

COLOUR Distinctively chestnut.

NOSE Rich sherry at first. Then malty nuttiness.
Raisins, dates. Finally floweriness.

BODY Big, oily.

PALATE Very dry. Thick-cut, bitter-orange and ginger marmalade on well-done toast. Then buttery, syrupy maltiness, developing to nutty, sherry sweetness. Strictly for the lover of powerfully oaked whiskies.

FINISH Richly fruity. Raisiny. Warming.

SCORE **95**

REPLICA EDITIONS

None of today's barley varieties existed in the 19th century, and malt was generally more heavily peated. The design of mash tuns and wort coolers was different, brewers' yeast was used, stills were fired with coal or coke. Sherry casks were used, but in a random fashion. The 19th century bottles that were opened to act as models for these replicas contained whiskies that, in some respects, tasted hauntingly reminiscent of today's Macallan (albeit, surprisingly, more delicate). In particular, the fruity esters seemed much the same. This seems to support the notion that a distillery's location and microclimate are formative influences on flavour. To try and replicate the individual characteristics of each bottle, large numbers of casks were nosed. To "recreate" the 1861, about 17,500 casks were sampled and 28 used.

"1876", 40.6 vol

This is the most "recent" vintage date in the series. It is also the
most recently created replica among the four reviewed here.
It seems a little thinner in body and palate than the other three.

COLOUR Dark, warm gold.

NOSE Very spicy and dusty. Honeyed.

BODY Firm.

PALATE Intense sweetness at first. Then perfumy. Lemony. Anis.
A hint of quinine dryness.

FINISH A touch of oakiness.

SCORE **94**

ESTABLISHED 1824
PRODUCE OF SCOTLAND

MACALLAN
THE 1874
Pure Highland Malt
Scotch Whisky

SELECTED BY WHISKY MAKER
F. A. NEWLANDS
AT THE MACALLAN DISTILLERY CRAIGELLACHIE SCOTLAND

"1874", 45 vol

The whiskies in this replica had an average age of just under 18, but included at least one
cask of 26 years. A key element was whisky with long maturation in fino sherry casks.

COLOUR Orange.

NOSE Ginger cake. Caraway. Cumin seeds.

BODY Medium. Firm. Smooth.

PALATE Dry, with softly orangey notes. Spices. Aniseed. Lemon grass.
The most estery of the bigger Macallans. Light peat.

FINISH Powerful. Dry. Just a hint of bitterness.

SCORE **95**

"1861", 42.7 vol

The original had a pronounced oak and sherry character, and
was rich in the spicy esters that arise during maturation.

COLOUR Bronze.

NOSE Spice cupboard. Flapjack. Syrup. Rose-water. Custard.

BODY Soothing. Syrupy.

PALATE Concentrated sweetness. Perfumy. Anis. Restrained fruitiness. Lemon.
Candied orange peel. Delicious sherry character. Great depth of flavour.

FINISH Toasty dryness. Sappy oak. Long.

SCORE **95**

"1841", 41.7 vol

The original was believed to have been bottled young, at between six and ten years old, and had a remarkably fresh character when opened more than 150 years later. It may have been one of the first bottled whiskies. In 1841, most whisky was still sold by the cask.

COLOUR Brilliant gold.

NOSE Very fresh. Fudge with vanilla essence and pistachio nuts.

BODY Silky.

PALATE Appetizing. Sweet but not cloying. Light, fresh, delicate notes of orange-blossom honey.

FINISH A very gentle acidity (dessert apples?) provides a balancing dryness.

SCORE **96**

EXCEPTIONAL SINGLE CASK RANGE
1981, ESC I, Fino Sherry Butt, Bottled 1999, 56 vol

COLOUR Chestnut to cherry.

NOSE Mint chocolate. Sherry. Slightly vinous. Oak.

BODY Firm, smooth. Thick. Demerara sugar.

PALATE Wafer-like. Crispy malt. Toffee. Forest berries. Oak. Some earthy notes.

FINISH Rummy. Warming. Very oaky, approaching astringency.

SCORE **92**

1980, ESC II, Sherry Butt, Cask No 4063, 59.3 vol

COLOUR Dark copper.

NOSE Madeira, in the hold of a ship crossing the equator (a hint of hot cylinder block and engine oil).

BODY Medium. Lapping on the tongue.

PALATE Hard treacle toffee. A quick gesture of sweetness, then burnt flavours., like chestnuts too long on a brazier.

FINISH Warming.

SCORE **90**

1980, ESC III, Sherry Butt, Cask No 17937, 51 vol

Mainly for the Swiss market.

COLOUR Distinctive pinkish amber. Palest in this flight.

NOSE Crème brûlée. Fruity. Pineapple.

BODY Medium. Luxuriously smooth.

PALATE Sweet. Sticky toffee pudding. Fruity esters. Apples. Cherries.

FINISH Coffeeish dryness. Bittersweet. Digestif.

SCORE **92**

1990, ESC IV, Sherry Butt, Cask No 24680, 57.4 vol

COLOUR Dark amber. Garnet tinge.

NOSE Smoky. Toasty. Malty.

BODY Big. Firm. Smooth.

PALATE Malty and fruity, with a slightly sharp edge
of smokiness (or is it charred oak?)

FINISH Slightly medicinal.

SCORE **91**

TRAVEL RETAIL

The whiskies under this heading are available at airports and ferry terminals,
on board some aircraft and ships, and in duty-free shops.

THE MACALLAN 10-year-old, 57 vol (100° proof)

COLOUR Attractive full amber.

NOSE Aromas very tightly combined and rounded, sherryish. Oaky. Resiny.
The faintest hint of peat. Flowering currants. Violets. A soft whiff of alcohol.

BODY Firm, smooth.

PALATE Sherry accent. Firm malt background.
Restrained fruitiness. Quietly intense.

FINISH Sherry, smoke, alcohol.

SCORE **89**

THE MACALLAN Elegancia 1990, 40 vol

COLOUR Warm gold to pale bronze.

NOSE Crisp. Spicy. Ginger ice cream.

BODY Smooth but light.

PALATE Restrained start. Gentle flavour development. Lean. Lightly creamy.
A suggestion of malted milk. Some concentrated sweetness.

FINISH Now the ice cream is rum-and-raisin.

SCORE **80**

THE DECADES SERIES

Travellers with time to kill and a few shelves of whisky to browse may find the labels on this series not only eye-catching but also apposite. Like the Replica bottlings, these attempt to recall the flavours of the past, by making vattings from stock. The initial bottlings, intended to evoke the 1920–50s, are identified by social motifs of each period, based on racing. The whiskies seem to highlight the Speyside character of Macallan. All are at 40 volume.

THE MACALLAN Twenties (racing car motif). Pale walnut colour. Passion fruit aroma. Notably light-bodied. Starts sweetly but quickly becomes dry. An elegant touch of oak. SCORE 92

THE MACALLAN Thirties (ocean liner motif). Pale apricot. Seville orange aroma. Smooth bodied. The sweetest and most fruity of the whiskies in this flight. SCORE 94

THE MACALLAN Forties (locomotive motif). The palest in colour, primrose. Also the most flowery, grassy, herbal. Some sweetness. Playful, lively. The least complex of this flight, but deliciously drinkable. SCORE 93

THE MACALLAN Fifties (airliner motif). Deep bronze. Closest in style to The Macallan today. Well balanced and rounded. Oak, sherry, malt, light spiciness. Long, soothing. SCORE 92

THE MACALLAN, Cask Strength, 58.6 vol

A new series of single-cask bottlings for the US market. The first cask was tasted in the fourth edition of Malt Whisky Companion, *as a work in progress. That vintage was described as "a very intense expression of a classic Macallan". So is this one, which is in the age range of 10 to 12 years.*

COLOUR Distinctive reddish mahogany.

NOSE Oak. Sherry. Winey. Faint suggestion of chocolate.

BODY Big, textured. Slightly abrasive.

PALATE Robust. Dry maltiness. Hard toffee, becoming chewy. Dried fruits. Nutty. Oily. Perfumy.

FINISH Oaky dryness. Slightly astringent (less so with water).

SCORE 88

RARE VINTAGES OF THE MACALLAN

THE MACALLAN Millennium 50-year-old, Distilled 1949, 46 vol

Offered in about 900 Caithness crystal decanters, with a copper insignia made from a retired still at Macallan. Price around £2,000/$3,000.

COLOUR Very dark orange.

NOSE Peaty, smoky, almost sooty.

BODY Lean, firm, slippery.

PALATE Oily, nutty, creamy. Almond cookies. Crème brûlée. Some burnt flavours. Becoming woody. Oaky. The oak is big but never quite overpowers the other elements.

FINISH Spicy. Peppermint. Smoky. Oaky.

SCORE 92

THE MACALLAN 1961, 54.1 vol

COLOUR Deep orange, with an inner glow. Sunrise.

NOSE Soft. Creamy. Fruity. Orange blancmange.

BODY Silky.

PALATE Firm. Hint of cedar. Cigar box, but it contains orange-crème pralines in very bitter chocolate. Subtle development of other citrus flavours, spices, and peppermint.

FINISH Clean, crisp, oaky bitterness.

SCORE 94

THE MACALLAN 1951, 48.8 vol

COLOUR Garnet with jade tinge.

NOSE Creamy, chocolatey, spicy.

BODY Silky.

PALATE Malt background like rich, dark fudge. Almost immediately, sherbety explosions of fruity and spicy flavours.

FINISH Very distinctive in the interplay of sweet spiciness and oaky dryness. Very lively and appetizing.

SCORE **93**

THE MACALLAN 1948, 46.6 vol

COLOUR Old gold.

NOSE Sherry not obvious – fino? Flowery, leafy, peaty, woody.

BODY Light but firm. Smooth.

PALATE An altogether more elegant, wistful style. Some sweetness and floweriness, but the outstanding feature is an astonishingly fresh peat-smoke flavour. Great Speyside whiskies once tasted like this.

FINISH Gentle but lingering and warming, leaving smoky memories.

SCORE **96**

THE MACALLAN 1946, 40 vol

COLOUR Bright full gold.

NOSE Much more estery-fruity.

BODY Light, smooth, almost slippery.

PALATE Firm, complex flavours. Flowery. Estery, but very delicately balanced. Sweet lime, lemon, and orange. A remarkably seductive whisky for its age.

FINISH Bitter orange. Grass. Peat. Again, long smokiness.

SCORE **95**

FINE & RARE VINTAGES

Most whiskies peak in their teens, but the heaviest ones can do
well in their twenties and even thirties. As the best-known heavyweight,
Macallan has made a great many outings at advanced ages.
The ticket price can be very high. Yet, given that most whiskies
do peak a decade or two earlier, it is not reasonable to expect the
performance of malts in their 30s, 40s, or 50s to be of the very best.

Some are, indeed, surprisingly good – whisky's counterparts to
Archie Moore or George Foreman – but their value is driven by their
antiquity and rarity. If a previously unknown Old Master is identified,
it may not be the painter's finest work, but it will command a great
price. If a recording of Buddy Bolden were found on a wax cylinder we
might know whether his cornet really could be heard on the far side of
Lake Ponchartrain. These tastings seem to confirm the widely held view
that Macallan was a peatier, smokier whisky until the 1950s. If it is true
of Macallan, it is probably true of other Speyside malts.

1926, 42.6 vol

Bottled as a 60-year-old in 1986. Very dark ("laburnum"
say Macallan). Medicinal, phenolic, peaty, and woody in aroma.
Surprisingly light on the tongue. Very dry and concentrated in palate.
Figs, treacle toffee. Molasses. Liquorice. Rooty. Finish is cedary
and oaky – dominated by the wood. SCORE 80

The vintages from 1937 to 1940 (*see p. 360*) were bought as bottled stock.
They were then rebottled for the Fine and Rare series, in 2002. The vintage
dates shown here represent the year of the original bottling.

1937, 43 vol

First bottled as a 37-year-old, in 1974. Dark gold. Green tinge.
Vanilla in the aroma. Rich, delicious, syrupy, malty middle. Sweetshop
flavours. Sufficiently soothing to calm the palate, but then somewhat abrupt
in its spicy, hot finish. Late smokiness, and some astringency. SCORE 87

1937, 43 vol

First bottled as a 32-year-old, in 1969. Bronze. Fragrant. Sweetish, spicy
aromas. Lively flavours with plenty of development. At first, bitter chocolate
pralines filled with ginger. Then with orange. Then with peppermint.
Finishes with spicy bitterness. Saffron? SCORE 85

1938, 43 vol

First bottled as a 31-year-old, in 1969. Ripe apricot colour. The same fruit is
suggested by the aroma. The body is prickly, almost spiky. It all suggests
tropical fruits, but the flavour doesn't develop much more than nutty toffee.
Nice surge of orangey spiciness in the finish. SCORE 84

1938, 43 vol

First bottled as a 35-year-old, in 1973. Deep, warm bronze. Sweetly
appetizing on the nose. Lightly syrupy. Falls away in the middle.
Crispy, spicy finish. A very elegant whisky. No doubt less vigorous than
it was, but still with great charm. SCORE 86

1939, 43 vol

First bottled as a 40-year-old, in 1979. Deep bronze. Appetizing, sweetly
nutty aroma and palate. Smooth to the point of urbanity. Seduces, then slips
away. Back later, to lift the finish gracefully, as though kissing a lady's hand.
Perfumy and dry. SCORE 85

1940, 43 vol

First bottled as a 35-year-old in 1975. Pale bronze, with green tinge.
Fragrant smoke, with subtle fruit and malt. Lean, firm, elegant.
Hint of anis. Remarkable emergence of peppermint in
the finish. Aperitif. SCORE 92

1940, 43 vol

First bottled as a 37-year-old, in 1977. Slightly darker than
the earlier bottling. Considerably maltier and sweeter. Lime
zest, cilantro, and garden mint. Finish very dry indeed,
but no astringency. SCORE 93

THE FOLLOWING VINTAGES WERE ALL BOTTLED IN 2002

1945, 51.5 vol

Bottled at 56 years old. Reddish orange. Mint humbugs and
butterscotch in the aroma. A very sweet whisky. Fruity, too. Perhaps
cherries, but especially green fruits. Also spicy, with lots of pepper.
Somewhat erratic, crochety. SCORE 82

1946, 44.3 vol

Bottled at 56 years old. Very attractive deep yellow, tawn colour. Spicy
aroma, especially cinnamon. Syrupy. Lapping on the tongue. Lemony.
Dry, herbal. Slightly medicinal. Phenol. Peat smoke. SCORE 92

1948, 45.3 vol

Bottled at 53 years old. Lovely, pink-tinged amber. The aroma of thick-cut
orange marmalade. Lightly syrupy, sweetish palate, gently becoming drier.
Orangey. Liqueur-like. Long, lively, dry, spicy finish. SCORE 85

1949, 49.8 vol

Bottled at 53 years old. Bright, reflective, deep gold. Very inviting.
Sweet, flapjack aroma. Full-bodied, smooth. Appetizing, oaty,
bittersweet. The trademark spicy finish. Some big whiskies
are belligerent brawlers. This one floats like a butterfly and
it kisses instead of stinging. SCORE 92

1949, 44.1 vol

Bottled at 52 years old. Garnet. Or morello cherry. The colour suggests
cherry pie, and alerts the nose to aromas of cooked fruit. Maderisation,
perhaps? Also some acidity. Tastes like a fruity herb bitters. SCORE 82

1950, 46.7 vol

Bottled at 52 years old. Warm, deep gold colour. Clean, dessert apple aroma (a typical Macallan characteristic, making its first indisputable appearance in this flight). Big-bodied, soft, embracing. Honeyed palate. Orange flower honey? Moves to long, gingery spiciness. Some cookie-like maltiness. Light smokiness. Clean and appetizing, with plenty of flavour development. SCORE 93

1950, 51.7 vol

Bottled at 52 years old. Slightly darker colour, toward bronze. Slightly sweeter and maltier aroma. Very creamy. Some vanilla. Malty. Appetizingly well-rounded peaty dryness in the finish. Over the full course of aroma, palate and finish, this rather austere expression emerges as being slightly drier than the version above, and perhaps marginally less complex. SCORE 92

1951, 52.3 vol

Bottled at 51 years old. Deep bronze. Clean, sweet, appetizing aroma, with some gingery, spicy notes. Instant hit of spiciness in the palate. As crisp as a karate chop. Then things slow to a more natural pace, and the spices present themselves one by one, against a background of malty sweetness. Finally, they meld into an endlessly soothing glow. SCORE 92

1952, 50.8 vol

Bottled at 50 years old. Deep gold. Floral, lemony aroma. Straight into a firm, malty base. The top notes are spicy from start to finish. Flowery and fruity characteristics persistently try to take over but never quite manage it. Nice touch of oak in the finish. SCORE 91

1952, 48 vol

Bottled at 49 years old. Deep copper red colour. Sherry, charred oak and anis in the nose. Rich, syrupy body. Liquorice and chewy malt in the palate. Woody finish, with some astringency. SCORE 84

1953, 52 vol

Bottled at 49 years old. Extraordinary garnet-to-ruby colour. Iron and passion fruit in the aroma. Dark, deep flavours. Alcohol-soaked fruitcake, studded with cherries, topped with marzipan and toasted sliced almonds. Warm, clovey spiciness and toasted oak in the finish. SCORE 86.

1954, 50.2 vol

Bottled at 47 years old. An even fuller ruby colour and a gently smoky aroma seem promising. The palate is intensely sweet. This whisky may have been drinkable when it was bottled. Now it is strictly collectable. NOT SCORED

1955, 45.9 vol

Bottled at 46 years old. Almost opaque. Black, with red tinges. Clovey aromas. Syrupy. Herbal. Fruity (prunes?). A wintry dram, but lacking in vigour. Toward the end of its life. SCORE 83

No stocks of 1956 or 1957 have been traced.

1958, 53.7 vol

Bottled at 43 years old. Sauternes-like colour. Earthy aroma, with suggestion of apples (a boxful, not peeled). Syrupy maltiness in the palate. Sugary, toffee-like. Toffee apples? Finishes with dusty spiciness. SCORE 85

1959, 47 vol

Bottled at 43 years old. Very dark orangey amber colour. Nutty, sugary, and deeply malty aromas. Like a spiced cake glazed with sugar and studded with cloves. Similarly wintry flavours: nutty, crystal sugar, ginger. Spicy, bittersweet finish. SCORE 84

No stocks of 1960, 1961, 1962, or 1963.

1964, 58.6 vol

Bottled at 37 years old. Pale, greeny gold colour. Very unusual for a Macallan. Fruity, creamy aroma, with some vanilla, and woody dryness. Syrupy body. Palate is sweet, with suggestions of green fruits – or chillis. Finishes with the burning sensation of having bitten into a chilli pepper. An interesting whisky, but not very Macallan-like. SCORE 76

1965, 56.2 vol

Bottled at 36 years old. Cerise. The colour suggests cherries and the aroma seems to follow suit. The palate is sweet, fruity, and toffeeish. Cherries, again, in the finish. Reminiscent of cherry "brandy" (the liqueur type, as famously made in Denmark). SCORE 79

1966, 55.5 vol

Bottled at 35 years old. Claret colour. Instant spicy, bittersweet attack. Peppery. Dry. Drying. Some astringency in the finish. Not very Macallan-like. Not very whisky-like. SCORE 77

1967, 56.3 vol

Bottled at 35 years old. Mahogany red. Sherry and malt in the aroma. Very sweet and toffeeish in the palate. Good wood extract. Spicy. Dusty. Lively, long finish, with slight astringency. SCORE 87

1968, 51 vol

Bottled at 34 years old. Bright yellow gold. Sweet and fruity in the aroma. Pineapple. Banana. Syrupy. Spicy. Vanilla. Creamy. Beautifully balanced between sweetness and dryness. A playful, refreshing demonstration of Macallan's fruity esters. Otherwise not at all typical. SCORE 80

1968, 46.6 vol

Bottled at 33 years old. Pale gold, faint green tinge. Oily, cereal-grain aroma. Sweet at first, then a dusty dryness. Finally, a huge, sweet fruitiness. Pineapple. Papaya. Custard apple. SCORE 78

1969, 52.7 vol

Bottled at 32 years old. Dark oak colour. Deep, malty aroma. Palate starts with sweet maltiness, developing chocolatey flavours, becoming rooty, resiny, and fruity. Very slight oaky astringency in the palate. SCORE 92

1969, 59 vol

Bottled at 32 years. Deep, refractive, gold to bronze. Lemony aroma. Fresh, lemony palate. Orange blossom. Flowery. Scenty. Delicate. Lively finish. SCORE 84

1970, 54.9 vol

Bottled at 32 years old. Dark claret colour. Oaky aroma, but Macallan spiciness and apple esters come through. Chewy, malty, sweet, rum-butter flavours. Sherryish. The finish is peppery and very long, with some woody astringency. SCORE 85

1970, 52.4 vol

Bottled at 31 years old. Dark chestnut. Sweet, fruity Christmas pudding aroma. Very smooth body. Sweetish palate. Malty, rooty, garden mint, resiny, fruity. Slight woody astringency in the finish. SCORE 89

1971, 56.4 vol

Bottled at 30 years old. Dark, tawny. Palate starts malty and very sweet. Becomes drier, with cocoa-like flavours. Long, lively, spicy. Reminiscent of root ginger. SCORE 90

1971, 55.9 vol

Bottled at 30 years old. Very dark oak colour. A surprisingly soft, gentle expression. Lightly syrupy. Brown sugar and cherry brandy flavours. Perfectly pitched spicy finish. SCORE 89

1972, 49.2 vol

Bottled at 29 years. Rosewood. Almost opaque. Passion fruit aroma. Palate has violets, bitter chocolate, fudge, and espresso. Bitterness of finish rather aggressive. SCORE 88

1972, 58.4 vol

Bottled at 29 years. Very dark mahogany. Fruity, calvados-like aroma. Fruity, resiny, spicy palate. Very lively. Slightly abrasive. Sappy, oaky finish. SCORE 89

SOME INDEPENDENT BOTTLINGS OF MACALLAN

Macallan is one of several distilleries that have on occasion brought legal pressure to stop their whisky being bottled and marketed by independents. This is also one of the intentions behind Macallan's use of the definite article. The Macallan implies that the bottling was "official", and carried out precisely as deemed by the company. There is an amusing twist to the adoption of this solution. Macallan was one of the dozen, or twenty, distilleries that for many years hyphenated their names with the word "Glenlivet", despite their remoteness from that glen. It was to distinguish itself from them that the original styled itself "The Glenlivet".

The confusing Glenlivets are gradually pruning themselves, but definite articles are sprouting like mushrooms. One independent bottler persisted for a time with the designation Macallan-Glenlivet, and others have used their own variations. A robust expression of Macallan called "As We Get It" once commanded a following. These two were reviewed in earlier editions of this book. Gordon & MacPhail compromise with "Speymalt from Macallan".

TASTING NOTES

 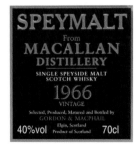

A Speymalt distilled in 1994 and bottled in 2003, at 40 vol, has a bright gold colour; a suggestion of marzipan in the aroma; a sweetish, spicy, well-balanced palate; and a very appetizing, confident, lemony finish. SCORE 86 From the same bottler, again at 40 vol, a 1966 distillation with an attractive reddish amber colour, is scenty, flowery, and distinctly herbal. SCORE 81

A 10-year-old, distilled in 1989 and bottled in 2000 at 50 vol, from Douglas Laing, has a burnished bronze colour; a malt accent that seems richer in the aroma than the palate; and lively spiciness in the finish. SCORE 86

A 1990, butt no 8747, at 57.6 vol, from Signatory, has a bright, golden colour and, again, a malt accent. It is a long, straightforward maltiness, light to medium in weight; dry at first, becoming creamy, honeyed and much sweeter; with a warming, spicy finish. SCORE 86

A 1990, cask no MM10242, bottled in 2001 at 46 vol, from Murray McDavid, has a dark walnut colour; a cinnamon spiciness in the aroma; a toffeeish malt background; and surprisingly intense smokiness. This whisky must have been made with a well-peated malt, but the flavour is more reminiscent of oak smoke. SCORE 91

A 12-year-old, distilled in 1989 and bottled in 2001 in the Whisky Galore series, at 46 vol, has a distinctively greeny gold colour. The colour perhaps suggests chlorophyll, but that aroma does seem to be present. There are grass aromas and the faintest hints of peat. The vegetation turns to lemon grass in the palate. Light, pleasantly sweet and refreshing, but lacking in flavour and structure. Not very Macallan-like. SCORE 79

A 1967, cask no 7676, at 51.2 vol, from the same bottler, has a more fragrant aroma and palate; flowery dryness in the beginning; a slightly bigger body; and a livelier, spicier finish. It is equally untypical. SCORE 79

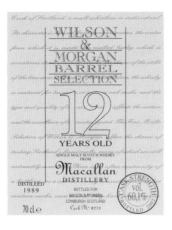 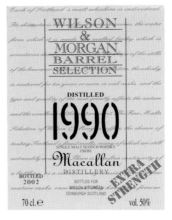

A 12-year-old, at 60.1 vol, a Wilson & Morgan Barrel Selection, has a bright, warm amber colour; the floral aroma of furniture polish; a rich, creamy texture; a buttery maltiness; and a concentrated sweetness in the finish. Like eating a cake (chocolate, coffee, walnuts?) with a butter-cream filling. Score 88

From the same enterprise, a vintage dated 1990 was released in 2002 at 50 vol. It has a full bronze colour; a nutty sherry character; and a buttery maltiness; with a touch of chocolate in the finish. Curiously labelled Extra Strength, it is a compromise between standard strength and cask strength. Score 89

These two bottlings are very close in style to the distillery's own principal expressions. A 1990 marsala finish, at 46 vol, has a full, yellowy gold colour; fresh "peat kiln" aromas; a slippery smooth body; with lemony and malty flavours. A good example of Macallan, but lacks marsala. SCORE 87

A 1988, bottled at 12 years old and 57.5 vol, was released by Adelphi in 2000. It had a full gold colour; cedar and peat in the aroma; rich cream toffee and fudge in the palate; with the typical Macallan "calvados" and flowering currant in the finish. SCORE 85

A 1980, at 57.8 vol, from James MacArthur, has a bright gold colour; a flowery aroma; a light body, and an engaging interplay of honeyed sweetness and estery spices. SCORE 89

A 1979, at 53.7 vol, from Scott's Selection, has a bright, yellowy gold colour; a dry, slightly sharp aroma; a rich maltiness, with clean, appetizing dessert apple flavours; and an attractive spiciness to round out the finish. SCORE 88

TASTED AS WORKS IN PROGRESS

(and therefore not scored)

From MacKillop's choice, all at cask strength:

1988 Sherry wood. Dark orange colour. Faintly smoky aroma, with vanilla. Soft, toffeeish maltiness. Lively spiciness in the finish.

1980 Sherry wood: Attractive full amber colour. Appetizing nutty sherry and barley sugar aroma. Clean, malty flavours. Depth of maltiness. Syrupy sweetness and warming spiciness combine in the finish.

1974 Full gold. Dessert apple and honey in the aroma – and in the palate. Soothing. Delicately spicy finish.

1973 Deep gold. Beautifully melded, restrained fruits and spices. Lightly creamy malt. Clean, rounded, spicy finish.

MANNOCHMORE

PRODUCER Diageo
REGION Highlands DISTRICT Speyside (Lossie)
ADDRESS By Elgin, Morayshire, IV30 3SF TEL 01343 862000
WEBSITE www.malts.com

THE BLACK WHISKY Loch Dhu was produced here. This curious product was aimed at "image-conscious young men". Given the fashionability of black among young women, they may have felt excluded. Diageo insists that the colour of the whisky derived from "a secret preparation, involving the double charring of selected bourbon barrels". The best guess is that the "preparation" – perhaps first a spraying and then a charring – involved caramelization.

The distillery is quite young itself, having been established in 1971–72. Its original role was to provide malt whisky as a component of the Haig blends, augmenting the production of its older neighbour, Glenlossie. The two are south of Elgin, and take their water from the Mannoch hills. With the same raw materials and location, the two make similar malts. Mannochmore's seems slightly less complex, but it is very enjoyable nonetheless.

HOUSE STYLE Fresh, flowery, dry. Aperitif.

SPEYSIDE
SINGLE MALT *SCOTCH WHISKY*
MANNOCHMORE
distillery stands a few miles *south* of Elgin in *Morayshire*. The nearby *Millbuies Woods* are rich in birdlife, including the Great *Spotted* Woodpecker. The *distillery* draws process *water* from the Bardon Burn, which has its *source* in the MANNOCH HILLS, and *cooling water* from the Gedloch Burn and the *Burn of Foths*. Mannochmore *single MALT WHISKY* has a *light, fruity* aroma and a *smooth, mellow taste.*

AGED **12** YEARS
43% vol   Distilled & Bottled in *SCOTLAND*, MANNOCHMORE DISTILLERY, Elgin, Moray, Scotland.   70 cl

MANNOCHMORE 12-year-old, Flora and Fauna, 43 vol

COLOUR White wine.

NOSE Fresh. Very flowery indeed.

BODY Medium, firm, drying on the tongue.

PALATE Becoming lightly fruity. Clean. Dry.

FINISH Perfumy, light, dry. Faint peat.

SCORE 72

MANNOCHMORE 22-year-old, Distilled 1974, Bottled 1997, Rare Malts, 60.1 vol

COLOUR Bright greeny gold.

NOSE Fragrant, flowery, faint peat.

BODY Very soft. Lightly smooth.

PALATE Oily, wintergreen, peppery fruit.

FINISH Robust, hot, faint peat.

SCORE **74**

This edition is in a 75cl bottling. Later the same year, a 70cl Rare Malts bottling at the same age seemed much cleaner and rounder. SCORE 76

LOCH DHU The Black Whisky, 10-year-old, 40 vol

COLOUR Ebony, with a mahogany tinge.

NOSE Liquorice, medicinal. Fruity, flowery, whisky aromas very evident.

BODY Medium. Softly syrupy.

PALATE Light, dryish. Liquorice. Hint of cough sweets. Fruit.
Scores for initiative, but not for the whisky lover.

FINISH Whisky flavours gently emerge. Liquorice root. Dryish. Hint of warmth.

SCORE **70**

INDEPENDENT BOTTLINGS OF MANNOCHMORE

Gordon & MacPhail offer a 1984, at 40 vol, in their Connoisseurs Choice range. This has a bright, buttercup colour; a distinctly buttery, flowery, grassy aroma; a very fat body; and flavours that develop from clotted cream to hard toffee; with nuts and ginger in the finish. SCORE 76

MILLBURN

PRODUCER DCL
REGION Highlands DISTRICT Speyside (Inverness)
SITE OF FORMER DISTILLERY Millburn Road, Inverness,
Inverness-shire, IV2 3QX

A S THE TRAIN FROM LONDON finishes its 11-hour journey to Inverness, it glides by recognizable distillery buildings that are now a pub-steakhouse. At least there is still drink on the premises.

Millburn is believed to have dated from 1807, and its buildings from 1876 and 1922. It was owned for a time by Haig's. The distillery closed in 1985. Whiskies distilled a decade earlier have been released at 18 years and now 25, as Rare Malts.

HOUSE STYLE Smoky, aromatic. Night cap.

MILLBURN 25-year-old, Distilled 1975, Bottled 2001, Rare Malts, 61.9 vol

COLOUR Yellow.

NOSE Vegetal. Peppery. Aromatic.

BODY Dry, firm chewiness.

PALATE Flavour development. Medium dry. Sooty. Smoky oaky. Sappy. Orange pith and zest.

FINISH Surprisingly lively, spicy. Faintly medicinal.

SCORE 75

MILLBURN 18-year-old, Distilled 1975, Rare Malts, 58.5 vol

COLOUR Greeny gold.

NOSE Oaky and aromatic.

BODY Lightly smooth.

PALATE Dryish, perfumy, smoky.

FINISH Oaky, sappy.

SCORE **74**

MILLBURN 18-year-old, Distilled 1983, Signatory Unchillfiltered Collection, 46 vol

COLOUR Bright, greeny gold.

NOSE Perfumy. Somewhere between mothballs and tar-like peat.

BODY Rich and creamy.

PALATE Sweetish. Emphatic sugared almonds. Hazelnuts.

FINISH Pistachios this time? Nutty dryness rounds out the palate. Very soothing and warming.

SCORE **75**

MILLBURN 1976, Gordon & MacPhail, Connoisseurs Choice, 40 vol

COLOUR Light amber.

NOSE Juicy and fruity. Vanilla, chocolate, candied peel, smoke, oak.

BODY Rich and full-bodied.

PALATE Mature with cooked apple. Typical Millburn succulence.

FINISH Long and fruity.

SCORE **80**

MILLBURN 1978, Gordon & MacPhail Cask Edition, 65.6 vol

COLOUR Bright, greeny gold.

NOSE Dry, lightly peaty, alcoholic.

BODY Smooth but drying.

PALATE Peaty, vegetal attack. Becoming sweeter.

FINISH Slightly musty. Some medicinal peat. Heady.

SCORE **74**

MILLBURN 1974, Connoisseurs Choice, 40 vol

COLOUR Gold to bronze.

NOSE Appetizing peat, perfume, and hint of sherry.

BODY Lightly oily.

PALATE Lightly malty, quickly becoming perfumy, then peaty.

FINISH Slightly aggressive. Dries on tongue.

SCORE **75**

MILTONDUFF

PRODUCER Allied Distillers Ltd
REGION Highlands DISTRICT Speyside (Lossie)
ADDRESS Elgin, Morayshire, IV30 3TQ
TEL 01343 547433

T HE BENEDICTINE PRIORY OF PLUSCARDEN, which still exists, was once a brewery – and provided the land on which the Miltonduff distillery stands. Although there is no other connection, the name of the Priory is invoked on the box that houses the Miltonduff bottle. The distillery, established in 1824, south of Elgin, was extensively modernized in the 1930s, and again in the 1970s. Its whisky is very important in the Ballantine blends.

For a time, the company also had a Lomond still on the site. This produced a malt with similar characteristics to Miltonduff, but heavier, oilier, and smokier, identified as Mosstowie. That still has been dismantled, but the malt can occasionally be found in independent bottlings. The Miltonduff malt is well regarded by blenders, and makes a pleasant single.

HOUSE STYLE Flowery, scenty, clean, firm, elegant. Aperitif.

MILTONDUFF 10-year-old, 40 vol

COLOUR Honeyed gold.

NOSE Fragrant, flowery. Very faint peat.

BODY Light to medium. Firm. Smooth.

PALATE Sweetish, firm, clean.

FINISH Firm. Lightly nutty. Soothing.

SCORE 75

MILTONDUFF 15-year-old, Special Distillery Bottling, 46 vol

COLOUR Gold.

NOSE Very soft fruits, toffee, pigskin, Viennese whirls.

BODY Velvety.

PALATE Aromatic herbs: rosemary, thyme. Toffee.
Soft and gentle. A demure dram.

FINISH Almond and chocolate.

SCORE **78**

MILTONDUFF 1968, Gordon & MacPhail, 40 vol

COLOUR Bronze.

NOSE Flowery, buttercup-like.

BODY Light to medium. Oily.

PALATE Fresh, flowery, oily. Lightly clean maltiness.

FINISH Flowery dryness.

SCORE **77**

MOSSTOWIE 1979, Gordon & MacPhail, Connoisseurs Choice, 40 vol

COLOUR Pale bronze.

NOSE Beeswax. Flowery.

BODY Oily and rich.

PALATE Orange-flower water. Jaffa cakes. Good malt background.

FINISH Cocoa powder.

SCORE **72**

MILTONDUFF 1968, 40 vol

An official bottling, now hard to find.

COLOUR Amber.

NOSE Light sherry and very gentle peat.

BODY Medium, textured.

PALATE Flowery, honeyish, lightly nutty. Hint of vanilla.

FINISH Long, peat-smoke fragrance. Perhaps better as a light digestif.

SCORE **78**

MORTLACH

PRODUCER Diageo
REGION Highlands DISTRICT Speyside (Dufftown)
ADDRESS Dufftown, Banffshire, AB55 4AQ
TEL 01340 822100 WEBSITE www.malts.com

A LL THE PLEASURES OF A GOOD SPEYSIDE single malt are found in
Mortlach: floweriness, peatiness, smokiness, maltiness, and
fruitiness. Its complexity may well arise from its extraordinary
miscellany of stills. In the course of a history stretching from the
earliest days of legal distilling, successive managers seem to have been
heretics: fiddling with the shape, size, and design of stills to achieve
the result they desired. It seems that they strayed so far from the
orthodoxies of the industry that they were never corralled, and the
whisky was so good that no one wanted to risk changing it. Nor does
anyone wholly understand how the combination of stills achieves its
particular result. The whisky has such individuality that its character is
not overwhelmed by sherry maturation. While UDV/Diageo has over
the years moved away from sherry, and argued for "distillery
character", Mortlach has not been bound by that orthodoxy, either.

HOUSE STYLE A Speyside classic: elegant and flowery yet supple and
muscular. Immensely complex, with great length. After dinner or bedtime.

MORTLACH 16-year-old, Flora and Fauna, 43 vol

COLOUR Profound, rich amber.

NOSE Dry oloroso sherry. Smoky, peaty.

BODY Medium to full, firm, smooth.

PALATE Sherryish, smoky, peaty, sappy, some fruitiness, assertive.

FINISH Long and dry.

SCORE *81*

MORTLACH 1980, Bottled 1997, Cask Strength Limited Bottling, 63.1 vol

COLOUR Very attractive. Bright, orangey amber.

NOSE Distinct peat character. Stalky. Lime skins.

BODY Big, rich.

PALATE Flowery. Buttercups. Syrupy. Rich sherry notes. Very big in the middle, with lots of flavour development. Soft mint humbugs.

FINISH More mint, becoming drier. An outstanding digestif.

SCORE *85*

MORTLACH 22-year-old, Distilled 1972, Rare Malts, 65.3 vol

COLOUR Very full gold.

NOSE Cereal grains. Fresh baked bread. Some smoky peat.

BODY Remarkably smooth, layered.

PALATE Hugely nutty. Developing from dryness to sweeter juiciness. Then sweet smokiness.

FINISH Complex, with barley-sugar nuttiness and surging warmth. Tremendous length.

SCORE *85*

MORTLACH AND THE SHERRY TRADITION:
SOME INDEPENDENT BOTTLINGS

From Coopers Choice, a 1989 Mortlach, matured in sherry and
bottled in 2000 at 40 vol, has the aroma of lemon curd;
a nectar-like palate; finding balancing dryness in a heathery
finish, with a clean, appetizing smokiness. SCORE 85

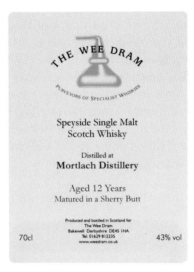

THE WEE DRAM

PURVEYORS OF SPECIALIST WHISKIES

Speyside Single Malt
Scotch Whisky

Distilled at
Mortlach Distillery

Aged 12 Years
Matured in a Sherry Butt

Produced and bottled in Scotland for
The Wee Dram
Bakewell Derbyshire DE45 IHA
Tel: 01629 812235
www.weedram.co.uk

70cl

43% vol

A 12-year-old, bottled at 43 vol for The Wee Dram, at Bakewell, England,
is notably spicy, from a gentle, simple aroma to a complex finish.
The mid-palate offers a rush of barley-sugar maltiness. SCORE 78

A sherry cask matured 12-year-old, at 46 vol from Hart Brothers,
has a nose of roasted nuts, treacle, struck match, charred raisin,
and a hint of leather; a big-bodied whisky; it is meaty but with
a sweet centre and raisin and treacle finish. SCORE 75

Blackadder has a 1989 sherry oak butt at 59.4 vol. The alcohol numbs the
aroma a little, but you can discern the smell of dunnage warehouse and
a slightly dull woodiness; the palate is savoury with touches of Bovril
and a concentrated sweetness; walnut finish. SCORE 70

Murray McDavid's 1989 fresh sherry vintage, at 46 vol,
balances the sweet and savoury well on the nose: roast lamb,
sulphur, flowers, and oak; the palate is powerful with a rich,
deep, meaty flavour with dried-fruit sweetness. SCORE 80

NORTH PORT

PRODUCER DCL/UDV

REGION Highlands DISTRICT Eastern Highlands

SITE OF FORMER DISTILLERY Brechin, Angus, DD9 6BE

T HE NAME INDICATES THE NORTH GATE of the small, once-walled city of Brechin. The distillery was built in 1820. The pioneering whisky writer, Alfred Barnard, who toured Scotland's distilleries in the 1880s, recorded that this one obtained its barley from the farmers around Brechin, and its peat and water from the Grampian mountains. The present-day writer, Derek Cooper, reports that the condensers were cooled in a stream that ran through the distillery. North Port was modernized in the 1970s, and closed in 1983. It has now been sold for redevelopment.

HOUSE STYLE Dry, fruity, gin-like. Aperitif.

NORTH PORT 19-year-old, Distilled 1979,
Bottled 1998, Rare Malts, 61 vol

COLOUR	Bright, pale gold.
NOSE	Dry, lightly smoky, grassy. Dry fruitiness.
BODY	Light to medium. Some viscosity.
PALATE	Light. Leafy. Dried apricot. Dried banana. Toasted marshmallow.
FINISH	Dry, spirity, sharp. Cedary.

SCORE **68**

NORTH PORT 23-year-old, Distilled 1971, Bottled 1995, Rare Malts, 54.7 vol

COLOUR Bright gold.

NOSE Aromatic, dry, almost sharp.

BODY Very light, smooth.

PALATE Light, with suggestions of mints, crystallized fruit, and pineapple.

FINISH Sharp.

SCORE **67**

NORTH PORT 36-year-old, Single Cask Bottling, Distilled 1966, Douglas Laing, 49.3 vol

COLOUR Deep, pinkish brown.

NOSE Cedary. Newly sawn wood. Resin. Oil of peppermint.

BODY Oily. Black chocolate. Bitter.

PALATE Cedary, Oily. Woody.

FINISH Drying. Musty.

SCORE **67**

NORTH PORT-BRECHIN 1981, Connoisseurs Choice, 40 vol

COLOUR Full gold.

NOSE Perfumy. Fresh bananas.

BODY Oily, smooth.

PALATE Bananas again. Lightly creamy flavour.

FINISH Leafy. Light spiciness. Fades quickly.

SCORE **66**

OBAN

PRODUCER Diageo
REGION Highlands DISTRICT Western Highlands
ADDRESS Stafford Street, Oban, Argyll, PA34 5NH
TEL 01631 572004
WEBSITE www.discovering-distilleries.com/www.malts.com VC

ENTHUSIASTS FOR THE WESTERN HIGHLAND malts sometimes dismiss Oban as being too restrained. With the 14-year-old augmented not only by the Montilla fino, but also by a 2002 Limited Release, there is now enough of an oeuvre to prove otherwise.

Oban is one of the few Western Highland distilleries on the mainland. It is a small distillery in a small town, but within that scale has a commanding position. Oban is regarded as the capital of the Western Highlands, and the distillery has a central site on the main street, facing the sea.

The principal expression of its whisky, the 14-year-old, has a label design incorporating a summary of the town's history: settled by Mesolithic cave dwellers before 5000BC; later by Celts, Picts, and Vikings. It was a fishing village, and in the era of railways and steamships became a gateway to the islands of the west, which it still is. Travellers following the muses of Mendelssohn, Turner, Keats, or Wordsworth to Mull or Iona, or Fingal's Cave, return to see a harbourfront centred on the distillery – backed by mossy, peaty hills whence its water flows.

A family of merchants in the town became brewers and distillers in 1794, though the present buildings probably date from the 1880s. The still-house was rebuilt in the late 1960s and early 1970s.

HOUSE STYLE Medium, with fresh peat and a whiff of the sea.
With seafood or game, or after dinner.

OBAN 14-year-old, 43 vol

COLOUR Full gold to amber.

NOSE "Pebbles on the beach", said one taster. A whiff of the sea,
but also a touch of fresh peat, and some maltiness.

BODY Firm, smooth, slightly viscous.

PALATE Deceptively delicate at first. Perfumy. Faint hint of fruity seaweed.
Then lightly waxy, becoming smoky. Dry.

FINISH Aromatic, smooth, appetizing.

SCORE **79**

OBAN 1980, Double Matured, Distillers Edition, 43 vol

Finished in Montilla fino wood.

COLOUR Amber.

NOSE Fragrant. Edible seaweed. Peaches. Very complex.

BODY Smooth, bigger.

PALATE Salty, nutty, peachy. Sweet in the middle, developing
notes of tobacco and seaweed.

FINISH The salt comes rolling back like an incoming tide.

SCORE **80**

OBAN 32-year-old, Limited Release of 6000, Bottled 2002, 55.1 vol

COLOUR Greeny gold. Ripe pears.

NOSE Sweet, sandy. A walk on the beach.

BODY Soft, oily, soothing.

PALATE Silky, teasing. Tightly combined flavours.
Oily creaminess. Sweet, edible seaweed.

FINISH Surprisingly assertive. Sandy. Almost gritty. Stinging, salty.

SCORE **83**

INDEPENDENT BOTTLINGS OF OBAN

A 1963, bottled at 30 years old and 52 vol by Cadenhead, is powerfully peaty,
slightly woody, with a huge, salty finish. SCORE 81. Earlier bottlings (in the late
1980s): a Cadenhead 21-year-old, at 46 vol, was maltier and smoky. SCORE 74.

OLD PULTENEY

PRODUCER Inver House Distillers Ltd
REGION Highlands DISTRICT Northern Highlands
ADDRESS Huddart Street, Wick, Caithness, KW1 5BD
WEBSITE www.inverhouse.com/www.oldpulteney.com
EMAIL enquiries@inverhouse.com

O NE OF WHISKY'S GREAT DEBATES (or was it a storm in a copita?) began here, and went public in 2003: do coastal whiskies really taste of salt? The debate surfaced in *Whisky Magazine*, but the salty suggestion had first been made in respect of Old Pulteney 25 years earlier, in the wine magazine *Decanter*.

Not only is the Pulteney distillery on the coast, it is the northernmost distillery on the Scottish mainland, at the town of Wick, in the famously peaty, rock-faced county of Caithness. Part of the town was designed by Thomas Telford and built by Sir William Pulteney in 1810 as a model fishing port. The distillery, founded in 1826, is in "Pulteneytown". It is thus one of the few urban distilleries, albeit only 250 yards from the nearest part of the harbour front. Even that walk can be sufficiently windy to demand a dram. "Caithness is a bare county, and needs a good whisky to warm it up," observed an early writer on the water of life, Professor R.J.S. McDowall. He was referring to Old Pulteney.

HOUSE STYLE Fresh, salty, appetizing. Pre-dinner.

OLD PULTENEY 12-year-old, 40 vol

COLOUR Deep yellow.

NOSE Dry. Peat, grass, sweet broom.

BODY Light, oily.

PALATE Light. Still honey and nuts, but oilier.

FINISH Oily. Soothing. Very salty.

SCORE **79**

OLD PULTENEY 18-year-old, Sherry Wood Finish, Cask No 1498, 59.9 vol

COLOUR Warm amber.

NOSE Hint of peat. Nutty. Earthy.

BODY Oily. Firm. Textured.

PALATE Very sweet. Distinctly nutty.
Toasted nuts. Peanut brittle.

FINISH Now the nuts are salted. That distinctly
maritime manzanilla character.

SCORE **81**

OLD PULTENEY 26-year-old, Highland Selection Limited Edition, 46 vol

COLOUR Full gold.

NOSE Rich, complex, creamy. Biscuity at first,
then sweeter, malty aromas.

BODY Smooth and silky.

PALATE Fresh, sweet, rewarding. Minty and malty.

FINISH Chewy. Lasting on soft spices and salt.

SCORE **81**

OLD PULTENEY 32-year-old,
Highland Selection Limited Edition, 56.2 vol

COLOUR Mahogany.

NOSE Full sherry. Rich dried fruit, figs, sultanas. Cherry liqueur chocolates. Tobacco. A balsamic touch (eucalyptus?).

BODY Full, syrupy.

PALATE A sherry burst-out. The distillery character is buried under assertive oak and punchy spices. Burnt wood. Bitter chocolate. Not typical of Old Pulteney.

FINISH Muscular, dry.

SCORE **75**

SOME INDEPENDENT BOTTLINGS OF OLD PULTENEY

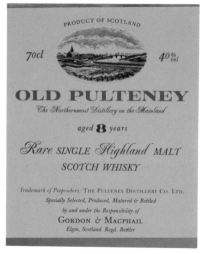

An eight-year-old at 40 vol, from Gordon & MacPhail, is as fresh as a day in the country; sweetly malty; with a touch of peat and salt in the finish. SCORE 80
From the same bottler, a 1990 at 59.4 vol, is heavily sherried to the point of being indelicate: harsh, astringent, sour. SCORE 69
A 1966, at 40 vol, has a sustained freshness of appetizing malt and complex fruit and spices. SCORE 80

A 12-year-old, at 55.6 vol from Hart Brothers, has a Chartreuse-like aroma; salt on the tongue; and a biting, dry finish. SCORE 78

A 19-year-old, at 51.9 vol from Adelphi, starts with wild flowers by the sea, develops sweet herbal flavours, and finishes with fresh, crushed nuts. SCORE 79

PITTYVAICH

PRODUCER Diageo
REGION Highlands   DISTRICT Speyside (Dufftown)
SITE OF FORMER DISTILLERY
Dufftown, Banffshire, AB55 4BR

Bulldozed in 2002, after a short and unglamorous life, the industrial-looking distillery was built by Bell's in 1975. In the late 1980s, enthusiasts for single malts began to wonder whether the product would become available to them. Then independent bottler James MacArthur released a 12-year-old, revealing a perfumy, soft-pear house character. The same bottler then added a 14-year-old that more assertively pronounces its dry finish. A bottling of the same age from the Scotch Malt Whisky Society was similar, but seemed to have more spicy dryness on the nose. In 1991 there was finally an official bottling, at 12 years old, in United's Flora and Fauna series. This has all the other characteristics, plus a hefty dose of sherry.

HOUSE STYLE Fruity, oily, spicy, spirity.
After dinner – a Scottish grappa, so to speak.

PITTYVAICH 12-year-old, Flora and Fauna, 43 vol

COLOUR	Deep amber red.
NOSE	Sherryish, perfumy, pear skin.
BODY	Light to medium. Firm. Dry.
PALATE	Very sherryish. Assertive. Some malty chewiness. Vanilla. Soft, sweet, pear-like fruitiness, moving to a spicy dryness.
FINISH	Spicy, perfumy, intensely dry, lingering on the tongue.

SCORE **69**

PORT ELLEN

PRODUCER Diageo
REGION Islay DISTRICT South Shore
SITE OF FORMER DISTILLERY Port Ellen, Isle of Islay, PA42 7AH
WEBSITE www.malts.com

WHICH WILL BE THE FINAL VINTAGE of this cult whisky? As stocks at the distillery diminish, and the fashionability of Islay soars, speculation mounts. Port Ellen is the rarest of Islay malts, despite a surprising number of independent bottlings. The distillery, near the island's main ferry port, was founded in 1825, substantially rebuilt and expanded during the boom years of the 1960s, then closed during the downturn in the 1980s. In the last two or three years, the modern parts of the distillery have been demolished, but the original pair of malt kilns have been preserved, complete with pagodas.

Adjoining the distillery is a modern maltings. The malt is supplied, in varying levels of peatiness, to all of the other Islay distilleries, including those which make a proportion of their own.

In 1995, Diageo started marketing whiskies from silent distilleries as The Rare Malts. These are vintage dated, so the number of bottles is determined by the amount of whisky held from a single year. In 1998, a 20-year-old Port Ellen was included in the range. In 2000, there was a further bottling of the same vintage at 22 years old. In order to vary the offerings, The Rare Malts had made it a rule not to feature the same distillery two years running. Such was the interest in the Port Ellen that it was decided to circumvent the rule. The Rare Malts selection ceased to include Port Ellen, which became a stand-alone Limited Edition. After three releases (see below), of 6000 to 12,000 bottles each, the final vintage seemed nigh.

HOUSE STYLE Oily, peppery, salty, smoky, herbal. With smoked fish.

PORT ELLEN 1979, 22-year-old, Limited Edition Numbered Bottles, First Release 2001, 56.2 vol

COLOUR Solid, greeny gold. Bright, refractive.

NOSE Fresh. Bison grass. Cereal grain. Oily.

BODY Firm, nutty, malty.

PALATE Earthy. Peaty. Salty. Quite hard. Austere.

FINISH Pronounced salt. Dry smokiness. Intensely appetizing.

SCORE **92**

PORT ELLEN 1978, 24-year-old, Limited Edition Numbered Bottles, Second Release 2002, 59.35 vol

COLOUR Lemony with golden hues.

NOSE Grassy and herbal. Dill, angelica, camomile.
A pleasant earthiness comes through.

BODY Tender.

PALATE Surprisingly smooth and sweet. A refreshing coolness.
Smokiness slowly emerges and hovers on menthol and vanilla.

FINISH Pleasantly dry and slowly dying.

SCORE **90**

PORT ELLEN 1979, 24-year-old, Limited Edition Numbered Bottles, Third Release 2003, 56.2 vol

COLOUR Pale gold. Faint green tinge.

NOSE Herbal. Slightly sour. Seaweedy. Sea breezes.

BODY Soft, textured.

PALATE Edible seaweed. Salty flavours reminiscent of
some vermouths. Developing spicy notes.

FINISH Powerful, peppery, warming.

SCORE **91**

PORT ELLEN 21-year-old, Anniversary Bottling, 58.4 vol

A rare "official" bottling, to celebrate 25 years of the maltings at Port Ellen.

COLOUR Bright gold.

NOSE Very medicinal, but clean and firm.

BODY Exceptionally oily, creamy.

PALATE Smooth and deceptively restrained at first, then the tightly
combined flavours emerge: bay leaves, parsley, peppercorns.

FINISH Slowly unfolding. Salty, smoky, oaky. Very warming. A subtlety and
complexity to which no aquavit or pepper vodka could quite aspire.

SCORE **83**

PORT ELLEN 20-year-old, Distilled 1978, Bottled 1998, Rare Malts, 60.9 vol

COLOUR Gold.

NOSE More assertive. Appetizing and arousing. Bay trees. Seaweed.

BODY Lightly oily.

PALATE More expressive, fruity, dryish flavours. Fruity olive oil. Parsley.

FINISH Salty. Smoky. Oaky. Extremely peppery.

SCORE **82**

PORT ELLEN 22-year-old, Distilled 1978, Bottled 2000, Rare Malts, 60.5 vol

COLOUR Pale yellow.

BODY Big, textured.

NOSE Fruity, seaweed, bay leaves, olive oil.

PALATE Big-bodied. Slightly sticky. Chewy. Edible seaweed. Parsley.

FINISH Hugely salty and equally peppery.

SCORE **85**

PORT ELLEN 11-year-old, Cadenhead, 64.1 vol

COLOUR Pale gold.

NOSE Leafy, slightly sour.

BODY Lightly oily.

PALATE Fruity, herbal, seaweedy.

FINISH Sweet, parsleyish. Then seaweedy, peppery, warming.

SCORE **79**

From the same bottler, an 18-year-old at 62.2 vol is smokier, oakier, drier, and more peppery, but slightly less complex. SCORE 79

PORT ELLEN 1980, Connoisseurs Choice, 40 vol

COLOUR	Deep gold to bronze.
NOSE	Leathery, oaky.
BODY	Lightly oily.
PALATE	Oaky, salty.
FINISH	Oily. Late saltiness.

SCORE **77**

PORT ELLEN 1975, 23-year-old, Cask Strength, Hart Brothers, 52.5 vol

COLOUR	Full gold.
NOSE	Clean. Lightly medicinal.
BODY	Lightly oily.
PALATE	Very sweet and parsleyish.
FINISH	Peppery.

SCORE **79**

SOME INDEPENDENT BOTTLINGS OF PORT ELLEN

A 1982 from Gordon & MacPhail, at 40 vol, shows classic distillery character: cod liver oil, black olive, dried seaweed, and smoke. The palate builds slowly, mixing these flavours within a firm structure. The finish has a dab of Germolene on it. SCORE 80

Douglas Laing's 23-year-old version, at 50 vol, is straw in colour and has a mix of oaky/malty aromas alongside light smoke, tar, and peanut oil. A succulent centre with tangerine, tarry peat, and a slightly austere finish. Great balance. SCORE 85

A 23-year-old, distilled in 1979, from Wilson and Morgan at 46 vol, has a pinky copper tinge. The nose is very soft and buttery, mixing European oak notes with fragrant peat smoke and on the palate balances sweet fruit and dry smoke. SCORE 85

Signatory's 1979, bottled at 43 vol, is sugary sweet on the nose with hints of sea thrift, linseed oil, and bay leaf. The feel is light and a little thin but there is good balance and a dry, smoky finish. SCORE 78

The same firm's 1978, bottled at 55 vol, is austere. The nose reminds you of stony beaches, dunnage warehouses, and pier heads all enlivened by a sprig of spearmint. The palate shows real intensity and good oily length before the stones come back on the finish. SCORE 78

Signatory has also finished a 1978 vintage in a port pipe. Bottled at 58 vol, it has a sunset pink glow. The sweet fruits work well against the firm structure. There is heather blossom and linseed oil on the palate; the finish is perfumed, fruity with some tar. SCORE 80

SIGNATORY BOTTLINGS OF PORT ELLEN

Without having quite cornered the market, this independent seems to have made something of a speciality of Port Ellen.

1983 at 43 vol: "White wine" colour; flowery aroma; light, oily body; clean hits of sweet, savoury, herbal, then oily. SCORE 77

1976 at 57.9 vol: Similar colour; drier aroma, with a hint of peat; firmer; more seaweed; slightly woody; comes to life in a seaweedy, peppery finish. SCORE 78

1975 at 43 vol: Very pale indeed. Flowery aroma; very light body; fruit and vanilla in palate; peppery finish. SCORE 76

23-year-old, distilled 1975, bottled 1998, at 56.1 vol, Signatory Silent Stills series, has a greeny gold colour; parsley aroma; light, firm body; lightly peaty, peppery finish. SCORE 79

ROSEBANK

PRODUCER Diageo
REGION Lowland DISTRICT Central Lowlands
SITE OF FORMER DISTILLERY Falkirk, Stirlingshire, FK1 5BW
WEBSITE www.malts.com

In 2002, THE QUEEN OPENED The Falkirk Wheel, a rotating lift to hoist boats between the Union canal and the restored Forth-Clyde canal. There had been hopes that the development of the canalside at Falkirk would include a tourist distillery to replace the silent Rosebank, but this prospect seems to have vanished.

Roses once bloomed on the banks of the Forth-Clyde canal, and a great deal of very early industry grew there. The Rosebank distillery may have had its origins as early as the 1790s. From the moment the canals lost business to the roads, the distillery's location turned from asset to liability. The road awkwardly bisected the distillery and as the traffic grew, it was difficult for trucks to drive in and out of the distillery. Rosebank was closed in 1993.

Rosebank's whisky at its best (i.e. not too woody) is as flowery as its name. It was the finest example of a Lowland malt, and was produced by triple distillation, in the Lowland tradition. It is a grievous loss.

HOUSE STYLE Aromatic, with suggestions of clover and camomile. Romantic. A whisky for lovers.

ROSEBANK 12-year-old, Flora and Fauna, 43 vol

This is a second version, released in 2003. It is a little drier and less lively than the first.

COLOUR Limey yellow.

NOSE Rosebank's typical camomile.

BODY Lightly creamy.

PALATE Flowery sweetness.

FINISH Mint imperials.

COMMENT Beginning to tire. Snatch a kiss while you can.

SCORE **76**

ROSEBANK 1981, Bottled 1997, Cask Strength Limited Bottling, 63.9 vol

COLOUR Lemony yellow.

NOSE Seductively aromatic. Clover. Camomile. Dry.

BODY Soft, caressing.

PALATE Creamy, lemony, flowery. Buttercups? Potpourri.

FINISH Fragrant, faintly smoky.

SCORE **78**

ROSEBANK 19-year-old, Distilled 1979, Rare Malts, 60.2 vol

COLOUR Vinho verde.

NOSE Shamelessly aromatic. Potpourri, camomile. Very flowery.

BODY Silky. Sensuous.

PALATE Delicious, lively flavours. Clover, lavender, fennel.

FINISH Very long indeed. Pulsating with sweet and hot flavours. Starts sweet, developing a rounded dryness.

SCORE **82**

ROSEBANK 20-year-old, Distilled 1981, Special Release, 62.3 vol

COLOUR Dull yellow. Faint green tinge.

NOSE Perfumy. Herbal. Vegetal.

BODY Soft. Very smooth. Sweet. Camomile.

PALATE Starts quietly, then explodes with flavours. Lemon grass. Very spicy. Very dry. Intense.

FINISH The same pulsating quality as in the 1979 above.

SCORE **80**

ROSEBANK 20-year-old, Distilled 1979, Rare Malts, Bottle No 2326, 60.3 vol

COLOUR Primrose. Greenish tinge.

NOSE Fresh, flowery, clean, vegetal. Belgian endive.
Moving toward old books.

BODY Firm. Very smooth.

PALATE Grassy. Dock leaves. Dandelion (needs water)? Peaty.

FINISH Intensely dry, herbal.

SCORE **79**

SOME INDEPENDENT BOTTLINGS OF ROSEBANK

A 20-year-old from Douglas Laing, at 50 vol, is mellow, with the scent of meadow flowers; a hint of rhubarb in the palate; and a dry, crisp spiciness in the finish. SCORE 77

A 1992 from Blackadder, at 60 vol, has an intense, almost prickly, aroma; a flowing, sweetly lemony palate; and a deftly rounded finish. SCORE 75

A 1992 Coopers Choice, at 43 vol, has the typical camomile aroma (or is it Earl Grey tea?) and a hint of lavender; a silky, oily, sweet palate (baked custard, dusted with icing sugar); and a suggestion of burnt sugar in the finish. SCORE 79

A 1992 Murray McDavid, at 46 vol, has the aroma of a flower garden on a summer's evening; a suggestion of mint tea in the palate; and a finish that is less dry than usual. SCORE 79

A 1991 Signatory, at 43 vol, has a suggestion of Turkish delight in the aroma; almond milk in the palate; and an interplay of hot and sweet in the finish. SCORE 78

A 1989 from Gordon & MacPhail, at 40 vol, has the aroma of lemon meringue pie; a biscuity palate; and a soothing but spicy and dry finish. SCORE 78

A 1989 from Lombard, at 50 vol, is slightly sharp in its floral aroma; effervescent in its zabaglione palate; with a sting of nettles in the finish. SCORE 81

A 1990 from Duncan Taylor has candied grapefruit in the aroma; sensuous tropical fruits (guava?) in the palate; and waves of spiciness in the finish. SCORE 79

OLDER EXRESSIONS NOW HARD TO FIND
ROSEBANK 1990, Fresh Sherry Cask, Murray McDavid, 46 vol

COLOUR Full gold to amber.

NOSE Sherry, honey, lemons, buttercups.

BODY Light, smooth.

PALATE The flowery youth of the whisky and the freshness of the sherry cask achieve an interesting harmony.

FINISH Smooth, appetizing. A teasing balance of sweetness and dryness.

SCORE **78**

A Murray McDavid bottling of the same age and strength, but from a bourbon cask, had a good, spearmint-like herbal note, but its flavours held together less well, and it was rather sharp. SCORE 76

ROSEBANK 1989, Signatory, 43 vol

COLOUR Lemony yellow.

NOSE Very aromatic. Flowery. Honeyed.

BODY Creamy.

PALATE Creamy, nutty, flowery.

FINISH Lemony. Buttercups. Fragrant.

SCORE **77**

ROSEBANK 1989, 9-year-old, Cadenhead, 58.8 vol

COLOUR White wine to pale gold.

NOSE Assertively flowery. Fragrant. Dry.

BODY Light.

PALATE Flowery, soft, grassily sweet, moving to very gentle, dry finish.

FINISH Flowery, very lightly nutty, nougat-like.

SCORE **80**

ROSEBANK 1988, Connoisseurs Choice, 40 vol

COLOUR Full gold.

NOSE Buttercups, clover, sweet grass, honey, and a tender touch of sherry.

BODY Light, soft, smooth.

PALATE Flowers softened and sweetened by sherry. Honey, junket, very light nutty dryness. A deft balance between the whisky's own character and the sherry.

FINISH Candied angelica, honey-coated nuts.

SCORE **79**

ST MAGDALENE

PRODUCER DCL
REGION Lowland DISTRICT Central Lowlands
SITE OF FORMER DISTILLERY Linlithgow, West Lothian, EH49 6AQ

THIS SITE ACCOMMODATED a leper colony in the 12th century, and later a convent, before a distillery was established, possibly in 1765. Production ceased in 1983 and some of the buildings have since been converted into apartments. The distillery has sometimes been known as Linlithgow, after its hometown west of Edinburgh and close to the river Forth.

HOUSE STYLE Perfumy, grassy, smooth. Restorative.

ST MAGDALENE 19-year-old, Distilled 1979, Released 1998, Rare Malts, 63.8 vol

COLOUR Full gold to pale amber.

NOSE Very aromatic. Burnt grass. Rooty. Liquorice root. Juicy oak.

BODY Medium to full. Firmly oily.

PALATE Big flavours. Chewy, liquorice-like maltiness.

FINISH Sudden robust hit of peaty, sappy bitterness, rounding out in lively flavours as it develops.

SCORE **78**

An earlier Rare Malts bottling of a 1970 St Magdalene had burnt grass, toffee, candy, and exotic fruit. SCORE 77

ST MAGDALENE 20-year-old, Distilled 1978, 62.7 vol

To celebrate the centenary of UDV's Engineering Department.

COLOUR Chestnut.

NOSE Polished oak.

BODY Big, smooth.

PALATE Winey sherry. Juicy oak. Burnt grass.

FINISH Nutty, syrupy, smoky. Delicious.

SCORE **79**

SOME INDEPENDENT BOTTLINGS OF
ST MAGDALENE/LINLITHGOW

Four distilled in 1982:

A Duncan Taylor bottling, as Linlithgow, is pricky on the nose, with a suggestion of bison grass; almost effervescent in the middle, with hot paprika; and very warm in a long, dry finish. SCORE 71

A Gordon & MacPhail bottling as St Magdalene, at 40 vol, has the aroma of a farmer's field where stubble has been burned; a palate suggesting toasted marshmallows or Belgian waffles; and a cedary finish. SCORE 76

A McKillop's Choice, at 62.6 vol, as Linlithgow, has a hugely powerful linseed aroma; a big, sweet, grassy palate; and a medicinal finish. SCORE 76

A Scott's Selection, at 61.6 vol, as Linlithgow, has a fragrant aroma, with a suggestion of butter cookies; an appetizingly fresh palate evoking mint chocolates; and an almondy dryness in the finish. SCORE 74

Two distilled in 1975:

A Blackadder, at 59.3 vol, as Linlithgow, has a subtle pepperiness in the aroma; a velvety maltiness in the palate; and a juicy, sappy oakiness in the finish. SCORE 75

A Signatory, at 51.5 vol, as Linlithgow, has an orchard fragrance; good flavour development in a palate accented toward cereal grains and malted milk; and a slightly hot but satisfying finish. SCORE 79

SCAPA

PRODUCER Allied Distillers Ltd
REGION Highlands ISLAND Orkney
ADDRESS St Ola, Kirkwall, Orkney, KW15 1SE
TEL 01856 872071

THE NEW APPRECIATION of island whiskies has heightened interest in Scapa, which already had its own following. The puzzle is the proprietors' apparent lack of enthusiasm. The distillery has in recent years been operated only intermittently, and marketed sporadically.

True, the functional buildings from the late 1950s lack romance, but a restored water wheel is a reminder of origins in the 1820s. Agreed, the distillery is not the northernmost, but it fails by only half a mile. Yes, there is a breezy elusiveness to the whisky, but that is the perfect foil to its rounded, grounded, northern neighbour.

Scapa's greatest asset is its evocative location. Scapa Flow, a stretch of water linking the North Sea to the Atlantic, is famous for its roles in both World Wars.

The water for the distillery's mash tun is from a stream called the Lingro Burn, and is very peaty. The distillery uses wholly unpeated malt. It has a Lomond wash still, which may contribute to a slight oiliness of the whisky. Maturation is in bourbon casks. Although the whisky is quite light in flavour, it has a distinctive complex of vanilla notes, sometimes suggesting very spicy chocolate, and nutty, rooty saltiness.

HOUSE STYLE Salt, hay. Oily, spicy chocolate.
After a hearty walk, before dinner.

SCAPA 8-year-old, 40 vol

Now hard to find.

COLOUR Full gold to amber.

NOSE Fresh, sea-breeze saltiness, new-mown hay, heather. Some bourbon character.

BODY Medium, silky.

PALATE Salty, slightly sharp, tangy.

FINISH Oily but dry, appetizing.

SCORE **76**

SCAPA 10-year-old, 43 vol

Hard to find.

COLOUR Full gold to amber.

NOSE Salt, hay, chocolate, bourbon. Delicious soft peatiness.

BODY Medium, silky.

PALATE Smooth, vanilla, chocolate. Rounded. Beautiful balance.

FINISH Appetizing bitterness. Rounded peat. Faint salt. Quick warmth.

SCORE **77**

SCAPA 12-year-old, 40 vol

COLOUR Bright full gold.

NOSE Softer. Hay. Warm.

BODY Light, smooth, salty.

PALATE Clean, sweetish. Vanilla, nuts, salt.

FINISH Late salt and pepper, with a hint of peat.

SCORE **76**

SOME INDEPENDENT BOTTLINGS OF SCAPA

A 1990 at 40 vol, from Gordon & MacPhail, has the aroma of white chocolate. Its palate suggests Orkney fudge and dry hay. The finish is spicy and dry but soothing. SCORE 74

A 1990 at 43 vol, from Signatory, has the aroma of freshly cut grass; coriander in the palate; and a warm, dry, salty finish. SCORE 76

A 13-year-old at 43 vol, from Dun Bheagan, has a hint of coconut in the aroma; a palate suggesting honeyed pipe tobacco; and a lingering spiciness in the finish. SCORE 75

A 23-year-old, at 50 vol, from Douglas Laing, has a winey, sherryish aroma; rich, dark chocolate and dried apricots in the palate; and a spicy, vanilla-pod oakiness in the finish. SCORE 76

SPEYBURN

PRODUCER Inver House Distillers Ltd
REGION Highlands DISTRICT Speyside (Rothes)
ADDRESS Rothes, Aberlour, Morayshire, AB38 7AG
WEBSITE www.inverhouse.com EMAIL enquiries@inverhouse.com

Pretty as a picture: both the growing range of whiskies (flowery and fruity) and the distillery (a much photographed Victorian classic, masked by trees in a deep, sweeping valley). Speyburn makes a spectacular sight on the road out of Rothes, toward Elgin. It was built in 1897 and, despite modernizations, has not undergone dramatic change. In the early 1990s, Speyburn was acquired by Inver House.

HOUSE STYLE Flowery, herbal, heathery. Aperitif.

SPEYBURN 10-year-old, 40 vol

COLOUR Solid gold.

NOSE Flowery.

BODY Medium, gentle.

PALATE Clean, lightly malty. Developing fresh, herbal, heathery notes.

FINISH Fresh, very sweet, lightly syrupy.

SCORE **71**

SPEYBURN 16-year-old, Limited Edition Highland Selection, 46 vol

COLOUR Shimmery greeny gold.

NOSE Sweet and fruity.

BODY Light. Very smooth.

PALATE Lots of flowers and fruit. Raspberry? Strawberry? One of the most assertive, flavoursome expressions of Speyburn.

FINISH Long. Echoes.

SCORE **78**

SPEYBURN 21-year-old, Single Cask 1979, Bottle No 468, Cask No 1132, 60.1 vol

This will eventually be replaced by a 25-year-old.

NOSE Very heavy sherry. Bitter chocolate. Heathery. Leafy.

BODY Very firm. Slightly oily.

PALATE Good malt background. Nutty. Spicy. Aniseed.
Lots of flavour and interest.

FINISH Peaty. Sappy. Very oaky. Woody.

SCORE **76**

SPEYBURN 27 year-old, 46 vol

COLOUR Full gold with pale copper hues.

NOSE Sherry tinted. Beeswax. Fruity, leafy. Ferns. Earthy.

BODY Smooth, medium.

PALATE Rich. Bitter chocolate. Marzipan. A mouthful of spices.

FINISH Heather root. Gently peaty. Long, dry oakiness.

SCORE **76**

SPEYBURN 1974, Gordon & MacPhail, 49 vol

COLOUR Medium gold with a bronze tinge.

NOSE Heathery, slightly earthy. Wet leaves.

BODY Medium, supple.

PALATE Smooth. Malty, opening on spices and
heathery notes (root rather than flowers).

FINISH Sweet and gentle, drying on soft spices.

SCORE **74**

SPRINGBANK

PRODUCER Springbank Distillers Ltd
REGION Campbeltown DISTRICT Argyll
ADDRESS Well Close, Campbeltown, Argyll, PA28 6ET
TEL 01586 552085 VC Summer only by appointment

SOME TIME DURING 2004, the Glengyle distillery, in Campbeltown, was due to restart production after more than 75 years' silence. The sense of revival was heightened by the use of stills that once produced Ben Wyvis, in the northern Highlands. The rebirth of Glengyle was ahead of schedule, only three years after the distillery buildings had been bought as an empty shell by Springbank, a couple of streets away.

Meanwhile, another revived Campbeltown malt, Hazelburn, was maturing well for its planned launch a year later, also slightly ahead of schedule. Hazelburn is being triple distilled, from unpeated malt, at Springbank. The original Hazelburn distillery, which closed in 1925, having existed since 1796, was an immediate neighbour of Springbank.

Springbank's own whisky is made from medium-peated malt, with a trajectory that amounts to two-and-a-half times distillation. With its brineyness, its oily, coconut-like flavours, and its great complexity, Springbank features in almost every whisky lover's top ten malts.

Springbank dates from the 1820s, and even earlier as an illicit still. Its present proprietor, and tireless revivalist of Campbeltown distilling, Hedley Wright, is a member of the founding Mitchell family.

In the early 1990s, Springbank revived its own floor maltings. It now uses only its own malt. (Among other distilleries with their own floor maltings, none is self-sufficient.) This has been of particular benefit in the production of another revivalist malt, Longrow, first released in 1985. Springbank first distilled Longrow in 1973–74.

Longrow is double distilled from heavily peated malt. With its own maltings, the distillery can achieve exactly the character of peatiness it requires. In their peatiness, oiliness, brineyness, and sense of restrained power, the Longrows are becoming cult whiskies. The original Longrow distillery closed in 1896. It adjoined the Springbank site.

Over the centuries, the town has had about 30 distilleries, some of which ruined their reputations by producing hurried whiskies for the US during Prohibition, and closed soon afterwards. Vestiges of them remain in a bus garage, a business park, and other manifestations. These sites have been diligently mapped by Frank McHardy, who manages Springbank. Campbeltown was the great whisky region in the age of coastal steamers, before the railways made Speyside more accessible.

As an isolated independent with its own underutilized bottling line, in 1969, J. & A. Mitchell bought the century-old firm of Cadenhead. This company, formerly based in Aberdeen, has always been an independent bottler. Both Springbank and Cadenhead use the same bottling line, in Campbeltown, but they are run as separate enterprises.

Neither company chill filters its whiskies, or adds caramel to balance the colour. Being long-established enterprises, they have a considerable inventory of casks. Some Springbank once even found its way into a couple of casks of acacia wood. As awareness of woods has increased in the industry, Springbank has mainly acquired bourbon barrels, to highlight the character of the whisky itself, but most bottlings are vatted to give a touch of colour and sweetness from sherry wood.

With a maltings, two distilleries, four single malts, an independent bottlings business, and a chain of shops (Eaglesome's in Campbeltown and Cadenhead's in Edinburgh and London), J. & A. Mitchell has ensured that Campbeltown remains a whisky centre. This surge of activity was the response of Hedley Wright to a suggestion that Springbank and its local rival, Glen Scotia, were insufficient justification for the town retaining its status (along with Islay, the Highlands, and the Lowlands) as one of the whisky regions. Mr Wright can be famously taciturn, but his actions are stentorian.

The geography itself is tenuous. Hanging from the coast by a neck of land only 1.6 kilometres (1 mile) wide, Kintyre looks like an island, but is actually a peninsula, stretching 65 kilometres (40 miles) south. Physically, either an island or a peninsula might better qualify as a region, but there are no distilleries until the town itself, which is near the southern extremity. At this point, the peninsula is at its broadest, but still less than 16 kilometres (10 miles) wide. Drive and climb to Crosshill Loch, and the sea is visible to both east and west, as are Islay and Arran on a clear day.

This loch has provided water for all the Campbeltown distilleries: an unusual situation that perhaps accounts for some similarities of character. To the immediate south of the town, the land narrows at the tip, or "mull" of the peninsula. This is the mull of Kintyre, where the mist rolls in from the sea just as Paul McCartney promised it would. It hangs over the back-street warehouses of the curiously urban distilleries, and entraps the ghosts of all those whiskies past. No wonder Springbank and Longrow have so much character.

HOUSE STYLE Springbank: salty, oily, coconut. Aperitif.
Longrow: piney, oily, damp earth. Nightcap.

SPRINGBANK 10-year-old, 46 vol

COLOUR Gold.

NOSE Light brine, spice, rounded malt, pear. Elegant for a youngster.

BODY Rich and oily. Mouth-coating.

PALATE Fantastic mix of dry and sweet, tinned pear, citrus. Suggestion of smoke.

FINISH Melon.

SCORE **83**

SPRINGBANK 12-year-old, 175th Anniversary, 48 vol

COLOUR Old gold.

NOSE Panettone, raisin, apricot, lilies, nut oil, smoke. Real complexity.

BODY Soft and oily.

PALATE Fascinating, subtle, and ever-changing. Great balance between sooty smoke, olive, dried peels, cashew, custard, brine. A classic Springbank.

FINISH Spicy, briny, long.

SCORE **90**

SPRINGBANK 12-year-old, 1989, Rum Wood, 54.6 vol

COLOUR Pale. Greenish tinge.

NOSE Sweetish. Fragrant. Smoky, with fruit behind.
Like an apple wood grill. Hint of salty sea air.

BODY Quite full-bodied. Soft. Marshmallowy.

PALATE Sweet red apples. Pears. Hedgerow fruit.

FINISH Small explosion of spiciness. Peppermint.

SCORE **90**

SPRINGBANK 13-year-old, Port Cask, 54.2 vol

COLOUR Pinkish gold.

NOSE Sweet. Blackberry, wild strawberry, cherry cake.
Attractive burnt notes.

BODY Thick and syrupy

PALATE Tinned fruits. Cherry ripe with soft feel. Good balance.

FINISH Fresh. Smoke and fruit.

SCORE **80**

SPRINGBANK 15-year-old, 46 vol

COLOUR Light amber.

NOSE Sophisticated. Dundee cake, vanilla, new leather,
pipe tobacco, dried apricot, peat, tea.

BODY Full and rich. Mouth-coating.

PALATE European oak is there, but not dominating. Sweet
tobacco, nut, smoke in the background. Complex.

FINISH Soot, malt.

SCORE **90**

SPRINGBANK 25-year-old, Limited Edition, 46 vol

COLOUR Apricot.

NOSE Sea air. Sherry oak. Very clean.

BODY Creamy.

PALATE Excellent sherry, but held in balance. Walnuts. Restrained
esters. Very faint suggestion of banana. Coconut. Salt.
Brine. A magnificently complex whisky.

FINISH Salty. Some peat. Dry.

SCORE **95**

SPRINGBANK Frank McHardy Anniversary, 1975, 46 vol

COLOUR Rich gold.

NOSE Nutty, spicy oak, mandarin/curaçao, macadamia, herbs, light smoke.
Oakiest of current expressions, but understated.

BODY Creamy and soft

PALATE Coconut, pine, citrus, coffee. Spices to the finish.

FINISH Nutty, sooty.

SCORE **90**

LONGROW

LONGROW 10 year-old, 1992, 46 vol

COLOUR Light gold.

NOSE Fuller than 1991. Sweeter and a little floral, but also
slightly more medicinal and earthy.

BODY Robust, succulent.

PALATE Peaches and soft fruit under the peat. Good, nutty depth.

FINISH Dry, peaty.

SCORE **83**

LONGROW 10-year-old, 1991, Bourbon Wood, 46 vol

COLOUR Straw.

NOSE Earthy yet fragrant and complex. Dried lavender,
charcoal, coconut. Good lift.

BODY Long and rich.

PALATE Dusty, chimney-like with a sweet centre.
Explosive: almond oil, smoked fish.

FINISH Long, smoky, and dry.

SCORE **90**

LONGROW 10-year-old, 1991, Sherry Wood, 46 vol

COLOUR Oily gold.

NOSE Very restrained, nutty sherry, with sea air
and peat smoke lurking behind.

BODY Textured.

PALATE Slightly sweeter, creamier, more rounded.

FINISH Almost a shadow of the nose. Nutty at first, then
the peat emerged, followed by the salt.

SCORE **90**

LONGROW 13-year-old, Sherry Cask, 53.2 vol

COLOUR Old gold.

NOSE Dundee cake, raisin, pecan, smoke. More sherry than smoke.

BODY Gentle and soft.

PALATE The peat bedded down in the rich fruitcake character given by the sherry cask. Subtle, rich, and weighty.

FINISH Oily.

SCORE **80**

HAZELBURN

HAZELBURN 1997, Cask Sample at Natural Strength

COLOUR Pale gold.

NOSE Very clean and high-toned. Vanilla, malting floor, mealy, custard, hazelnut spread.

BODY Light, sweet.

PALATE Firm and youthful but with great citric sweetness. Apple and banana. Beautiful balance.

FINISH Clean and fresh.

COMMENT Tasted as a work in progress.

SOME INDEPENDENT BOTTLINGS OF SPRINGBANK

Blackadder bottles a 1991 vintage at 57.4 vol. The nose is like old-fashioned lemonade or ginger beer. The body is gentle with gingery notes on the palate. Some dry smoke on the finish. SCORE 77

A 1974 from Chieftain's Choice, at 46 vol, has an elegant nose with marzipan and vanilla. Soft and gentle in the mouth, it is toasty with the distillery's characteristic oily feel and briney, sooty finish. SCORE 80

The firm's 1972 bottling, at 57.8 vol, has a resinous nose reminiscent of deck oil and sweet amontillado. Unchillfiltered, water makes it go a murky brown and brings out coffee cake and smoke. Well balanced, but strange looking. SCORE 80

Duncan Taylor's 1967 vintage, at 40.7 vol, has an aroma of pine, canvas, soot, coconut, pear, and juicy malt. A soft, light body with ripe fruits and spices on the palate. SCORE 82

A 1969 from the Signatory stable, at 56 vol, has hints of sesame, mink oil, soft leather. Very concentrated – essence of Springbank? A silky body, the flavours extend across the palate, showing real saltiness and light smoke. The finish is reminiscent of green tea. SCORE 90

STRATHISLA

PRODUCER Chivas Brothers
REGION Highland DISTRICT Speyside (Strathisla)
ADDRESS Seafield Avenue, Keith, Banffshire, AB55 3BS
TEL 01542 783044 VC

Hardly surprisingly, the new owners of Chivas will continue to use as their showpiece the oldest distillery in the north of Scotland. In the 13th century, Dominican monks used a spring nearby to provide water for brewing beer. The same water, with a touch of calcium hardness and scarcely any peat character, has been used in the distillation of whisky since at least 1786.

Strathisla, which has also at times been known as Milltown, began its life as a farm distillery. It started to take its present shape from the 1820s onwards, especially after a fire in 1876. In 1950 it was acquired by Chivas. Over the years, it has been restored, and features have been added to make it a somewhat idealized traditional distillery.

Lightly peated malt is used, as well as wooden washbacks and small stills. Although wooden washbacks are by no means unusual, Strathisla believes that fermentation characteristics play a very important part in the character of its dry, fruity, oaky malt whisky.

HOUSE STYLE House style Dry, fruity. After dinner.

STRATHISLA 12-year-old, 43 vol

COLOUR Full, deep gold.

NOSE Apricot. Cereal grains. Fresh, juicy oak.

BODY Medium, rounded.

PALATE Much richer than previous bottlings. Sherryish, fruity.
Mouth-coating. Then Strathisla's teasing sweet-and-dry character.

FINISH Smooth and soothing. Violets and vanilla.

SCORE **80**

STRATHISLA 25-year-old, Official Limited Bottling of 600, 43 vol

COLOUR Old gold.

NOSE Potting shed (earth, clay pots, moss) hessian,
dry tobacco, and dried fruits. Oaky.

BODY Gentle and rich. Good grip.

PALATE Tea-like. Light chocolate orange, woodland/woodsmoke.
Soft fruits in the centre.

FINISH Slightly tannic.

SCORE **78**

SOME INDEPENDENT BOTTLINGS

Strathisla has been one of the mainstays of the Gordon & MacPhail range
for many years. The golden-hued 1987 vintage, at 40 vol, has a floral, lightly
citric nose: spring-like with a nice, crispy dryness. The body is creamy and
soft; the palate has a tingle of citrus peel cream, blossom, spices.
Great balance and a zesty finish. SCORE 85

A 25-year-old, at 40 vol, is richer in colour and more elegant; lilies,
heather, and cigars in the aroma; then a burst of flavour in the palate, with
Bakewell tart, orange peel, coffee beans, allspice, and nuts. A sparkling,
complex, effervescent dram. SCORE 90

The firm's 1963, at 40 vol, shows oily maturity of old whisky (and old
style Speyside). There is fragrant wood, dried apple, kumquat, mace,
and red plum. The body is quite oaky but the palate still dances
in the manner of great Strathisla. SCORE 85

The venerable 1953, at 40 vol, has a nose like a woodland walk
(fungal, mulch) with the faint hint of citrus. The firmest of the range,
the palate has a smoky note, dried apple, grilled nut. The finish is
of ash and orange. SCORE 83

STRATHMILL

PRODUCER Diageo
REGION Highlands DISTRICT Speyside (Strathisla)
ADDRESS Keith, Banffshire, AB55 5DQ
TEL 01542 885000 WEBSITE www.malts.com

GRAPES HAVE TO BE CRUSHED; grain has to be milled. The town of Keith must once have been a considerable grain-milling centre. The Glen Keith distillery was built on the site of a corn mill. Strathmill, as its name suggests, went one better. It was rebuilt from a corn mill, in 1891, when the whisky industry was having one of its periodic upswings. Three years later, it was acquired by Gilbey, of which Justerini & Brooks became a subsidiary through IDV (Diageo). Arguably, it has been in the same ownership for more than a century. Its whisky was for many years central to the Dunhill/Old Master blends, but does not seem to have been available as a single until a bottling of a lusciously sweet 1980 by the wine merchant chain, Oddbins, in 1993.

HOUSE STYLE The whisky world's answer to orange muscat. With dessert.

STRATHMILL 12-year-old, Flora and Fauna, 43 vol

COLOUR Lively gold.

NOSE Grassy and malty. With a delicate, floral touch. Clover. Orange peel.

BODY Smooth and flowing.

PALATE Sweet and fulfilling. Appealing freshness. Honeycomb, orange. Hint of mint.

FINISH Drying on a resiny but soothing note.

SCORE 78

TALISKER

PRODUCER Diageo
REGION Highlands ISLAND Skye
ADDRESS Carbost, Isle of Skye, IV47 8SR
TEL 01478 614308
WEBSITE www.discovering-distilleries.com/www.malts.com VC

ALREADY VOLCANICALLY POWERFUL, Talisker has boosted its impact in recent years by adding new expressions. However many versions there may be, it remains a singular malt. It has a distinctively peppery character, so hot as to make one taster's temples steam. The phrase "explodes on the palate" is among the descriptions used for certain whiskies by blenders at UDV; surely they had Talisker in mind when they composed this. "The lava of the Cuillins" was another taster's response. The Cuillins are the dramatic hills of Skye, the island home of Talisker. The distillery is on the west coast of the island, on the shores of loch Harport, in an area where Gaelic is still spoken. The local industry was once tweed.

After a number of false starts on other sites, the distillery was established in 1831 and expanded in 1900. For much of its life, it used triple distillation, and in those days Robert Louis Stevenson ranked Talisker as a style on its own, comparable with the Islay and Livet whiskies. It switched to double distillation in 1928, and was partly rebuilt in 1960. The distillery uses traditional cooling coils – "worm tubs" – which can make for a fuller flavour than a modern condenser.

Some malt lovers still mourn the youthfully dry assertiveness of the eight-year-old version that was replaced by the current, more rounded version a couple of summers older. For a time, this was the only expression, but official bottlings have multiplied. As if to balance an equation, independent bottlings seem to have vanished.

The island is also home to an unrelated company making a vatted malt called Poit Dubh, and a blend, Te Bheag. Both are said to contain some Talisker, and their hearty palates appear to support this suggestion. A dry, perfumy, blended whisky called Isle of Skye is made by the Edinburgh merchants Ian Macleod & Co. The style of whisky liqueur represented by Drambuie is also said to have been created on the Isle of Skye, though its origins actually remain somewhat clouded in Scotch mist.

HOUSE STYLE Volcanic. A winter warmer.

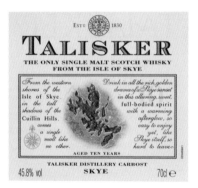

TALISKER 10-year-old, 45.8 vol

COLOUR	Bright amber red.

NOSE	Pungent, smoke-accented, rounded.

BODY	Full, slightly syrupy.

PALATE	Smoky, malty sweet, with sourness and a very big pepperiness developing.

FINISH	Very peppery, huge, long.

SCORE **90**

TALISKER Natural Cask Strength, No Age Statement, Bottled 2000, 60 vol

Available at the distillery.

COLOUR	Very bright. Yellow with an olive tinge.

NOSE	Wild garlic. Blanched spinach with cracked black pepper.

BODY	Oily.

PALATE	Starts smoothly and has huge development toward earthy, chive-like, seaweedy, medicinal notes.

FINISH	Soft and smooth on the tongue, drying toward a late surge of salt, ground white pepper and lactic acidity (ricotta cheese?)

SCORE **77**

TALISKER "Double Matured", 1986, Distillers Edition, 45.8 vol

Finished in amoroso sherry wood.

COLOUR Orange.

NOSE Toffee, bitter chocolate, and toasted nuts, with late salt and pepper.

BODY Full, textured.

PALATE Toffeeish, then toasty. The richness of these flavours introduces a shock of contrast when the seaweed and pepper suddenly burst through.

FINISH Powerful salt and pepper.

SCORE 90

TALISKER 1982, 20-year-old, 58.8 vol

COLOUR Gold, with green tinge.

NOSE Scorched earth. Harbour aromas. Seaweed.

BODY Medium to full. Firm.

PALATE Distant thunder. Seems to rumble and reverberate as the volcanic heat builds ever so slowly. Hot, slightly sour, peppery. Very tightly combined flavours, reluctant to unfurl. When they did, the earth moved.

FINISH Quite quick and sharp. A thunderflash.

SCORE 93

TALISKER 25-year-old, Bottled 2001, 59.9 vol

COLOUR Peachy, tan.

NOSE Warm. Minerally. A hint of sulphur.

BODY Quite rich.

PALATE Nutty, with a suggestion of artichoke. A touch of salt, then a burst of freshly milled pepper.

FINISH Volcanic. Reverberating.

SCORE 92

TAMDHU

PRODUCER The Edrington Group
REGION Highlands   DISTRICT Speyside
ADDRESS Knockando, Morayshire, AB38 7RP

THIS DISTILLERY IS STILL somewhat overshadowed by its charismatic neighbour, Macallan, six or seven miles down river. Both malts are significant contributors to The Famous Grouse, the biggest selling blend in Scotland. As singles, their fortunes differ. Since Macallan and Tamdhu came under the same ownership, the former has been promoted as the group's Speyside malt at the expense of the latter.

Like several Speyside distilleries, Tamdhu shares its name with a station on the railway that ran up and down the valley. Tamdhu station is more elaborate than most, with two full-length platforms and a signal box. The distillery was founded in 1896, and largely rebuilt in the 1970s. Water comes from the Tamdhu burn, which flows through woodland into the Spey.

Tamdhu has a sizeable and impressive Saladin maltings, providing for all its own needs and those of several other whisky makers. A modest reminder of this is the stylized ear of barley that appears on the label of the principal version of Tamdhu. The distillery is impeccably well kept, and has its own touches of tradition, notably its enthusiasm for wooden fermenting vessels.

HOUSE STYLE Mild, urbane. Sometimes toffee-nosed. Versatile.

TAMDHU **No Age Statement, 40 vol**

COLOUR Bright gold.

NOSE Flowery. Faintly lemony. Cereal grain.

BODY Light, soft.

PALATE Clean, sweet. Very slightly toffeeish. An easily drinkable,
malt-accented introduction to singles.

FINISH Flowery. Very faint hint of peat.

SCORE **74**

SOME INDEPENDENT BOTTLINGS OF TAMDHU

A 15-year-old, at 55.3 vol, from Adelphi, has an aroma reminiscent of
cooking apples; the flavours of intensely sweet, fruity pears in rich syrup;
and a clovey, woody dryness in the finish. SCORE 72

From Chieftain's, a 1985 Tamdhu, at 16 years old and 46 vol,
finished in a rum cask, has aromas reminiscent of Demerara sugar,
nutmeg, lime, and ripe banana in the aroma; a caressing sweetness
in the palate; and a tender nuttiness in the finish. SCORE 77

A 1981 Gordon & MacPhail Reserve, at 43 vol, has aromas reminiscent of
sweet limes; a lemony, flowery palate; and a peppery finish. SCORE 78
A 1961, at 40 vol, from the same bottler, is very heavily sherried.
It has a copper-red colour; a resiny aroma; a spicy, minty, treacly
palate; and a sweetly fading finish. SCORE 73

A 1968, at 40.1 vol, from Duncan Taylor, opens slowly, with
cumin seeds and burnt leaves in the aroma; and a palate that is
unusually peaty for Tamdhu. SCORE 76

A 1966 from Kingsbury, at 33 years old and cask strength, has an
attractive fragrance of light, fresh peat smoke; black treacle and
butterscotch in the palate; and oaty dryness in the finish. SCORE 78

A 34-year-old, at 50 vol from Douglas Laing, is aristocratic and intense,
with saddlery and polished oak in the aroma; a scrumptious display of rich
Christmas flavours; and a spicy finish. A beautiful dram. SCORE 79

TAMNAVULIN

PRODUCER Whyte and MacKay Ltd
REGION Highlands   DISTRICT Speyside (Livet)
ADDRESS Ballindalloch, Banffshire, AB37 9JA

O N THE STEEP SIDE OF THE GLEN of the Livet, the river is joined by one of its tributaries, a stream called Allt a Choire (in English, "Corrie"). This is the site of the Tamnavulin distillery, taking its name from "mill on the hill". The location is more often spelled Tomnavoulin, but such discrepancies are hardly unusual in Scotland.

Part of the premises was formerly used for the carding of wool. The distillery, built in the 1960s, has a somewhat industrial look. Tamnavulin has been mothballed since 1996.

Among the malts produced in and around the glen of the Livet river, the elegant Tamnavulin is the lightest in body, although not in palate. In taste, it is a little more assertive than Tomintoul, with which it might be most closely compared.

HOUSE STYLE Aromatic, herbal. Aperitif.

TAMNAVULIN 12-year-old, 40 vol

COLOUR Vinho verde.

NOSE Very aromatic. A touch of peat, hay, heather, herbal notes. Slightly medicinal.

BODY Very light indeed, but smooth.

PALATE Lemon, flowering currant. Winey. Vermouth-like.

FINISH Aromatic. Juniper?

SCORE 76

TAMNAVULIN 22-year-old, 45 vol

COLOUR Deep amber to copper.

NOSE Almondy sherry, junipery aroma, and oak.

BODY Light but firm.

PALATE Sherry. Lemon pith. Stalky. Aromatic.

FINISH Spicy. Crisp.

SCORE **77**

TAMNAVULIN 29-year-old, Stillman's Dram, 45 vol

COLOUR Gold.

NOSE Herbal and nutty. Chestnut. A hint of beeswax.

BODY Medium, firm.

PALATE Sweet, mouth-coating. Malt, liquorice and peppermint,
beautifully combined.

FINISH Fresh and crisp.

SCORE **78**

TAMNAVULIN 1966, Single Cask 52.6 vol

COLOUR Deep amber.

NOSE Assertive sherry. Toasted sandalwood. Stewed prunes.
A touch of sour apple.

BODY Medium, very firm.

PALATE Muscular, almost biting. Bitter chocolate. Raisins. Prunes.

FINISH Long, tangy, and oaky. Reminiscent of an old armagnac.

SCORE **74**

TAMNAVULIN 1977, Scott's Selection, 53.8 vol

COLOUR Greeny gold.

NOSE Herbal. Freshly cut grass. Apple skin. Almond milk.

BODY Light but firm.

PALATE Sweet start followed by an explosion of ginger.

FINISH Soothing, grassy. Very refreshing.

SCORE **73**

TEANINICH

PRODUCER Diageo
REGION Highlands DISTRICT Northern Highlands
ADDRESS Alness, Ross-Shire, IV17 0XB
TEL 01463 872004 WEBSITE www.malts.com

THIS LESSER KNOWN NEIGHBOUR of Glenmorangie and Dalmore is beginning to develop a following for its big, malty, fruity, spicy whisky: not before time. Teaninich was founded in 1817, as an estate distillery, and later provided whisky for such well-known blends as VAT 69 and Haig Dimple. It gained a classic DCL still-house in the 1970s. The tongue-twisting name Teaninich (usually pronounced "tee-ninick", but some say "chee-ninick") began to be heard more widely in the 1990s, when the malt was bottled in the Flora and Fauna series. Three Rare Malts bottlings followed.

HOUSE STYLE Robust, toffeeish, spicy, leafy. Restorative or after dinner.

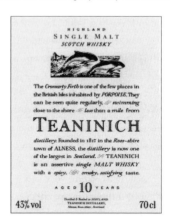

TEANINICH 10-year-old, Flora and Fauna, 43 vol

COLOUR Pale gold.

NOSE Big, fresh aroma. Fruity. Hints of apple. Smoky.

BODY Medium, rich.

PALATE Sweet and dry. Chocolate limes. Fruity. Remarkably leafy. Lightly peaty. Gradually warms up until it fairly sparks with flavour. Very appetizing.

FINISH Cilantro. Herbal. Rounded.

SCORE 74

TEANINICH 1972, 27-year-old, Bottled 2000, The Rare Malts, 64.2 vol

COLOUR Full, bright gold.

NOSE Very perfumy. Incense, sandalwood, vanilla.

BODY Big.

PALATE Intense sugared almonds, but big and profound.

FINISH Powerful, explosive. Gunpowder tea.

SCORE 77

A 1973 Teaninich from Rare Malts, at 57.1 vol, was harder and more authoritarian. SCORE 76. An earlier (1998) release of 1972, at 64.95 vol, was very similar to the 2000 bottling, but more creamy and toffeeish. SCORE 76

SOME INDEPENDENT BOTTLINGS OF TEANINICH

A 12-year-old, at 40 vol, in Lombard's Golfing Greats series, has an easy, affable approach, with suggestions of caramelized almonds, custard, and summer fruits. Stalky dryness to balance the finish. SCORE 76

A 19-year-old from Cadenhead, at 58.7 vol, has an especially sparkling golden hue; vanilla and toffee in the palate; finishing with a lively warmth reminiscent of ginger and lemon tea. SCORE 74

A 1973, at 29 years old and 43 vol, from Berry Brothers & Rudd, does not offer convincing evidence of its sherry ageing. Its evocative scents are of a summer's evening: green apples and almonds; ginger and nutmeg in the palate; dryish oak in the finish. SCORE 75

A 31-year-old from Adelphi, at 57.8 vol, has honey and stewed fruits in the aroma; a spicy, muscular palate; and black pepper in a warm, dry finish. SCORE 72

TOBERMORY

PRODUCER Burn Stewart Distillers plc
REGION Highlands DISTRICT Mull
ADDRESS Tobermory, Isle of Mull, Argyllshire, PA75 6NR
TEL 01688 302645 WEBSITE www.burnstewartdistillers.com
EMAIL enquiries@burnstewartdistillers.com VC

IF THE ART OF DISTILLATION was brought from Ireland over the Giant's Causeway, it must have arrived in Fingal's Cave, on the tiny island of Staffa. A later immigrant from Ireland, St Columba, founded an abbey on nearby Iona and urged the community to grow barley. One and a half thousand years later, a whisky called Iona was launched.

Both Staffa and Iona are off Mull, where the harbour village of Tobermory gives a home and a name to the local distillery. (Lovers of trivia may know that this name was also given to a talking cat by the Edwardian author Hector Hugh Munro, better known by his pen-name Saki). The village was once known as Ledaig (sometimes pronounced "ledchig", and meaning "safe haven" in Gaelic). The distillery traces its origins to 1795, but has a much interrupted history and many owners.

Various owners have at times used the name Tobermory on a blend and a vatted malt, but it now appears on a clearly labelled single malt, produced after the distillery reopened in 1989–90. This version has a peatiness, albeit light, derived entirely from the water. The barley-malt is not peated. The name Ledaig was for some years used for older versions of the whisky, employing peated malt. Ledaig is now being made again, and its peatiness gradually being increased.

The maritime character of the whiskies was diminished when the warehouses were sold by previous owners during a financial crisis to make room for apartments.

HOUSE STYLE Faint peat, minty, sweet. Restorative.

TOBERMORY 10-year-old, 40 vol

COLOUR Full gold.

NOSE Light but definite touch of peat. Some sweetness.

BODY Light to medium. Very smooth.

PALATE Faint peat. Enjoyable interplay of malty, nutty dryness,
and toffeeish, faintly minty sweetness. Slightly weak in
the middle, but recovers well.

FINISH Light, soft, becoming sweeter.

SCORE **69**

LEDAIG No Age Statement, Sherry Finish, 42 vol

COLOUR Bright gold.

NOSE Sweet. Custardy, with an appetizing fruitiness.
Sherry enhances oak. Toffeeish.

BODY Medium and smooth.

PALATE Mellow roundness. Elegant combination of fruit and oak.
Good balance. A hint of peat in the back.

FINISH Drying, with soft spices but satisfying.

SCORE **74**

LEDAIG 7-year-old, 43 vol

COLOUR Lemony gold.

NOSE Definitely maritime. Peaty with phenolic notes and a quickly fading
iodine accent. Fresh garden herbs. Thyme and mint.

BODY Light and crisp.

PALATE Assertive spiciness. Fizzy. Fruity. Pear drop.
Peat and smoke linger in the back.

FINISH Dry and spicy, amazingly long for its youth.

SCORE **80**

LEDAIG Over 15 Years, 43 vol

The preposition is superfluous; all ages on labels represent the youngest whisky in the bottle.

COLOUR Gold to bronze.

NOSE Soft, full peatiness.

BODY Light but smooth.

PALATE Slightly thin. Toffeeish, then spicy.

FINISH Sweet, smoky, full peatiness. A hint of the sea in this one.

SCORE **73**

LEDAIG Over 20 Years, 43 vol

COLOUR Pale amber.

NOSE Slightly musty.

BODY Creamy.

PALATE Dull start, but some burnt grass, cream, and mintiness develops.

FINISH Late peatiness.

SCORE **71**

IONA Single Malt, 4-year-old, 40 vol

Created for sale at distillery only.

COLOUR Almost white. *Eau-de-nil.*

NOSE Lichen. Moss on the rocks. Cockles and mussels.

BODY Lightly oily.

PALATE Broth-like. Miso. Hot-smoked salmon.

FINISH Wintergreen. Iron.

SCORE **78**

SOME INDEPENDENT BOTTLINGS OF LEDAIG

A 1992 at 10 years old, from Cadenhead, is the colour of white wine; with the aroma of a freshly cut lawn; light and crisp, with malty sweetness, spicy dryness, and an echo of malt in the finish. SCORE 71

A 1990 at 40 vol, from Gordon & MacPhail, has a touch of burnt grass in the aroma, with cider apple, custard, and fudge. SCORE 72

A 1975 at the same strength, from the same bottler, has rich sherry and luscious caramelized fruits, with a whiff of sea air. A beautiful whisky that would have been sensational at cask strength. SCORE 75

TOMATIN

PRODUCER The Tomatin Distillery Co. Ltd
REGION Highlands DISTRICT Speyside (Findhorn)
ADDRESS Tomatin, Inverness-shire, IV13 7YT
TEL 01808 511444 WEBSITE www.tomatin.com
EMAIL info@tomatin.co.uk VC

IF YOU POSSESS A PAIR OF BINOCULARS, look out for new products
from the lofty heights of Tomatin, at 315 metres (1028ft). So far,
only the new 12-year-old single malt has appeared, but there will be
more. Tomatin has begun to understand the pleasure of selling whisky
by the bottle. It has perhaps been encouraged by its success with
The Antiquary, a much-loved blend acquired from UDV in the fallout
from the creation of Diageo.

Tomatin, on the upper reaches of the Findhorn, was established in
1897, but saw its great years of expansion between the 1950s and
the 1970s. During this period, it became the biggest malt distillery in
Scotland, just a little smaller than Suntory's Hakushu distillery in
Japan. Both have scaled down volume since those heady days: Tomatin
by removing almost almost half of its stills; Hakushu by mothballing
its biggest still-house. Tomatin might just remain the largest in
Scotland; though neck-and-neck with Glenfiddich.

As a large distillery, Tomatin developed a broad-shouldered malt as
a filler for countless blends during the boom years. It is neither the
most complex nor the most assertive of malts, but it is far tastier than
is widely realized. For the novice wishing to move from lighter single
malts to something a little more imposing, the climb to Tomatin will be
well worthwhile.

HOUSE STYLE Malty, spicy, rich. Restorative or after dinner.

TOMATIN 12-year-old, 40 vol

Slightly softer and more "accessible" than the earlier 12-year-old which it replaces.

COLOUR Bright, greeny gold.

NOSE Biscuity sweetness. Vanilla. Soft mint tablets.

BODY Smooth, velvety.

PALATE Mellow and round. Toffeeish. Soft spices. Pine nuts.

FINISH Sweet with a pleasant refreshing mintiness.

SCORE **75**

SOME INDEPENDENT EXPRESSIONS OF TOMATIN
TOMATIN 12-year-old, James MacArthur & Co. Ltd, 43 vol

COLOUR Chartreuse-like gold.

NOSE Malty. Malt flour. Touch of honey. Distant apple.

BODY Medium, coating, smooth.

PALATE Sweet maltiness. A refreshing aniseed note.
Develops on spices. White pepper, touch of ginger.

FINISH Warm but soothing on sweeter notes.

SCORE **75**

TOMATIN 1989, Signatory Vintage Co., 46 vol

COLOUR Pale, lemony gold.

NOSE Intense, malty, and nutty. Fudgey sweetness.
Touch of burnt leaves. Fresh lemon peel.

BODY Medium and firm.

PALATE Crisp, clean with luscious malty/minty notes. Quite chewy.
Sour cider-like note. Opens up on spices. Paprika, ginger.

FINISH Lingering, gingery, drying on nutty notes.

SCORE **76**

TOMINTOUL

PRODUCER Angus Dundee Distillers plc
REGION Highlands DISTRICT Speyside (Livet)
ADDRESS Ballindalloch, Banffshire, AB37 9AQ

THE VILLAGE OF TOMINTOUL (pronounced "tom in t'owl") is the base camp for climbers and walkers in the area around the rivers Avon and Livet. Nearby, Cromdale and the Ladder Hills foreshadow the Cairngorm Mountains. It is about 13 kilometres (8 miles) from the village to the distillery, which is on the edge of a forest, close to the river Avon.

The distillery was built in the 1960s and is modern in appearance. The wildness of the surroundings contrasts with the delicacy of the district's malts. Tomintoul has traditionally seemed the lightest among them in flavour, though there is an almost effervescent fruitiness to the new 16-year-old, the first release under the new owners.

HOUSE STYLE Delicate, grassy, perfumy. Aperitif.

TOMINTOUL 10-year-old, 40 vol

COLOUR	Full, sunny gold.
NOSE	Grassy. Lemon grass. Orange flower water.
BODY	Light, smooth, slippery.
PALATE	Sweetish. Crushed barley. Potpourri.
FINISH	Lively and lingering gently. Nutty. Lemon grass.

SCORE 77

TOMINTOUL 16-year-old, 40 vol

COLOUR Pale bright orange.

NOSE Orange-cream icing on a cheesecake.

BODY Silky.

PALATE Finely grated, zesty, citrus peels. Syllabub. Zabaglione. Nougat.

FINISH Refreshing but also warming, like the sherry in a trifle.

SCORE **78**

SOME INDEPENDENT BOTTLINGS
TOMINTOUL 1966, Official Bottling,
Single Cask No 6073, 46.5 vol

Apparently from the last bottle in existence. A beautiful rich and fulfilling single malt.

COLOUR Full gold with a bronze hue.

NOSE Rich fudginess. Vanilla. Polished oak.
A floral honeyish note. Appetizing toffee.

BODY Syrupy, oily.

PALATE Sweet, luscious, creamy. Nougat, coffee, toffee.
Touch of cucumber.

FINISH Sweet, long, rewarding, warming up on spices.

SCORE **79**

TOMINTOUL 1966, Single Cask No 3405,
Cask Strength, Mackillop's Choice

Tasted as a work in progress.

COLOUR Glittering full gold.

NOSE Rich, grassy/herbal. Sherry tinge. Raisiny.
A touch of wet earth (humus). Beeswax.

BODY Medium, silky.

PALATE Sweet at start then opening up on spices. Pepper.
Marmalade. Nuts and raisins chocolate.

FINISH Long, dry and spicy.

COMMENT Not the most elegant sherryness. A bit harsh on nose
and palate (burning spices). But rich and complex.

TORMORE

PRODUCER Allied Distillers Ltd
REGION Highlands DISTRICT Speyside
ADDRESS Advie by Grantown-on-Spey, Morayshire, PH26 3LR
TEL 01807 510244

THE MOST ARCHITECTURALLY ELEGANT of all whisky distilleries. With a musical clock, belfry, and ornamental curling lake, it looks like a spa offering a mountain-water cure. In a sense, it does: the water of life, uisge beatha. Tormore, among the Cromdale Hills, overlooking the Spey, was designed by Sir Albert Richardson, president of the Royal Academy, and erected as a showpiece in 1958–60, during a boom in the Scotch whisky industry.

The whisky was originally intended as a component of Long John, and later became an element of Ballantine's. Admirers find it aromatic, sweet, and easily drinkable, but the more cautious deem its firmness "metallic". The distillery does not have tours, which seems a wasteful denial of its original purpose as a visual celebration.

HOUSE STYLE Nutty. Firm, smooth. Versatile. Perhaps best as a restorative.

TORMORE 12-year-old, 40 vol

COLOUR	Bright, sunny gold.
NOSE	Nutty. Hint of barley sugar. Soft pear in a fudgey sauce.
BODY	Medium, smooth.
PALATE	Sweet, soft. Caramelized walnuts. Braised artichokes.
FINISH	Rounded.

SCORE **73**

TULLIBARDINE

PRODUCER Tullibardine Ltd
REGION Highlands DISTRICT Midlands
ADDRESS Stirling Street, Blackford, Perthshire, PH4 1QG
TEL 01764 682252 WEBSITE www.tullibardine.com

THE REOPENING OF TULLIBARDINE under new ownership in 2003 was followed by the announcement of a 1993 vintage, to be launched in 2004. Such news items are welcome in a region with a strong – but in recent years silent – tradition of brewing and distilling. Brewing is more strongly associated with the south of Scotland and distilling with the north; here in the Midlands, they met and overlapped. Water from the Ochil Hills gave rise to both industries. Fuel was handy in the form of coal from Fife, or via coastal steamers on the firth of Forth. Steamers could also bring barley or malt from the Borders. The main brewing centre was the town of Alloa, which shipped dark Scottish ales to England. The last two sizeable breweries in Alloa closed in recent years.

Tullibardine Moor is in the Ochil hills. In this area, the village of Blackford is the source of Highland Spring bottled water. The hills and their springs have provided water for brewing since at least the 12th century. In 1488, a Tullibardine brewery brewed the ale for the coronation of King James IV at Scone. A former brewery site accommodates the distillery. There may have been whisky making there in the late 1700s, but it was not until 1949 that the present distillery was erected. It was built by Delmé Evans, a noted designer of distilleries, whose functional styling can also be seen at Glenallachie and Jura. Evans, who was at school with the son of an excise officer, was fascinated by breweries and distilleries. He first visited a distillery at the age of 12. One of his enthusiasms was the "tower" brewery design, popular in the late 1800s. In this system, a water tank on the roof and a malt loft disgorge their contents, which flow by gravity, without pumps, through the processes that lead to a cellar full of beer. At Tullibardine, he sought to incorporate gravity-flow into a distillery. Evans died just before the distillery reopened. It is in the Highland region, though south of Perth and half-way to Stirling.

HOUSE STYLE Winey, fragrant. With pre-dinner pistachios. More sherried versions with a honeyish dessert (baclava?).

TULLIBARDINE 10-year-old, 40 vol

COLOUR Bright gold.

NOSE Soft, lemony, malty, sweetish.

BODY Medium, firm, oily, smooth.

PALATE Full, with clean, grassy-malty, buttery sweetness. Only medium-sweet. Develops to a fruity, almost Chardonnay-like wineyness.

FINISH Sweetish, fragrant, appetizing, big. Vanilla-pod spiciness.

SCORE 76

TULLIBARDINE 27-year-old, 45 vol

An "official" bottling, now hard to find.

COLOUR Full gold to bronze.

NOSE Touch of sherry. Then expressive, scenty, luscious, inviting.

BODY Medium, smooth, clean.

PALATE Softened by the sherry. Still grassy, but slightly nuttier.

FINISH Lemon grass. Honeyed but dry. Nutty.

SCORE 77

TULLIBARDINE 30-year-old, Stillman's Dram, 45 vol

COLOUR Amber.

NOSE Dry honey.

BODY Medium to full. Rounded.

PALATE Honey, butter, nuts, sherryish wineyness.

FINISH Sherryish. Sweet. Nutty. Spicy.

SCORE 77

WHISKY WORLDWIDE: THE FAMOUS FIVE

EACH OF THE FIVE great whisky nations has a different claim to this status. Scotland is by far the greatest. It makes the most whisky, has the most distilleries, the most single malts, and the most styles of whisky. Form an adjective from Scotland and "whisky" is understood.

Whether the Gaelic word that became "whisky" was Scottish or Irish, and in whichever of those two countries the evolution of the spirit began, both are the charter members of the famous five. Ireland has its own style of whiskey, but also produces malts and blends.

Canada has its own style, and has only tiptoed into malts, at Nova Scotia's Glenora distillery. Its Glen Breton malt has shortbread and pastis notes, proposing a nouvelle alliance. SCORE 71. In the United States, the local styles are produced in Kentucky and Tennessee, but the new microdistilleries making malts are mainly in the west.

The fifth great whisky nation is Japan. When the country opened up to Western trade in the late 1800s, it developed a taste for British luxuries, of which Scotch whisky remains the quintessence.

Japan qualifies as a great whisky nation on the grounds of both volume and quality. It makes malt whisky by the same methods as the Scots, and does so with a typical blend of traditionalism and technical skill. Its whiskies cannot be called Scotch, as they are Japanese, yet they do not represent a local style. Their most local feature is that they are sometimes matured in Japanese oak, which can impart an aroma reminiscent of joss-sticks.

IRELAND

Whiskey permeates Irish lore and literature, but the nation has only three distilleries. Bushmills is in the village of the same name, in County Antrim, in the far north. Triple distillation is used, exclusively from malt, but the principal Bushmills products are blends (with grain whiskey from the Midleton distillery, in County Cork). The first, very tentative, malt was the 10-year-old, launched in 1987.

Bushmills and Midleton are both owned by Pernod Ricard. The distillery specializes in the Irish pot still type. The independent Cooley distillery is on the peninsula of the same name, just inside the Republic. It produces malt and grain whiskies, in separate still-houses.

Some versions of Bushmills Malt (40 vol, except madeira)

The 10-year-old has a very fresh, cookie-like, aroma. The palate is reminiscent of apple pie in cream; the finish minty, oily. SCORE 76. The 12-year-old Distillery Reserve, on sale at Bushmills, has considerably more flavour development, with toasted almonds; an apricot-like oily sweetness; and a winey oakiness. SCORE 79. The 16-year-old is sub-titled "TripleWood". Bushmills malt matured in bourbon casks is married with a smaller amount aged in oloroso sherry butts. Both are 16 years old. They are then recasked in port pipes for six to (more often) 12 months. Wonderful complexity: Fragrant smoke and anis in the nose; tongue-coating marshmallow; raspberries. SCORE 83. A 21-year-old madeira finish, at cask strength and 51.4 vol, is lively and elegant. It has garden mint in the aroma; glazed almonds and marzipan in the palate; and a dusting of ginger in the finish. SCORE 83.

Cooley's Principal Malts

Connemara Peated single malt, no age statement, 40 vol. Made entirely with peated malt. Pungent. Smoky, rather than peaty. Aromas and flavours young and fresh. Mouth-filling. Sweet grass. Earthy. Sesame oil. Spicy. SCORE 81. Connemara Cask Strength (this bottling 59.6 vol), no age statement. Each batch has its own label, because of variations in strength. Slightly sooty aroma. Bigger palate. Slightly hot finish. SCORE 82. Locke's Single Malt, eight years old, 40 vol, has the faintest hint of peat in the nose, with grass and lemon grass; the palate has creamy malt and baked peaches; and the finish toasted coconut. SCORE 77. Tyrconnell. The scent of unpeeled apples. Light, oily, grassy, cereal-grain palate. Lightly malty and cookie-like. Some vanilla sweetness. Crisp, clean, finish, with a hint of charcoal. SCORE 75.

UNITED STATES

For lovers of food and drink, the world's new frontier is the west coast of the US, especially the stretch between San Francisco Bay and Seattle. A youthful population, adventurous ("Go West, young man"), well educated (famously at Stanford and Berkeley), now prosperous, has fostered a new appreciation of local produce, of new world wines, of microbrewed beers, and now of spirits.

Wine country gave rise to brandies, and now brewers and distillers are exploring whiskey. Here in the west, Fritz Maytag has been inspired by the oldest style of American whiskey, the original rye of the east (historically, it was produced in Maryland and Pennsylvania; today, rye is a sideline for bourbon distillers in Kentucky).

Anchor Distillery

Old Potrero (SCORE 88) is made exclusively from rye, all malted, and pot stills are used. (Regulations require only 51 per cent rye, not necessarily malted. In most distilleries, the remainder of the grist comprises corn and barley malt, and column stills are typically used). Old Potrero has a more assertive rye character than any other whisk(e)y anywhere in the world. The aroma is like spearmint toffee; the texture soft, rich, and smooth; the palate starts sweetly, becoming drier, with liquorice and rooty notes. The first distillate was matured in new, uncharred oak, and bottled at one year old. It had some raw-boned hits of alcohol.

Subsequent numbered editions ("essays" is the word used on the label) have additionally used second-fill casks, toasted, and have been matured for longer periods. The sample tried and rated here was distilled in December 1997 and bottled in July 2000 at 62.1 vol. SCORE 88.

Clear Creek

There are more beer breweries in Portland, Oregon, than in any other city in the world. The successful Widmer microbrewery uses peated malt to make a wash which is supplied to the town's Clear Creek distillery. There, the wash is transformed into McCarthy's Single Malt (40 vol, no age statement), with a barbecue smokiness and mustardy spiciness. SCORE 68. Clear Creek's principal activity is the distillation of Poire Williams from local pears. It was set up for that purpose by Steve McCarthy, who previously practised as a lawyer, specializing in environmental issues.

St George Spirits

In the Bay Area at Alameda, California, this distillery pioneered *eaux-de-vie*. It now also produces a St George Single Malt. The grist includes crystal malt and roasted barley, and proportions are smoked over alder and beech. This sounds more like the grist for a beer. The whisky has an intensely fruity and curiously nutty character. SCORE 62. The distiller is a former beer brewer, and the founder, Jorg ("St George") Rupf, a former attorney in the German ministry of culture.

More single malts are breaking ground around these western pioneers, and there is the odd example in middle America and the east.

JAPAN

Fourteen malts from Japan were reviewed in the fourth edition of Malt Whisky Companion. Since then, releases from Japan's malt distilleries have swollen from a trickle into a torrent. Recent releases from each distillery have been tasted for this edition. Here are some highlights, in alphabetical order by proprietor.

Chichibu

This company, with a whisky distillery at Hanyu, about 80 kilometres (50 miles) northwest of Tokyo, originally made the Japanese spirit shochu. Its Flying Horse malts, at various ages, tend toward lightly creamy sweetness, with some citrus. Top-of-the-line Chichibu 14-year-old is more citric, nuttier. and very well structured. SCORE 78.

Kirin, Gotemba

The brewers Kirin are now sole owners of this distillery, but the past partnership with Seagram remains evident in its portfolio. The distillery is at Gotemba, at the foot of Mount Fuji. Its Japanese identity is proclaimed in Fuji Pure Malt Whisky. Some of the malt was distilled in a column. The result is a flowery whisky, lean-bodied, but with an interplay between dry and sweet maltiness. SCORE 77.

Mercian, Kariuzawa

A wide selection of vintages is offered by this tiny distillery (formerly Sanraku Ocean) in the mountain resort of Kariuzawa. It also has a range of regular ages. The whiskies are inclined to oakiness. Kariuzawa 17-year-old is a well-balanced example, with rich, chocolatey notes. SCORE 78.

Nikka, Sendai

The company's "Lowland" distillery may be identified with a big city but the site is in nearby countryside. It is a handsome distillery, producing honeyed, flavoursome whiskies. Sendai Single Malt, at 12 years old, has a lively development and a touch of sherry. SCORE 80.

Nikka, Yoichi

The original Nikka distillery is not so much "Highland" as coastal. It is in the harbour village of Yoichi, on Hokkaido: an island, but the size of Scotland. Yoichi has bottled a wide range of ages, some peated, others not. The distillery is especially known for peaty expressions such as Yoichi 1986, bottled by the Scotch Malt Whisky Society. This had a leafy, menthol-like, aroma; piney notes in a complex palate; and a dry, resiny finish. SCORE 85.

Suntory, Hakushu
Both of Suntory's malt distilleries have recently launched their principal expressions globally. From the company's "Highland" distillery, Hakushu 12-year-old, has a leafy, "forest-floor" aroma; a creamy-tasting palate; and an appetizingly bittersweet, spicy, faintly smoky finish. It is drier and more assertive in flavour, but lighter in body, than its "Lowland" partner. SCORE 85.

Suntory, Yamazaki
This whisky seems to have gained in confidence and intensity over the years. Yamazaki 12-year-old is lightly syrupy, honeyed in flavour, perfumy, with a cookie-like dryness in the finish. SCORE 80. Yamazaki 1979 Oak Cask is more zesty, with notes of kumquat, cypress, and beeswax. This was matured in Japanese oak. SCORE 83. A great many other versions have been released in recent years.

REST OF THE WORLD: ASIA
The Scots having been so influential in the British Empire, a taste for whisky remains in some Commonwealth countries. Just as the Scottish distilleries have given a new emphasis to single malts, so have the handful in the Commonwealth.

Australia
Cradle Mountain Malt Whisky, 43 vol, distilled in Ulverstone, Tasmania: white wine colour; earthy-fruity (apple core?) aroma; and a grainy dryness. SCORE 61. This whisky is vatted with Scotland's Springbank to create the livelier, salty, lemony Double Malt (54.4 vol). SCORE 69. Sullivan's Cove Single Malt, 40 vol, distilled in Hobart, Tasmania: full gold; smooth; leathery and dry. SCORE 63.

India
McDowell's Single Malt: vegetal, medicinal, very warming; malty dryness. SCORE 65.

New Zealand
Lammerlaw Single Malt, 43 vol, no age statement, from Dunedin: Sunny, gold; light, clean, peat, grass, and apricot in the aroma; firm, maltiness; warm finish, with peat returning. SCORE 70. No longer in

production, but Cadenhead released a 10-year-old in 2002. This was drier: toasty, nutty, peppery. SCORE 73. Lammerlaw also produced a more herbal 10-year-old under the Milford name. SCORE 69.

Pakistan
Murree Single Malt, 43 vol, no age statement (8–10 years): pale, greeny gold "vinho verde" colour; grassy, flowery aroma and finish, with sugary, "boiled sweets" character throughout, vanilla, and some syrupy maltiness. SCORE 62.

REST OF THE WORLD: EUROPE
As Europe unites, Scotland asserts its nationhood. The Scottish Highlands and islands are rediscovered as Western Europe's romantic great outdoors. In France and Germany especially, there is a fascination with Celtic myth, history, and culture – often indulged with a glass of Scottish or Irish whisk(e)y. France's own Celtic fringe, Brittany, takes particular inspiration from its cousins across the sea. Continental distillers of brandies and schnapps began to make whiskies after the Second World War. Since the 1980s and 1990s, the trend has been to single malts. Here is a sampler:

Austria, Waldviertel
"Roggen" is the German word for rye. This perhaps obliges a distillery in a hamlet called Roggenreith to make a straight rye whisky. Roggenreith is in a region called the Waldviertel, northwest of Vienna, in the direction of the Czech border. The Waldvierteler distillery has at least four variations on a rye theme, among nine or ten whiskies.

The range includes a 100 per cent rye, labelled as Roggen-Malzwhisky, with a menthol, mint-toffee palate: firm, focused and lively. SCORE 75. A 100 per cent barley-malt distillate, Gersten-Malzwhisky, has the aroma of clean linen, saddlery, linseed, and sesame; oily, creamy, nutty flavours; and a lively, spicy, gingery finish. SCORE 77. (Both at 41 vol.) An oat version (surely a natural for Scotland), labelled Hafer Whisky, is surprisingly dry and briar-like, with suggestions of privet, garden mint, and peppermint, at 69 vol. SCORE 68.

Czech Republic
King Barley Malt Whisky, over 12 years, at 43 vol, is one of a range from the Dolany distillery, in the town of the same name, north of Olomouc and Brno, in Moravia. The whisky has a peachy colour; a

hint of peat in a grassy, nutty aroma; a clean, syrupy, malty sweetness; and a spicy finish. SCORE 67.

France
Armorik Single Malt de Bretagne, 43 vol. This Breton whisky has the aroma of the forest, and perhaps a wood-fired oven; flavours of reminiscent of nuts, orange fondant, and black chocolate; and a spicy, gingery finish. SCORE 74.

Germany
Blaue Maus, at 40 vol, is neither blue nor a mouse. It is gold, big, and deliciously liqueur-ish: an anis-tasting whisky in the range of Robert Fleischmann, the pioneer of malt distilling in Germany. SCORE 73. Fleischmann started distilling in 1983, and released his first whisky in 1994. The distillery is at Eggolsheim, near the malting and brewing town of Bamberg, in Franconia.

Slyrs Bavarian Whisky, at 43 vol, is made from barley grown locally, in the Munich basin malting and brewing region. The distillery is in Schliersee about half-way between Munich and the Austrian town of Innsbruck. The whisky is creamy and sweetish, with a delicate perfumy-spicy dryness and warmth in the finish. SCORE 68.

Schwäbischer Whisky, at 43 vol, is produced by Inge and Christian Gruel in the oddly-named small town of Owen/Teck, near Stuttgart, in the region known as Swabia. The whisky is described as a single grain, but is actually made from malted wheat. It has a pale, vinho verde colour; seems drying at first, with a chlorophyl note, then sweetens and seems to become more viscous. SCORE 68.

Switzerland
Holle Single Malt, 42 vol. This whisky is named after the traditional fairytale character whose scattering of goose feathers is responsible for snow, although such untidiness sounds unlikely in Switzerland. The use of barley to make spirits was, if not actually sinful, illegal in Switzerland until 1999. Ernst Bader was the country's first legal whisky maker. His latest expression employs beechwood-dried malt from the German city of Bamberg (the home of smoked beer). The distillery is in Lauwil, near Basel, Switzerland. The whisky has an ash-like aroma; a light body; and is only gently smoky, with some woody fruitiness. SCORE 67.

VATTED MALTS

The smooth, sweeter one; The Rich, Spicy One; and The Smoky, Peaty One – those are the names of three whiskies launched in the UK for Christmas of 2003/04. They are the first malt whiskies to be be named according to their flavour characteristics. The Smooth One is a single malt from the Cooley distillery, in Ireland, but the other two are vatted malts.

In order to achieve the Rich, Spicy character, the big tastes of Highland Park were melded with the more sweetly complex Glenrothes and the herbal Bunnahabhain and that palette of flavours set against a background of Tamdhu's mild maltiness. The end product is syrupy and full of flavour: SCORE 79.

The Smoky, Peaty One employed Ledaig along with four Islay malts: Laphroaig, Bowmore, Caol Ila, and again Bunnahabhain. This vatting also included Highland Park. The end result has an attractive aroma of log fires, but is light in body and restrained in flavour. SCORE 72

With their simple, descriptive names, and flavours to match, these whiskies are intended to catch the eye and engage the palate of younger drinkers. The advertising seems to address what the British call the laddish market. To create products from scratch for a specific market is a radical departure in an industry where evolution is the norm. This approach suggests a new role for vatted malts, a category of whiskies that has in the past had difficulty in holding down a steady job.

A similar use of vatting was developed by Compass Box, with its Eleuthera. This was vatted from Caol Ila and two versions of Clynelish, to meld smokiness with softness and sweetness. The result is big and oily, with a pronounced maritime character. SCORE 83.

With its elegant packaging, Compass Box clearly has a more upscale orientation. The company was established in 2000 by John Glaser, formerly with Johnnie Walker.

A direction for the future?
Compass Box has erudite labels and unusual whiskies. The vatted malt Eleuthera is reviewed above. The bittersweet Hedonism (its label is shown here) is a vatted grain whisky.

GETTING THE MOST OUT OF YOUR MALT

WHEN WE ENJOY DRINK, or food, we use all our senses: sight, smell, taste, and hearing. Do you listen to your food and drink? You do when you hear the steak sizzling in the pan, the whisky being poured from the bottle, or the clink of glasses.

Lovers of malt whisky want to enjoy to the full its subtleties of colour, its arousing bouquet, and its complex flavours. Malt lovers tend to dislike the cut-glass tumbler that is often regarded as the traditional whisky glass. The bevels in the glass may illuminate the colour of the whisky, but they also distort it. More important, the tumbler shape does a poor job of delivering aroma.

The size of the tumbler does accommodate ice, but a frozen tongue cannot taste properly. When the tumbler assumed its role, whisky was a hugely popular drink, but it had not yet inspired the connoisseurship it enjoys today.

Malt lovers prefer a brandy snifter, sherry copita, or something similar. These glasses were designed to showcase the special characteristics of noble and complex drinks. The growing connoisseurship of malts has led to the evolution of whisky glasses based on a similar, tulip-like shape.

Having tried every glass on the market, the author has observed that the tiniest variations in shape can make a huge difference in the delivery of aroma and flavour. Based on his experience, he has designed his own Whisky Connoisseur Glass, with spirits consultant Jürgen Deibel. The bowl of the glass has no decoration, so that the colour of the whisky can be appreciated to the full. The inward curve above the bowl holds in the aroma. Then the slight flare directs the bouquet to the nose. There is a lid to retain the aroma between sniffs and swallows.

THE QUESTION OF WATER

It is conceivable that the heroes of Scottish history drank their whisky neat; however, contrary to myth, today's Highlanders do not. "Half and half,

Sweet smell?
The successful shape is a variant of the copita.

with lots of water" is a common prescription. Some malt zealots do resist dilution – on principle. Others feel that the texture of the bigger, richer, sherryish malts is spoiled by water.

The problem is that neat whisky can numb the palate. This can be countered with a glass of water with which to chase down their whisky. In the whisky itself, even a drop of water, by disturbing the molecular composition of the whisky, can open the aromas and flavours. To avoid chlorine notes, bottled water (without carbonation) is preferred.

MALT WHISKY WITH FOOD

Anyone who enjoys a whisky after work, or in the early evening, is arguably treating it as an aperitif. A light, flowery, dryish dram best suits that purpose. Increasingly, some of the richer, creamier, more oaky malts are being offered after dinner.

Although there is no tradition of accompanying a meal with whisky, some malt lovers like to offer "the wine of Scotland". The first public manifestation of this was a whisky dinner organized by the author in the early 1990s, at the University of Pennsylvania's Museum of Anthropology and Archaeology.

The object was to help highlight the aromas and flavours of whisky by relating them to the tastes in the meal, which employed materials typically found in Scotland. It was a simple demonstration of possible affinities. The starter was smoked salmon marinated in the salty Oban and garnished with seaweed. The accompanying whisky was the lightly piney Isle of Jura, served in a small sherry copita. The main course was venison in a sauce made from Perthshire raspberries marinated in Blair Athol. This was served with the spicy Royal Lochnagar. The dessert was a butterscotch flan, flavoured with the honeyish Balvenie and served with the nutty Macallan 18-year-old.

Collaborations followed with Oregonian chef Christopher Zefiro (at The James Beard House, New York's shrine to gastronomy) and with French writer-cook Martine Nouet (in Scotland, initially at the Aberlour distillery). Nouet began to write a regular cookery column in *Whisky Magazine*. This publication has also run blindfold tastings to match malts with sushi, cheese, chocolate, and coffee. The materials in sushi – grain, fish, and seaweed – are superbly accompanied by some maritime malts. A sushi-and-whisky lunch, prepared by a former chef to the Emperor of Japan, was a highlight in a series of meals presented by Diageo.

The post-prandial cigar might well have been a smoky Lagavulin. In different company, it could be Dalmore's Cigar Malt – or Glenfiddich's Havana Reserve.

WHISKY SHOPS

Malt whisky is far easier to find today than it was when the first edition of this book was published 15 years ago. Some of the ground-breaking retailers double as independent bottlers, and are therefore listed at the foot of p. 81.

Among those, The Vintage House, of Old Compton Street, London, opened a tasting room in 2003. Its Soho neighbour, Milroy's, of Greek Street, pioneered this idea. Milroy's is now part of the La Réserve group. Visitors to London, on returning through Heathrow, Gatwick or Stansted airports, will find an excellent selection and knowledgeable staff at half a dozen specialist shops called Whiskies of the World. These are separate from the supermarket-style former duty-free shops.

In Scotland, people visiting Campbeltown or Islay by road might find Inverary a good place to break the journey – and visit Loch Fyne Whiskies. Such shops are institutions. The same is true of Park Avenue Liquors, in Manhattan. (The last is in fact not on Park Avenue but on Madison, between 40th and 41st).

BIBLIOGRAPHY & FURTHER INFORMATION

HISTORY
The Whisky Distilleries of the United Kingdom,
Alfred Barnard.
(Accounts of visits to distilleries. 1887 classic, with reprints in 1969, 1987, 2002, 2003)

The Making of Scotch Whisky,
John R. Hume and Michael S. Moss.
Canongate, 1981. Updated 2000. (Standard work)

The Scotch Whisky Industry Record, Charles Craig.
Index Publishing Limited, 1994. (Includes year-by-year chronology from 1494)

Scotch Whisky: A Liquid History, Charles MacLean.
Cassell, 2003. (Social history/commentary, by a whisky specialist)

REFERENCE
The Whisk(e)y Treasury,
Walter Schobert.
Neil Wilson Publishing, 2002. Originally published by Wolfgang Krüger Verlag, 1999. (A to Z lexicon of brand-owners, distilleries and industry terms)

The Scotch Whisky Industry Review (annual),
Alan S. Gray.
Sutherlands, Edinburgh.
(Industry statistics, financial analysis and commentary)

PRACTICAL
Appreciating Whisky,
Phillip Hills.
HarperCollins, 2000.
Reprinted 2002. (The physiology, psychology and chemistry of taste)

Scotland and its Whiskies,
Michael Jackson.
Duncan Baird, 2001. (From the sea-spray to the scorched moorlands ... treading the terroir that shapes the whiskies; with landscape photographer Harry Cory Wright)

The World Guide to Whisky,
Michael Jackson.
Dorling Kindersley, 1987.
Reprints 1990, 1991, 1992, 1994, 1996, 1997. (The geography of the spirit – recognizing at first hand the qualities of Japanese, North American, and Irish whiskies alongside those of Scotland)

MAGAZINES & WEBSITES
Whisky Magazine
(Published in the United Kingdom)
www.whiskymag.com

Malt Advocate
(Published in the United States)
www.maltadvocate.com

Celtic Malts
(International news, issues and debates, among devotees. Online magazine)
www.celticmalts.com/default. htm

Ulf Buxrud is a Swedish computer entrepreneur and devotee of Macallan, whose personal website offers an extraordinary compilation of news, sources of reference, useful addresses, titles of publications, and general information of assistance to the whisky lover.
www2.sbbs.se/hp/buxrud/ whisky.htm

For official websites devoted to particular malts, see distillery entries.

AUTHOR'S ACKNOWLEDGMENTS

Whatever I know about malts has been absorbed over decades, some of it directly from the glass; more from people who share my enthusiasm; yet more from those who make or market whisky. The diversity of their knowledge and opinions provide a broad foundation for my own, for which I take complete responsibility.

Although I keep notes of whiskies tasted in bars and restaurants, during distillery tours, and with my colleagues, that is an exercise in monitoring. The whiskies newly described and scored in this edition were sampled specifically for the book.

With more than a thousand tasting notes and scores, the gathering of samples was a massive task. For their generous time and effort in helping with this edition, I thank the following. If your name is not there, and should be, my apologies. I will put that right next time.

Pauline Agnew, Nick Andrews, Bridget Arthur, Elaine Bailey, Liselle Barnsley, Rachel Barrie, Michael Barton, Thierry Benitah, Bill Bergius, Jérôme Bordenave, David Boyd, Neil Boyd, Derek Brown, Lew Bryson, Alec Carnie, Rick Christie, Neil Clapperton, Paula Cormack, Isabel Coughlin, Simon Coughlin, Andrew Crook, Jim Cryle, Bob Dalgarno, Lucy Drake, Jonathan Driver, Gavin J.P. Durnin, Anthony Edwards, Hans-Jürgen Ehmke, Kate Enis, Robert Fleming, John Glaser, Alan Gordon, Jim Gordon, Lesley Gracie, Heather Graham, George Grant, Alan S. Gray, Peter Greve, Natalie Guerin, Donald Hart, Ian Henderson, Stuart Hendry, Robert Hicks, Sandy Hislop, David Hume, Brigid James, Richard Jones, Kiran Kuma, Fred Laing, Stewart Laing, Christine Logan, Richard Lombard-Chibnall, Jim Long, Bill Lumsden, Lorne Mackillop, Fritz Maytag, Anthony McCallum-Caron, Jim McEwan, Frank McHardy, Douglas McIvor, Claire Meikle, Marcin Miller, Euan Mitchell, Matthew Mitchell, Shuna Mitchell, Mike Miyamoto, Lindsay Morgan, Nicholas Morgan, Malcolm Mullin, Margaret Nicol, B.A. Nimmo, The Patel Family, Richard Paterson, Lucy Pritchard, Annie Pugh, John Ramsay, Stuart Ramsay, Kevin Ramsden, Kirsty Reid, Mark Reynier, Rebecca Richardson, Dave Robertson, Geraldine Roche, Dominic Roskrow, Colin Ross, Fabio Rossi, Colin Scott, Jacqui Seargeant, Catherine Service, Euan Shand, Raj Singh, Sukhinder Singh, David Stewart, David Stirk, Kier Sword, Andrew Symington, Elodie Teissedre, Jens Tholstrup, Graeme Thomson, Margaret Mary Timpson, Hide Tokuda, Robin Torrie, Robin Tucek, The Urquhart Family, Alistair Walker, Ian Weir, Amy Westlake, Alan Winchester, Arthur Winning, Gordon Wright, Kate Wright, Vanessa Wright.

Countless other people in the industry have helped me over the years, and their assistance is much appreciated.

Dorling Kindersley would like to thank Chris Bernstein for compiling the index, Pamela Marmito and Gary Werner for editorial assistance, and Ritzenhof Cristal for Michael Jackson's tasting glass (*see p. 440*), which is available from De Hoeksteen Projects b.v./www.hoeksteen-glasses.nl.

All photography by Ian O'Leary except Anchor Brewing Co. (9), Asahi-Nikka (10), Bruichladdich Distillery Co. (12), Chivas Brothers (22), Paul Harris (82), Diageo plc (42), The Edrington Group (53), Glenmorangie plc (15), Steve Gorton (1, 2–3, 5, 440), Cathy Turner (23).

INDEX